THE AUTHENTIC MARK TWAIN

For Dolan
from his
great admirer

Everett Emerson

11/4/86

Mark Twain, 1874. (Reproduced with permission of Mark Twain Papers, the Bancroft Library)

THE AUTHENTIC MARK TWAIN

A Literary Biography
of Samuel L. Clemens

EVERETT EMERSON

University of Pennsylvania Press · *Philadelphia* · *1985*

Design by ADRIANNE ONDERDONK DUDDEN

Library of Congress Cataloging in Publication Data

Emerson, Everett H., 1925–
  The authentic Mark Twain : a literary biography of
Samuel L. Clemens.

  Bibliography: p.
  Includes index.
  1. Twain, Mark, 1835–1910.   2. Authors, American—
19th century—Biography.   I. Title.
PS1331.E47 1983   818'.409 [B]   83–10626
ISBN 0-8122-1214-2

Printed in the United States of America

This Book Is for Henry Nash Smith

CONTENTS

Illustrations

Preface

MARK Twain is America's favorite writer and a world favorite as well. A great personality, he lived a life and created a whole library of books that have an enormous interest, and their intersection is the subject of the following pages. "To me," Mark Twain wrote near the end of his life, "the most important feature of my life is its literary feature."[1] Samuel Clemens drew attention to his identity as a writer by his use of a pen name—he often called it his *nom de plume* and sometimes his *nom de guerre*—but unlike some other writers who adopted this practice, he never encouraged people to forget that he was also Samuel L. Clemens: he signed letters with both names, and the two names appeared together on the title pages of his books. In the early part of his career he was referred to as "Mark Twain," as if it were a sobriquet, and in his review of *The Innocents Abroad* Bret Harte reminded his readers that "Mark Twain" is "a very eccentric creation of Samuel Clemens."[2] It was one of the writer's voices, first among many; Hank Morgan's (he was the Connecticut Yankee) and Huck Finn's are but two others.

There are tides in literary taste, but the Mark Twain tide has not yet gone out. Although he is not as popular today as he once was in England, where his books appeared simultaneously with American publication, Mark Twain is still much admired and read in Germany and the Soviet Union. In the United States he is inescapable, omnipresent. His image and his writings are before us everywhere, on television, in airline magazines, in drugstore paperback racks. Both his tiny boyhood home in Hannibal and his Victorian mansion in Hartford attract thousands each year.

Though he all but gave up writing for a time in his early fifties and often devoted only his summers to composition, he wrote a huge quantity of books over a long career: travel books, novels, stories, plays, essays, sketches, poems, autobiographical writings. Previously unpublished works from his pen continue to appear: half a dozen volumes in the last fifteen years, with more to follow. In 1896, he told an interviewer that he "liked literary work for its own sake,"[3] and yet he allowed a large part of his literary career to be shaped by his somewhat imperfect sense of the literary marketplace.

While he is an unusually accessible writer, some knowledge of the forces at work in his life as well as a recognition of the nature of his talent is useful for an understanding of his writings. One important consideration was his own perception of himself as a writer. Early in his career, in February 1868, Clemens wrote to his friend Mary Mason Fairbanks: "There is nothing that makes me prouder than to be regarded by intelligent people as 'authentic.' A name I have coveted so long—& secured at last! *I* don't care anything about being humorous, or poetical, or eloquent, or anything of that kind—the end & aim of my ambition is to be authentic—is to be considered authentic." His concern was not so much to *be* authentic as to be *considered* authentic. This concern is manifested in the way he presented himself—or rather presented Mark Twain: a personage palpably present in his words, an irreverent skeptic, irrepressible, humorous, unpretentious but self-assured, and often victimized, usually by his own illusions. Sometimes there are two different Mark Twains, a "before" version and an "after." Then one meets either a naive and youthful innocent, one who is not very bright, easily misled but well-meaning, *or* an experienced, confident, humorous, perhaps impudent veteran, who knows the world, especially its underside, thoroughly. Whichever it is, Mark Twain seems like the genuine article. Both the vulnerability of the innocent and the casual ease of the veteran assure the reader that whoever touches his book touches a man.

Early in his career, in Nevada and California, he also developed a second technique that contributed to authenticity: he created another kind of voice, that of a storyteller, usually an older man and often a Westerner, who has had a long career as a miner, a sea captain, a riverboat man. This narrator speaks in the vernacular and is distinctly antigenteel. He is usually an innocent, or rather pretends to be, and he tells tall tales, but with a straight face. After Clemens came east and became more and more "sivilized" (Huck Finn's word), he had more and more need to employ such a vernacular commentator as a subtle indicator of his own inner rebelliousness. Late in life he began a novel, "Indiantown," about one David Gridley who by "working a deception" marries an "archangel," though he knows that "there were things in his make-up which would distress this dear unworldly creature." Therefore he let her remake him, but while "training and teaching can alter the outside of him," they cannot alter "the inside." The "elaborate sham" that she constructed was of course a hypocrite, and he knew it, to his shame.[4] Here Clemens told the story of his life with his adored wife, perhaps to acknowledge his sense that he had betrayed part of his true self.

Each year we learn new things about Samuel Clemens and his remarkable literary career, as the work he left unpublished at his death in 1910 is published, as well as notebooks, newly discovered letters, and better texts of the books published in his own time. Few readers, even devoted admirers, have any comprehension of the scope of Mark Twain's output. One estimate, probably conservative, is that his more than eight hundred surviving pieces fill about eighteen thousand pages. During a sabbatical leave in 1979–80 and again during the summer of 1982, when I enjoyed a grant from the National Endowment for the Humanities, I was privileged to work in the Mark Twain Papers, the headquarters of most of these recent publications. Housed in the Bancroft Library of the University of California, Berkeley, these papers have as their nucleus the manuscripts, correspondence, clippings, photographs, and memorabilia that were the charge of Albert Bigelow Paine, Clemens's authorized biographer, when he became Clemens's literary executor in 1910. Paine's successors—Bernard DeVoto, Dixon Wecter, Henry Nash Smith, Frederick Anderson, and now Robert Hirst—have augmented as well as organized the collection. It now includes photocopies of materials in other collections; editions, early and late, of Mark Twain's works; and books and articles about him, including unpublished dissertations. Another of its resources is a staff of experts involved in editing his notebooks, letters, and published and unpublished writings. (Many of his best-known works have desperately needed reediting, as the following pages will show.) I owe a debt to the staff of the Mark Twain Papers, especially to Henry Nash Smith, who returned from retirement to his old post there on the death of Frederick Anderson, and to Robert Hirst. I am also grateful to staff members Lin Salamo, Dahlia Armon, Kenneth Sanderson, Victor Fischer, Harriet Smith, Michael Frank, and Paul Machlis, who helped me in innumerable ways. I am especially indebted to Professor Louis Budd, whose visit to the Papers in January 1980 enriched my own; his subsequent readings of the manuscript delivered me from a number of errors, and his suggestions proved invaluable. I thank too my son Stephen, John Seelye, and Jules Chametzky, who made helpful suggestions, as did Alan Gribben. My friend Alberta Booth read the whole manuscript with care and proposed hundreds of valuable improvements, chiefly stylistic. I owe a debt to the supportiveness of my wife Katherine and my friends Mae and Sidney Roger, and to Ted Pearson; and I owe much to the students with whom I have studied the writings of Mark Twain over the last twenty-five years, especially at the University of Massachusetts, Amherst. I am deeply grateful for permission to quote from manuscript materials of Mark Twain Papers, University of California, Berkeley; also to the Mark Twain Memorial, Hartford, Connecticut; the libraries of Washington University, St. Louis, Missouri; the Beinecke Rare Book and Manuscript Library of Yale University; the McKinney Papers of Vassar College, Poughkeepsie, New York; the Henry W. and Albert A. Berg Collection, New York Public Library, Astor, Lenox, and Tilden Foundations; and the Pierpont Morgan Library, New York. My thanks too go to the staffs of the libraries of the University of Massachusetts, Amherst; Amherst College, and the University of California, Berkeley, especially the Bancroft Library.

In the pages that follow, I have told the story of Samuel L. Clemens's literary career often by means of his own words, especially from unpublished materials or writings that, though published, are inaccessible to many readers. Sources from works published in many "complete" editions are provided by identifying the work, if short, or the chapter, if long, in which it appears. The abbreviations I employ are derived from a list used at the Mark Twain Papers.

To avoid burdening the reader with footnotes, I have usually cited only by date in my text Samuel Clemens's letters appearing in *Collected Letters* (forthcoming, University of California Press), the first three volumes—covering the period through January 30, 1874—of which I was privileged to see in proof in July 1982; also cited only by date are letters from Clemens to William Dean Howells and from Howells to Clemens, which appeared in *Mark Twain–Howells Letters* (Harvard University Press, 1960), and letters from Clemens to H. H. Rogers, which appeared in *Mark Twain's Correspondence with Henry Huddleston Rogers* (University of California Press, 1969). References to the three volumes so far published of *Mark Twain's Notebooks & Journals* (University of California Press, 1975–79) should be locatable from the text. In addition, these volumes are well indexed.

While I have attempted to examine closely the whole of Samuel Clemens's career in a way not attempted before, I have not discussed or even mentioned everything that he wrote, since there are many pieces that I judge to be of very little value. I have tried to address the interests and needs of readers who know little as well as those who know much about Mark Twain and his writings. While the shape of Clemens's life should be apparent from these pages, readers who are interested in knowing more are referred to the biographies by De-Lancey Ferguson (published in 1943, and so somewhat outdated) and Justin Kaplan (1966), which regrettably opens when Clemens was thirty-one.

Anyone who in the last quarter of the twentieth century seriously studies Mark Twain soon discovers that many have been there already. Thomas Tenney's massive *Mark Twain: A Reference Guide*, with six supplements as of 1982, cites nearly seven thousand items, with 116 for the year 1978 alone. Although I have not read all of that work, Dr. Tenney's guide has made it possible to locate from that mammoth library of criticism and scholarship what seemed most relevant to my task. Finally, a disclaimer: most of the humor in this book will be found to be Mark Twain's, not my own. His is a hard act to follow.

CHAPTER ONE

The Creation of Mark Twain

SAMUEL Langhorne Clemens's childhood in Hannibal, Missouri, the story of which he tells in some of the best passages in his not always reliable *Autobiography*, was a source he drew on repeatedly in his best works. When he was just sixteen, he published a description of Hannibal in the Philadelphia *American Courier*. "The town is situated on the Mississippi river, about one hundred and thirty miles above St. Louis, and contains a population of about three thousand. . . . Among the curiosities of this place we may mention the *Cave*, which is about three miles below the city. It is of unknown length; it has innumerable passages, which are not unlike the streets of a large city."[1] This cave, Hannibal's steep hill, the steamboats, the islands in the river, his uncle's farm not far from Clemens's birthplace, the town of Florida— all these Mark Twain would make into memorable aspects of the American literary landscape. Of his boyhood summers he was to recall in "Early Days" (1897–98):

> I spent some part of every year at the farm until I was twelve or thirteen years old. The life which I led there with my cousins was full of charm, and so is the memory of it yet. I can call back the solemn twilight and mystery of the deep woods, the earthy smells, the faint odors of the wild flowers, the sheen of rain-washed foliage, the rattling clatter of drops when the wind shook the trees, the far-off hammering of woodpeckers and the muffled drumming of wood pheasants in the remoteness of the forest, the snapshot glimpses of disturbed wild creatures scurrying through the grass—I can call it all back and make it as real as it ever was, and as blessed.

For several pages he conjured up the sights, tastes, touches, sounds, and smells of his past. Sentence after sentence begins "I know how" and "I know" and "I can remember."

People too he remembered. When he was sixty-one he wrote "Villagers of 1840–3," which recalls an amazing number—168—of his Hannibal townsfolk, described at length. Here are two samples.

> *Ouseley.* Prosperous merchant. Smoked fragrant cigars—regalias—5 apiece. Killed old Smar. Acquitted. His party brought him huzzaing in from Palmyra at midnight. But there was a cloud upon him—a social chill— and he presently moved away. [From this memory Mark Twain derived Colonel Sherburn in *Huckleberry Finn.*]

> *Letitia Honeyman.* School. Married a showy stranger. Turned out to be a thief and swindler. She and her baby waited while he served a long term. At the end of it her youth was gone, and her cheery ways.[2]

The writer remembered his own father, and his death. (His memory was vivid but imprecise.)

> Judge C. was elected County Judge by a great majority in '49 [actually John Marshall Clemens died in 1847 before the election], and at last saw great prosperity before him. But of course caught his death the first day he opened court. He went home with pneumonia, 12 miles, horseback, winter—and in a fortnight he was dead. First instance of affection: discovering that he was dying, chose his daughter from among the weepers, who were kneeling about the room and crying—and motioned her to come to him. Drew her down to him, with his arms about her neck, kissed her (for the first time, no doubt), and said "Let me die"—and sunk back and the death rattle came. Ten minutes before, the Pres[byterian] preacher had said, "Do you believe on the Lord Jesus Christ, and that through his blood only you can be saved?" "I do." Then the preacher prayed over him and recommended him. He did not say goodbye to his wife, or to any but his daughter.[3]

Judge Clemens was a man of dignity with a good standing in this community, but at his death he left his family very little. In the 1820s and 1830s he had purchased thousands of acres in Tennessee, and for years members of his family would imagine that it was to make them rich. But they were mistaken.

The presence of the preacher at John Clemens's deathbed probably was the responsibility of Jane Lampton Clemens, Samuel's mother. She saw to it that Sam went to Sunday school, first at the Methodist church, later at the Presbyterian church that she joined. Subsequently the writer was to recall his Sunday school experiences in *Tom Sawyer*. In Hannibal, revivalism was strong, and there was a good deal of spiritualism as well. Sam was a troublesome child, plagued by illnesses. His behavior was often eccentric, and he had a tendency to wander away from home. His formal education, soon to be interrupted, was what such a small town could offer. The far from negligible education that he was to obtain later was of necessity picked up elsewhere than in schools. Clemens was only eleven years old when his father died. Soon after, Sam undertook part-time work, and in 1848, when his schooling came to a close, he was introduced to an occupation that would lead to a career. After serving as delivery and office boy, he became a printer's apprentice for his hometown newspaper, the Hannibal *Courier*. He was following in the footsteps of his brother Orion, nearly six years his elder, who had become an apprentice in 1839. After a stint in St. Louis, Orion returned to Hannibal, and in early 1851 Sam went to work for his brother as a journeyman printer on Orion's newspaper, the Hannibal *Journal*. Even before this time, Sam had published his first paragraph, "A Gallant Fireman," in the Hannibal *Union* for January 16. Soon he was showing signs of literary ambition. On May 1, 1852, he published in the Boston comic weekly *The Carpet-Bag* a short sketch entitled "The Dandy Frightening the Squatter." The piece is not in itself striking; it resembles a sketch that its author may well have read in the Hannibal *Courier* of 1850, "Doin' a Dandy." Yet it is notable that this short sketch, signed "S.L.C.," appeared in remote Boston. Sixty years later, the writer would say of this sketch and of his description of Hannibal published the same year, "Seeing them in print was a joy which rather exceeded anything in that line I have ever experienced since."[4]

His Boston publisher was B. P. Shillaber, creator of Mrs. Partington, a character later to influence the creation of Tom Sawyer's Aunt Polly. Shillaber's publication was only one of many comic periodicals flourishing in America at this time, and these had a strong influence on Clemens, especially in his youth. The first was created as early as 1831 by William T. Porter, a Vermonter: the *Spirit of the Times* described itself as a "Chronicle of the Turf, Agriculture, Field Sports, Literature, and the Stage." Addressing a masculine audience, it published chiefly tales based on the oral humor of the frontier. Many other magazines soon followed its example. Though never very remote from the real life of the people they portrayed, the stories they published were frequently tall tales. To increase his credibility, the teller was likely to maintain a poker face while he ostensibly provided a report.

The theme of many of these tales is the distinction between the real and the false, between the unsophisticated and the pretentious. Sometimes the teller is himself the unconscious victim in his story; often it is an Easterner who is outsmarted, even humiliated, for he is likely to be innocent, ignorant, green. (Sometimes it is the reader who is taken in.) Clemens found particularly congenial to his talents and attitudes this concern with victimization and humiliation: it became a central theme in many works, such as *Huckleberry Finn* and "The Man That Corrupted Hadleyburg." Clemens adopted another technique of these stories, the use of slang and elaborate misspellings, only for a short time. Like many of the writers of this school, he would adopt a pen name. Among the writers closest in one way or another to Clemens were George Horatio Derby, who became John Phoenix and told of his adventures in the California of the 1850s; H. W. Shaw, who as Josh Billings wrote about farming, exploration, riverboating; and David Ross Locke, who adopted the name "Petroleum Vesuvius Nasby, late pastor uv the Church uv the New Dispensation, Chaplain to his excellency the President, and p. m. at Confederate roads, Kentucky." Most successful of all was Charles Farrar Browne, later to become Artemus Ward, crusader against insincerity and sentimentality, chiefly as a comic lecturer. Clemens was to meet Ward in 1863 and later make his humor the subject of a much-repeated lecture.

Frequently coarse, violent, and emphatic, the humor of these writers is only feebly reflected in young Clemens's "Dandy" anecdote. Set in Hannibal when "the now flourishing young city . . . was but a 'woodyard,'" it tells of a would-be gentleman, obviously from the east, who seeks to demonstrate his manliness to some young women by frightening a woodsman. But the Easterner ends up in the river. The dandy is "astonished" and humiliated. Clemens gives no characterization to his narrator, and the story is not told in dialect.

After demonstrating that his work could be published in the East, Clemens turned his attention to local publication. While his brother Orion was absent from home for a time in September 1852, Sam was able to publish several items, some as a consequence of his getting into an argument with the editor of the Hannibal *Tri-Weekly Messenger*, whom he tried to embarrass. Nearly forty pieces in all have been located in Hannibal newspapers: verses, burlesques, local items. They show much energy but little control. Several are signed "W. Epaminondas Adrastus Perkins," who later became simply "Blab" or signed his pieces by his initials, W.E.A.B. "Historical Exhibition—A No. 1 Ruse" is such a piece, an anticipation of the confidence games played

by the Duke and the King in *Huckleberry Finn*. Here young Jim C——
is the victim. He pays his five cents to see "Bonaparte crossing the
Rhine," exhibited by a local merchant. What he gets to see is the bony
part of a hog's leg crossing a piece of hog's rind. Some other pieces,
mostly very brief, use the pen names of the Rambler, the Grumbler,
and Peter Pencilcase's son, John Snooks. Somewhat more personal is
"Oh, She Has a Red Head!" by a redhead who signs himself "A Son
of Adam" and who argues that "red is the natural color of beauty."
Here the future public personality acknowledges his love of display,
which was to be lifelong. A satire of the Democratic governor and
legislature, "Blabbing Government Secrets," anticipates another of his
future interests, public affairs.[5]

In May 1853, Orion Clemens awarded young Sam "Our Assistant's Column." There he criticized newspapers that borrow without
credit and attacked one "Mr. Jacques," whose drunken mistreatment
of his children he believed should be punished with tarring and feath-
ering and being ridden out of town on a rail, a form of punishment
that Huck was to think cruel when applied to the Duke and the King.
While Orion was away, Sam published a headline in the paper:

TERRIBLE ACCIDENT!
500 MEN KILLED AND MISSING!!!
We had set the above head up, expecting (of course) to use it, but as the
accident hasn't yet happened, we'll say
(To be continued)[6]

Hannibal was a very small world, remote from the life of literature, but as a journeyman printer Sam Clemens could soon find work
elsewhere. At the age of seventeen, after a visit to his sister Pamela in
St. Louis, he made his way, without telling his mother in advance, to
New York City. Two letters he wrote to her in August appeared in
Orion's newspaper. Sam explains how he traveled to New York, by
steamboat and train, in five days, with a little sightseeing in Chicago,
Rochester, and Syracuse. In New York he saw "the wild men of Bor-
neo," a magnificent "fruit salon," and the ships of New York harbor.
Young Clemens had already picked up a literary technique he was to
make good use of throughout his career, notably when he uses Huck
to tell his story: emphasizing the writer's own response to what he
sees. Of the wild men he wrote, "Their faces and eyes are those of the
beast, and when they fix their glittering orbs on you with a steady,
unflinching gaze, you instinctively draw back a step, and a very un-

pleasant sensation steals through your veins." In these early letters home Sam identifies himself not so much as a fledgling writer—but as a printer, proud of his ability to set clean proof. He is a reader too, for he has found satisfaction that the New York printers have two libraries where he can "spend my evenings most pleasantly." He would later become a lover of books and libraries.

Other letters, written in September and October to his sister Pamela Moffett of St. Louis, were not published until after his death. They are full of descriptions of New York sights, including the theater. Soon Sam moved on to Philadelphia, and from there he wrote a series of letters that were published in the Muscatine (Iowa) *Journal*, which was then partly owned by Orion, who had moved 120 miles up the river in September. After printing a portion of a letter dated October 26, 1853, apparently without permission, Orion invited his brother to write letters for publication, and Sam accepted. The first three letters are somewhat impersonal accounts of Philadelphia and of Washington, D.C., from whence he wrote in February 1854. With deep respect the young Clemens visited the monuments of American history, the grave of Benjamin Franklin, the Liberty Bell, and objects associated with George Washington. He saw Philadelphia as continuing the European cultural tradition; his attitude comes close to reverence. Some of this respect was borrowed, for the two Philadelphia letters apparently were written with R. A. Smith's *Philadelphia as It Is in 1852* open in front of him. In Washington, his tone is similar as he describes the Capitol, the senators, and the members of the House of Representatives. In the West he would learn to be more critical. After a year's interruption, in February and March 1855, two more letters appeared in the Muscatine *Journal*, from St. Louis, where Clemens was working. Signed S.L.C., these letters reflect much more of his tastes and are perhaps the first strong indication of the writer that was to be. Young Sam reports, for instance, on *The Merchant of Venice*: "I had always thought that this was a comedy, until they made a *farce* of it. The prompters found it hard matter to get the actors on stage, and when they did get them on, it was harder still to get them *off* again. 'Jessica' was always 'thar' when she wasn't wanted, and never would turn up when her services were required." There is a freshness of diction even in his comments about the weather: "Yesterday and to-day were as bright and pleasant as anyone could wish, and fires were abolished, I hope for the season."

How seriously Sam Clemens took this newspaper assignment is impossible to say. He wrote little for publication during the year and a half that followed, when neither he nor his brother Orion was connected with a newspaper. Then they both lived in Keokuk, Iowa—between Hannibal and Muscatine. Sam spoke at a printer's banquet celebrating the 150th anniversary of Benjamin Franklin's birth—Franklin the patron saint of American printers—and according to the Keokuk *Gate City* for January 19, 1856, his speech was "replete with wit and humor."

The origins of Samuel Clemens's interest in humor and in writing appear to be his pleasure from books. In printers' libraries and later in his own substantial one, Clemens was a great reader. His early work was influenced by his familiarity with the writings of such English and American literary comedians as Laurence Sterne, Thomas Hood, and George W. Curtis, whose *Potiphar Papers* (1853) burlesques religious hypocrisy and snobbery. In a March 1860 letter to Orion, Clemens identified Oliver Goldsmith's *Citizen of the World* and Cervantes's *Don Quixote* as his "*beau ideals*" of fine writing. In time Cervantes would provide him with a model for expressing both realistic and romantic viewpoints in the same work. A different kind of reading, undertaken a little later, had an impact too: when Clemens was a cub pilot, he read Thomas Paine's *The Age of Reason* "with fear and hesitation, but marveling at its fearlessness and wonderful power."[7] It reinforced his penchant for skepticism.

In the late summer or early fall of 1856 Clemens left Keokuk. Once again we can follow his travels from the letters he wrote for publication, this time actually for money. He was paid $5.00 a letter, later increased to $7.50, for what he wrote to the Keokuk *Post*. He now adopted a pen name and a pen personality: he was Thomas Jefferson Snodgrass, an innocent ready to be victimized in his city encounters. The three letters in this series show the strong influence of another of the frontier literary comedians, William Tappan Thompson, author of *Major Jones's Sketches of Travel* (1847). The first letter, dated October 18 from St. Louis, is Snodgrass's report of his visit to a performance of Shakespeare's *Julius Caesar*. This bumpkin's visit is largely predictable, especially to those who remember Jonathan's similar experiences as a theater-goer in Royall Tyler's post-revolutionary war play *The Contrast*, though Snodgrass's quotation from Dickens's *Little Dorrit* may surprise the reader today. A month later Snodgrass reports again. Just as he had been ejected from the theater in St. Louis because of his ignorance of proper behavior, here his innocence leads to misadventures. He had traveled eastward through Chicago, of which he reports: "When you feel like tellin a feller to go to the devil, tell him to go to Chicago—it'll anser every purpose, and is perhaps, a leetle more expensive."[8]

The third and most ambitious letter, dated Cincinnati, March 14, 1847, explains that the writer had "pooty much quit scribblin" until now when he has at last "a adventure" to report. The innocent has been victimized again, this time by a young woman who asked him to hold her basket while she went around the corner. Snodgrass obliges and uses the waiting time to daydream of marrying the woman, who he supposes is a rich heiress. An hour and a half later, he starts after her, whereupon he hears from the basket the howls of "the ugliest, nastiest, orneriest he-baby I ever seed in my life." Snodgrass does not know what to do. He keeps the baby for a day, then tries to "poke the dang thing through a hole in the ice" on the river. He is arrested and fined, then released. Such is his adventure.[9]

The Snodgrass letters, the last of which was written when Clemens was twenty-one, do not show the author-to-be discovering his métier. Not surprisingly, he now left journalism for an extended period, and also not surprisingly—for one who had lived in Hannibal, St. Louis, Keokuk, Muscatine, and Cincinnati—he was attracted to the river. Later he was to explain that he had planned to go from Cincinnati to the Amazon in order to become a trader and make a fortune,[10] but instead he became an apprentice pilot to Horace Bixby, a story he told brilliantly, though with exaggeration, in "Old Times on the Mississippi" (1875). This phase of his career lasted four years, until Clemens was twenty-five. Very little he wrote during that time has survived: some letters, six published pieces of journalism, all slight, and two pieces of fiction that he did not publish. A few letters do give the impression, however, that the pilot was still interested in writing. A letter to Annie Taylor in 1857 describes effectively the French Market of New Orleans and a cemetery of vaults and tombs in the city. Clemens was to have a continuing interest in cemeteries, morgues, and death, as *The Innocents Abroad* and *Huckleberry Finn* show. To his sister Pamela he wrote a rather literary letter on March 11, 1859. Here he provides a description of the Mardi Gras parade in New Orleans: "The procession was led by a Mounted Knight Crusader in blazing gilt armor from head to foot, and I think one might never tire of looking at the splendid picture."

Clemens's continuing interest in Charles Dickens is suggested by a long quotation in a November 1850 letter to his brother from *Martin*

Chuzzlewit concerning Mrs. Gamp's interest in alcohol. But these years on the river seem to have been so deeply gratifying to Clemens that he was not for a long time tempted to try another career. Throughout his life he was to remember as a reference point his experiences as a pilot, sometimes with pleasure, sometimes with relief that he had escaped. In January 1866, some four years after he had left the river, he wrote to his mother, "I wish I was back there piloting up & down the river again. Verily, all is vanity and little worth—save piloting." Toward the end of his piloting years, in February 1861, Clemens made a visit to a fortune-teller that he seems to have found especially significant. According to a long letter he sent to Orion, she told him, "You have written a good deal; you write well—but you are out of practice; no matter—you will be *in* practice some day."

One of six known publications of these years relates to the obscure and muddled history of Clemens's pen name. Some forty years later, in his *Autobiography*, Clemens explained that while a pilot he wrote a "rude and crude satire" of a riverboat man who wrote under the pen name of Mark Twain.[11] In 1874 he wrote, "Mark Twain was the *nom de plume* of one Capt. Isaiah Sellers, who used to write river news over it for the New Orleans *Picayune*. He died in 1863, & as he would no longer need that signature I laid violent hands upon it without asking permission of the prophet's remains."[12] In a sketch written in 1899–1900 he wrote merely that he began to sign his Nevada newspaper letters "using the Mississippi leadsman's call, 'Mark Twain' (two fathoms = twelve feet) for this purpose."[13] But Sellers did not die until a year after Clemens began to call himself Mark Twain, and no evidence has been found that Sellers used that pen name. On the other hand, Clemens did indeed satirize Sellers, whom he calls "Sergeant Fathom" in "River Intelligence," a piece he published in the New Orleans *Crescent* in May 1859. Here he has Sellers reminisce outlandishly and offer predictions of phenomenally high water. "In the summer of 1763 [ninety-six years before the date of the report] I came down the river on the old *first* Jubilee. She was new, then, however; a singular sort of a single-engine boat, with a Chinese captain and a Choctaw crew. . . ." According to the account in Mark Twain's *Life on the Mississippi* (chapter 50), this satire deeply affected Sellers, to the regret of the young Clemens.

Four pieces have just been discovered. Three were published in 1858. One pays tribute to the steamboat *John H. Dickey*, on which Clemens was working; another discusses Memphis and the Cotton trade; and a third offers some slight comic correspondence about a performing dog. More ambitious is "Soleleather Cultivates His Taste for Music," which appeared in the New Orleans *Crescent* in 1859. In it the brash narrator tells of his experiences at a St. Louis boarding-house, where he soothes a sick fellow boarder with his attempts to play first a violin, then a trombone. "Soleleather" is a version of Snodgrass, but better educated.[14] The sixth surviving piece is "Pilot's Memorandum," which burlesques the standard reports on river traffic appearing in newspapers. Its humor assumes a good deal of familiarity with the steamboating of that day.

Of the two attempts at fiction Clemens made during his years on the river, one is a gothic tale of murder and revenge set in Germany, but with a plot borrowed from Robert Montgomery Bird's *Nick of the Woods* (1837), and the other tells of a pilot who returns from the dead to perform an unusually difficult task of piloting. The stories suggest Clemens's continuing serious interest in writing more significantly than do the three published pieces.

With the coming of the Civil War, Clemens left the river, even though he might have chosen to serve as a pilot for either of the adversaries. Instead he returned home to Missouri, where he joined a group of volunteers who were taking the Confederate side in the conflict, but in two weeks he left them. This service was too informal and irregular for it to be said that he was a deserter, as is sometimes reported. Nearly twenty-five years later he was to render a somewhat fictionalized account of his "war" experiences in "The Private History of a Campaign That Failed." Sam's next adventure was more important. In July 1861 he accompanied his brother to the West, where Orion was to serve as secretary of the territory of Nevada. Sam was eventually hired to be a clerk at eight dollars a day, not Orion's official secretary, as Sam reported in the entertaining but not wholly reliable account in *Roughing It* (1872).[15]

After the long, slow journey westward to the territory, Sam found himself in a world of strange ugliness and beauty. He soon undertook some exploring and examined Lake Tahoe, only twenty miles or so from his headquarters, Carson City. The beauty of the lake affected him deeply, despite the negligence that resulted in his starting a forest fire there. He wrote a vivid account of the lake and the fire to his mother and sister in the early fall. A letter written a little later, in October, is one of his best-written early pieces; it shows Sam succumbing to the get-rich-quick fever of the silver miners. It also provides a description of the landscape.

> It never rains here, and the dew never falls. No flowers grow here, and no green thing gladdens the eye. The birds that fly over the land carry their provisions with them. Only the crow and the raven tarry with us. Our city lies in the midst of a desert of the purest—most unadulterated, and compromising *sand*—in which infernal soil nothing but that fag-end of creation, "sage brush," ventures to grow. If you will take a lilliputian cedar tree for a model, and build a dozen imitations of it with the stiffest article of telephone wire—set them one foot apart and then try to walk through them, you'll understand (provided the floor is 12 inches deep with sand) what it is to wander through a sage-brush desert. When crushed, sage brush emits an odor which isn't exactly magnolia and equally isn't exactly polecat—but, is a sort of compromise between the two. It looks a good deal like greasewood, and is the ugliest plant that was ever conceived of.

A version of this letter was published in the Keokuk *Gate City* in November. Two subsequent letters, written in January and March 1862 and also addressed to Clemens's mother, seem to have been intended for publication; they also appeared in the *Gate City*. In them Clemens assigns Jane Clemens the role of romantic disciple of Fenimore Cooper and admirer of the Noble Savage, and he himself is conceived to be a disenchanted old-timer. Later, when he was to take up some of these same materials in *Roughing It*, he played both roles himself: he had arrived in the West, he explains, as an innocent tenderfoot, full of book-learning, but years later he was writing as a hardened veteran. While the 1872 version is deservedly better known, these letters are a valuable indication of Clemens's development as a writer: he was beginning to assign himself more interesting roles. The discovery would have the most crucial consequences in his career.

The second of these early Nevada letters describes a trip Clemens and three others made to Unionville, Humboldt County, where silver was being discovered and mined. Here Clemens mixes information and anecdote just as he was to do in his travel books. In the third letter, he responds to an imagined plea from his mother to "tell me all about the lordly sons of the forest." And he does, at length. To him the Native Americans are far from lordly. Though Clemens was later to lose much of his inherited racist attitude toward Negroes, he was to remain quite as scornful of the Indians as he is in this letter. The description of a representative Indian, whose name is given as Hoop-de-doodle-do, is thoroughly repulsive. Clemens's advice is, "Now, if you are acquainted with any romantic young ladies or gentlemen who dote on the loves of Indians, send them out here before the disease strikes in." In 1897, Mark Twain wrote that in his youth "any person would have been proud of a 'strain' of Indian blood"; Cooper's great popularity was responsible.[16]

These long descriptive letters home indicate not merely that Clemens was interested in writing, but also that he was beginning to experiment creatively and to enjoy playing the skeptic. Chiefly, however, he wanted to get rich quick, and the means was obviously silver. In a letter written to Orion on May 11 and 12, 1862, he reports that he owns a one-eighth interest in a ledge, and "I *know* it to contain our fortune." In the same letter he observes that he assumes Orion was seeing his letters in the local newspaper, the *Enterprise*. By June he was thinking seriously of his work as a writer, for after complaining about the unsatisfactory printing of a letter in the local paper, he instructs Orion, "Put all of my Josh's letters in my scrap book. I may have use for them some day." (The letters signed "Josh" were written for the Virginia City *Territorial Enterprise*; they have not survived.) A month later he told Orion to write to the Sacramento *Union* or to members of its staff to announce that "I'll write as many letters a week as they want, for $10 a week—my board must be paid. Tell them I have corresponded with the N. Orleans Crescent, and other papers—and the Enterprise. California is full of people who have interests here, and its d——d seldom they hear from this country." The explanation for his job-hunting is that he was in debt, and now "The fact is, I must have something to do, and that *shortly* too."

What happened next is not quite clear, though it turned out to have great consequences. According to the account in his autobiography, Clemens now became so desperate that he "stood on the verge of the ministry or the penitentiary." Fortunately, he recounted, he found occasion to submit to the *Enterprise* for publication a burlesque of a speech by the chief justice of Nevada—just when the city editor of the *Enterprise*, Dan De Quille (William E. Wright) was planning a trip home to Iowa. The piece was admired, and Sam was hired.[17] Perhaps a more likely story is that Sam was hired so that the *Enterprise* printing house would get patronage from Orion's brother, the territorial secretary.[18] At any rate, within a short time Clemens as a full-time writer for the *Enterprise* adopted the pen name "Mark Twain," though for a time he probably used his real name for serious news stories.

The development of Samuel Clemens as a writer is not fully documented, since the great bulk of what he wrote for publication in

Nevada is lost. It has been estimated that he published fifteen hundred to three thousand local items, but since there is no file of the *Enterprise*, one must consult such sources as the slim gathering of clippings in a surviving Clemens notebook, and those pieces reprinted in other newspapers that have survived. These provide a total of fewer than fifty items, although many of them are among his more notable pieces. The earliest extant pieces signed "Mark Twain" are three letters from Carson City dated January 31 and February 3 and 6, 1863. Written while he was on a week's vacation, they are notable chiefly for their tone: good-natured, confidential, nonchalant. For instance, discussing a wedding he'd attended, Mark Twain writes that it was "mighty pleasant, and jolly, and sociable, and I wish to thunder I was married myself. I took a large slab of the bridal cake home with me to dream on, and dreamt that I was still a single man, and likely to remain so, if I live and nothing happens—which has given me a greater confidence in dreams than I ever felt before." This is the voice of the authentic Mark Twain.

For the *Enterprise*, Mark Twain wrote local items, unsigned editorials, and reports from San Francisco, Carson City, and the territorial legislature and constitutional convention. (For the convention, he and another reporter provided full and in part verbatim accounts. These are of no literary value; it is impossible to distinguish Clemens's writing from that of his co-worker.[19] They are not included in the reckoning cited earlier.) Even routine items frequently have a humorous touch. He suggests, for example, in "The Spanish Mine" that "stout-legged persons with an affinity for darkness" might enjoy an hour-long visit to the mine on which he was reporting. Such unsigned items as the following appeared soon after Clemens joined the *Enterprise* staff. "A beautiful and ably conducted free fight came off in C street yesterday, but as nobody was killed or mortally wounded in manner sufficiently fatal to cause death, no particular interest attaches to the matter, and we shall not publicize the details. We pine for murder— these fist fights are of no consequence to anybody." In this piece— written before the earliest appearance of Clemens's *nom de plume*—one hears for the first time the voice that was to become famous. Excitement made life tolerable in the dull towns of the West, and Clemens was to make much of his boyish appreciation of it. Violence was especially exciting, but if necessary one could always resort to theatrics, even those of the hoax.

In Nevada, Mark Twain was a successful journalist, with his stories being picked up by other papers, especially in California, even though few of these early pieces—the surviving ones—give an indication of what he would later be able to do. As much as anything, in Nevada he became identified with hoaxes; they were preparations, perhaps, for Huck Finn's imaginative deceptions. One of the earliest hoaxes dates from October 15, 1862. It reports the discovery of a "petrified man," found "in a sitting posture" with "the right thumb resting against the side of the nose; the left thumb partially supporting the chin, the forefinger pressing the inner corner of the left eye and drawing it partly open; the right eye was closed, and the fingers of the right hand spread apart." "This strange freak of nature" was examined by a local judge, "Justice Sewell or Sowell of Humboldt City," who convened a jury to hold an inquest, according to the account. (Mark Twain later explained that one of the objects of the piece was to make the judge look ridiculous.[20]) The jury concluded that "deceased came to his death from protracted exposure." Published in the *Enterprise*, this account was picked up by other newspapers, twelve in Nevada and California. The San Francisco publication, headed "Washoe Joke" (Washoe was a name for Nevada), was presumably captioned by someone who recognized that the petrified man was winking and thumbing his nose.

At the *Territorial Enterprise*, Mark Twain was associated with other writers, such as the twenty-four-year-old editor, Joseph Goodman, and Dan De Quille, with whom he roomed. (De Quille had already written up an effective hoax about a personal portable air-conditioning system.) The new journalist soon discovered that his work was not arduous. Reporters from other journals were ready to swap "regulars," reports from continuing sources of news such as the courts and the registry of bullion. If news was short, it could be invented. In this career Clemens for a time lost his ambition, drank a good deal, and was soon making a reputation for flippancy, bohemianism, and irreverence. He was proud enough of his direct language to defend it in print: "If I choose to use the language of the vulgar, the low-flung and the sinful, and such as will shock the ears of the highly civilized, I don't want him [a printer] to appoint himself an editorial critic and proceed to tone me down."[21]

The *Enterprise* period was a beginning. Mark Twain was discovering himself—or, perhaps more accurately, Sam Clemens was beginning to create "Mark Twain." He was discovering that there is a close connection between the comic and the forbidden—those aspects of life not to be mentioned in polite society. He was discovering that humor is gratifying because it relaxes a repressive atmosphere. Obviously the frontier environment encouraged this discovery, though he was never able to determine accurately how far he could go without being offensive—even if he was aware, usually, of his inability to judge. He knew that he could amusingly violate inhibiting strictures by satirizing the fastidiousness of the genteel and genteel attitudes: romantic love, admiration for the "sublime" in nature, idealized childhood, grand opera, even benevolent humanitarianism. He could offend the pretentiousness of the proper by referring to the unmentionable: sows, nose-picking, vomit, spit, warts, singed cats, body odor. He was never to outgrow the conviction that bad smells are funny. A mild specimen of this brand of humor is Mark Twain's August 1863 account of his adventures after taking a tonic called "Wake-up Jake." It affected him for forty-eight hours. "And during all that time, I could not have enjoyed a viler taste in my mouth if I had swallowed a slaughter house." He almost died, he says, of vomiting and other forms of elimination.

This sketch is one of the few in which Mark Twain is a victim. More often he asserts in exaggerated form his own superiority. The roles he assigns himself are, in one critic's words, those of the "Social Lion, the Nabob, the Entertainer, and the Ladies' Man."[22] He saw his assignment to be insulting and humiliating to others. It would be some time before he learned how much more funny he could be if he himself was humiliated, especially by becoming, in James Cox's phrase, the fool of his own illusions.

San Francisco was a long 150 miles from Washoe, with the Sierra Nevadas on the way west. The trip took thirty hours. But California was the source of supplies for Nevada; all the bullion was shipped there in bars, with three stages a day each way. Clemens visited San Francisco a number of times during his years in Nevada, at least three times in 1863. His first trip, which lasted two months, occasioned this parting shot from the May 3 *Enterprise*: "Mark Twain has abdicated the local column of the *Enterprise*, where by the grace of Cheek, he so long reigned. . . . he has gone to display his ugly person and disgusting manners and wildcat on Montgomery Street."[23] In one of his letters he describes the trip "Over the Mountains" and in it introduces perhaps the first of his antigenteel narrators. Much of the letter is devoted to Mark Twain's account of what the driver of the stagecoach said about a man who, having fallen asleep while riding up with the driver, fell off his seat, "and in a second there wasn't anything left of him but a promiscuous pile of hash." The use of such a figure was soon to become an important part of Mark Twain's literary repertoire.

These narrators, usually veterans of long service in their occupations (as miners, ship captains, or stage drivers), are utterly lacking in self-consciousness, perhaps because they are authority figures. As the man behind the writer became more interested in moving upward in the social scale, he found that when he wished to avoid presenting Mark Twain as too "low," too vulgar a personage, he could introduce a narrator such as the coach driver to tell his tale. Mark Twain especially enjoyed describing characters who were both profane and innocent.

Another letter on his adventures in California went not to Virginia City but to New York, where it was published in the *Sunday Mercury* for February 21, 1864. Artemus Ward, who visited Virginia City in late 1863, had suggested that he write occasionally for that Eastern paper. In "Those Blasted Children," Mark Twain describes his suffering at the Lick House in San Francisco, where noisy "young savages" pestered him. "It is a living wonder to me that I haven't scalped some of those children before now," he comments unsentimentally. "I expect I would have done it, but then I hardly felt well enough acquainted with them." The cures for illnesses in children indicate his approach. For worms, "administer a catfish three times a week. Keep the room very quiet; the fish won't bite if there is the least noise."

While in San Francisco, Clemens obtained a commission to write a series of letters to a local newspaper, the *Daily Morning Call*, and in the summer of 1863 ten letters from Mark Twain in Nevada appeared. The *Call* announced that these letters "set forth in his easy, readable style the condition of things in Silverland."[24] Very competent journalism with a good deal of wit interspersed, the pieces both helped spread his reputation and prepared the way for a later position on that San Francisco newspaper. Ready to make much ado about the vast difference between the San Francisco climate and that of Virginia City, he reports in his second letter that "last week the weather was passably cool, but it has moderated a good deal since then. The thermometer stands at a thousand, in the shade, today. It will probably go to a million before night." In another letter Mark writes that Mr. G. T. Sewell was among those bruised recently in travel accidents; he reminds his readers that Sewell is the man who held the inquest on the death of the petrified man. An amusing piece explains that crime is much more common in Nevada than in California. "Nothing that can be stolen is neglected. Watches that would never go in California, generally go fast enough before they have been in the Territory twenty-four hours."[25]

One passage, "A Rich Decision," is particularly interesting because it tells a story that Mark Twain was to return to twice, in "The Facts in the Great Landslide Case" in the Buffalo *Express* for April 12, 1870, then (in only slightly revised form) in chapter 34 of *Roughing It*. In this 1863 version, Mark Twain lets the reader know from the start that "some of the boys in Carson" were playing a hoax on old Mr. Bunker, an attorney, who was employed to bring suit for the recovery of Dick Sides's ranch after Tom Rust's ranch slid down the mountain and covered it. In the later versions, the hoax is played on the unwary reader as well, and the story, three times as long, is elaborated and dramatized.

In addition, Mark Twain wrote a few sketches from Nevada for the *Golden Era*, a weekly founded to encourage the development of literature in the area. Albert Bierstadt had designed the masthead, and among the local writers were Joaquin Miller, Charles W. Stoddard, and Bret Harte, whose "M'liss" was the first memorable story of the California frontier. The editors of the *Enterprise* had been apprentices on the *Golden Era*, and its founder, Rollin M. Daggett, had also founded the *Enterprise*. Many items by Mark Twain appeared in the *Golden Era*, but probably only a few were written especially for it. They include "How to Cure a Cold," published September 20, and "The Lick House Ball," published September 27, both in 1863. The former is one of the earliest to find a place, in revised form, in the first American collected editions of Mark Twain's writings. After appearing in 1867 in his first book, it was collected in *Sketches New and Old* (1875). It tells of the author's efforts to get rid of that most common of ailments by adopting the many suggested cures offered by well-meaning people: cold showers, drinking a quart of salt water (which caused him, he reports, to throw up everything, including, he believes, his "immortal soul"); then a mixture of molasses, aquafortis, turpentine, and drugs; then gin, then gin and molasses, and gin and onions; then travel; a mustard plaster, and steam baths. He survives, with difficulty. The account is still amusing; Mark Twain did well to save it.

During his Nevada years, Mark Twain created the first fully developed character to flout the genteel. A rival reporter, actually a friend named Clement T. Rice, undertook to criticize Mark Twain's reports of a session of the Nevada legislature. He replied that Rice's accounts were a "festering mass of misstatements the author of whom should be properly termed the 'Unreliable.'"[26] Thereafter "the Unreliable" was to make frequent appearances in Mark Twain's writings of the period, both as the butt of his humor and as Clemens's alter ego—the coarser side. The Unreliable borrows, without permission, Mark Twain's most elegant clothes, his boots, his hat, his "white kid gloves," and his "heavy gold repeater." Mark Twain finds him in this garb attending an evening party, where he devours huge quantities of food and drink, including a roast pig, and sings a drunken song. Mark Twain offers to duel with him, "boot-jacks at a hundred yards." The Unreliable swindles a San Francisco hotel when the two visit it. He is constantly obnoxious, reprehensible, boorish. When Mark Twain plans to send back to Nevada a report on the San Francisco weather, "something glowing and poetical," the Unreliable tells him, "Say it's bully, you tallow-brained idiot! that's enough; anybody can understand that; don't write any of those infernal, sick platitudes about sweet flowers, and joyous butterflies, and worms and things, for people to read before breakfast. You make a fool of yourself that way; everybody gets disgusted with you; stuff! be a man or a mouse." The Unreliable is— as Mark Twain frequently chose to be—the sworn enemy of sentimentality.

In one letter Mark Twain writes as the Unreliable—or rather he renders an account of the Unreliable's drunken remarks on his visit to San Jose, "Sarrozay." Rice was to get even when Clemens was ill with a cold and arranged for Rice to attend to *Enterprise* chores. Over Mark Twain's name Rice published an apology to all those whom he had ridiculed, especially "the Unreliable," and promised to go "in sackcloth and ashes for the next forty days." The next day Clemens was recovered enough to publish a retraction of "his" apology and a denunciation of Rice as a reptile and jackass-rabbit. Rice was a real person, little resembling "the Unreliable"; later Mark Twain was to create a similar but wholly fictional character of much fuller dimensions, the outspoken Mr. Brown. The still-developing author was seeking a means of expressing himself frankly, but without dirtying himself.

Few of the surviving pieces from the *Enterprise* could be called sketches. One of these, "Ye Sentimental Law Student," quotes a letter, identified as probably by the Unreliable, expressing effusively the writer's devotion to "Mary, the party of the second part." "The view from the lonely and segregated mountain peak," he continues, "of this portion of what is called and known as Creation, with all and singular the hereditaments and appurtenances thereunto appertaining and belonging, is expressively grand and inspiring. . . ." For Mary's benefit he extends his legalistic description. Another sketch provides a learned essay on Washoe in response to an innocent inquiry from a Missourian. He tells him, for instance, that it may rain for four to seven days in a row, after which "you may loan out your umbrella for twelve months, with the serene confidence which a Christian feels in four aces."

One of the most famous, even notorious, of Mark Twain's writings of his Western years is "A Bloody Massacre near Carson" (October 1863). His purpose, he was later to explain, was to compose a "reformatory satire" on the "dividend-cooking system" of misleading investors, but nobody ever saw the point of the satire.[27] In this hoax he reported that one Hopkins, who lived in the old log house between Empire City and Dutch Nick's, at the edge of a forest, had been driven to despair by the loss of his savings through financial manipulations in San Francisco. He died after having ridden into town, his throat cut ear to ear, with his wife's bloody scalp in his hand. The husband was discovered to have brutally murdered six of his children. The report stressed many bloody details. But this Hopkins was in fact a bachelor; there was no forest—none for many miles—and Dutch Nick's and Empire City were one and the same. If the reader did not know this geography, he might have detected the hoax nonetheless: Hopkins's riding four to five miles with throat cut ear to ear ought to have seemed unlikely. But the nearby Gold Hill *Daily News* picked up the story as fact, as did other papers. When Mark Twain wrote in the next issue of the *Enterprise*, "I take it all back," he was widely attacked. California newspapers, such as the Sacramento *Daily Union*, demanded that he be discharged. Eventually the "massacre" became part of the local lore, frequently alluded to in newspapers.

In the following spring Mark Twain's often obnoxious ways brought about his departure from Nevada. He had been feuding fiercely, in print, with the publisher of the Virginia City *Union* when by chance a piece he had written—but then rejected on advice from Dan De Quille—appeared in the *Enterprise*. The story had to do with local efforts to raise money for the Sanitary Fund, a Civil War organization somewhat like the Red Cross. It had been stated, Mark Twain wrote, that funds raised for the organization had been misdirected to "a Miscegenation Society somewhere in the East." He then asserted that the charge was "a hoax, but not all a hoax, for an effort is being made to divert these funds from their proper course."[28] Soon there was an uproar, and the likelihood of a duel; Sam Clemens, partly through his love of mischief, partly because of what was considered malice, partly through mischance, had become persona non grata. He wrote to Orion's wife that "the Sanitary expedition has been disastrous to me," and on May 29 Clemens and his friend Steve Gillis left Nevada, for good.

The Gold Hill *Daily News* bid good riddance: "Shifting the *locale* of his tales of fiction from the Forest of Dutch Nick's to Carson City; the *dramatis personae* from the Hopkins family to the ladies of the Sanitary Fair; and the plot from murder to miscegenation—he slopped. The indignation aroused by his enormities has been too crushing to be borne by living man, though sheathed with the brass and triple cheek of Mark Twain." But the Virginia City *Old Piute* was kinder: "We shall miss Mark. . . . To know him was to love him. . . . God bless you, Mark!"[29]

The newborn, original—in more than one sense—and authentic Mark Twain was a product of Nevada. There Samuel Clemens found that he could become a writer by dramatizing a portion of himself and then wearing this identity when he wrote. Who was "Mark Twain"? He was, first of all, a writer who had imbibed deeply of what he was to describe in chapter 4 of *Roughing It* as "the vigorous new vernacular of the occidental plains and mountains." His adoption of an anti–Fenimore Cooper style was natural, as was the style. It derived from the writer's adoption of the ways of the old-timers who had found, before him, that genteel Eastern ways did not fit in the West. It was derived from a rejection of artificiality, superficiality, the hypocritical cult of polite conformity. More specifically, this Mark Twain was a skeptic in religion, and irreverent too. Where there was an establishment, as he would soon find there was in San Francisco, he was anti-establishment, though by no means an alienated loner, for he had enjoyed and valued his membership in the *Enterprise* group. He was more humorous than funny, though he was increasingly fond of burlesquing, with hilarity, genteel attitudes. He was not able now or later to create a fully consistent literary personality—perhaps not interested in the attempt, but he made his hallmark a self-assured, confidential, unhurried tone. Another aspect of this Mark Twain, soon to increase in importance, was an appreciation of "characters": people less cultured than himself but honest, natural, straightforward, manly—these he described as "simple-hearted" or characterized by "simplicity." They have been called "vernacular" characters because their conversational style and manners are by implication antigenteel and because words such as "low," "common," "vulgar," or even "folk" connote a spirit of condescension that Mark Twain seldom if ever expressed. Samuel Clemens's contribution to the achievement of American literature in the twentieth century lies in his discovery of vernacular values and his creation of "Mark Twain."[30]

CHAPTER TWO

California, Hawaii, and the East

THE *Golden Era* welcomed Mark Twain to California; he was addressed as "The Sage-Brush Humorist from Silver Land."[1] He soon sent back to the *Enterprise* a piece, "'Mark Twain' in the Metropolis," written sometime in June. For a long-time resident of Washoe, he explained, life at San Francisco's Occidental Hotel is "Heaven on the half shell." He reported on the city's varied entertainments and celebrated its climate. That anyone who knows Washoe could be unhappy with the city seemed to him very unlikely. He also wrote two striking pieces for the *Golden Era*, published in June and July, "The Evidence in the Case of Smith vs. Jones" and "Early Rising, as Regards Excursions to the Cliff House." The first of these is something of an anticipation of the chapter on "Buck Fanshaw's Funeral" in *Roughing It*. Mark Twain reported on the absurdly contradictory testimony provided by witnesses to a fight. Each account seems especially designed to entertain its giver and to outrage the judge, who objects to such expressions as "busted him in the snoot" and "d——n you old tripe." He insists that they "refrain from the embellishments of metaphor and allegory as far as possible." Faced with the impossible task of sorting out truth from falsehood, he continues the case. The effect is to make the judge's formality ridiculous. This sketch seems to have been Mark Twain's longest to date, some seventeen thousand words. It makes heavy use of dialogue, with several colorful characters adding to the humor.

"Early Rising" is an attack on romanticism. Mark Twain repudiates the maxim "Early to bed, early to rise, makes a man healthy, wealthy, and wise" by contrasting the anticipated pleasures of an early-morning trip to the beach with the actuality of the experience. He joins George Washington, who he finds also stood in disagreement with Benjamin Franklin. The "gorgeous spectacle of the sun in the dawn of his glory; the fresh perfume of flowers still damp with dew"— Mark Twain is having none of it. The misadventures of his trip were "only just and natural consequences of the absurd experiment of getting up at an hour when all God-fearing Christians should be in bed." The sketch epitomizes the identity that Mark Twain presented in 1864: lazy, skeptical, self-indulgent, open, outspoken, humorous without trying to be funny. If he at this time wished to appear authentic, he was successful. The writer's lack of pretense is engaging.

Fortunately, when Clemens arrived in San Francisco after his hasty departure from Nevada, he had a convenient place to head for regular work, the *Daily Morning Call*, a paper with the largest circulation of the five local newspapers, about ten thousand. There he was employed as a reporter for four months, from June to October 1864. Again his responsibility was to report on local events, but this time a file of the paper survives, though it is not always easy to distinguish his anonymous writings from those of other reporters: he was not often writing as "Mark Twain." One scholar has tentatively identified nearly five hundred items.[2] Clemens's work on the *Call* did not permit him the kind of freedom he had enjoyed in Nevada, but many of the pieces he wrote are amusing. A particularly playful one explains how the earthquakes of June 23 affected the city. Entertainment was to be welcomed, in his view, even from a near catastrophe. "There were three distinct shocks, two of which were very heavy, and appeared to have been done on purpose, but the third did not amount to much. Heretofore our earthquakes—as all old citizens experienced in this sort of thing will recollect—have been distinguished by a soothing kind of undulating motion, like the roll of waves on the sea, but we are happy to state that they are shaking her up from below now. The shocks last night came straight up from that direction; and it is sad to reflect, in these spiritual times, that they might have been freighted with urgent messages from some of our departed friends."[3]

Another piece may amuse those who remember Huck Finn's analysis of the loot picked up on the steamboat *Walter Scott*. Mark Twain similarly catalogs the contents of a drunkard's pockets:

> Two slabs of old cheese; a double handful of various kinds of crackers; seven peaches; a box of lip–salve, bearing marks of great age; an onion; two dollars and sixty-five cents, in two purses, (the odd money being

considered as circumstantial evidence that the defendant had been drinking beer at five-cent houses;) a soiled handkerchief; a fine-tooth comb; also one of coarser pattern; a cucumber pickle, in an imperfect state of preservation; a leather string; an eye-glass, such as prospectors use; one buckskin glove; a printed ballad, "Call me pet names;" an apple; part of a dried herring; a copy of the Boston Weekly Journal, and copies of several San Francisco newspapers; and in each and every pocket he had two or three chunks of tobacco, and also one in his mouth of such remarkable size as to render his articulation confused and uncertain.[4]

Among other still-readable items are reports on horse races, theatrical performances, political meetings, and sensational crimes. There are no sketches. The one distinctive development to be noted is that at this time Clemens was becoming sensitive to political corruption and the incompetence of public officials. Of his work on the *Call*, Mark Twain wrote an account in his autobiography, and there he tells of preparing a fiery report on how some hoodlums chased a heavily burdened Chinese laundryman, a policeman observing "with an amused interest—nothing more." His story did not appear, however, because, as the editor explained to Clemens, the *Call* had to respect the prejudices of its readers.[5] The work becoming boring and tedious, Clemens hired an assistant. But soon Clemens was fired, or as he put it in his autobiography, "retired" "by solicitation of the proprietor."[6] Some of his energies at this time were going into the preparation of a book, apparently about his Nevada experiences, since in a letter written to Orion and his wife (dated September 28, 1864) he noted that he expected to ask Orion to send the "files" that he kept of his writings.

Bret Harte had just begun to edit *The Californian*, a rival to the *Golden Era*—Harte being an established California writer who had been there since 1854. In the fall, Clemens began to contribute regularly, and he and Harte began a long association, including the co-authorship of a play. For a time Clemens enjoyed the relationship, but eventually he came to despise Harte for his insincerity, callousness, and dishonesty, as we shall see.[7]

At the *Call*, Clemens had been paid twenty-five dollars a week. For a weekly article for *The Californian*, which Clemens called in a September letter to his mother "the best weekly literary paper in the United States," he was paid just fifty dollars a month. While little of what he wrote at this time has much continuing literary worth, it was a crucial period in Clemen's life. Now he could write at length and at leisure, and from October 1 through December 3, each issue of *The Californian* contained a piece by him. He chose to write accounts of adventures, real and imaginary; visits to the Industrial Fair, to the Cliff House to see a whale on the beach, and to the opera. The fourth piece deserves attention. In *The Californian* it is called "Whereas"; later published versions, such as the much-abridged one in *Sketches New and Old*, are entitled, "Aurelia's Unfortunate Young Man." Here Mark Twain looks, askance, at the subject of romantic love. Alleging that his advice has been sought by one Aurelia Marie, of San Jose, he recounts her sad story. She is "almost heart broken by the misfortunes she has undergone." Her fiancé lost first his good looks through smallpox, then a leg by walking into a well, then one arm by "premature discharge of a Fourth of July cannon," then the other to a carding machine. Her heart was "almost crushed by these latter calamities." Then her lover lost his eyesight to erysipelas, next his other leg, then his scalp to Indians. What SHOULD she do? Aurelia asks. Mark Twain's advice is that she should furnish her lover with "wooden arms and wooden legs, and a glass eye and a wig, and give him another show." If he survives ninety days, she should marry him. Her risk will be slight, he notes, since the man will not live long—he is obviously accident prone.

The account of the unfortunate young man's mutilations is somewhat amusing black comedy. Mark Twain's interest, however, is not in the man but in Aurelia's responses, as is shown by the author's matter-of-factness in describing the young man's experiences. The focus is on Aurelia: "It was a sad day for the poor girl when she saw the surgeons reverently bearing away the sack whose use she had learned by previous experience, and her heart told her the bitter truth that more of her lover was gone." It is not her lover's suffering that interests Aurelia; it is her own inner life. The sketch is one of Mark Twain's freshest and most original.

In "Lucretia Smith's Soldier," Mark Twain aims at a somewhat similar target. It is a burlesque of a popular type of literature of the day, the Civil War romance, in the form of a "condensed novel," a genre then cultivated among San Francisco's literary bohemians. Bret Harte published a volume of such parodies in 1867, and this was Mark Twain's second "novel." (The first is the very brief "Original Novelette," published in the July 4, 1864, *Call.*) The satirist was soon to write several more, such as "The Story of the Bad Little Boy" (1865) and "The Story of the Good Little Boy" (1870). Lucretia's story is by "M. T.," who identifies himself as "an admirer of those nice, sickly war stories in *Harper's Weekly.*" He has now soared "happily into the realms of sentiment and soft emotion," inspired by "the excellent beer manufactured at the New York Brewery." The story tells of how Lucretia Smith, seeking to make up for her earlier rejection of her lover, devotedly tends for a long time in the hospital a wounded soldier she takes to be her man, only to discover the truth when the bandages are removed. "O confound my cats," Lucretia exclaims. "If I haven't gone and fooled away three mortal weeks here, snuffling and slobbering over the wrong soldier." The sketch was widely reprinted in the East, where it hit its target resoundingly. Somewhat toned down, it was included in Mark Twain's first book. Though the piece now seems slight and rather silly, it is another indication of the antiromantic and skeptical frame of mind Clemens had developed.

At this time Mark Twain was once again writing for the *Enterprise*, as San Francisco correspondent, and again nearly all of what he wrote is lost. Some of the pieces, it is known, criticized the San Francisco police and made him unpopular with their chief. When Steve Gillis, for whom Clemens had stood bond after a barroom brawl, fled to Virginia City, Clemens chose to leave town too rather than contend with the police. On December 4, 1864, he went to the Sierra foothills, to the Mother Lode country of Calaveras County, California, where he stayed with Steve Gillis's brother Jim at Jackass Hill and Angel's Camp. There he heard several tales that he was to make much of later. In his autobiography he recalled:

> Every now and then Jim would have an inspiration, and he would stand up before the great log fire, with his back to it and his hands crossed behind him, and deliver an elaborate impromptu lie—a fairy tale, an extravagant romance—with Dick Stoker as the hero of it as a general thing. Jim always soberly pretended that what he was relating was strictly history, veracious history, not romance. Dick Stoker, gray-headed and good-natured, would sit smoking his pipe and listen with a gentle serenity to these monstrous fabrications and never utter a protest.[8]

In the notebook he began to keep on New Year's Day 1865 he recorded several items that were to serve as reminders. Among them are these: "The 'Tragedian' & the Burning Shame. No wo*men* ad*mitted*." "Mountaineers in habit telling same old experiences over & over again in these little back settlements. Like Dan's old Ram, which he always drivels about when drunk." "Coleman with his jumping frog—bet stranger $50—stranger had no frog, & C got him one—in the meantime stranger filled C's frog full of shot & he couldn't jump— the stranger's frog won." The first of these would serve as the basis of one of the Duke and the King's performances in *Huckleberry Finn*, and the story of the old Ram would be attributed to Jim Blaine in *Roughing It.* The third item was to see earlier use. The notes also mention Ben Coon, a former riverboat pilot who appeared in his writings almost immediately.

Clemens left the mountains on February 25 and was back in San Francisco the next day, when in his notebook he recorded: "Home again—home again at the Occidental Hotel—find letters from 'Artemus Ward' asking me to write a sketch for his new book of Nevada Territory travels which is soon to come out. Too late—ought to have got the letters 3 months ago. They are dated early in November." Now Mark Twain wrote fourteen more pieces for *The Californian,* published between March and December. In the first of these, "An Unbiased Criticism," he referred to his experiences in the Big Tree region of Calaveras County, where he had "a very comfortable time." Pretending to be a review of the paintings at the new California Art Union, this sketch is a parody of art criticism, or rather what passed for criticism, for like the targets of his satire, "An Unbiased Criticism" is full of irrelevancies. By far the most engaging is a long comment from Ben Coon, who becomes one of Mark Twain's vernacular narrators. He tells the history of his Webster's Unabridged, which has made the rounds of the mining camps: "But what makes me mad, is that for all they are so handy about keeping her sashaying around from shanty to shanty and from camp to camp, none of 'em's ever got a good word for her."

Soon Mark Twain renewed his attack on the genteel through a thoroughly amusing imagined "Important Correspondence" concerning the vacancy in the pulpit of San Francisco's Grace Cathedral. The position was open at the time, and each of Mark Twain's "correspondents" had in fact been invited to fill it, as a story in the San Francisco *Evening Bulletin* reported.[9] A letter to Bishop Hawks, D.D., of New York encourages him to take it, despite the terms, for Mark Twain argues that he has "a great deal of influence with the clergy here" and "can get them to strike for higher wages any time." The reply concocted for the bishop is full of gratitude. Both writers suggest that they understand the game, with its formalities, pretenses, and hypocrisies. Hawks writes:

> I threw up my parish in Baltimore, although it was paying me very handsomely, and came to New York to see how things were going in our line. I have prospered beyond my highest expectations. I selected a lot of my best sermons—old ones that had been forgotten by everybody—and once a week I let one of them off in the Church of the An-

nunciation here. The spirit of the ancient sermons bubbled forth with a bead on it and permeated the hearts of the congregation with a new life, such as the worn body feels when it is refreshed with rare old wine. It was a great hit. The timely arrival of the "call" from San Francisco insured success to me. The people appreciated my merits at once. A number of gentlemen immediately clubbed together and offered me $10,000 a year and agreed to purchase for me the Church of St. George the Martyr, up town, or to build a new house of worship for me if I preferred it.

Mark Twain manages to create just the right tone for the bishop, with biblical echoes and pious sentiments mixed skillfully with frank expressions of opportunism. Moreover, the satirist had his facts straight about the New York reaction to his "call." Following a long and witty commentary on the bishop's letter, Mark Twain promises that he'll publish in the next issue the replies of two other clergymen, the Rev. Phillips Brooks of Philadelphia and the Rev. Dr. Cummings of Chicago. But instead he published their telegrams, urging him not to do so and each offering five hundred dollars to discourage him. But now, he reports, he has become overwhelmed by other ambitious clergymen, each seeking his support, some even turning up to be his guests, with good appetites. The combination of affected charity and actual vulgarity makes this whole "correspondence" funny, fresh, and on target, one of the high points of Mark Twain's writing career in California. Indeed, some readers must have found these pieces highly offensive. Later, when his prospective father-in-law wished to get letters of recommendation concerning Clemens, the author must have had second thoughts about these sketches. At that time, he was expressing sentiments quite consistent with the values of his other pieces. He had developed a skeptical attitude and a style with vernacular features to go with it. Making fun of clerical ambitiousness and the hypocrisy associated with it was part of the same attitude that dismissed romantic love and sentimental attitudes toward nature.

In June 1865, *The Californian* announced a new department, "Answers to Correspondents," a parody of the "Dear Abby" columns featured in many periodicals then as now, though at that time literary advice was sometimes sought as well as more personal kinds of advice. Mark Twain wrote six columns and in 1867 included parts in his *Jumping Frog* collection. One item is a poem, prefaced by a letter from the poet "Simon Wheeler" of Sonora, California. These demonstrate Mark Twain's continuing interest in vernacular characters, especially narrators, and his increasing skill in rendering their language and their values. Soon Simon Wheeler would achieve wide and lasting fame.

Composing these *California* pieces and sending occasional letters to the Napa County (California) *Reporter* did not provide enough to live on. Here is Mark Twain's account of the period, in *Roughing It*: "When my credit was about exhausted (for I had become too mean and lazy, now, to work on a morning paper, and there were no vacancies on the evening journals), I was created San Francisco correspondent of the *Enterprise*, and at the end of five months I was out of debt, but my interest in my work was gone; my correspondence being a daily one, without rest or respite, I got unspeakably tired of it. I wanted another change" (chapter 62). His boredom is reflected in his contrived *Enterprise* letters, at least in the surviving ones.

Although most of the pieces written at this time indicate a lack of development, there are two important exceptions, a letter and a story. The letter is Clemens's first real indication of a commitment to writing, to literature. On October 19, 1865, he shared with his brother Orion his life's ambitions. He explains that in his early years he had been interested in becoming a pilot and a preacher; he had achieved the first goal but not the second, because he had never had a call. "But I *have* a 'call' to literature, of a low order—i.e., humorous. It is nothing to be proud of, but it is my strongest suit." The tone of resignation in this letter presumably comes partly because he had now reconciled himself to the fact that the stocks he owned, shares in the Hall and Norcross mines on the Comstock Lode, were never going to be worth much, as he had strongly believed, and partly from the fact that humorists did not enjoy a good reputation, on the West Coast or elsewhere. If he accepted the role of humorist, he would have to produce a new and distinctive kind of humor—literary burlesque was commonplace—in order to obtain much-needed self-respect.

About the time that he wrote this letter, Mark Twain produced the first solid evidence that he had been *called*, nearly a year after he heard the frog story. Two surviving false starts show that he was being very deliberate in composing this piece; he must have known that he had good materials to care for. One of these early versions, less than one thousand words, is entitled "Angel's Camp Constable." It deals with one of the vernacular narrator Simon Wheeler's pet heroes. The other, too, is only a fragment; it never gets around to its announced topic. Like the version that was at last completed and published, it is a letter addressed to Artemus Ward, who—it will be recalled—had written to Clemens in the fall of 1864 asking for a sketch for his Nevada book. This second fragment, recently published for the first time, is entitled "The Only Reliable Account of the Celebrated Jumping Frog of Calaveras County, together with some reference to the decaying city of Boomerang, and a few general Remarks concerning Mr. Simon Wheeler, a resident of the said city in the day of its Grandeur." The fact that the story was nine months in gestation suggests that the writer was just beginning to realize what he was to emphasize often in his later years in his comments about literature, notably in "How to Tell a Story," that the "humorous story depends for its effect upon the manner of telling."

The version of Mark Twain's story that was published in the New York *Saturday Press* of November 18, 1865, is entitled "Jim Smiley and His Jumping Frog." (It had arrived too late for publication in *Artemus Ward, His Travels.*) Told with infinite care, the story is narrated by two tellers, Mark Twain, who introduces his account somewhat pompously, and Simon Wheeler, the garrulous vernacular storyteller who sets forth his story for Mark Twain's ears. Simon Wheeler, the erstwhile poet, was kin to Ben Coon of Angel's Camp, who (according to Mark Twain's 1897 account) had told him the story.[10] The addition of a second narrator, carefully characterized, enriches the sketch greatly. There is irony in both tellings. Mark Twain pretends that he has had to put up with a preposterous bore as the result of Artemus Ward's request that he look up the Rev. Leonidas W. Smiley; and Simon Wheeler, whom he meets on his search, pretends that there is nothing funny about the story he tells in response. Wheeler possessed what Mark Twain had called in his 1864 sketch " 'Mark Twain' in the Metropolis" "the first virtue of a comedian, which is to do funny things with grave decorum and without seeming to know that they are funny." Moreover, Wheeler's artfully told story appears to be never-ending and pointless. This double irony gives readers the pleasure of feeling superior to Mark Twain, the narrator, though an alert one sees that Mark Twain is playfully portraying himself as having been victimized.

That the technique of the story focuses attention on the narrator as victim is quite appropriate, since victimization is also a theme of the story. Jim Smiley, the optimistic and compulsive gambler, always looking for a little excitement, can be fooled by a stranger because he lacks the caution of the experienced Westerner. But before Simon Wheeler reveals Smiley's gullibility in the climax of the yarn, he creates great interest in the gambler, as well as in his animals, which are exaggerated to heroic proportions. The story moves from a catalog of Jim's interests, including chicken fights and straddle-bug races, to a discussion of his horse's surprising abilities and the distinct personality of his dog, the well-named Andrew Jackson. Now Wheeler is ready to tell about Smiley's frog, Dan'l Webster. Dan'l too is humanized; he resembles his namesake. Wheeler comments, admiringly, "You never see a frog so modest and straightforward as he was, for all he was so gifted."

As the story moves to its climax, the narration moves to drama, and we hear conversations between Jim and the stranger, whose coolness more than matches Jim's studied indifference. Jim thinks he has entrapped the stranger when the latter observes, "I don't see no points about that frog that's any better'n any other frog." Jim's search for a frog for the stranger, to compete with Dan'l, provides the stranger with time to fill what was to become known as the celebrated jumping frog of Calavaras County "pretty near up to his chin" with quail-shot. Thus the stranger's frog is permitted to win, whereupon the winner comments, again coolly, "*I* don't see no points about that frog that's any better'n any other frog," and leaves.

It is Mark Twain's control of point of view that makes the story so rich. We see the narrator's view of Simon Wheeler, and Wheeler's view of Jim Smiley; each is consistent, and subtle. The story gave Mark Twain a new sense of his capabilities. Even before it was published, the New York *Round Table* in an article on "American Humor and Humorists" had called him "foremost among the merry gentlemen of the California press." Clemens saw the article, for it was quoted in at least two San Francisco publications. In January, Clemens sent his mother a clipping from the New York correspondent of the San Francisco *Alta California*: "Mark Twain's story in the *Saturday Press* of November 18, called 'Jim Smiley and His Jumping Frog,' has set all New York in a roar, and he may be said to have made his mark. I have been asked fifty times about it and its author, and the papers are copying it far and near. It is voted the best thing of the day. Cannot the *Californian* afford to keep Mark all to itself? It should not let him scintillate so widely without first being filtered through the California Press." The *Californian* of December 16 reprinted the piece.

Mark Twain's Eastern reputation was spread through a series of eight pieces appearing in the New York *Weekly Review* in 1865 and 1866, the first being an account of the October 7 San Francisco earthquake. But there was no sudden change in Mark Twain's fortunes. He continued to write for the *Enterprise*, many of his letters being reprinted in the *Golden Era*. In the letter to Orion about his call to humorous literature, he announced that he was beginning work as a reviewer for the San Francisco *Dramatic Chronicle*. Though it was the earliest version of San Francisco's current leading newspaper, it was a poor thing, a four-page advertsing handout, in which Mark Twain's work consisted of squibs and fillers in addition to reviews—all anonymous. Only one short sketch appeared there, "Earthquake Almanac." The pages of the *Chronicle* mention Mark Twain frequently during his two months of employment, but usually he is identified as the *Enterprise* correspondent. He also contributed two pieces to the San Francisco *Examiner*, and one ridiculing women's fashions to the *Evening Bulletin*.

Six new pieces appeared in *The Californian* in late 1865 and early 1866. One deserves mention. "The Christmas Fireside for Good Little Boys and Girls. *By Grandfather Twain*," subtitled "The Story of the Bad Little Boy That Bore a Charmed Life," was published on December 23. The story takes all the conventions of the moralistic children's fable and naughtily turns them upside down. This bad little boy has none of the appeal of Tom Sawyer; in fact, he is thoroughly wicked. "And he grew up, and married, and raised a large family, and brained them all with an axe one night, and got wealthy by all manner of cheating and rascality, and now is the infernalist wickedest scoundrel in his native village, and is universally respected, and belongs to the Legislature." Here Mark Twain presents himself as the satirical outsider.

Such sketches required a fertile imagination; finding something to write about was a constant strain. Clemens still had in mind the idea of a book, which he mentioned in a letter to his mother and sister on January 20, 1866, but, as he explained, "nobody knows what it is going to be about but just myself." After complaining in this letter that his life was uneventful and that he wished he had accepted an invitation to take a round trip on the *Ajax* to the "Sandwich Islands" (the Hawaiians), he visited Sacramento, and there the *Daily Union* commissioned him to write twenty or thirty letters from Hawaii. He was to go on the next voyage of the *Ajax*. This experience was pivotal, for it provided him with an opportunity for sustained writing. The assignment combined travel and observation, a combination that was to prove fruitful both in travel books and in novels.

Clemens left San Francisco on March 7 and did not return until August 13. Concerning this visit he wrote one letter for the New York

Saturday Press, one for the New York *Weekly Review*, and twenty-five letters to the Sacramento *Union*. He stayed much longer than he expected, as he explained in a letter to Will Bowen, an old friend from Hannibal days, in a letter from Maui, written in May.

> I contracted with the Sacramento Union to go wherever they chose & correspond for a few months, & I had a sneaking notion they would start me east—but behold how fallible is human judgment!—they sent me to the Sandwich Islands. I look for a recall by the next mail, though, because I have written them that I cannot go all over the eight inhabited islands of the group in less than five months & do credit to myself & them, & I don't want to spend so much time. I have been here two months, & yet have only "done" the island of Oahu & part of this island of Maui, & it is going to take me two more weeks to finish this one & at least a month to "do" the island of Hawaii & the great volcanoes—& by that time, surely, I can hear from them.
>
> But I have had a gorgeous time of it so far.

He visited only the three islands he names.

Later Clemens prepared his Hawaiian letters into a book manuscript but was not able to publish it. (In recent years the original versions have been collected into a book more than once.) He did, however, use the letters as the basis of chapters 63 to 77 of *Roughing It*. While readers of *Roughing It* usually find the Hawaiian chapters weaker than the earlier ones on Nevada and California, the explanation is simply that these earlier chapters were written later, after Clemens's trip to Europe and the publication of the book he wrote about the trip; he was then a rapidly maturing writer.

Mark Twain's growth from a writer of sketches and news stories, humorous and otherwise, created a change that would lead to severe tensions in his career. Hitherto, in Nevada and California, he had been a critic of the dominant culture. He had chided the clergy, the courts, and the police. He had ridiculed women's fashions. He had even criticized children and romantic young women. He had presented himself as an associate of the disgusting "Unreliable." He was an outsider, a bohemian. In the increasingly sophisticated San Francisco, he was identified as being from Washoe, and he constantly reminded his readers of his origins. He was lazy, often a loafer. As a writer he was a hoaxer and a humorist, a man of limited education and uncertain ambition. All this was to change, though underneath he was to remain not so different.

In Hawaii, he discovered, he was a man of importance, on an assignment that gave him prestige. As a result he associated with people of a sort that he would not have known on the mainland. He visited the king; he met the American minister, and he was befriended by Anson Burlingame, who was on his way to an important position in China. When Burlingame asked him to show him his writings, Clemens provided, as he told his mother in June, "pretty much everything I ever wrote." Soon Burlingame was helping him to prepare a news story that was to spread his reputation. He was especially proud of this account of the burning of the clipper ship *Hornet* and the survivors' story. Burlingame advised him, he was to recall at the end of his life, that he should "avoid inferiors. Seek your comradeship among your superiors in intellect and character, always climb."[11] The advice was to be heeded, and Samuel Clemens would climb, sometimes leaving Mark Twain far behind, often with unfortunate results for the writer.

Mark Twain was still a humorist, but the invention of a companion for the traveling writer, Mr. Brown, permitted him to appear much less vulgar. To Brown he assigned anything crude or earthy he wished to say. This technique Mark Twain may have picked up from the English humorist William Combe, who created a sentimental traveler who was accompanied by a servant with a quite different point of view. Dickens's Mr. Pickwick and his servant Sam Weller are of the same pattern. Reporting the adventures of two travelers gave Mark Twain two levels of action: what the travelers saw, and the byplay between the two. Mark Twain calls Brown "this bitter enemy of sentiment." When Brown is nauseated but unable to find relief, Mark Twain reads him sentimental poetry. " 'It is enough. God bless you!' said Brown, and threw up everything he had eaten for three days." When Mark Twain reports how much he likes the islands, Brown reads the account and proposes that he go on to describe the "cockroaches, and fleas, and lizards, and red ants, and scorpions, and missionaries."[12]

The best passages are those in which Mark Twain is neither the admiring visitor nor his vulgar companion, but the witty, skeptical, and ironic commentator—the writer produced by his Western experience. For example, on the subject of the old pagan religion, when human sacrifice was practiced, he observes:

> The simple child of nature, yielding momentarily to sin when sore tempted, acknowledged his error when calm reflection had shown it to him, and came forward with noble frankness and offered up his grandmother as an atoning sacrifice—in those old days when the luckless sinner could keep on cleansing his conscience and achieving periodical happiness as long as his relations held out; long, long before the missionaries braved

a thousand privations to come and make them permanently miserable by telling them how impossibly beautiful and how blissful a place heaven is, and how nearly impossible it is to get there; and showed the poor native how dreary a place perdition is and what necessarily liberal facilities there are for going to it; showed him how, in his ignorance, he had gone and fooled away all his kinsfolks to no purpose; showed him what rapture it is to work all day long for fifty cents to buy food for next day with, as compared with fishing for pastime and lolling in the shade through eternal Summer, and eating of the bounty that nobody labored to provide but Nature. How sad it is to think of the multitudes who have gone to their graves in this beautiful island and never knew there was a hell! And it inclines a right thinking man to weep rather than to laugh when he reflects how surprised they must have been when they got there.[13]

Just as Herman Melville had developed religious skepticism from his Pacific islands experience, so did Mark Twain—unless his Hawaiian experience merely enhanced his views.

Despite amusing aspects, the Hawaiian letters are now chiefly interesting as historical accounts. They treat geography, the character of the native Hawaiians, politics, industry, and religion. The visitor makes a strong case for San Francisco becoming a whaling center to replace Honolulu. He makes other proposals, such as the use of "coolie" labor in the production of sugar. Even on his way back to San Francisco he was undertaking straight reporting, a fuller account of the *Hornet's* burning and its aftermath that was to be published in *Harper's Magazine* in December 1866, entitled "Forty-three Days in an Open Boat." (This was published anonymously but in the index is ascribed to "Mark Swain.") Later he proudly called the publication of *this* article (not the "Jumping Frog") "My Debut as a Literary Person."

On his return to California, Sam Clemens found that he had some money for once: he collected eight hundred dollars from the *Union*. He also had an improved and widened reputation. But he was not sure what to do with himself. In his notebook for August 13 he recorded: "San Francisco—Home again. No—*not* home again—in prison again—and all the wild sense of freedom gone. The city seems so cramped & so dreary with toil & care & business anxiety. God help me, I wish I were at sea again." The passage suggests that Clemens had much in common with Tom Sawyer and Huck Finn: a love of freedom and a hatred of routine. He needed some excitement and found it where he could. He took advantage of his reputation as an authority on Hawaii to lecture on the subject, and on October 2 he drew a crowd of perhaps eighteen hundred to Maguire's Academy of Music in San Francisco. This was not Clemens's first public lecture, for he had contributed his services to a fund-raising effort for a Carson City church in 1864, but it was the first intended to be profitable to the lecturer. His handbill ominously warned, "The trouble will begin at eight." This lecture was such a success that soon he was delivering the same lecture, with variations, in Sacramento, Marysville, Grass Valley, and eventually in Virginia City. Though it contained information, the lecture was full of comic digressions and funny asides. Making direct contact with his audience, standing before them not so much as the conveyor of information but as the public personality "Mark Twain," now one of the best-known writers in the West, Clemens was rapidly discovering, by trial and error, what it was he could do best. For a good while lecturing was stimulating, exciting. The lecturer was nearly always able to avoid pomposity; it was not difficult for this drawling humorist. He could control an audience. The discovery of his talent as a lecturer was to have an important effect on Clemens's life. It both contributed to the creation of the authentic "Mark Twain," and diverted his energies from writing at several points in his career. He became very much in demand as a lecturer, and lecturing was lucrative, a ready source of funds. Eventually he was to switch to reading selections from his writings, as Dickens had done. But in time Clemens's laziness, the enormous success of his 1870 book, and his dislike of routine would keep him from a career on the platform.

Because of his Hawaiian experience, Mark Twain as a lecturer and as a writer could play a new role, that of mock-serious moralist. In a short piece in *The Californian*, dated August 20, he applied for the editorship of that journal as "The Moral Phenomenon." He had served, he declares, as "a missionary to the Sandwich Islands, and I have got the hang of that sort of thing to a fraction." As editor, he would replace sentimental tales, wit, humor, and elevated literature with morality, just what he believes is really called for.[14] If Clemens was now ambitious, ready to undertake the social climbing Burlingame had urged, he was not yet willing to stifle his irreverence. He now added to the cluster of "Mark Twain's" attributes the pretense of being, sometimes, a moralist.

Samuel Clemens had not been home to Missouri for five and a half eventful years. Tired of the West, he contracted with the San Francisco *Alta California* to supply a weekly letter "on such subjects and from such places as will best suit him," during a trip that would, according to the expectations of the *Alta* proprietors, take Clemens to Europe, India, China, Japan, and back to San Francisco. He left for New York on December 15, 1866. The *Alta* published his farewell the day before his departure. He declared that he was leaving San Francisco "for a season . . . to go back to that common home we all tenderly remember in our waking hours and fondly visit in dreams of the night—a home that is familiar to my recollections but will be an unknown land to my unaccustomed eye."[15]

In the next eight months, twenty-six letters signed "Mark Twain" appeared in the *Alta*. Though he did nothing more with them, they were collected in 1940 into a book aptly titled *Mark Twain's Travels with Mr. Brown*, since the traveler is accompanied, at least in the early pages, by his vulgar companion. Not as well known as the Hawaiian letters and probably not taken as seriously by their author (who was not now traveling in order to write for a newspaper), these letters are nonetheless attractive, and significant in the growth of the writer. Through them one follows Clemens on his trip from San Francisco to Nicaragua, across the Isthmus, then up to Key West and on to New York. On the first leg of the journey he met Captain Edgar Wakeman, who was to appear again and again in Mark Twain's works, including *Roughing It*, where he is Captain Ned Blakely, and in "Captain Stormfield's Visit to Heaven," which Mark Twain began in 1868 but did not publish until the end of his life. In his *Alta* letters he had a good deal to say about Wakeman, but the more hearty comment, though incomplete, is in his notebook: "I had rather travel with that portly, hearty, jolly, boisterous, good-natured old sailor, Capt Ned Wakeman than with any other man I ever came across. He never drinks, & never plays cards; he never swears, except in the privacy of his own quarters, with a friend or so, & then his feats of blasphemy are calculated to fill the hearer with awe & admiration. His yarns—" Here he broke off.

In one of his *Alta* letters Mark Twain lets Wakeman tell tall tales of rats. Later, long after he found it difficult, if not impossible, to call up his early literary personality, Mark Twain was able to return to the spirit of his earlier self by the use of a vernacular narrator, and a favorite was Captain Wakeman. Here Wakeman tells how rats saved his life by indicating that a ship was not safe.

> We were going passengers from the Sandwich Islands in a bran-new brig, on her third voyage, and our trunks were below—he [his friend Jose-

phus] went with me—laid over one vessel to do it—because he warn't no sailor, and he liked to be conveyed by a man that was—felt safer, you understand—and the brig was sliding out between the buoys, and her headline was paying out ashore—there was a woodpile right where it was made fast on the pier—when up come the biggest rat—as big as an ordinary cat, he was, and darted out on that line and cantered for the shore! and up come another! and another! and another! and away they galloped over the hawser, each one treading on t'other's tail, till they were so thick you couldn't see a thread of cable, and there was a procession of 'em three hundred yards long over the levee like streak of pismires, and the Kanakas [Hawaiians], some throwing sticks from that woodpile and chunks of lava and coral at 'em and knocking 'em endways every shot—but do you suppose it made any difference to them rats?—not a particle—not a particle on earth, bless you!—they'd smelt trouble!—they'd smelt it by their unearthly, supernatural instinct!—they wanted to go, and they never let up till the last rat was ashore out of that bran-new beautiful brig.[16]

Wakeman and his friend wisely followed the rats' example and, since the ship was never seen again, thereby saved their lives.

Elsewhere in Clemens's notebook record of the voyage he took with Wakeman there is evidence of his concern that his letters should be well written, but what he would do next was not clear to the journalist. On January 15, just three days after he arrived in New York, Clemens wrote to E. P. Hingston, who had been Artemus Ward's manager, to report that he was planning a lecture tour but needed Hingston to manage him. He wrote to Orion's wife from New York in February that he had been made good offers by newspapermen, and he arranged for the New York *Weekly Review* to publish five of his Sandwich Island letters, but by early March he had discovered that "Prominent Brooklynites are getting up a great European pleasure excursion for the coming summer . . . ," as he explained to his California readers. His account describes at length how he and a fellow journalist had visited the chief officer of the excursion, with his friend entertaining himself by introducing the Rev. Mark Twain of San Francisco. Playing along, Clemens explained that "I have latterly been in the missionary business." Clemens's friend elaborated the joke and arranged for him to preach on the vessel, at sea. The next day Clemens went back to book passage for himself and reveal his true identity. The cruise was intended to have a strong religious orientation, with a visit to the Holy Land as a feature. When the letter describing all this appeared in the *Alta*, readers were notified by the editor that Mark Twain's plans had been authorized by his employers.[17] He would leave for Europe in June.

In the interim, Clemens went on to Missouri, to St. Louis, where he lectured on the Sandwich Islands and wrote a series of funny pieces on "Female Suffrage"[18] and then on to Hannibal. His visit to his home town caused him to recall Jimmy Finn and the excitement he brought to Hannibal. Finn was to be portrayed as Huck's "pap." How close to fact the portrait of the town drunkard is in the novel may be suggested by this 1867 account of Finn's reformation and its aftermath.

> Jimmy Finn, the town drunkard, reformed, and that broke up the only saloon in the village. But the temperance people liked it; they were willing enough to sacrifice public prosperity to public morality. And so they made much of Jimmy Finn—dressed him up in new clothes, and had him out to breakfast and to dinner, and so forth, and showed him off as a great living curiosity—a shining example of the power of temperance doctrines when earnestly and eloquently set forth. Which was all very well, you know, and sounded well, and looked well in print but Jimmy Finn couldn't stand it. He got remorseful about the loss of his liberty; and then he got melancholy from thinking about it so much; and after that, he got drunk. He got awfully drunk in the chief citizen's house, and the next morning that house was as if the swine had tarried in it.[19]

Perhaps because of this Hannibal visit Mark Twain soon wrote up another anecdote from his boyhood memories. A request for a contribution to the New York *Sunday Mercury* resulted in "Jim Wolf and the Tom-Cats." While he had some references to boyhood memories in the *Alta* and elsewhere, notably his experience as a "Cadet of Temperance," this is the first extended piece on the subject. The hero, or victim, is Sam's bashful friend Jim, some sixteen years of age, whose efforts one winter night to chase away noisy cats that had awakened him from his sleep leads him on to an icy roof in nothing but his short shirt. He slips and ends up in the midst of a group of girls having a candy pull. The story purports to be, however, not what the author remembers but a story he heard from Simon Wheeler, who had once again caught his visitor and made him listen. The story is a funny one; the theme is humiliation, but pain and pleasure are artfully mixed. While Wheeler takes pleasure in Jim's acute embarrassment, his humor also helps him to preserve his sense of proportion—and the reader's too.[20] The story was widely reprinted.

In the *Alta* letters Mark Twain reports the limited success of his ambitions to publish a book. When the publishers of Artemus Ward's collection (in which the "Jumping Frog" was to have appeared) rejected his manuscript, Charles Henry Webb, former editor of *The*

Californian and now in New York City, arranged to publish *The Cele-brated Jumping Frog of Calaveras County, and other Sketches* in late April. Described as "Edited by John Paul," Webb's pen name, it contains twenty-seven pieces. Mark Twain and Webb revised the sketches and stories selected for publication by removing local references and allu-sions to gambling, alcohol, sex, and damnation. This first censorship was largely self-inflicted. The prefatory advertisement in the volume explains, playfully, that "the somewhat fragmentary character of many of the sketches" resulted from "detaching them from serious and moral essays with which they were woven and entangled." In his *Alta* letter Mark Twain praises the "truly gorgeous frog" on the cover, so beau-tiful that maybe it will be well to "publish the frog and leave the book out."[21]

More than half the items collected appeared originally in *The Californian*. Four came from the *Enterprise*, one from the *Golden Era*, and one from the *Dramatic Chronicle*. Four pieces in addition to the "Jumping Frog," were originally published in New York periodicals. Only three came from Hawaii via the Sacramento *Union*, since the writer was still hoping to publish a book on the Hawaiians. (In June he wrote to his family, "I have withdrawn the Sandwich Islands book—it would be useless to publish it in these dull publishing times.") *The Jumping Frog* was not a great success; it brought some publicity but no money to Clemens. His disappointment may have made him more eager to profit from his next book.

Neither from this collection nor from the *Alta* letters of the period does one get a strong sense of Mark Twain's identity as a writer. He appears particularly divided on the question of his social standing. Did he want to climb, as Burlingame had urged? He had discreetly cleaned up his earlier pieces for book publication. He was sensitive to the differences between East and West, as his comments in an *Alta* letter show: Sut Lovingood's collection of humorous sketches "will sell well in the West, but the Eastern people will call it coarse and possibly taboo it" (p. 221). Was he to be of the West or of the East? His fortunes seemed to be carrying him east, and his comments in his letters about his New York experience seem to show an increasing liking for it. And New York was where he must succeed. "Make your mark in New York," he wrote to the *Alta*, "and you are a made man. With a New York endorsement you may travel the country over . . . but without it you are speculating on a dangerous issue" (p. 176). On the other hand, he was willing to describe the night he spent in jail as a result of trying to stop a fight: he seems to have enjoyed meeting the prisoners there. He delighted in the conversation of bootblacks; their speech and sentiments are reported appreciatively. He is gladdened when his "old Washoe instincts that have lain asleep so long are waking up here." The newspapers are full of violence—murders, suicides, assassinations, fights. "It is a wonderful state of things," he reports (p. 232). The coarseness that he had identified with, even cultivated, in the West—what part was it to have in the continuing development of the literary personality of Mark Twain? Samuel Clemens obviously did not know.

Mr. Brown was disappearing from his *Alta* letters. He appears frequently in the earlier ones, but later he makes appearances only when Mark Twain seems at a loss for something to write about. He is absent from the nonhumorous letters written in May, one about a visit to the Bible house of the American Bible Society, one about an asylum for the blind. These institutions could scarcely be treated comically, and the writer had decided to report on more serious subjects. When Mark Twain visits an exhibition at the Academy of Design, he does feel free to make jokes and profess pride in his ignorance: he is "glad the old masters are dead, and I only wish they had died sooner" (p. 239). But his comments are not vulgar or outspoken, as they would be later, when he saw the old masters' paintings in Europe. He was even now working his way to a position that he was to set forth more fully eight years later in "Old Times on the Mississippi." Here he writes:

> It is a gratification to me to know that I am ignorant of art, and ignorant also of surgery. Because people who understand art find nothing in pictures but blemishes, and surgeons and anatomists see no beautiful women in all their lives, but only a ghastly stack of bones with Latin names to them, and a network of nerves and muscles and tissues inflamed by disease. The very point in a picture that fascinates me with its beauty, is to the cultured artist a monstrous crime against the laws of coloring; and the very flush that charms me in a lovely face, is, to the critical surgeon, nothing but a sign hung out to advertise a decaying lung. Accursed be all such knowledge. I want none of it (p. 238).

Later he would compare the antiromantic outlook of the physician and that of the riverboat pilot, who can no longer appreciate the beauty of the river.

This appreciation of the blessings of innocence and ignorance contrasts sharply with another observation, one that shows he had not forgotten that his Western experiences had led him to shed some of his romantic illusions. He writes, "I am waiting patiently to hear that they have ordered General Connor out to polish off those Indians, but the news never comes. He has shown that he knows how to fight the kind of Indians that God made, but I suppose the humanitarians want somebody to fight the Indians that J. Fenimore Cooper made. There is just where the mistake is. The Cooper Indians are dead—died with their creator. The kind that are left are of altogether a different breed, and cannot be successfully fought with poetry, and sentiment, and soft soap, and magnanimity" (p. 266).

Despite uncertainties about his literary identity, Mark Twain tried out a version of his Sandwich Islands lecture; in May he appeared twice in Manhattan and once in Brooklyn. He considered these lectures "a first-rate success"; he "came out handsomely" (pp. 178–79). Later he was to build on this success effectively; now his real interest was the trip he was about to undertake. He wrote to his mother on June 1 of being "wild with impatience to move—move—*move!*" A week later he complained that he had written himself "clear out" in his letters to the *Alta*, "the stupidest letters that ever were written from New York." He had written ten letters in less than three weeks, letters vastly better written than the bulk of his Western journalism. He was also writing for the New York *Sunday Mercury*, where six pieces appeared, in addition to "Jim Wolf and the Tom-Cats." Presumably his impatience was chiefly over his dissatisfaction with his career as a writer and his failure to achieve any sense of fulfillment. He was thirty-one years old and had not yet discovered fully his métier. He was growing, intellectually, very fast, even though he considered himself, he wrote his mother, "so worthless that it seems to me I never do anything or accomplish anything that lingers in my mind as a pleasant memory." Meanwhile, his European trip was in his mind not a great opportunity but—as he wrote to his friend Will Bowen—simply an occasion for fun.[22]

CHAPTER THREE

The Turning Point

IN his last work written for publication, "The Turning Point of My Life," Mark Twain described the composition of *The Innocents Abroad* as "the last link" in the chain of events that made him a member of the literary profession. All the links he described no doubt were important, but the good fortune of being in a position to travel through the Mediterranean on the *Quaker City*, on assignment, was crucial. The voyage, which lasted just over five months, from June to November 1867, was the first exclusively pleasure trip made by a ship to the Old World. Clemens was to see the Azores, Gibraltar, Tangiers, Marseilles, Paris, several Italian cities, Athens (just a peep, because the ship was quarantined), Istanbul, Sevastopol, Yalta (where he met the czar), Ephesus, Beirut, Damascus, Jerusalem and the Holy Land, Egypt, and Spain. He was also to see, more closely than he might have wished, the seventy-five other passengers and the ship's officers. He soon found they were, as he wrote in October to Joseph Goodman back in Virginia City, "the d——dest, rustiest, ignorant, vulgar, slimy, psalm-singing cattle that could be scraped up in seventeen States," and following his return he referred in a letter to John Russell Young to "the Quaker City's strange menagerie of ignorance, imbecility, bigotry, & dotage." His associates on ship were not, however, very different from the readers he would address when he came to write a book about his experiences, though the passengers were obviously wealthier.

His immediate task, he had been instructed, was "to write at such times and from such places as you deem proper, and in the same style that heretofore secured you the favors of the *Alta California*."[1] He was expected to write, according to his later testimony, fifty letters,[2] and in due time the *Alta* published that number. He wrote several others that never arrived. He also had commissions from the New York *Tribune*—(for it he wrote only seven letters, far fewer than he had planned) and for the New York *Herald* (only three unsigned pieces appeared). Half the trip expenses were to come from the fees the *Alta* was to pay him; he expected to profit chiefly from the other assignments, ones that he could only partially complete. It was difficult to write on board ship, he complained in a letter written from Naples in August, and he could not write on shore because of his need to be sight-seeing. Thus in his October 1 *Alta* letter he reported that he was on the *Quaker City* for the first time in six weeks, but there his "anticipations of quiet are blighted" by "one party of Italian thieves fiddling and singing for pennies on one side of the ship, and a bagpiper, who knows only one tune, on the other."[3]

The letters Mark Twain produced for the *Alta* were written for the audience he had been addressing for years. Not intended to constitute a complete account of the voyage, they focus somewhat erratically on this and that. At the end of his sixth letter he is in Paris, though he has little to say about that great city; the next is from Genoa, where he announced, "I want to camp here"; the beautiful women were the attraction. A few pages later he is inspired to write an account of his companion Brown's French composition to his hotel keeper in Paris. The casual journalistic style of Mark Twain permitted him to move forward and back in time.

In most ways these *Alta* letters are like the earlier ones about Mark Twain's American travels and adventures. Brown appears once again, intermittently. There are humorous passages and serious ones, a good deal of irreverence, and a good deal of chauvinism. Few things that he saw struck the traveler as better than what America had to offer. Sometimes he stretched a point to demonstrate to Europeans that America was in every way more advanced. When the head of the Russian railroad system told him that he employed ten thousand convicts, Mark Twain topped him: "I said we had eighty thousand convicts employed on the railways in California—all of them under sentence of death for murder in the first degree." "That," he explained, "closed *him* out" (p. 162).

A significant new feature is that the writer now has a continuing narrative, determined by the announced itinerary of the *Quaker City*. What, one wonders, will Mark Twain do and say in Venice, or in Jerusalem? There is also the letter-writer's running feud with his fellow voyagers, the "pilgrims," who were entirely different from his usual associates. Their piety and hypocrisy offended him, especially in the Holy Land. For example, when he drank at "Ananias's well," he noted that "the water was just as fresh as if the well had been dug only yesterday." He then went on: "I was deeply moved. I mentioned it to the old Doctor, who is the religious enthusiast of our party, and he lifted up his hands and said, 'Oh, how wonderful is prophecy!'. . . . I started a bogus astonisher for him every now and then, just to hear him yelp" (p. 202).

Another new feature is that Mark Twain is now putting more emphasis on his reactions, his personal experiences, and less on the places he visited. He knew that he was not the first visitor to write about travels in the Old World; the special nature of his accounts was to come from their being his: Mark Twain's anticipations and surprises. Since his forte was comedy, he would have ridiculous expectations so that his actual experiences would be startling to him. Thus in Venice "the fairy boat in which the princely cavaliers of the olden time were wont to cleave the waters of the moonlight canals" turned out to be "an inky, rusty old canoe with a sable hearse-body clopped on to the middle of it" (pp. 97–98). Sometimes the technique is resorted to merely as a filler, as when he reports that "after a good deal of worrying and tramping under a roasting Spanish sun, I managed to tree the Barber of Seville, and I was sorry for it afterwards. With all that fellow's reputation, he was the worst barber on earth. If I am not pleased with the Two Gentlemen of Verona when I get there next week, I shall not hunt for any more lions" (p. 551). He put less emphasis on his ridiculous self in the last letters, when the fact that he had few notes and many letters to write caused him to pad his account with Bible stories and even to translate biblical idiom into flat prose. The *Alta* apologized for the thirty-fifth letter, with the reporter's "strange conduct in presenting . . . information to the public with such a confident air of furnishing news" (p. 229).

Since Mark Twain heavily revised his letters after his return to the United States to produce a work of continuing interest, further discussion of his *Quaker City* adventures will appear later in these pages. But it should be noted that even while he was traveling, the writer had begun to set higher standards for himself—or rather more genteel ones. On the *Quaker City* he had met Mary Mason Fairbanks, who was also writing newspaper accounts of the voyage, and she served as his critic during the preparation of the last twenty or so letters. He refers to her in a revealing letter (a passage of which was quoted earlier) to J. R. Young of the New York *Tribune* on his return. "I stopped writing for the Tribune, partly because I seemed to write so awkwardly, & partly because I was apt to betray glaring disrespect for the Holy Land & the Primes and Thompson's [authors of pious travel books] who had glorified it," a disrespect that his travels had bred. But, he explained, "coming home I cramped myself down to at least something like *decency* of expression, & wrote some twenty letters, which have survived the examination of a most fastidious censor on shipboard and are consequently not incendiary documents. There are several among these I think you would accept, after reading them. I would so like to write some savage letters about Palestine, but it wouldn't do." He enclosed the letters he thought suitable, with the not very encouraging comments, "The letters I have sent you heretofore have been—well, they have been worse, much worse, than those I am sending you now."

Clearly the writer was insecure. Exactly what was suitable for an Eastern audience? Soon he was to meet a woman who would represent that audience for him; she would serve as his censor for many years. Olivia Langdon's brother, who had been Clemens's shipmate, would provide the necessary introduction. The immediate consequences of his trip, however, were not especially striking. He returned to New York on November 19, 1867, and went almost immediately to Washington, D.C., where he served for a short time as secretary to Senator William Stewart of Nevada, a position he had accepted while still in Europe. Expecting the experience to be "better than lecturing for $50 a night for a literary society in Chicago," he spent the winter in Washington. His familiarity with the political capital was to prove useful in the writing of a novel. He gave a humorous account of his Washington activities in "My Late Senatorial Secretaryship."[4] He made the New York *Tribune* office in Washington his headquarters. By December 4 he was writing a new series of letters for the Virginia City *Territorial Enterprise*, eleven letters in all, the last dated March 2, 1868. He identified himself as a *Tribune* "'occasional,' *Alta* 'special,'" with "propositions from the *Herald*."[5] For the *Alta* he wrote fourteen letters, the earliest on the day after his arrival in New York, later ones in July 1868, and two in July 1869. He was soon to begin a series of letters for the Chicago *Republican* and some for the *Herald*. He was open to anything. As he wrote to his old Nevada friend Frank Fuller on December 2, "If you know of any villainy here that has money in it, let me know." He was a highly ambitious journalist who could augment his income on the lecture platform. The successful Western journalist was becoming a successful Eastern one. His trip had cured his depression, but it had not yet changed his life. What he wrote now is worth describing as a way of indicating the author's literary personality at this time.

His little-known letters to the *Enterprise* deserve attention. (At last a full batch of surviving *Enterprise* pieces!) They are much better than the letters written at the same time for the *Alta*. According to his first letter, "To write 'EDS ENTERPRISE' seems a good deal like coming home again." Mark Twain is full of admiration for Washington, especially the Capitol, which he has examined several times, "almost to worship it, for surely it must be the most exquisitely beautiful edifice that exists on earth today"[6]—this from his vantage point as world traveler. He is soon exploring political corruption and problems of poverty in New York, a city which he found much livelier on a brief visit. After describing life in a tenement, the struggles of a sixty-year-old ex-circus clown, now a "rag-picker and a searcher after old bones and broken bottles," and the plight of poor little girls who nevertheless enjoy showing off their wretched "rusty rag dolls," he presents the lessons he has learned about the possibilities of political action to redress social injustice.

> In this city, with its scores of millionaires, there are to-day a hundred thousand men out of employment. It is an item of threatening portent. Many apprehend bread riots, and certainly there is a serious danger they may occur. If this army of men had a leader, New York would be in an unenviable situation. It has been proposed in the Legislature to appropriate $500,000 to the relief of the New York poor, but of course the thing is cried down by every body—the money would never get further than the pockets of a gang of thieving politicians. They would represent the "poor" to the best of their ability, and there the State's charity would stop.[7]

The longer he made Washington his headquarters, the more disenchanted Clemens became. He wrote a memorable brief account of the disappointments of an office-seeker, "The Man Who Stopped at Gadsby's," later to be developed into a chapter of *A Tramp Abroad*. He could find nothing, he wrote, that an honest man could do about political corruption. He reminded his Western readers that he saw the East as they might, for his Washoe adventures were vivid in his mind. "To find a petrified man, or break a stranger's leg, or cave in an imaginary mine, or discover some dead Indians in a Gold Hill mine tunnel, or massacre a family at Dutch Nick's were feats and calamities we never hesitated about devising when the public needed matters of thrilling interest for breakfast." "The seemingly tranquil ENTERPRISE office was a ghastly factory of slaughter, mutilation, and general destruction in those days."[8]

In the letters, four in all, that he wrote for the Chicago *Republican* in January and February, Mark Twain worked hard at being funny. Valentine's Day, he explained in one letter, has special meaning for him. "For the last sixty years I have never seen the day approach without emotion." He is moved by the valentines he receives, especially those intended "to conceal the real passion that is consuming the young women who send them." One such reads in part: "SIR: our metallic burial cases have taken the premium at six State Fairs in this country, and also at the great Paris Exposition. Parties who have used them have been in each instance charmed with them. Not one has yet entered a complaint. . . . Families supplied at reduced rates." Other "valentines" received on February 14 deal with a "patent Cancer-Eradicator," "double-back action, Chronometer-balance, incombustible wooden legs," gravestones, and one "fraught with a world of happiness for me. It—it says: 'SIR: You better pay for your washing. Bridget.'"[9]

Two other pieces from Washington, D.C., are sketches. The earlier, published in the New York *Citizen* of December 21, 1867, and entitled "The Facts in the Case of the Senate Doorkeeper," is signed "Mark Twain, Doorkeeper *ad interim*." He tells how as doorkeeper he was "snubbed" every time he attempted to speak on the Senate floor. Eventually he was impeached for a variety of causes, among them charging senators fifty cents admission. Here the writer might justly be called an inspired lunatic.[10] In "The Facts Concerning the Recent Important Resignation," published in the New York *Tribune* of February 13, 1868, he tells how as secretary of the Senate Committee on Conchology he never met the courtesy due him from other members of the cabinet.[11] Again it is the inspired idiot who writes. This pose, in which the writer presents himself as a humorist and nothing more, suggests strongly that "Mark Twain" had nowhere to go.

Just after Clemens arrived in New York after his trip abroad, a man who was to play a crucial role in his life wrote to him. Elisha Bliss, Jr., of the American Publishing Company of Hartford asked Clemens for "a work of some kind, perhaps compiled from your letters from the East, &c, with such interesting additions as may be proper."[12] Clemens replied in early December that he could "make a volume," but sought more information. He believed, he wrote, that he could revise the letters, "weed them of their chief faults & inelegances of expression," and write some other new pieces. In early January 1868, he wrote to his mother and sister to request that they "cut my letters out of the *Alta's* and send them to me in an envelope."

For a conference with Bliss in late January, Clemens visited Hartford, and on January 27 wrote to him to accept the proposition that he furnish "MSS sufficient for a volume of 500 to 600 pages, the subject to be the trip of the *Quaker City*, the voyage, description of places, etc., and also embodying the substance of letters written by me during the trip." The agreement called for the manuscript to be ready in just six months. The writer would have a great deal of revising to do, but he was encouraged by the fact that he was expecting the book to be highly remunerative, at a time when he was looking desperately for some project that would pay him well. As he explained to his family, "I wasn't going to touch a book unless there was *money* in it, & a good deal of it." (He was to make a royalty of 5 percent of sales.) He expected, however, to continue to write for newspapers. The new project seems not to have created any great sense of anticipation or possible fulfillment.

By January 31 he was writing to Emeline Beach, who had been on the *Quaker City*, for names and other information that he had not remembered. He was also consulting the published letters of three other *Quaker City* passengers. But shortly after receiving copies of his own *Alta* letters from his family he learned that the *Alta* proprietors intended to publish his letters in book form and that they were not willing to let him use them as he had planned. About the middle of March he therefore headed for San Francisco, a trip he described in a letter to the Chicago *Republican* for May 19. He was happy to go, he wrote, because "a business call in any given direction is a most comfortable thing when your inclinations call you in the same direction." His voyage from the isthmus to San Francisco was once again with Captain Wakeman, who this time told him a story that he would develop into one of his very best pieces, "Captain Stormfield's Visit to Heaven." But he reported to the *Republican* simply that "The old gentleman told us his remarkable dream."[13]

In San Francisco, Clemens successfully arranged with the *Alta* to publish the *Quaker City* letters in revised form. He undertook the work while in California, with the help of Bret Harte. In November in a letter to Webb he reported that "Harte read all of the MS of the 'innocents' & told me what passages, paragraphs, & *chapters* to leave out—& I followed orders strictly." A surviving manuscript has a few of Harte's notes; one indicates that a description of seasickness should be deleted because it is a hackneyed subject, treated by Dickens, Thackeray, and Jerrold.[14]

After completing his revisions in California, he lectured there on his travels abroad. He promised to make his lecture "somewhat didactic. I don't know what didactic means, but it is a good, high-sounding word, and I wish to use it, meaning no harm whatsoever."[15] He lectured in San Francisco before a full house, even though he was in deep disfavor with some California clergymen, who called him "this son of a devil," one who ridiculed "sacred scenes and things." After a less-than-successful first effort, he "got the hang of the sermon," as he put it, and thereafter he spoke with "that confidential tone that breaks down . . . barriers between the man on the stage and people occupying the seats,"[16] as a newspaper reported. He went on to lecture in Sacramento, Marysville, Nevada City, Grass Valley, and Virginia City, and he reported his experiences to the readers of the Chicago *Republican*. After returning to San Francisco for a final lecture on Venice, he left California in July for the last time to return to New York, which was now to serve as his headquarters, and from thence to Hartford to deliver his much-revised manuscript.

On his return trip to the East he drafted two sketches in his notebook. One concerns an imagined personage, "Mamie Grant, the Child Missionary." The complete sketch, preserved in the notebook, is as good an indication of the state of the author's mind and art at this time as one could wish. Mamie is an eager, devoted Sunday school student, just nine years old, deeply read in pious tracts. In her earnest attempts to save the souls of those who call at her uncle's house on business, she manages to stop his newspaper subscription, antagonize the tax collector, and prevent the return of one thousand dollars desperately needed to prevent foreclosure on the mortgage. But she is content. "I have saved a paper carrier, a census bureau, a creditor & a debtor, & they will bless me forever. I have done a noble work to-day. I may yet see my poor little name in a beautiful Sunday School book." Mark Twain's skepticism found do-goodism the target most ready at hand for his satire. The burlesque of moral tracts is devastating. Mamie is speaking to the census-taker. She shows a remarkable grasp of "the dreadful game of poker."

Take these tracts. This one, entitled, "The Doomed Drunkard, or the Wages of Sin," teaches how the insidious monster that lurks in the wine-cup, drags souls to perdition. This one, entitled, "Deuces *and*, or the Gamester's Last Throw," tells how the almost ruined gambler, playing at the dreadful game of poker, made a ten strike & a spare, & thus encouraged, drew two cards & pocketed the deep red; urged on by the demon of destruction, he ordered it up & went alone on a double run of eight, with two for his heels, & then, just as fortune seemed at last to have turned in his favor his opponent coppered the ace and won. The fated gamester blew his brains out & perished. Ah, poker is a dreadful, dreadful game. You will see in this book how well our theological students are qualified to teach understandingly all classes that come within their reach. Gamblers' souls are worthy to be saved, & so the holy students even acquaint themselves with the science & technicalities of their horrid games, in order to be able to talk to them for the saving of their souls in language which they are accustomed to.

The census-taker has had enough and makes a quick departure.

Mark Twain's immediate inspiration for this sketch was his skeptical reading of Elizabeth Stuart Phelps's *The Gates Ajar* (1868), a religious novel. But on his way to the East, he knew that such irreverence was not likely to advance his career: "Mamie Grant" was not offered for publication.

The Innocents Abroad is substantially different from the *Alta* letters from which it was derived. For example, new sections were added about Paris and Egypt, and notably one on the Sphinx. Also added were accounts of the narrator's movement from place to place. In attempting to address a different audience, an Eastern one, he dropped local references and eliminated some coarse expressions, such as "slimy cesspool" and "bawdy house." He also removed some but not all of the irreverent comments that had characterized his treatment of the Holy Land. The character Brown was completely eliminated, never to reappear in Mark Twain's writings, but while dropping Brown's vulgar remarks, he retained the ignorant ones and assigned them to others. Some he kept for himself, as he sought to develop the character of the narrator. Perhaps to compensate for such changes, Mark Twain added to his criticisms of the hypocritical pilgrims. The presence of the theme is underscored by the subtitle he gave his book, *The New Pilgrims' Progress*.

More important, Mark Twain sought to give the account a shape, a sense of design, by developing theme and attitude. He made the account more subjective by placing more emphasis on the narrator. As he noted in the preface, the book suggests "to the reader how *he* would be likely to see Europe and the East if he looked at them with his own eyes instead of the eyes of those who had traveled in those countries before him." The eyes of Mark Twain were unique, however, for they saw what was funny, what evoked personal memories, and how reality often differed from expectations. In the West he had made fun of the genteel and the naive tenderfoot and identified himself as a skeptical veteran. Now he himself is often an innocent as his illusions are stripped away.

What is Europe for the visiting American? Often it is a misrepresented product, created by years of anticipation. Nothing proves to be as advertised, neither Parisian barbers, Arabian horses, nor the Holy Land itself. Even Jesus Christ, Mark Twain explained, would never visit *there* again, since he had the misfortune of seeing it once, which was enough. The author is the victim of misleading expectations, though frequently he has no one to blame but his naive self. Nonetheless, he gets revenge by exploding superstitions, myths, and legends by means of parody and burlesque with such success that it is sometimes difficult to distinguish passages of genuine sentiment from burlesque imitation, especially since the "genuine" passages were written in a deliberate effort to gratify his audience. For example, the drafts surviving at Vassar College of the Sphinx description show that he worked hard at this passage, which became a favorite in his lectures. He knew his audiences liked such purple prose:

> After years of waiting, it was before me at last. The great face was so sad, so earnest, so longing, so patient. There was a dignity not of earth in its mien, and in its countenance a benignity such as never anything human wore. It was stone, but it seemed sentient. If ever image of stone thought, it was thinking. It was looking toward the verge of the landscape, yet looking *at* nothing—nothing but distance and vacancy. It was looking over and beyond everything of the present, and far into the past. It was gazing out over the ocean of Time—over lines of century-waves which, further and further receding, closed nearer and nearer together, and blended at last into one unbroken tide, away toward the horizon of remote antiquity. It was thinking of the wars of departed ages; of the empires it had seen created and destroyed. . . . [Chapter 58]

The passage goes on and on.

In *The Innocents Abroad*, Mark Twain presents an identity, though he does not wear it consistently. He is the honest innocent who is ready to become the skeptic; the iconoclastic democrat; and, at worst, the ignorant philistine. Usually his good nature and sense of humor permit him to maintain and even enhance the reader's acceptance of him, so that his report remains good fun. But sometimes his skepticism is not so much a weapon as a limitation; his constant shifts from present to past, from the serious to the humorous, from topic to topic, and from places to person, both keep the book alive and keep it superficial.

Again and again Mark Twain contrasts reality with his own expectations, sometimes by quoting what previous visitors, especially pious ones, had reported. He was particularly disappointed by the Sea of Galilee, which he found to be "a lake six miles wide and neutral in color; with steep green banks, unrelieved by shrubbery; at one end bare, unsightly rocks, with (almost) invisible holes in them of no consequence to the picture; eastward, 'wild and desolate mountains' (low, desolate hills, he [William C. Grimes] should have said); in the north a mountain called Hermon, with snow on it; peculiarity of the picture, 'calmness'; its prominent feature, one tree." To this he adds, "No ingenuity could make such a picture beautiful—to one's actual vision" (chapter 48). Perhaps aware that the reality he encountered was not what his readers wanted, he provided a second account that emphasizes not the actual lake but what had been associated with it.

> Night is the time to see Galilee. Gennesaret under those lustrous stars has nothing repulsive about it. Gennesaret with the glittering reflections of the constellations flecking its surface almost makes me regret that I ever saw the rude glare of the day upon it. Its history and its associations are its chief charm in any eyes, and the spells they weave are feeble in the searching light of the sun. *Then* we scarcely feel the fetters. Our thoughts wander constantly to the practical concerns of life and refuse to dwell upon things that seem vague and unreal. But when the day is done, even the most unimpressible must yield to the dreamy influences of this tranquil starlight. The old traditions of the place steal upon his memory and haunt his reveries, and then his fancy clothes all sights and sounds with the supernatural. In the lapping of the waves upon the beach he hears the dip of ghostly oars; in the secret noises of the night he hears spirit voices; in the soft sweep of the breeze, the rush of invisible wings. Phantom ships are on the sea, the dead of twenty centuries come forth from the tombs, and in the dirges of the night wind the songs of old forgotten ages finds utterance again. [Chapter 48]

Readers of Mark Twain's *Alta* letters may be excused from believing that he yielded to the dreamy influences of the place.

One of the writer's most difficult problems in transforming his wisecracking letters into a book acceptable to Middle Americans was coping with his skepticism. He could scoff, freely, at Roman Catholic traditions, such as those associated with Veronica's handkerchief, but he could not make fun of the Church of the Holy Sepulcher or even the piety of those who visited it. Still he found an outlet, a permissible one, by reporting his ecstasy in being able to visit "Adam's tomb," which he places within the same church. Burlesquing the responses of such visitors as William C. Prime, author of *Tent Life in the Holy Land* (1857), he exclaims:

> The tomb of Adam! How touching it was, here in a land of strangers, far away from home, and friends, and all who cared for me, thus to discover the grave of a blood relation. True, a distant one, but still a relation. The unerring instinct of nature thrilled its recognition. The fountain of my filial affection was stirred to its profoundest depth, and I gave way to tumultuous emotion. I leaned upon a pillar and burst into tears. I deem it no shame to have wept over the grave of my poor dead relative. Let him who would sneer at my emotion close this volume here, for he will find little to his taste in my journeyings through Holy Land. [Chapter 53]

The passage, only part of which is quoted here, is stressed in the original publication, where a picture shows Mark Twain shedding pious tears.

Though often undercut, Mark Twain's dominant purpose was to show reality as it is, uncolored by pretense, conventionality, and gentility, his familiar enemies. Here these enemies are often specifically *literary*, with Grimes's and Prime's guidebooks at the head of the list. Mark Twain's weapon was style. In order to tell the truth, he showed what it is not. Sometimes what it is not is his invention, a kind of exercise in literary absurdity, as in the affectations of the tomb of Adam speech or in the description of a Roman holiday slaughter as it might be described in the *Spirit of the Times*. These experiments are among the high points of the book, and they remind the reader constantly that it is a piece of writing that he is reading, at a significant remove from the ostensible subject. The author in his first book—as distinguished from his "Frog" collection—is not quite the same Mark Twain that readers had encountered earlier. Now he is specifically an author, and one who draws attention to his stylistic repertoire.

Mark Twain's iconoclasm is limited, however, as Bret Harte noted when he reviewed the book in the *Overland Monthly*. If he rejected the art of the old masters, he shared with many Americans the bad taste that led him to admire such meretricious works of architecture as the Milan Cathedral. Sometimes his uncertainty about what he could accept and what reject leads to amusing passages, such as when he attends a performance of the cancan in Paris. "I placed my hands before my face for very shame. But I looked through my fingers" (chapter 14).

The final revisions of *The Innocents Abroad* were made while Clemens was courting Olivia Langdon, who helped with the proofreading and began her long career as his editor. It was for her, for his fellow voyager Mrs. Fairbanks, and for the audience they represented that Mark Twain composed sentimental rhetoric, such as the descriptions of the Sphinx and of the Sea of Galilee at night. And it was passages such as these that helped make the book a success. *The Innocents Abroad, or The New Pilgrims' Progress* was a great success. Published in July 1869, it sold 77,800 copies during its first sixteen months, and some 125,000 in the United States during its first decade. The advertisements called Mark Twain "the people's author," and indeed he was. Reviews were generally favorable, both American and English, including one by William Dean Howells, who wrote in the December *Atlantic Monthly*, "There is an amount of human nature in the book that rarely gets into literature." Clemens was so pleased with these words that he sought out Howells in Boston, and soon the two became friends. Before long Howells would serve as Mark Twain's unpaid editor.

While the *Innocents* has now almost classic status and is the most popular travel book ever written by an American, it is not wholly satisfying. The chief difficulty is the aforementioned shifting perspective of the narrator. He is a purveyor of information, an on-the-spot observer, a satirist who too often strains for effect, a poetic rhapsodizer, a humorous storyteller, an amiable idiot. The author himself put his finger on the problem of inconsistency when he observed to his publisher Bliss that "the irreverence of the volume appears to be a tip-top feature of it, diplomatically speaking, though I wish with all my heart that there wasn't an irreverent passage in it." The wish made by the famous "Wild Humorist of the Pacific Slope" presumably came from his desire to please the woman he was courting, who thought "a humorist is something perfectly awful"—as he explained in January 1869 to his friend "Mother Fairbanks." What he would have liked to make fun of was now "forbidden ground," he had reported to this same friend a few months earlier.

After his return from California, the author had several occasions to visit Hartford, to see his publisher; later Hartford was to become his home, and there he discovered the huckleberry. The little-known passage in which he announces his discovery is in his best humorous style.

> I never saw any place before where morality and huckleberries flourished as they do here. I do not know which has the ascendency. Possibly the huckleberries, in their season, but the morality holds out the longest. The huckleberries are in season now. They are a new beverage to me. This is my first acquaintance with them and certainly it is a pleasant one. They are excellent. I had always thought a huckleberry was something like a turnip. On the contrary, they are no larger than buckshot. They are better than buckshot, though, and more digestible.[17]

Strange that Mark Twain was to use the name of a berry he discovered in Hartford for a character intimately associated with his boyhood in Missouri.

During the fall and winter of 1868–69, Clemens lectured in New York, Pennsylvania, and Ohio and continued his courtship of Olivia Langdon. Their engagement to be married was announced in February. Mark Twain was still writing, but much less than he had been before. In the *Spirit of the Times* for November 7, 1868, one of his funniest pieces yet written made its appearance, though he did not select it for republication in his later American collections. It shows his ability to make much of little on the subject of the "Private Habits of Horace Greeley." While expressing admiration for the man, he manages to make much good-natured fun. He notes, for example, that Greeley "snores awfully." "In a moment of irritation, once, I was rash enough to say I would never sleep with him until he broke himself of the unfortunate habit. I have kept my word with bigoted and unwavering determination."[18]

He was acutely conscious that he had written little during the time he was revising the *Innocents*, lecturing, and courting. He called the period in a letter to his family written in June 1869 "the idlest, laziest 14 months I ever spent in my life. . . . I feel ashamed of my idleness, & yet I have *no* inclination to do anything but court Livy." He did have a plan for his future, however, as he explained: to "buy into a paper." Despite the book he had written, he still thought of himself as a journalist. Among the pieces written at this time are several sketches: "George Washington's Negro Body-Servant," published in *Galaxy* magazine in February 1868; "Cannibalism in the Cars," published in the English journal *The Broadway* in November, and "Personal Habits of the Siamese Twins" in *Packard's Monthly* in August 1869. The latter two were collected in *Sketches New and Old*.

One of these sketches was probably solicited by the American agent of George Routledge and Sons, the English publisher whose pirated *Celebrated Jumping Frog* had sold well. It had appeared both in a Routledge edition and in one published by another pirate, John Camden Hotten: over thirty thousand copies altogether. Routledge paid generously for the sketch, a fact that Mark Twain was not to forget. Another sketch, "Personal Habits of the Siamese Twins," deserves attention because it is the first real indication of what was to become an abiding interest: the subjects of twins, duality, and the problem of identity, themes to be associated in his writing with role-playing. Though there were actual Siamese twins being exhibited in the United States, Mark Twain was writing a humorous sketch about the complications of two separate people being physically connected. That the consequences of the actions of each one were the same for both fascinated him: imprisonment and drunkenness for both, though one is blameless. Though not explicitly, the twins are by implication an instance of dual identity. One may assume that Mark Twain's interest in the subject resulted from his attempting, in his thirties, to assume a new identity, that of a candidate for gentility, in Van Wyck Brook's phrase. In a letter from Olivia's mother to Mrs. Fairbanks, the former noted that "a great change has taken place in Mr. Clemens, that he seems to have entered upon a new manner of life, with higher and better purposes actuating his conduct." She wondered if this change made "an immoral man a moral one."[19] Clemens too might have asked who he really was. Was he switching sides in the battle between authenticity and pretentious gentility?

After reading proof on the *Innocents*, Clemens devoted some attention to the question of where he would settle. "I want to get located in life," he told Olivia in May. In his thirty-third year he did not have much to show for his life so far, or so it clearly seemed to the man approaching marriage. For a time Cleveland attracted him; there the husband of Mrs. Fairbanks was publisher of the *Herald*. But he decided against it because, as he told her in August, "It just offered *another* apprenticeship—another one, to the tail end of a foolish life *made up* of apprenticeships. I believe I have been apprentice to pretty much everything—& just as I was about to graduate as a journeyman I always had to go apprentice to something else." Instead, Clemens purchased a one-third interest in the Buffalo *Express* and became its associate editor, to "do a little of everything," as he reported to Mrs. Fairbanks. The money needed was advanced by Jervis Langdon, Olivia's father.

In his "Salutation" published in the *Express* on August 21 he promised—as if announcing his reformation, somewhat begrudgingly, "I shall not make use of slang and vulgarity upon any occasion or under any circumstances, and shall never use profanity except when discussing house rent and taxes. Indeed, upon a second thought, I shall never use it even then, for it is unchristian, inelegant, and degrading; though, to speak truly, I do not see how house rent and taxes are going to be discussed worth a cent without it. I shall not often meddle with politics, because we have a political Editor, who is already excellent and only needs a term or two in the penitentiary to be perfect." Here one can see the old Mark Twain as well as an indication of the new manner of life the writer was entering, uneasily.

During the next thirteen months Mark Twain published some fifty pieces in the *Express*, mostly in the period through April 1870, including a column of fillers entitled "People and Things" and a later one entitled "Browsing Around." Ten *Express* pieces were to appear in *Sketches New and Old*. "Rev. Henry Ward Beecher, His Private Habits" suggests a preoccupation with his need to eliminate his habit of swearing, a frequent topic in his letters to Mrs. Fairbanks. "Mr. Beecher never swears. In all his life a profane expression has never passed his lips. But if he were to take it in his head once, he would make even that disgusting habit beautiful—he would handle it as it was never handled before, and if there was a wholesome moral lesson in it anywhere, he would ferret it out and use it with tremendous effect."[20] "The Legend of the Capitoline Venus," a condensed novel, tells the story of an artist who is denied the hand of the woman he loves until he raises fifty thousand dollars, a story that has autobiographical overtones because it was written while under pressure to demonstrate his eligibility for Olivia's hand to her father.

Mark Twain's most ambitious project for the *Express* was a series of letters written on the basis of an idea that engaged him for several years: writing travel letters while staying home by using the reports of an actual traveler as grist for his mill. Charles Langdon, Olivia's brother, was to make another trip, this time a grand tour around the world, accompanied by a tutor, Professor D. R. Ford, who would send back accounts of their experiences. Mark Twain describes his imaginative scheme in the pages of the *Express*. "These letters are [to be] written jointly by Professor D. R. Ford and Mark Twain. The former does the actual traveling, and such facts as escape his notice are supplied by the latter, who remains at home." So Mark Twain announced on October 16. But none of the letters published was in any sense by Ford, since none arrived soon enough to serve Mark Twain's purpose. Nonetheless he wrote eight, and materials from six would find their way into Mark Twain's next book. Based on his own travels, they are pieces on Mono Lake, California; Silver City nabobs; California mining; and the glorious story of Dick Baker's curious cat Tom Quartz. The second letter is a wholly fictitious account of Haiti, and the last, on Hawaii, is based on a letter Mark Twain had written in 1866.

Though an occasional piece from his pen, in addition to the "Around the World Letters," appeared in the *Express* during the late fall and winter, Mark Twain was largely occupied with another lecture tour begun on November 1. This time he appeared, with appropriate anxiety, in Boston, where his topic was the one he used throughout the tour, "Our Fellow Savages of the Sandwich Islands." He was well received, went on to suburbs of Boston, then to Connecticut, where he made a highly successful appearance in Hartford, and then on to Brooklyn, Philadelphia, Washington, then back to Pennsylvania, New York, Connecticut, and Massachusetts.

At the end of his tour, on February 2, 1870, Samuel Clemens and Olivia Langdon were married; as planned they settled in Buffalo. Soon the author was undertaking another new project, writing a series of pieces to appear in *The Galaxy*, a monthly magazine to which he had already contributed two sketches. On March 11, he wrote to the editor, Francis P. Church, "If I can have entire ownership of what I write for the *Galaxy*, after it has appeared in the magazine, I will edit your humorous department for two thousand dollars ($2000) a year. . . ." But first he had to meet his obligations to the *Express*, and after his lecture tour he produced a spate of pieces for the newspaper—ten during February, March, and April, and thereafter an occasional piece, only four during the remainder of his tenure as associate editor.

For *The Galaxy*, Mark Twain had to supply material for ten pages of printed copy a month. He did not limit himself to humor but announced in the first issue, "I would always prefer to have the privilege of printing a serious and sensible remark, in case one occurred to me, without the reader's feeling obliged to consider himself outraged."[21] In all he wrote eighty-seven pieces, many slight, some even flimsy, and some gems. Several of the pieces are reminiscences, of "My First

Literary Venture" as a contributor to the Hannibal *Journal*; on "A Couple of Sad Experiences," his publication of the petrified man and bloody massacre hoaxes; some memories of Hawaii; some on his experiences in the San Francisco police courts and with the treatment of the Chinese there. In addition, he capitalized on his California memories to write a series of seven "serious and sensible" imaginary letters from "Goldsmith's Friend Abroad Again," in which—following the example of Oliver Goldsmith's "Citizen of the World" letters—he has his letter-writer, a Chinese immigrant to the United States, tell the story of his American experiences. An Song Hi's reports, in the face of great expectations, are uniformly painful. He who "wanted to dance, shout, sing, worship the generous Land of the Free and Home of the Brave" is beaten from his very arrival in San Francisco. He is later imprisoned, attacked by his fellow prisoners (whose wickedness and crimes he catalogs), then found guilty of disorderly conduct after a farcical trial.[22]

Some other pieces of social criticism are included: "About Smells," which concerns a Brooklyn clergyman's objections to the smells of common working people in his church, and a critique of a minister who would not officiate at the funeral of an actor. Most of the pieces, however, fulfill his assignment as a humorist, such as his account of how he edited an agricultural paper despite abysmal ignorance. He discusses oyster beds under the heading "Landscape Gardening" and recommends the importation of the guano, "a fine bird." Perhaps the most amusing piece is a review of *The Innocents Abroad*, ascribed to the London *Saturday Review* (that journal had reviewed the book favorably, with great condescension). Mark Twain has fun taking his own humor with high seriousness and in the process fooling many readers into believing that his hoax had actually appeared in England. He quotes from letters of readers who accepted it, as well as one from the Cincinnati *Inquirer*, which argued that Mark Twain had failed to see that the English review was not serious. (He thought that the Cincinnati editors must be children to be so naive.)

Mark Twain's review finds much exaggeration in the *Innocents* and expresses shock at the author's "stupefying simplicity and innocence," "his colossal ignorance." "He did not know, until he got to Rome, that Michael Angelo was dead! And then, instead of crawling away and hiding his shameful ignorance somewhere, he proceeds to express a pious, grateful satisfaction that he is gone and out of his troubles!" "The book is absolutely dangerous," the reviewer complained, "considering the magnitude of the misstatements, and the convincing confidence with which they are made." "The poor blunderer mouses among the sublime creation of the Old Masters, trying to acquire the elegant proficiency in art-knowledge, which he has a gripping sort of comprehension is a proper thing for the traveling man to display."[23] The author of *The Innocents Abroad* proves to be the ideal victim of Mark Twain's irony.

Some thirty-three of the *Express* and *Galaxy* pieces are preserved—mostly in revised form—in *Sketches New and Old*, the selection from his short pieces that Mark Twain published in 1875. Except for the social criticism, the *Galaxy* and *Express* pieces represent no new development in the writer's career but rather a continuation of the sketch-writing he had begun in the West. He himself called it "periodical dancing before the public."[24]

This continuity is shown by his publication of several pieces in the late 1860s and early 1870s in California newspapers other than his regular ones for the *Alta*. In these he chose to present himself as he had formerly done, perhaps because he supposed he might have to return one day to his earlier literary personality. One piece, which may not be canonical, tells of his misadventures in New York City without any money. Ejected by one hotel for nonpayment, he then directs a hackman to take him to a "cheap but respectable hotel." "'And the cheaper it is,' I added, 'the more respectable I shall consider it.'" Unable to pay the hackman, he suffers the indignity of having his trunk broken open. "But the contents of that trunk are far from valuable, for I carry it filled with sawdust. It looks just as respectable, and in an emergency of this kind is invaluable."[25] Samuel Clemens was working at looking respectable as Olivia's husband, but he was willing to share with old friends the fact that he was putting on an act.

It was the success of the *Innocents* as well as the strain of producing sketches on schedule that would turn Mark Twain to other kinds of writing, though he continued to write a few sketches. He declared to a correspondent on March 3, 1871, that he was determined to write no more for periodicals but instead to write books. He made a similar protest in print, as an introduction to "My First Literary Venture." Most of the later short pieces, until the 1890s, are properly stories or essays, such as the damning attack on Commodore Vanderbilt he published in *Packard's Monthly* in March 1869.[26] Compared with the 365 pieces being published in the new edition of *Early Tales and Sketches, 1851–1871*, only thirty-one pieces are scheduled to appear in *Later Tales and Sketches, 1871–1895*. (But both collections omit social criticism, shorter travel pieces, and literary criticism, since separate volumes will include writings under these headings.) In the late 1890s, Mark Twain looked back at his early work with distaste. "I find that I cannot *stand* things I wrote a quarter of a century ago. They seem to have two qualities, gush and vulgarity."[27] The pieces are decidedly uneven, but a few, such as "Some Learned Fables" and "Aurelia's Unfortunate Young Man," are still amusing and deserve more attention than they have usually received as specimens of Mark Twain's comic artistry.

Strange as it may seem, Mark Twain's writings after he came east had much wider publication in book form in England than in the United States; this was due partly to the activities of literary pirates, who gathered his pieces without authorization from either the writer or his American publishers. Two thin volumes, *Eye Openers* and *Screamers*, collected *Express*, *Galaxy*, and other sketches in 1871. Besides other small volumes, a fat collection of sixty-six pieces was published by Routledge in 1872 as *Mark Twain's Sketches*; this one was authorized. In it a prefatory note from the author states, "This book contains all of my sketches which I feel willing to father." Though he himself prepared this volume for publication, he used the versions of his work that had appeared in England in 1871 as the basis for the printer's copy of a number of the pieces, even though these versions had been heavily edited by the unauthorized publisher, John Camden Hotten. Hotten himself drew attention to this strange practice of accepting a stranger's unsought editing in a letter to the English journal *The Spectator* published June 8, after the 1872 *Sketches* was published. He noted, for example, that he had found "A rather strongly-worded article entitled 'Journalism in Tennessee'" likely to profit from the elimination of "certain forcible expressions," such as "bumming his board" and "animated tank of mendacity, gin, and profanity"; and so he performed the pruning. Now in an authorized edition the same changes appeared.

Hotten later published a volume of 107 sketches, along with the *Innocents*, combined as *The Choice Humorous Works of Mark Twain* (1873). After Hotten's death in June 1873, he was succeeded by the man who was to become Mark Twain's authorized publisher, Andrew Chatto, whose firm became Chatto and Windus. Chatto gave the American writer the opportunity to revise his work, and he did so, deleting seventeen sketches and making revisions. In 1874 *The Choice Humorous Works* "Revised and Corrected by the Author," appeared. None of these volumes appeared in the uniform edition Mark Twain prepared toward the end of his career. Only *Sketches New and Old* serves there to represent his early work.

Although Mark Twain was to concentrate on writing books after 1871, just what he would undertake next was not clear to him for a time. As early as August 1869 he had written to his sister that he had begun a project, perhaps the one he wrote to Elisha Bliss about in January 1870, a "Noah's ark" book. He supposed, with hope, that "maybe it will be several years before it is *all* written—but it will be a perfect lightning striker when it *is* done." Nothing of this work appears to have survived. Rather more to the point is a letter written to Mrs. Fairbanks a little earlier. Here he explained that the success of the *Innocents* had so encouraged him that he intended "to write another book during the summer."

The popularity of the *Innocents* was to have a great effect on the writer's career. In the preface to the second volume of an English edition of the work, he described his modest expectations. "I did not seriously expect anybody to buy the book when it was originally written—and that will account for a good deal of its chirping complacency and freedom from restraint: the idea that nobody is listening, is apt to seduce a body into airing his small thoughts with a rather juvenile frankness." As noted earlier, the frankness of the book is much less striking than that of the original letters.

In March, after his marriage, Clemens was still thinking about a book. He wrote to Olivia's parents that the *Galaxy* chore occupied him only six days a month. He needed time, he explained, "to write a book in." One of his *Express* pieces, published in April, was about the West, "The Facts in the Great Landslide Case," and in May he wrote to Mrs. Fairbanks that his publishers wanted another book, "& I doubt if I could do better than rub up old Pacific memories & put them between covers along with some eloquent pictures." But he did not commit himself to a book until July 15, when he signed a contract with Bliss while he was in Elmira, New York, where Jervis Langdon, Olivia's father, was fatally ill. He contracted to complete the book in less than six months and immediately began preparation by writing to his brother Orion about their journey to Nevada in 1861. "I propose to do up Nevada & Cal., beginning with the trip across the country in the stage." This time he had no rough draft, such as his *Alta* letters from Europe, to get him started. But he was excited and optimistic, since he was getting the biggest royalty "ever paid on a subscription book in this country," 7.5 percent.

Like the *Innocents*, the book that Mark Twain was to write about the West belongs to a special class, addressed to a specific readership. The American Publishing Company sold its books not in stores but through agents, who sought subscribers in advance of actual publication by showing a prospectus and sample selections. The typical buyer lived in a small town and was without access to a bookstore. He wanted, or it was supposed by such publishers that he wanted, *big* books with many pictures. (*The Innocents Abroad* had 234 illustrations—many *not* freshly prepared for the book.) He did not want "literature" but information. The typical subscription book therefore was nonfiction, often a first-person narrative with some kind of current appeal. Appearance too was important: several styles of bindings, usually with illustrations on the cover, were offered. Most authors with literary pretensions had no use for such books. William Dean Howells later observed that "no book of quality was made to go by subscription except Mr. Clemens's books, and I think they went because the subscription public never knew what good literature they were."[28] In the city, Howells knew, agents were "a nuisance and a bore," "a proverb of the undesirable."[29] But the success of the *Innocents* not surprisingly caused Mark Twain to undertake another lengthy subscription book, even though by the time he had finished his first he complained in June to Mrs. Fairbanks that he had "lost very nearly all my interest in it long ago." He judged—as he later told "Uncle Remus," Joel Chandler Harris—that "when a book *will* sell by subscription it will sell two or three times as many copies as it would in the trade; and the profit is bulkier because the retail price is greater."[30]

The American Publishing Company, which was at this time releasing only two books a year, was distinctly a commercial operation. Though he was eventually disenchanted with it because he believed he had been cheated by its officers, Mark Twain was to write most of his books specifically for a subscription audience, all of them prepared with the memory of the success of the first one before him. As late as 1897 he was still producing sequels. At one point he intended to call his book about his round-the-world tour *The Latest Innocent Abroad* or *The Surviving Innocent Abroad*.

For an effective subscription book, a major consideration was its size, which was stipulated in the contract for the new book. Mark Twain was to write "a 600-page 8 vo book (like the last) for my publishers," he wrote his family in late July 1870. That would be 240,000 words. But the writing did not go as scheduled. Family crises intervened: the death of Olivia's father; the illness of a house guest who eventually died in the master bedroom of Samuel and Olivia Clemens's Buffalo house; Olivia's collapse from exhaustion. In November, ten months after her marriage, Olivia gave birth prematurely to a son,

Langdon. The new father continued to write as best he could under the trying circumstances. In January he wrote to Bliss that he would write "night and day" and send him "200 pages of MS. every week" in order to finish by April 15. But he was unable to finish then because of the demands on him from Olivia, who was still very weak. In addition, he decided in March that he had to undertake a major revision, he told Orion, in order to "alter the whole style of one of my characters and re-write him clear through to where I am now." Probably the "character" was the "hero." As published, the book provides a portrait of the narrator as a very young and thoroughly innocent young man. His innocence and the adventures it leads to are central in the book.

Before he was finished writing, Clemens found that his experiences in Buffalo had soured him on the place. He decided that he, his wife, and young Langdon Clemens should leave Buffalo and that he should dissolve his connection with the *Express*. By March 3, he told J. H. Riley, he had come to "loathe Buffalo so bitterly (always hated it)" that he had advertised his house for sale. "I want to get clear away from all hamperings, all harassments," he wrote Bliss. In March the Clemenses moved temporarily to Quarry Farm, outside Elmira. The farm, which belonged to Theodore Crane and his wife, Olivia's adopted sister Sue, was to provide the Clemens family with a setting for many happy summers, and there Mark Twain was to produce much of his best work. In April his old friend Joe Goodman, his editor when he was a reporter for the *Territorial Enterprise*, arrived for a two-month visit. Goodman's admiration of the manuscript was encouraging. *Roughing It* was completed by August, though the author himself had digressed from his task during June to prepare lectures he was planning to deliver in the fall, in order to make money he would need to establish his family with a new home.

The last part of the book was much the easiest to prepare, since fifteen of the last seventeen chapters are merely revisions of the Sandwich Island letters Mark Twain had written six years earlier. But even when he thought he was through, there was more editing and more revising. To make the book long enough, he added three long appendixes, one on Mormon history, others well larded with quotations from documents. This device was to prove useful in stretching later subscription books to adequate length.

Though generally less admired, *Roughing It* is a distinctly better book than the *Innocents*. Whereas the earlier book was a revision of on-the-spot reports, the new book was based on memories artfully shaped—except for the Sandwich Island chapters, which were composed much as the *Innocents* had been. *Roughing It* tells the story of Samuel Clemens's life in Nevada, California, and Hawaii, but though autobiographical in outline, it is controlled by important shaping concerns. Here the author looks back over nearly ten years to an earlier self. A few years earlier he had taken a quick look backward, when in November 1868 he had written to Olivia, "I have been through the world's 'mill'—I have traversed its ramifications from end to end—I have searched it, & probed it, & put it under the microscope & *know* it, through & through, & from back to back—its follies, its frauds, & its vanities—all by personal *experience* & not through dainty *theories* culled from nice moral books in luxurious parlors where temptation never comes." Despite his status as a candidate for gentility, the author presents himself in *Roughing It* as a man of experience. He reminds the reader repeatedly in the early chapters that he has traveled to Europe and to the Holy Land; he suggests that those experiences, as well as the ones he is telling about, made him what he is now. As a result, the reader is encouraged to feel that he is in the presence of the authentic Mark Twain. Here he is providing his autobiography—not that of Samuel Clemens but of the personality we meet in the best pages of his book. Here the writer provides answers to some implied questions. How did there come to be this humorist, this skeptical, sometimes cynical character? This frank, confidential, vulnerable, justice-seeking comic writer, whose graceful but firm prose seems to fit him like a glove? The writer's Western experience provides explanations. Chapter 1 begins with the writer mocking his youthful self—the "before" to be contrasted with the present "after." He makes the ex-journeyman printer and experienced ex-pilot of twenty-six sound ten years younger as he describes the jealousy of the younger brother contemplating the older.

> [Orion] was going to travel! I never had been away from home, and that word "travel" had a seductive charm for me. Pretty soon he would be hundreds and hundreds of miles away on the great plains and deserts, and among the mountains of the Far West, and see buffaloes and Indians, and prairie dogs and antelopes, and have all kinds of adventures, and maybe get hanged or scalped, and have ever such a fine time, and write home and tell us about it, and be a hero. . . . What I suffered in contemplating his happiness, pen cannot describe.

This naive youth will go West and there through initiation lose his innocence. It is a retelling of an old familiar story, but in Mark Twain's words it is a fresh and original one. As an exploration of the values that come into existence when the restraints of an ordered life are relaxed, the book is a celebration of freedom. The loss of that innocence, and later that freedom, is recalled with considerable nostalgia, at the same time that Mark Twain sees the civilization of the East to be marked by pretense and vanity.

All the romantic features of the West are here: the buffalo hunt, the bucking bronco, the pony-express rider, the desperado, the tall tale. Early in the book two incidents suggest the ways of the West. Chapter 5 describes the coyote, "not a pretty creature or respectable either," especially to "a dog that has a good opinion of himself." The coyote attracts his attention, leads the dog on, misleading him into thinking that he can be caught, and the dog becomes "more and more incensed to see how shamefully he has been taken in by an entire stranger." At length this coyote "turns and smiles blandly upon him once more," then runs off with a speed that makes the dog's "head swim." Once so taken in, once so humiliated, the dog is unlikely to be victimized again soon. Such lessons were ones that the newcomer had to learn, as in chapter 24, when the narrator is persuaded to buy "a Genuine Mexican Plug" that proves to be unrideable. After several painful attempts to master the beast, an "elderly-looking comforter" tells him, "Stranger, you've been taken in." To emphasize the point he has been making, Mark Twain ends his chapter with this moral: "Now whoever has had the luck to ride a real Mexican plug will recognize the animal depicted in this chapter, and hardly consider him exaggerated—but the uninitiated will feel justified in regarding his portrait as a fancy sketch, perhaps."

Many other stories have a similar point. When in chapter 32 Mark Twain and two companions are lost in a snowstorm, then lose their horses and decide that they cannot survive, each ceremoniously prepares for the end by giving up his dearest vice: his bottle of whiskey, his playing cards, his pipe, each in a spirit of sincere reformation. Then "oblivion comes." But in the morning (in the next chapter) the three wake to discover that they are "not fifteen steps from . . . a stage station." Their situation is "painfully ridiculous and humiliating," and they soon shamedly gather up what they had thrown away and vow never to say more about reformation.

Others are taken in, too, in Mark Twain's collection of somewhat imaginative recollections, such as one he had told before, of how General Buncombe was taken in by a practical joke played on him in the landslide case and failed to recognize how he had been victimized for two months. One of the earliest stories in *Roughing It* suggests how a victim might cope with his situation. When in chapter 7 Mark Twain's traveling companion Bemis "ended up in disaster and disgrace" by being thrown from his horse and chased up a tree by a wounded buffalo, he avoids humiliation by resourcefully telling a fanciful tale, full of circumstance, of how after the buffalo frightened his horse into a long and hot chase—the buffalo chasing horse and rider, until Bemis's saddle separated and left him on foot. He climbed "the only solitary tree," only to find the buffalo climbing after him. So he lassoed him, fired his revolver at the beast, and "shinned down the tree and shot for home," leaving the buffalo "dangling in the air, twenty feet from the ground." Bemis's tale restores him to comradeship with those who heard it, and it has the further virtue of inculcating skepticism.

Roughing It is dedicated to a friend of Clemens's Western days, Calvin H. Higbie, "In Memory of the Curious Times When We Two WERE MILLIONAIRES FOR TEN DAYS." The story of how such riches were obtained, though far from true, is central to Mark Twain's account of a land where great wealth was won and lost overnight. Only a few pages are devoted to Mark Twain's *Enterprise* journalism, with Clement T. Rice, the Unreliable, here being referred to as Boggs. Instead there are memorable and hilarious stories of Scotty Briggs's efforts to communicate with a minister who cannot understand his vernacular, of Ned Blakely (Captain Wakeman), of Jim Blaine's grandfather's ram and Dick Baker's cat. For the subscription book buyer there is abundant factual information about that very curious subject, Mormon polygamy, a beautiful description of Lake Tahoe, about which the author had pleasant memories, and a sympathetic analysis of the situation of the Chinese in California. Samuel Clemens's adventures are a good part of the story, but Mark Twain never forgot the maxim "Don't spoil a good story for the truth."

In *Roughing It*, victimization and humiliation are constant themes, but the victim is seldom hurt for long, and the tone is good-natured, compassionate, seldom hostile or sadistic. Instead, the book emphasizes the solidarity and community that belong to those who have achieved status by being initiated into the fellowship of Western skeptics. The theme of initiation is lost in the Sandwich Island portion, even though Mark Twain seems to have intended to use it from early in his planning. For those readers who appreciate the accomplishments of the first four-fifths of the book, these chapters may be left unread, though there is a falling-off even earlier, after the protagonist forsakes the pursuit of wealth for the life of a newspaperman.

Clemens's years in the West had not been financially rewarding. Only two fifths of the way through the book, in chapter 28, the narrator recognizes that his hopes are never to be realized. "So vanished my dream. So melted my wealth away. So toppled my airy castle to the earth and left me stricken and forlorn." The writing of *Roughing It* brought home to its author that the West had not brought him the rewards he had expected and that he had better look elsewhere. He ended his account with what he called the moral of the story: "If you are of any account, stay at home and make your way by faithful diligence; but if you are 'no account,' go away from home, and then you will *have* to work, whether you want to or not." This notion of hard work as a formula for success may have been not so much what Clemens eagerly embraced as what he feared he had now committed himself to.

In October 1871, after their summer at Quarry Farm, the Clemenses took up residence in a rented house in Hartford, and two weeks later Mark Twain began an unusually extended lecture tour, nearly eighty appearances in Pennsylvania, Delaware, New England, New York, New Jersey, Ohio, Michigan, Indiana, West Virginia, and Maryland. His experiences were interesting enough, he wrote Olivia in January, to be the subject of a book. As his tour ended, his Western book was published, in February 1872. Though not so successful as the *Innocents*, *Roughing It* sold very well, over 72,000 copies in the first two years. Reviews were favorable too. One found his genius "characterized by the breadth, and ruggedness, and audacity of the West."[31] With a second success on the heels of the first, Mark Twain was established, at last.[32]

In 1863, after years as printer and riverboat pilot, Samuel Clemens adopted the pen name of Mark Twain while a Nevada journalist. This name was derived from the Mississippi leadsman's call that indicated that the river was two fathoms deep. Here is how he appeared in 1864. (Reproduced with permission of Mark Twain Memorial, Hartford, Connecticut)

In 1867 Clemens went to Europe on assignment for a California newspaper and as a result wrote The Innocents Abroad. *Another result was meeting Olivia Langdon, sister of a shipmate and ten years younger than Clemens. They were married in 1870. (Reproduced with permission of Mark Twain Memorial, Hartford, Connecticut)*

The Innocents Abroad *was an unexpected financial success. It was sold by subscription, as were such later books as* Roughing It *and* Tom Sawyer. *Mark Twain's publisher was the American Publishing Company of Hartford, Connecticut, the president of which was Elisha Bliss, Jr. (Reproduced with permission of Mark Twain Memorial, Hartford, Connecticut)*

In 1874 the Clemenses moved into a spacious house built for them in the Nook Farm section of Hartford. Restored in recent years, it attracts many visitors. (Reproduced with permission of Mark Twain Memorial, Hartford, Connecticut)

Because of social obligations, Mark Twain wrote little in Hartford. Summer was his writing time, and then he worked in this study at Quarry Farm, Elmira, New York. (Reproduced with permission of Mark Twain Memorial, Hartford Connecticut)

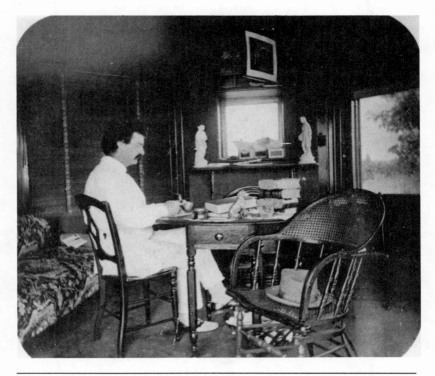

In his Elmira study, built especially for him by his wife's sister, Mark Twain wrote Tom Sawyer, Huckleberry Finn, *and* A Connecticut Yankee in King Arthur's Court, *among other works. (Reproduced with permission of Mark Twain Memorial, Hartford, Connecticut)*

Especially in his early years in the East, Mark Twain devoted much energy to lecture tours. Here is an 1873 poster that identifies him with the work that made him famous in 1865, the story of "Jim Smiley and His Jumping Frog." (Reproduced with permission of Mark Twain Memorial, Hartford, Connecticut)

CHAPTER FOUR

Something Old and Something New

EVEN before he had finished *Roughing It*, Mark Twain was making plans for another book, based on much the same scheme as the one that had failed to work earlier in the preparation of the "Around the World" letters for the Buffalo *Express*. On December 2, 1870, he wrote to J. H. Riley to propose what he described as "the pet scheme of my life." Just a little earlier he had drawn up an admiring sketch of this same man, "Riley—Newspaper Correspondent," published in the November *Galaxy*, where he explained that Riley wrote on assignment in Washington, D.C., for the San Francisco *Alta*. Now he proposed to send this experienced reporter, a friend of his from his days as a Washington newspaperman, to South Africa, there "to skirmish, prospect, work, travel, & take pretty minute notes, with hand and brain, for 3 months, I paying you a hundred dollars a month for you to live on. (Not more, because sometimes I want you to have to shin like everything for a square meal—for *experiences* are the kind of book-material I want.)" Riley would then write up his adventures, which might, Clemens thought, include getting rich from diamonds, and Clemens would then edit his report, adding parenthetical remarks as well.

On December 4, Riley replied by wire: "Long letter rec'd. Plan approved. Will get ready to go," and on December 6, Riley wrote a letter confirming his acceptance and making further arrangements with Clemens. On that same day Clemens signed a contract with Elisha Bliss to prepare a book on the subject of "the Diamond fields of Africa," based on "notes of adventures" prepared by "a proper party," with the manuscript to contain "matter enough to fill at least 600 printed octavo pages." The work was to be delivered by March 1, 1872. A fallback clause permitted substitution of another subject by mutual agreement.[1] The trip was financed to the extent of two thousand dollars by the American Publishing Company. Clemens had told Bliss in November that the book "*will have a perfectly beautiful sale*" and is "brim-full of fame and fortune for both author [and] publisher."

To meet their agreement, Riley started promptly, and on March 3, 1871, Clemens wrote to him, appreciatively, "Your letters have been just as satisfactory as letters could be, from the day you reached England till you left it." By October 1871 Riley had completed what turned out to be a hazardous journey to South Africa and was back in the United States. But Clemens was unable to see him, he declared in a letter, because of illness in the family and lecture-tour obligations. On January 4, Clemens wrote again, naming early March as the time when they would meet. "I shall be ready for you. I shall employ a good, appreciative phonographic reporter who can listen first rate, & enjoy, & even throw in a word, now & then. Then we'll light our cigars every morning, & with your notes before you, we'll talk & yarn & laugh & weep over your adventures." Clemens wrote again, on March 27, to describe the qualities needed by the stenographer and to report that he anticipated some thirty thousand words of material from Riley's notes. But the scene so vividly described was never to take place. Riley was now ill and could not visit Hartford; he proposed that Clemens visit him in Philadelphia. But they never met, and in September Riley died. Thus ended this unlikely scheme, which had been intended to produce a sequel to *Roughing It*. His next effort at a travel book was not much more successful.

Following his 1871–72 lecture tour, Clemens was busy with family matters, as he had told Riley. The second of the Clemens children, Olivia Susan (called Susie and later Susy) was born in March, and in June the first child, Langdon, died. Eighteen months old, he had never been strong. Later the father assumed a needless burden of guilt for the death. Perhaps Clemens felt inadequate as a result of his efforts to adapt to the ways of the genteel Langdons, and this feeling was a source of his guilt. Whatever the cause, he was to find much to feel guilty about, and being "found out" was to become a theme in many of his works.

But his native sense of humor seldom deserted the writer for long. One delightful piece, published over a pseudonym in the July 20, 1872, Hartford *Courant*, is entitled "The Secret of Dr. Livingston's Continued Voluntary Exile." An account of David Livingston's briefing on what happened during his five years in darkest Africa, it ends with Livingston being so unwilling to believe that Southerners would support Horace Greeley as the Democratic candidate for the presidency that he refuses to return to civilization. It has not been reprinted.

After a summer without much literary productivity, Clemens—alone—went to England for his first visit on August 21, 1872. His purposes were two. The first was somewhat pressing: to arrange for British publication of his books. He had lost much to pirates, and while he had arranged with George Routledge for publication in England of *Roughing It*, he was eager to make secure regular arrangements for British copyright. Second, he was interested in looking at the possibility of writing a book about England, one like the *Innocents*. In London he saw the sights and met many famous people, including the writers Charles Reade and Thomas Hood. He was asked to lecture, but decided that lecturing should await a return trip, the next year, when he would have Mrs. Clemens with him. "I came here," he wrote in November to his family, "to take notes for a book. But I haven't done much but attend dinners & make speeches." Though he took many notes, he wrote little in England and left on November 12. During the winter of 1872–73 he lectured a few times in Hartford and New York, and he prepared two long articles for the New York *Tribune* on the Sandwich Islands. He wrote up some English sketches and began *Tom Sawyer*. That, however, was to be his second novel.

For some time Mark Twain had been thinking of writing a novel. As early as April 6, 1871, he had written to the publisher of *The Galaxy*, "I begin to think I can get up quite a respectable novel, & I mean to fool away some of my odd hours in the attempt, anyway," Instead, his first complete novel was to be begun during the winter of 1872–73 as a "partnership novel" with his Hartford friend and neighbor, Charles Dudley Warner. The collaboration was the result of a conversation about the inadequacy of recent novels. Albert Bigelow Paine describes the origin in this way.

> At dinner one night, with the Warners present, criticisms of novels were offered, with the usual freedom and severity of dinner-table talk. The husbands were inclined to treat rather lightly the novels in which their wives were finding entertainment. The wives naturally retorted that the proper thing for the husbands to do was to furnish the American people with better ones. This was regarded in the nature of a challenge and as such was accepted—mutually accepted: that is to say, in partnership. On

the spur of the moment Clemens and Warner agreed that they would do a novel together, that they would begin it immediately.[2]

Warner was a newspaperman and essayist; like Clemens, he had never written a novel. According to Paine, Mark Twain had in mind from the beginning that the book would be about a character modeled after his mother's eccentric cousin, James Lampton. The plan was to hatch "the plot day by day," then each would take a turn in writing. It was, Warner noted, "a novel experiment."[3] Next, as Mark Twain told Mrs. Fairbanks, the writers and their wives gathered nightly "to hear Warner & me read our day's work; & then they have done a power of criticizing, but have always been anxious to be on hand at the reading & find out what has happened to the dramatis personae since the previous evening." By the end of April the book was finished.

The Gilded Age is long—subscription-book length—badly plotted, and uneven. Perhaps the best thing about the book is its title, which gave a name to the postwar Grant era. Clemens correctly observed later that the two authors' "ingredients refused to mix, & the book consisted of *two* novels—& remained so, incurably & vexatiously, spite of all we could do to make the contents blend."[4] Because it was a partnership novel, one seldom senses Mark Twain's literary personality in the telling of the story, though incidents and scenes resemble his earlier work. Nonetheless, there is much of value and interest, at least in Mark Twain's portion. Many of the events and characters are based on real people that he knew or knew of. The first eleven chapters introduce the subject of the "Tennessee Land" that John M. Clemens purchased before the family moved to Missouri, and it provides as well a version of the adventures of the Clemens family before Samuel Clemens's birth. The picture of Obedstown, Tennessee, and the riverboat scene are effective, but the chief feature of these early chapters is the introduction of Washington Hawkins, a character based on Orion Clemens, and Colonel Sellers, one of the most vivid of Mark Twain's creations, who was modeled after James Lampton.

So vital is the character of Colonel Sellers that he became the inspiration for a dramatization and sequels. He is both a courtly gentleman of the Old South and a true believer in his own fantastic inventions—schemes for getting rich quick. There is an element of self-portrait in the character, for his creator too was an inventor and an investor in inventions that were bound to produce riches. (Clemens had told Riley that their book would "sweep the world like a besom of destruction."[5]) Sellers's wealth would come, he was convinced, from such inventions as his "Infallible Imperial Oriental Liniment and Salvation for Sore Eyes," for which he would soon have factories and warehouses in Cairo, Ispahan, Peking, and other trade centers, with headquarters at Constantinople (chapter 8). Seller's situation as a result of his outrageous optimism is frequently embarrassing, and so despite his foolishness he is presented as a sympathetic character. Later Mark Twain was to insist to Warner in July that Sellers is "always genial, always gentle, hospitable, full of sympathy with anything that any creature has at heart." He is, he wrote another correspondent, "a perfectly *sincere*, pure-minded & generous-hearted man."[6]

Sellers's efforts take him to Washington, D.C., where "for the first time in his life his talents had a fair field" (chapter 40). The Washington scene gave Clemens a chance to utilize his knowledge of the capital and its politics. The picture of the relationships between speculators, lobbyists, and politicians is memorable, but too often the satire and the plot are at odds with each other, as in the visit in chapter 36 of Laura, the *femme fatale*, to a bookstore, where the clerk's efforts to sell the trash of the day result in his being given a lecture on the subject much more suitable to come from Mark Twain's mouth than from his character's. Because both Warner and Mark Twain created sets of characters, the novel is heavily populated, but it is Laura Hawkins, an adopted daughter of the fictional version of the Clemens family, who provides the focus of the plot, as distinguished from the theme, in which Sellers is central. Laura is tricked into a false marriage by a Confederate officer and then abandoned. Thereafter she seeks to capitalize on her beauty in Washington's political society and meets with some success until her seducer, now properly married, reenters the scene only to desert her once again. She follows him to New York and murders him there. Tried on a murder charge, she is acquitted. She then tries to exploit the notoriety that her trial gives her by appearing on the lecture platform, "that final resort of the disappointed of her sex." There she is humiliated by the small crowd gathered there for the purpose, and dies humbled.

Subtitled "A Tale of To-day," *The Gilded Age* fails badly as a novel but is valuable as a portrait of its age. It offers no cure for the corruption it depicts and no criticism of President Grant, who was later to become a friend of Clemens. Its angle of vision is that of the genteel society of which Clemens was becoming a member and to which Warner had already been admitted. There is little that is egalitarian or even humanitarian about the book. But in passages like this one it effectively suggests the spirit of the times:

> Beautiful credit! The foundation of modern society. Who shall say that this is not the golden age of mutual trust, of unlimited reliance upon human promises? That is a peculiar condition of society which enables a whole nation to instantly recognize point and meaning in the familiar newspaper anecdote, which puts into the mouth of a distinguished spec-ulator in lands and mines this remark:—"I wasn't worth a cent two years ago, and now I owe two million dollars." (Chapter 26)

At first *The Gilded Age* was a great success. That is to say, it out-sold *The Innocents Abroad* and *Roughing It* during its first two months. But later sales fell off; only fifty thousand copies were sold the first year. Some reviewers denounced the book. The Chicago *Tribune* re-viewer wrote that the authors had "willfully degraded their craft, abused the people's trust, and provoked a strong condemnation."[7] But before the book was published, Mark Twain had turned his interest back to England and his anticipated English book. The partnership novel had served only as brief interruption. In May 1873 the Clemens family left for a five-month visit to England, with side trips to Scotland, Ireland, and France. Mark Twain lectured for a week in London, then after delivering his wife and daughter back to America, he returned for two months of very successful lecturing.

However successful he was now, as the author of two books about his experiences, as a nascent novelist, and as a lecturer with a follow-ing on both sides of the Atlantic, Mark Twain was still deeply uncer-tain of himself, as he told his secretary-companion during his 1873–74 London season of lectures. Finding an old friend of California days in London when he was feeling very much alone, he hired Charles Warren Stoddard, who was himself to have a strange career as a writer, and the two lived together "in a kind of gorgeous seclusion that was broken only by our nightly trip to the Lecture Hall," Stoddard re-membered. Clemens shared his deepest fear with him, his belief that the time would soon come when he could neither write nor lecture and would therefore be unable to support his family. "I used to go to sleep," Stoddard reported, "night after night with that word of woe in my ears, that Mark would die in the poorhouse."[8]

Perhaps he had more reason to worry than may appear to those with the advantage of knowing how his life was to be lived. For one thing, there was to be no English book. At first the writer's problem was that he didn't know enough, he thought. He wrote to his wife in

October 1872, "One mustn't tackle England in print with a mere superficial knowledge of it. I am by long odds the most widely known & popular American author among the English & the book will be read by pretty much every Englishman—therefore it must not be a poor book." Then, after he had written a few English sketches, he abandoned the notion. He later explained: "I couldn't get any fun out of England. It is too grave a country." He found England "not a good text for hilarious literature."[9] In addition, he liked the English, who had received him with enthusiasm. He wrote to the London *Evening Post* in June 1873, "There may be no serious indelicacy about eating a gentleman's bread & then writing an appreciative & complimentary account of the ways of his family, but still it is a thing which one naturally dislikes to do."

In 1874 Mark Twain published three sketches that were to have been parts of his English book, each labeled "From the Author's Unpublished English Notes." They are "A Memorable Midnight Experience," about a visit to Westminster Abbey; "Rogers," and "Property in Opulent London." Two years later he published, most obscurely, "Some Recollections of a Storm at Sea [Being an Extract from Chapter III, of a Book Begun Three Years Ago, But Afterwards Abandoned]." Five other pieces survive. Two paragraphs, "An Expatriate" and "Stanley and the Queen," appear in Paine's biography, and Paine's successor as literary executor, Bernard DeVoto, published "The Albert Memorial," "Old Saint Paul's," and "The British Museum." All these pieces are worth reading, but none is remarkable. Had Mark Twain completed the book on England, it would have been pleasant and readable but probably not an advance over his two earlier accounts of his travels and adventures.*

When the Clemenses went to England in May 1873 they were accompanied by a young theological student, S. C. Thompson, hired as shorthand secretary for the English book. (Mark Twain was apparently interested in how the English talked.) In June he contracted with the New York *Herald*'s London office to write a series of papers about a visit of the shah of Persia to London. Thereupon he and Thompson traveled to Ostend, with Thompson taking notes. (He appears in the letters as Mr. Blank.) After observing the city, they recrossed the channel with the shah and in London and later at Windsor Castle witnessed

---

*Mark Twain left a bit of trivia behind in England, a slight sketch called "Magdalen Tower," which appeared in an Oxford undergraduate publication, *The Shotover Papers*, in its October 17, 1874, issue. It describes, good-naturedly, the responses of members of Mark Twain's English audience to his deliberately ignorant reference to the tower.

the elaborate receptions given the distinguished visitor. The accounts Mark Twain wrote, collected by Albert Bigelow Paine into book form in 1923 in *Europe and Elsewhere*, are among his weakest performances. He acts the buffoon, on assignment not to write letters but to deliver the shah. "If I got him over, all right. But if I lost him? if he died on my hands? if he drowned?" Then the author asks himself exactly what he is supposed to do and concludes that his task is to impress the shah. Thereafter he constantly questions which of the events of the trip will impress him. Mark Twain himself is impressed by the ceremonies he witnesses, for example by young Prince Arthur, with a "whole broadside of gold and silver medals on his breast—for good behavior, punctuality, accurate spelling, penmanship, etc., I suppose, but I could not see the inscriptions." Despite a few funny touches, these letters are embarrassingly bad—Mark Twain parodying himself, it would seem. Another explanation, the author's own, is that the "humor was not his but was added by a *Herald* employee, without authorization."[10]

When he had begun this assignment, he was excited. As he started on the first of his letters, he wrote to Bliss in June that he should "seize them as they appear & turn them into a 25 cent pamphlet (my royalties 10 per cent) & spread them over the land your own way, but be quick." After he wrote the last letter, he was more modest. Along with the shah letters he planned to publish "certain sketches of mine which are little known or not known at all in America, to the end that the purchase of the pamphlet may get back a portion of his money and skip the chapters that refer to the Shah altogether."[11] Apologetically he explained, "It is not my desire to republish these New York Herald letters in this form." When a pamphlet finally appeared, *Mark Twain's Sketches. Number One*, the shah letters were absent. He had seen what was published and had no desire to extend its life.

When he returned to Hartford in January 1874, following his London lectures, Clemens might well have seen that his various literary plans—at least three that he had counted on—had not worked. But he had the satisfaction of seeing that the spectacular house where he and his family would live happily for many years was going up. An expensive house, it would eventually cost—land, building, and furnishings—some $120,000. The project was to prove an enormous distraction—the house, the many servants required to keep it going, the entertaining, the guests that almost constantly filled its rooms, and the occasional but extensive renovations. More and more the author found that he could not find time to write there. In April the Clemenses retreated again to Quarry Farm, where Mark Twain spent an unusually productive spring and summer. By July he had produced a dramatic version of some of his parts of *The Gilded Age*. "I don't think much of it, as a drama," he wrote to Howells, then, "but I suppose it will do to hang Col. Sellers on." *Colonel Sellers, or The Gilded Age* was written as the result of the production, in San Francisco, of an unauthorized dramatization of the novel. Though no text survives, it has been assumed that Mark Twain revised the version that had been performed in California. With John T. Raymond, a skillful and popular actor, performing the part of Sellers, it was a considerable success, and Clemens profited to the extent of about fifty thousand dollars, though he was never happy with Raymond's vulgarization of Sellers's part. Perhaps these profits partially compensated Clemens for the two books he had not written; they definitely convinced him that there was gold for him in the theater.

During his 1874 stay at Quarry Farm, Mark Twain wrote his first piece to be published in the *Atlantic Monthly*. This piece, which he called "A True Story. Repeated Word for Word as I Heard It" is an account as told to Mark Twain by the Quarry Farm cook, Auntie Cord, of her painful experiences as a slave. It is in dialect and, according to Clemens's September letters to Howells, "not altered . . . except to begin at the beginning, instead of the middle, as she did—and traveled both ways."[12] Capturing the language and the personality was not easy, but the exercise helped prepare him for his writing work of the summer, since it brought him back to the atmosphere of the pre–Civil War South and memories of his own boyhood. Moreover his conversations with Auntie Cord would soon provide him with information that he would use in *Huckleberry Finn*. In an unpublished piece called "A Family Sketch" (1906) he told how Auntie Cord filled the heads of his children with Negro superstitions about spiders, cobwebs, snakes, the weather, the phases of the moon, the eccentricities of animals.[13]

In February 1870, soon after he was married, Clemens had written a letter to Will Bowen, whom he called his first, oldest, and dearest friend. He recalled in it the experiences of his youth, memories of which had suggested to him how far he had come since his Hannibal days. The excitement behind this long letter, which is very detailed, was warranted. Mark Twain was making one of the great discoveries of his career: that he had a highly usable past. Many of the incidents recounted in the letter soon were retold in *Tom Sawyer*, partly as a result of these renewed memories.

He had, however, never forgotten his boyhood, as is shown by such pieces as "Jim Wolf and the Tom-Cats" (1867); the episode in chapter 18 of *The Innocents Abroad* in which he describes finding a corpse in his father's office; and the pictures of Washington Hawkins and his youthful daydreams in *The Gilded Age*. Not long after writing his letter to Bowen, Mark Twain sketched what has been called the "Boy Manuscript," the diary of Billy Rogers. The story of Billy's romance with eight-year-old Amy, it suggests how Mark Twain was approaching his boy-hero Tom Sawyer. In this early version, for example, Billy prepares a love letter for his Amy:

> *Darling Amy*
> I take my pen in hand to inform you that I am in good health and hope these fiew lines will find you injoying the same god's blessing I love you. I cannot live & see you hate me & talk to that Jim riley which I will lick every time I ketch him and have done so already
> I do not wish to live any more as we must part. I will pisen myself when I am done writing this & that is the last you will ever see of your Billy forever. I enclose my tooth which was pulled out newyears, keep it always to remember me by, I wish it was larger. Your dyeing BILLY ROGERS[14]

The story is reminiscent of Mark Twain's earlier burlesque condensed novel, "Lucretia Smith's Soldier," though the fun that he makes of the children's romance is far gentler. Much of what Billy does in response to Amy, Tom Sawyer was later to imitate.

Another step toward *Tom Sawyer* was the composition in London in 1872 of the episode in which Tom tricks his friends into whitewashing the fence. The writing of the novel as it is now known was begun after the author's return from London and before he turned to *The Gilded Age*. He wrote about one hundred pages then. In April 1874 he returned to the book, and by September he had written about half, inspired in part by a new study at Quarry Farm, a little building by itself where he could write, often without interruption, even though that season there were distractions. His family was growing—a second daughter, Clara, was born on June 8. Nonetheless, in early September he wrote to a friend that his new book had been his real concern. He was "wrapped up in it and so dead to anything else." *Tom Sawyer* was not a book written to meet the demands of a contract, nor was it a sequel to the *Innocents*, as the diamond mine book and the English book were to have been. It was composed readily, from within, as suggested by the author's comment that in writing it he had "pumped myself dry" by summer's end.[15] In 1906 he described what had happened. At page 400 of his manuscript, "the story made a sudden and determined halt and refused to proceed another step. . . . I could not understand why I was not able to go on with it. The reason was very simple—my tank had run dry; it was empty. . . ."[16]

Perhaps a better reason for his inability to continue was that he had to solve a problem concerning Tom's future. When Tom leaves Joe Harper and Huck Finn on Jackson's Island at the end of chapter 15, he prepares a note for Joe. With it he leaves "certain school-boy treasures of almost inestimable value." Thereby the author hinted that Tom was about to leave St. Petersburg for greater adventures. But he was uncertain. On the manuscript itself at this point Mark Twain wrote a series of notes about how the story might be continued; they reflect this uncertainty.

So he put it aside until the following May, when he began it again, in Hartford—for in the previous September the family had moved into their new house and would stay there for the summer of 1875. Although he told Howells in June that "there is no plot to the thing," he later noted that "there was plenty of material now, and the book went on and finished itself, without any trouble."[17] The second half was shaped by two decisions: first, to have Tom remain in St. Petersburg (the boys return from Jackson's Island to their own funeral), and second, to show Tom in a heroic light. Some of what he wrote in 1875 before the decision showed an immature Tom; these passages, on the graduation exercises and Tom's joining the Cadets of Temperance (as young Clemens had done) were now placed *before* Tom's heroic performance at the trial in chapter 23. By July 5 the book was finished, though the author was uncertain whether or not he was right in "closing with him as a boy" instead of continuing Tom's story, as he then told Howells he had planned. His original intention, as shown by a note on the manuscript, was to write a four-part novel, of which he had completed only some of the first. "1. Boyhood & youth; 2 Y[outh] & early manh[ood]; 3 the Battle of Life in many lands; 4 (age 37 to 40) return to meet grown babies & toothless old drivelers who were the grandees of his youth. The Adored Unknown a faded old maid & full of rasping puritanical vinegar piety." The "new girl" who becomes Becky Thatcher is identified in chapter 3 as "The Adored Unknown."[18] Later Mark Twain would attempt to write a version of part 4, but with the "boys" returning as old men.

The Adventures of Tom Sawyer had its origins in three quite different interests of its creator. First, he was still fascinated by the concept of innocence. He had emphasized his own youthfulness and naiveté in *Roughing It*, and for him to move from young adulthood to boyhood was natural. Second, he was now aware that he could write, without notes or reminders, fiction based on his own childhood.[19] Tom is a version of Sam Clemens the boy, innocent but mischievous and deep-dyed in literary romanticism. Third, he was still entertained by the ideas of his early sketches about good boys and bad boys preserved in *Sketches New and Old* (1875). Moreover, many other writers were beginning to write about the "bad" boy—like the hero of *The Story of a Bad Boy* (1869) by Clemens's good friend Thomas Bailey Aldrich. Tom Sawyer differs from most such boys chiefly in that he is brought to maturity through the initiation process that had interested Mark Twain in *Roughing It*.

Tom Sawyer was a real breakthrough for Mark Twain. He was not revising an earlier account, working from his brother's notes, editing someone else's reports, or working with a partner; he was relying on his memories: of his mother for Tom's Aunt Polly; of the cave where the real "Injun Joe" had been lost (but did not starve); of the schoolhouse.[20] "Most of the adventures recorded in this book really occurred," he stated in the preface; "one or two were experiences of my own, the rest those of boys who were schoolmates of mine." He told an interviewer in 1895, "I knew those boys so well that it was easy to write what they said and did."[21] Tom himself is not a single individual, he explained in the preface, but is a combination of three boys "and therefore belongs to the composite order of architecture." If St. Petersburg is more attractive than Hannibal, the reason is the author's affection for his own youthful days. The scenes he paints from these memories are the best parts of the book.

Though autobiographical and highly original, *Tom Sawyer* reflects Mark Twain's reading. The grave-robbing scene is drawn from *A Tale of Two Cities*, Clemens's favorite Dickens novel. The relationship of Tom and Aunt Polly derives from B. P. Shillaber's books about Mrs. Partington as well as real-life experiences. Mrs. Partington's nephew Ike, like Tom, plays tricks on the cat, steals doughnuts, misbehaves in church, feigns illness to stay home from school, and is inspired by *The Black Avenger* of "Ned Buntline" (E. Z. C. Judson). The graduation chapter owes much to Mary Ann Harris Gay's *The Pastor's Story and Other Pieces; or, Prose and Poetry*, as the author acknowledged at the end of the chapter. He used the simple expedient of pasting pages of Gay's collection onto his manuscript. Many other authors influenced the composition: Tennyson, Poe, A. B. Longstreet, George Washington Harris, Carlyle. The cave episode was probably inspired by a news story published in April 1873 about children lost in the Hannibal cave. The chief elements of the plot, such as the love story and the treasure hunt, were widely used in contemporary books about boys. Indeed, in his first solo flight as a novelist, Mark Twain was consciously attempting to write a story after the model of other books about boys. Like Aldrich's boy, Tom Bailey, Tom Sawyer is a bookish boy and the book as a whole has a bookish, "Eastern" quality, as if the author had chosen to forget his experiences in Nevada and California. He presents himself as one familiar with Mont Blanc and wealthy English gentlemen, and in chapter 25 he observes that "every rightly constructed boy's life" includes a desire to hunt for buried treasure. Mark Twain kept Tom's adventures at a distance so that the reader is fully aware that he is reading a book. An early reviewer of its sequel, *Huckleberry Finn*, asked whether "the most marked fault" of *Tom Sawyer* "is not its too strong adherence to contemporary literary models." For him, "the modern novel exercises a very great influence" on *Tom*.[22] One senses that Mark Twain is doing what he has seen other writers do.

The central theme of *Tom Sawyer* is suggested by one of Mark Twain's lectures of 1871, entitled "Boy" and advertised as "An Appeal in behalf of extending the Suffrage to Boys."[23] In his novel the author provides a continuing comparison between the privileges, pleasures, and excitements of boyhood and the boredom, required conformity, and routine of adulthood. The virtues of being a boy are suggested by the fact that Tom is provided no satisfactory role models. He is fatherless. Judge Thatcher, the most eminent man in the book, presides in the county seat, not in St. Petersburg, and he enters the novel only briefly in chapter 4 and again in chapter 32. Tom's teacher, the sadistic Mr. Dobbins, spends his free time perusing an anatomy book—a book with pictures of naked people in it. Another dominant male is Injun Joe, whose presence is always sensed. Lest his rebelliousness prove appealing, he is made to suffer a painful death. The qualities of boyhood are thus enhanced by the demonstrated lack of anything to do and anyone to be like after growing up. Beginning with the opening word, a peremptory "Tom!" adults make demands on children. One child who had capitulated to adult tyranny is the hated Willie Mufferson, the "model boy," who is destined to grow up into a rigid Mr. Walters, the Sunday school superintendent, whose stiff collar "compelled a straight look ahead, and turning of the whole body when a side view was required" (chapter 4). Two of the chief weapons of adults, as Aunt Polly's behavior shows, are pity and guilt, from which children are early made to suffer. Tom's world is dominated by such women. In many ways the book thus suggests the superiority of boyhood to adulthood. Both children and adults enjoy "showing off," but the children are not hypocritical about their enjoyment. Adults such as Aunt Polly admire children's mischievous deeds as an escape from boring routine, though they feel obliged to qualify their approval in order to justify it: such actions are what children are permitted *before* they are required to conform to adult standards.

The world of Tom Sawyer is gratifying to readers, both adults and children. In it wishes—even impossible ones—are granted, and the gratification is greater than in legends and fairy stories because the events in the book are not greatly removed from daily life. Tom heroically wins Becky Thatcher and is lionized by adults after rescuing her from the cave, a much more gratifying achievement than winning the Bible (and afterward suffering humiliation) earlier. Tom and his friends escape, run away, and for a time enjoy an idyllic life, vastly appealing, on Jackson's Island. This long episode ends with Tom's pleasure at what many have wished for and few achieved—a triumphal return to his own funeral. Even the boys' unhappiness with school discipline leads to wish fulfillment. The odious father-figure, the schoolmaster Dobbins, is completely humiliated at the school ceremonies in chapter 21, when his students display beneath his wig "their master's bald pate," gilded by the sign-painter's boy.

Such pleasures as these may lead the reader to overlook some of the failings of the book: the variation in point of view from nostalgia to burlesque; the author's occasional abandonment of his role as storyteller to comment on the action and tell his reader what to think, even as a mock-serious "great and wise philosopher" in chapter 2. The strands of the narrative belong together thematically but are only loosely coordinated into a plot. The most successful achievement of *Tom Sawyer* is that in it Mark Twain was able to combine his desire to write a popular, appealingly upbeat book and his belief that small-town America had little to offer a person who would live both freely and intensely. Tom's search for something better than the restrictive institutions and attitudes of St. Petersburg leads again and again to terror, most fully and climactically in the cave. There Tom and Becky find that the unknown is the ultimate threat. Finally Tom renounces there his dreams when he admits, "I was such a fool! Such a fool! I never thought we might want to come back" (chapter 31). His experiences give him a change of heart, demonstrated when at the end of the story he successfully badgers Huck, the very embodiment of rebelliousness, into accepting respectability. Tom's own submission is a defeat, for he embraces values that the book as a whole does not recommend. Huck's reluctant abandonment, under pressure, of his comfortable smoking and cussing echoes Clemens's report to a friend in 1874 that "I was a mighty coarse, unpromising subject when Livy took charge of me 4 years ago. . . . She has made a very creditable job of me."[24] Few readers, however, are eager for Widow Douglas to take charge of Huck. Since Tom has sought adult approval, his gradual acceptance of adult standards is understandable, perhaps inevitable—but not Huck's.

His recent conversations with Auntie Cord may have reminded the author of how much cruelty was associated with slavery, for blacks have almost no place in the world of *Tom Sawyer*. Only a black boy, little Jim, is introduced. He happily joins the crew that whitewashes the fence for Tom. It was difficult for Mark Twain to reconcile nostalgia for his lost youth and a recognition of the place of slavery in Missouri.

The novelist considered publishing *Tom Sawyer* in the *Atlantic Monthly*, a most unlikely medium, for he wished to compete with his former friend Bret Harte, whose novel *Gabriel Conroy* was being published by *Scribner's Magazine*, with Harte receiving a handsome fee. The fact that he was considering the *Atlantic* shows the author's confusion concerning what he had written. In July he described it to Howells as "not a boy's book" but one that was "written for adults." Only after considering the matter for six months was the author able to accept his wife's judgment—and Howells's—and agree that "the book should issue as a book for boys, pure and simple," as he wrote to Howells.

The author's correspondence with Howells concerning *Tom Sawyer* demonstrates one of his limitations as a writer, his inability to discriminate, to judge his own writing. It was for this reason, as well as his eagerness to avoid offending the genteel, that he submitted his work to his wife and Howells for approval. The experienced *Atlantic* editor's reading led him to propose in July the pruning of the last chapter plus "some corrections and suggestions" in what Howells described as "faltering pencil." Clemens's response in January was simple and forthright. "Instead of *reading* the MS., I simply hunted out the pencil marks & made the emendations which they suggested." Some of these were significant. He shortened the episode in which Becky

examines Mr. Dobbins's anatomy book, "tamed the various obsceni-
ties," and eliminated from the description of the dog sitting down on
a pinch-bug in chapter 5 the phrase "with his tail shut down like a
hasp," which Howells described in November as "awfully good but a
little too dirty." Howells later described his friend's responses to his
suggestions as "a mush of concessions," although he had supposed
that he was merely making "suggestions for improvement" that he
hoped would be "never acted on."[25]

While *Tom Sawyer* was written with spontaneity, Mark Twain had
not failed to think of prospective income from the book. He took "a
vile, mercenary view of things," he admitted to Howells in July, "but
then my household expenses are something almost ghastly." He had
high expectations. He wrote to a correspondent in April 1876, "I am
determined that Tom shall outsell any previous book of mine, and I
mean he shall have every possible advantage."[26] Despite its virtues,
Tom Sawyer did not provide its author what he expected. A Canadian
pirated edition, selling in the United States for seventy-five cents in
paper and one dollar in cloth, took the edge off the market for the
American Publishing Company subscription edition. Even with 160
illustrations and large print, the book filled only 275 pages, far less
than the typical book sold to subscription-book readers. Only 23,638
copies were sold by the publisher during the first year, and less than
29,000 by the end of 1879, and it provided only half the income of
The Gilded Age.

The English publication preceded the American, which was much
delayed. The English reviewers liked it, though they judged that it
was addressed to adults, not to children. Most American periodicals
simply ignored it. Although Howells was enthusiastic, his review appeared too long before the book. Another review, otherwise favorable, protested against the powerful presence of violence in the book:
besides "revenge," talk of "slitting women's ears," and "the shadow
of the gallows," there is "an ugly murder in the book, over-minutely
described and too fully-illustrated, which Tom and Huck see, of
course."[27] Mark Twain's penchant for violence was far more evident
in a children's book than in his Western sketches.

Between seasons devoted to *Tom Sawyer*, Mark Twain composed what
is probably his best work of less than book length. Like *Tom*, it was
composed from inspiration. In the fall of 1874 Howells had requested
a sequel to "A True Story" for the *Atlantic Monthly*. Clemens replied

that he had nothing to offer, but that same day he talked with his friend Joseph Twichell during a long walk and, as he reported to Howells, "got to telling him about the old Mississippi days of steamboating glory & grandeur (during 5 years) from the pilot house." He soon decided that he could write not simply a single reminiscence but a whole series on piloting. The satisfaction he could anticipate from sharing in that glory and grandeur was a strong motivation. By late November he had finished one installment. In all, the *Atlantic* published seven segments of "Old Times on the Mississippi." Soon after he began, he decided to expand his work into a book about the Mississippi River, a subscription book, of course. Since the 1860s he had been nursing the idea, but he had not intended to describe his own experiences until that walk with Twichell. Fortune played a major role in the writer's career.

"Old Times" aroused Clemens's enthusiasm. "I am the only man alive," he wrote Howells in December, "that can scribble about the piloting of that day. . . . If I were to write fifty articles they would all be about pilots and piloting." "Old Times" is not, however, chiefly a series of essays on how a Mississippi riverboat pilot performs his task. It is the story of a cub pilot's education, or to put it another way, of the narrator's confrontation with a task and with reality, the reality of river currents and sandbars. That Mark Twain was writing specifically for an *Atlantic* audience is suggested by one of the themes running through the installments. Before this educated readership, the writer must have been conscious of his own limited schooling, for he put the best face he could on his experiences as a cub pilot. The process of learning the river he finds analogous to education from books. The river itself is described in the third installment as if it were a volume in Latin and Greek, "a book that was a dead language to the uneducated passenger." Titles of installments emphasize the point: "Perplexing Lessons" and "Completing My Education." But it is a humorous account, mainly, with an underlying seriousness—none of the forced high jinks of the shah letters, and below the seemingly simple, straightforward account is a complex mix of attitudes and feelings.

Clemens often looked back on his experiences as a pilot with satisfaction, and while writing the *Atlantic* installments, he thought of returning to the river again. "I am a person who would quit authorizing in a minute to go piloting, if the madame would stand it," he alleged.[28] A few years later, he responded to the query, Would you be a boy again? by answering yes—providing that "I should emerge from boyhood as a 'cub pilot' on a Mississippi boat, & that I should by &

by become a pilot & remain one."[29] On the other hand, he had lifelong dreams about being "obliged to go back to the river to earn a living. It is never a pleasant dream, either."[30] In his notebook he recorded more specifically: "My nightmares, to this day, take the form of running down into an overshadowing bluff, with a steamboat."[31] In "Old Times" the strength of these feelings of nostalgia and fear undergird the narrative. Mark Twain was writing more seriously than ever before, though his skill as a comic writer is nearly always apparent. He was writing about what he knew, but it was not simply his familiarity with the subject that informs the narrative. It is that he brings to his account a newly achieved sensitivity to the large issues of innocence and experience. "Old Times" is as entertaining as *Tom Sawyer*, and up to the last installment, which he thought was "odious" and should be left out,[32] the writing went easily. It was not, however, inspired by emotion recollected in tranquillity.

When Mark Twain wrote "Old Times," the satisfactions of his achievements as a writer were tempered by his recent failure to create a suitable sequel to his two successes and by his increasing sense that he was obliged to write what his audience expected. In the sixth installment he generalized his predicament: "Writers of all kinds are manacled servants of the public. We write frankly and fearlessly, but then we 'modify' before we print." The sense of repression that Mark Twain refers to has been much discussed; here it is sufficient to note that he found that pilots were unlike writers, kings, parliaments, editors: the pilot of the 1850s "was the only unfettered and entirely independent human being that lived on earth." This exaggerated authority assigned to the pilot is further emphasized by the fact that the earlier self that the writer portrays as the cub pilot is much younger than Clemens really was when he began piloting. Whereas in reality he was twenty-one, he appears in the first installment to be only about sixteen, pleased even to be sunburned: "I wished that the boys and girls at home could see me now." The comedy of "Old Times" results from the repeated exposure of the young cub's ignorance and innocence, and from his embarrassment and humiliation. The humor is often on the verge of being painful, as when the cub is exposed to a practical joke before an audience assembled to watch, but because the author is obviously enjoying the telling of his story and because the reader suspects that Mark Twain is deliberately emphasizing the cub's naiveté, there is little vicarious suffering in the reading.

The story gives as much attention to the master as to the apprentice. Horace Bixby is the most powerful authority figure in Mark

Twain's writings. While he is a strict, demanding teacher, he offers the cub the opportunity to be like him, and in the process provides protection from such fear as the author, in 1874–75, associated still with piloting. Early in his education they work together on a "big New Orleans boat," "a grand affair" where the boy is respectfully "sir'd" by "the regiment of natty servants," and his experience encourages him to anticipate the day when he too will be a Bixby, whose prowess is demonstrated early in the sequence in a virtuoso performance that Mark Twain entitled "A Daring Deed." The recognition that Bixby is given for his achievement is not lost on the cub. And in the third installment the cub learns: "The face of the water, in time, became a wonderful book" and he "mastered the language." The boy is successful. Mark Twain does not thereafter describe his experience as a licensed pilot, since the substance of the humor concerns his failures and his embarrassment, but instead he suggests what it means to belong to the community of river men, with their sense of solidarity and tradition. He suggests, too, that the process by which he learned to be a pilot was useful, perhaps even essential, to his becoming an effective writer.

Before the comedy is over, it is qualified. It is the cub's task to lose his ignorance and thereby lose his innocence. It was an observation that Mark Twain had made before, but here—in the context of a narrative about innocence and knowledge—it takes on greater significance. "I had made a valuable acquisition," he recognizes, "but I had lost something too. I had lost something which could never be restored to me while I lived. All the grace, the beauty, the poetry, had gone out of the majestic river! . . . All the value any feature of it had for me now was the amount of usefulness it could furnish toward compassing the safe piloting of a steamboat." Unlike the passenger who sees "all manner of pretty pictures" as he looks at the river, the pilot sees "the grimmest and most dead earnest of reading matter." Mark Twain was wrong if he supposed that he had lost the ability to respond to the poetry of nature, as both *Tom Sawyer* and *Huckleberry Finn* —and "Old Times" itself—demonstrate. But his appreciation of youthful innocence served as a justification for the sense with which he viewed himself, the "rough, coarse, unpromising subject" that Livy had taken charge of. It is worth noting that the passage about the difference between the pilot's perception and the passenger's is, ironically, clothed in Mark Twain's most genteel rhetoric.

Soon after he began the "Old Times" installments, Clemens was seeking to persuade Howells to travel with him to New Orleans to gather materials for the book he planned to make about the river. In January he commented to Howells that "the piloting material has been uncovering itself by degrees, until it has exposed such a huge hoard to my view that a whole book will be required to contain it if I use it. So I have agreed to write a book for Bliss." That same day he described his intention more specifically: he would "stop in September with the ninth chapter [i.e., installment] & then add fifty chapters more & bring the whole out in book form in November."[33] This was a highly optimistic forecast. Neither the trip to New Orleans nor the continuation beyond the *Atlantic* installments was to be realized for several years.

At the end of 1874, while he was beginning "Old Times," Mark Twain began to put into shape a substantial collection of his sketches for an American audience. While he called the book *Sketches New and Old*, most were old, though he continued the revising process by eliminating coarseness as he had in preparing his sketches for English readers. Some of the new pieces are slight, such as an after-dinner speech he had delivered in London. The longest of the new pieces, "Some Learned Fables, for Good Old Boys and Girls," had been rejected by Howells when Mark Twain had sent it to him in September. It is a beasts' fable, with some pleasant touches. The hero of the piece is Tumble Bug, who seems to have just arrived from the West to insult the pompous Dr. Bull Frog, Professor Snail, and other dignitaries. Though too long and unfocused, the sketch suggests that Mark Twain still had a good word to say for the values he had adopted in the West. It is in striking contrast to another piece, "Experience of the McWilliamses with Membranous Croup," the first of several McWilliams stories, which provide an oblique look at life in the Clemens household. The "Livy" figure of the story, extremely solicitous for the welfare of her child, makes heavy demands on her husband, usually in the most delicate and indirect way. The family picture is amusing; the sketch may be read as the author's subtle revenge. Howells thought that it "must read like an abuse of confidence to every husband and father."[34]

In the preparation of this collection, Mark Twain wrote to Howells in September, "I destroyed a mass of sketches, & now heartily wish I had destroyed more of them." As a whole the work represented his past, about which he had become thoroughly ambivalent. He could see that he had become a better writer and that his earlier work was that of an apprentice. "Every man," he told his brother, "must *learn* his trade—not pick it up. God requires that he learn it by slow and painful processes."[35] But he could also see that among his older pieces were ones like "The Scriptural Panoramist," written for *The Californian* in 1864. Therein a brief tale is told of a showman who hires a pianist, "a wooden-headed old slab," to provide a suitable musical accompaniment to both a showing of religious pictures and the showman's own pious rhetoric. But again and again the pianist undercuts him. A picture of the Prodigal Son, for instance, is introduced with comments about "the ecstasy beaming from the uplifted countenance of the aged father, and the joy that sparkles in the eyes of the excited group of youths and maidens, and seems ready to burst into the welcoming chorus from their lips. The lesson, my friends, is as solemn and instructive as the story is tender and beautiful." Thereupon the pianist bangs out:

> Oh we'll all get blind drunk
> When Johnny comes marching home!

After the third such juxtaposition, "all the solemn old flats got up in a huff to go—and everybody else laughed till the windows rattled." The showman thereupon "grabbed the orchestra and shook him" and ordered him to "vamose the ranch." Mark Twain's sympathies are clearly with the pianist and his successful, if unintentional, deflation of the pretentious genteel rhetoric of the showman. Publication of this piece in 1875 was to remind readers such as Howells of the identity Mark Twain had gained during the first thirty-two years of his life.

As usual, Howells befriended Clemens by publishing a review of the volume, and what he found was quite different from what Mark Twain had any reason to suppose he would: "a growing seriousness of meaning in the apparently unmoralized drolling" of a "subtile humorist." He objected to nothing and even listed "The Scriptural Panoramist" as a familiar favorite.[36] Olivia Clemens expressed her deep gratitude to Howells, with her husband explaining that "the thing that gravels her is that I am *so* persistently glorified as a mere buffoon." Mark Twain was trying to profit from the publication of another subscription book; he told Howells in October that his friend was "heroically trampling the truth underfoot in order to praise" him. Despite the kind words, the work sold poorly, fewer than twenty-four thousand copies by the end of 1879—less well than *Tom Sawyer*.

The "growing seriousness" of Mark Twain that Howells thought he saw in October 1875 may have been a response not to the *Sketches* but to a piece that Howells published that month—anonymously, at the author's request. "The Curious Republic of Gondour" was inspired by Clemens's sense of belonging to an elite class. In the utopia that he describes, universal suffrage "had seemed to deliver all power into the hands of the ignorant and non-taxpayer classes," with unhappy results. The remedy was to give additional votes beyond the basic one to those possessing wealth or education—the more money or learning, the more votes. But "learning being more prevalent and more easily acquired than riches, educated men became a wholesome check upon wealthy men, since they could outvote them."[37] Mark Twain's brief piece might have been designed to appeal to the *Atlantic* readers, and if *they* did not know the author's identity, the editor did. Howells asked in August for "some more accounts of that same country." None, however, were forthcoming.

After sending Howells the lightweight "A Literary Nightmare," later called "Punch, Brothers, Punch!"—which was, Howells reported in January 1876, "an immense success"—Mark Twain submitted something far better than either. In January 1876 he drafted "The Facts Concerning the Recent Carnival of Crime in Connecticut." It was inspired both by the author's experience and the treatment of morality and conscience in a book he had been reading, William E. H. Lecky's *History of European Morals*, which became one of his favorite books. Deliberately distinguishing his narrator from himself (the narrator, for instance, is the father of *sons*) Mark Twain tells a revealing story about his double, "a shriveled, shabby dwarf . . . not more than two feet high," forty years old, a distorted figure but with "a sort of remote and ill-defined resemblance" to himself. This figure has Samuel Clemens's famous drawl, a resemblance underscored by being noted three times. The narrator, a prosperous and successful writer, lives comfortably and well. He has a cook; his fame has recently brought a would-be writer to his door. But his conscience, the dwarf, will not leave him alone and rehearses his misdeeds. "It is my *business*—and my joy," his conscience announces, "to make you repent of *every*thing you do." The narrator thereupon tells how he found relief from his conscience's tormentings—he rose up, tore apart and killed his conscience, a deed that freed him to undertake a "carnival of crime in Connecticut."

If in "Gondour" Mark Twain had indicated his willingness to embrace the cultural values of the respectable New England community of which he was now a part, "The Carnival of Crime" shows that he was not ready to submit to the discipline of the social demands being made of him without a statement of protest, though he chose to disguise it in humor. To get the full good out of the "Carnival," he read it to his Hartford club, and according to Joseph Twichell, his clergyman friend there, Mark Twain made it "vastly funny," though Twichell recognized its serious intent.[38] Huck Finn too would have problems with his conscience, and the subject is brought up repeatedly in Mark Twain's writings, including his letters, often humorously, sometimes painfully, at times asociated with humiliation.

He wrote a friend toward the end of his life that his conscience had been troubling him: "I was afraid I had blundered into an offense in some way and had forfeited your friendship—a kind of blunder I have made so many times in my life that I am always standing in a waiting and morbid dread of its occurrence."[39] More humorously, he could explain, "I've had an awful accident. I have coughed up my conscience. I wouldn't have taken $40 for her, she was just out of the repair shops and had fresh paint on and new rubber tyres. . . ."[40] His fullest and bitterest complaint is in a letter to Howells in April 1882: "Oh, hell, there is no hope for a person built like me;—because there is no cure, no cure. If I could only *know* when I have committed a crime; then I could conceal it & not go stupidly dribbling it out, circumstance by circumstance, into the ears of a person who will give no sign till the confession is complete; & then the sudden damnation drops on a body like the released pile-driver, & he finds himself in the earth down to his chin. When he supposed he was merely being entertaining."

In "The Carnival of Crime," Mark Twain created a funny, serious, personal work—not a document but a small, a domestic masterpiece. In it Mark Twain's authentic voice is heard, perhaps more clearly than anywhere else. He is a victim, his own victim, and society's too. He is being confidential, even confessional, but not embarrassingly so. He is irreverent. His latent violence finds an acceptable outlet. From the curious title onward the work exhibits masterful control. The theme is significant and interesting; the story belongs with other *doppelgänger* stories such as Conrad's "The Secret Sharer" and Dostoevski's "The Double."

Another, quite different means by which Mark Twain released himself from his sense of being "manacled" is shown by a piece he wrote later in the same year, 1876, at Quarry Farm, where he once again spent the summer. "1601, or Conversation As It Was By the Social Fireside, in the Time of the Tudors," was written, according to the author's later remembrance, while he was reading "ancient English books" preparatory to writing *The Prince and the Pauper.* He found that "frank indelicacies of speech" were "permissible among ladies and gentlemen in that ancient time." The conversation he wrote, somewhat masked by attempts at archaic English, makes much of farts and codpieces in a somewhat adolescent way. Queen Elizabeth asks, "In God's name who hath favoured us? Hath it come to pass that a fartte shall fartte itself? Not such a one as this I trow. Young Master Beaumont? But no, 'twould have wafted him to Heaven like down of goose's body. Twas not ye little Lady Helen,—nay, ne'er blush, my childe, thou'lt tickle thy tender maiden-hedde with many a mousie squeak before thou learn'st to blow a hurricant. Wasn't you, my learned and ingenius Jonson?" The fact that royalty, the nobility, and the great writers of the age talked in such a "picturesque and scandalous way" was what amused the author,[41] who sent the piece to his friend Twichell—partly because he thought he would enjoy it and partly because Twichell was a clergyman, a symbol of gentility. (There is no record of his showing it to Mrs. Clemens.) Later, according to his notebook, he sent it anonymously to a magazine editor who said that he was looking for a "new Rabelais." "How the editor abused it & the sender," noted the author. Others, such as John Hay, called it a classic.[42] By 1879 Mark Twain felt that "it should only be shown to people who are learned enough to appreciate it as a very able piece of literary art."[43] After a few copies were printed in 1880, the author himself arranged for the printing of fifty copies of 1882 by the press of the U.S. Military Academy at West Point. Many other editions have since been published, though "1601" does not appear in editions of Mark Twain's works. It is too self-conscious, too much the work of a naughty boy playing hookey, to be of much interest—except to those who seek to understand the author.

During the summer of 1876 Mark Twain's chief literary activity was to begin a sequel to *Tom Sawyer,* which he had finished the year before. He had thought when finishing *Tom* of writing about another boy, this time in the first person. By the end of the summer he had come to a stopping place in what he was calling "Huck Finn's Autobiography," the place where Huck's and Jim's raft is destroyed by a steamboat. He liked what he had written "only tolerably well," as he told Howells in August, and now put it aside for three years. Two months later he accepted a proposal from Bret Harte, who visited him in Hartford, to write a play together and "divide the swag," as Clemens told Howells. (Harte's *Two Men of Sandy Bar* had been unsuccessfully produced only a month or so earlier.) The two writers put together a play set in the Mother Lode mining country of California, with a plot about a Chinese laundryman, miners, and a snob, centering on an apparent murder, disguises, and mistaken identity. Mark Twain's chief contribution was to translate Harte's stilted dialogue into the vernacular; the broken English supplied the actor who played "Ah Sin" was Harte's responsibility. The two hoped to capitalize on Harte's immensely popular "Plain Language from Truthful James," in which the famous "Heathen Chinese" is named Ah Sin. Other characters in the play had also appeared in Harte's earlier writings.

By February 1877 the work was finished, and in May it was performed in Washington, D.C., and then at the end of July in New York. Charles T. Parsloe was admired for his comic performance as Ah Sin, but the play had nothing else to recommend it and soon closed in New York. Later it was performed in St. Louis and in upstate New York, but it left the stage finally and permanently in October. Though Mark Twain's part in the composition was not great, he took responsibility for it when Harte stepped out before the first performance. Soon after, Clemens was calling it "that dreadful play."[44] (By then he had produced an even worse one, *Simon Wheeler*, single-handed.) But now he broke, permanently and violently, with Harte. Though there was much friction between the two during the composition, the determining source seems to have been Harte's criticism of Mrs. Clemens while he was a guest in the Hartford house.

Mark Twain was even less productive during the three-year period after the fall of 1876 than the three years after the completion of *Roughing It*. During the earlier period he had the profitable *Gilded Age* and *Colonel Sellers* to show; he had even less for the later. He had begun an unlikely story—perhaps it was to have been a novel—that he called "The Mysterious Chamber," the personal narrative of a bridegroom trapped for years in a room where he must improvise ingeniously to survive.[45] It is not clear whether the work has autobiographical overtones; its literary sources include *Robinson Crusoe* and the novels of Dumas *père*. A second aborted effort resulted when Mark Twain and Howells concocted a plan by which each of twelve writers was to produce a work from the same plot. The 8,500-word story that Mark Twain wrote, "A Murder, a Mystery, and a Marriage," was the only result; it has no real characters, only a farfetched plot. It has never been published.[46] Equally poor is the story of the transcontinental and transoceanic telephone romance, "The Loves of Alonzo Fitz

Clarence and Rosannah Ethelton," which appeared in the *Atlantic Monthly*. More ambitious than any of these is "Orion's Autobiography," begun in late March 1877 before the first rehearsals of *Ah Sin*. Orion Clemens had changed careers and religions frequently, each time with the utmost conviction, always full of hope that all would be well. His younger brother was both amused and exasperated. Eventually he would encourage Orion to write his own autobiography, but now Mark Twain began one for him. He introduced him, he wrote Howells as he began, "at 18, printer's apprentice, soft and sappy, full of fine intentions, & shifting religions, & not aware that he is a shining ass." The project was given up after a few weeks; the surviving fragment, entitled "Autobiography of a Damned Fool," was first published in 1967. What the narrator undertakes and what he suffers as a result of his ridiculous projects—such as trying to start a harem of middle-aged women—is not amusing. Rather, it is embarrassing to think that the author could make such cruel fun of his brother. Twenty years later, Mark Twain became almost obsessed with his brother as model for a fictional character and introduced versions of him into a whole series of story fragments, most effectively and sympathetically as Hotchkiss in "Schoolhouse Hill."

Still another indication of the failure of Mark Twain's creativity at this time is the series of four papers that he wrote as the result of a nine-day trip to Bermuda with Joseph Twichell in May 1877. "Some Rambling Notes of an Idle Excursion" first appeared in the *Atlantic Monthly*. He soon had reservations, too late, about the first two pieces, and his Quarry Farm listeners did not like the second two.[47] The trip had been made, Clemens told his sister-in-law before he left, "to get the world & the devil out of my head so that I can start fresh at the farm early in July."[48] But because he had kept full notes of his voyage and experiences, such as they were, and had enjoyed himself, he decided to write an account. The pieces make agreeable reading, with some good conversation recorded, but what is remarkable is that they are not by "Mark Twain" but by Samuel Clemens. That is, the literary personality of the earlier personal writings is almost completely gone. Instead, the "Notes" are by an observant, curious, rather dignified man of forty-two, who records, for example:

> The next day, in New York, was a hot one. Still we managed to get more or less entertainment out of it. Toward the middle of the afternoon we arrived on board the staunch steamship Bermuda, with bag and baggage, and hunted for a shady place. It was blazing summer weather, until we were half way down the harbor. Then I buttoned my coat closely; half

an hour later I put on a spring overcoat and buttoned that. As we passed the light-ship I added an ulster and tied a handkerchief around the collar to hold it snug against my neck. So rapidly had the summer gone and winter come again!

The disappearance of Mark Twain requires consideration. Was it Clemens's choice? He was writing for the *Atlantic* readership, "the only audience that I sit down before in perfect serenity," he had told Howells in December 1874, because they do not "require a 'humorist' to paint himself striped & stand on his head every fifteen minutes." Perhaps the title "Some Rambling Notes" was intended to prepare the reader not to expect much, but one could surely expect what was signed "Mark Twain" and purported to tell his adventures to have some of the qualities of the genuine article. Mark Twain would reappear in several works after 1877, but only when the subject encouraged the writer to be authentic, and few occasions offered themselves while he was writing about Bermuda.

Significantly, the author introduces into his rather stolid account one lively talker, and his words give the account a little of the earthiness and authenticity one identifies with Mark Twain. The ship's captain was a dull fellow; his one function is to provide the occasion for some reminiscences of Captain Ned Wakeman, this time named "Hurricane Jones," and his biblical "interpretations" brightens the piece up for a time, but it soon subsides to commonplaces again. This reminiscence was at second hand; Clemens's friend Joseph Twichell, with whom he traveled to Bermuda, had told him the story. Twichell had met Wakeman after Clemens had alerted him to what a great talker the seaman was, and Wakeman had told Twichell how to understand miracles.

After the "Notes," Mark Twain turned to a project that pleased him so much that he wrote fifty-four pages the first day and finished it within a week. He was inspired by the encouragement he had received from Chandos Fulton, a New York theater impresario, who had written him in March that he wanted a piece for two comedians and thought the plot Clemens had outlined to him six months earlier had in it "the germ of a good acting play."[49] *Captain Simon Wheeler, The Amateur Dectective. A Light Tragedy* was written as a satire of Allan Pinkerton's methods and as a burlesque of his books, such as *The Expressman and the Detectives, Mississippi Outlaws and the Detectives*, and *Poisoner and the Detectives*. Simon Wheeler is from the "Jumping Frog" but has little else to recommend him. The plot, very much like that of *Ah Sin*, revolves around a murder that did not take place. Three

New York detectives, as well as Wheeler, seek to discover the murderer. Each has outlandish theories. One believes that the murder weapon was a hymnbook and collects all the hymnals he can find. Like Tom Sawyer, Hugh Burnside, the central figure, attends his own funeral, though in disguise; he is thought to be the murdered man. There has in fact been a killing, an accidental one; the murdered man proves to be the desperate "pirate" Jack Belford—a member of the Canadian publishing firm that had profited from the unauthorized publication of *Tom Sawyer*. In addition to a ridiculous plot, the play is full of absurd passages of dialogue. After finishing his play, which the author conceded was not a comedy but a farce, he diligently altered, amended, and rewrote it. Then he went to New York to arrange for performance, as well as to see the production there of *Ah Sin*. He told Howells in August that Dion Boucicault, a leading figure in the New York theater, had described *Simon Wheeler* as a much better play than *Ah Sin*. But to the surprise of no one who has read the play, he could find no producer.

Howells encouraged him to rewrite the work as a novel, and in the fall and winter of 1877–78 he began the task but gave it up before he was half through. The novel fragment is far more interesting than the play, both because Mark Twain was a much more skilled writer of fiction than of drama and because he added several new elements to his story. There is now a vividly realized setting: a little Missouri town where the two leading families, from Kentucky and Virginia, have inherited a feud that foreshadows the Grangerford-Shepherdson feud of *Huckleberry Finn*. Judge Griswold resembles Colonel Grangerford, as well as Judge John Marshall Clemens. Hugh Burnside is now a poet, of the same sentimental school as Emmeline Grangerford. Captain Wheeler tells of a dream that is an early version of "Captain Stormfield's Visit to Heaven," perhaps because Howells suggested in October that his amateur detective "ought to be as like Captain Wakeman as you can make him." Marred by the continuing effort to satirize detectives, the novel is nonetheless readable. It differs from most of Mark Twain's longer efforts at fiction in that it has a love interest.

On December 17, 1877, while still working on the novelization of his play, Clemens attended an *Atlantic Monthly* dinner honoring John Greenleaf Whittier in Boston. Such dinners were the occasion of much speech-making, and Mark Twain had participated in a good many. He was now a regular contributor to the pages of the *Atlantic*; sixteen of his pieces had appeared there. Still, as a Western humorist he was much less admired in Boston than in the rest of the United States or in England. The speech he chose to deliver was made in the character of Mark Twain—quite naturally, since he was aware of how much he differed in background and in literary interests from the genteel writers of New England, many of whom were present that evening. He chose to "drop lightly into history," to tell a tale of his Western days, when he was "callow and conceited," just establishing himself as a writer, and ready to "try the virtue of my *nom de plume.*" He spoke of being in the Mother Lode country, at nightfall, when he had his chance and identified himself as he sought to gain admittance to a miner's cabin. Inside, the miner was soon telling him how he had been visited just the night before by "a rough lot," men who identified themselves as Henry Wadsworth Longfellow, Ralph Waldo Emerson, and Oliver Wendell Holmes. (The three writers were among the guests to whom Mark Twain spoke.) The men had eaten the miner's food and drunk his whiskey and stolen his boots and recited their poetry. They had threatened him when he protested. Now with Mark Twain's arrival, he judged that he'd have to move. "I ain't suited to a literary atmosphere."

> I said to the miner, "Why, my dear sir, *these* were not the gracious singers to whom we and the world pay loving reverence and homage; these were imposters."
> The miner investigated me with a calm eye for a while, then he said, "Ah—imposters, were they?—are *you*?" I did not pursue the subject; and since then I haven't traveled on my *nom de plume* enough to hurt. Such is the reminiscence I was moved to contribute, Mr. Chairman. In my enthusiasm I may have exaggerated the details a little, but you will easily forgive that fault, since I believe it is the first time I have ever deflected from perpendicular fact on an occasion like this.[50]

The speech is masterful and, delivered in Mark Twain's skillful manner, must have been a delight. No doubt there was an element of hostility behind the speech, a suggestion that the writers' gentility had an element of phoniness in it, but most of the audience was entertained. Howells, who introduced the speaker, was not; he believed the performance was offensive and was convinced that others thought so too. Some newspaper reports were highly critical. Soon Mark Twain was apologizing to the three writers, and even years later he was still smarting from what Howells called, after Clemens's death, "the amazing mistake, the bewildering blunder, the cruel catastrophe." The "awful speech," in Howells's opinion, came "near being the death of us all."[51] Howells too had come from the "West," and one suspects he was afraid that his friendship with Clemens might lead to his own status being challenged.

Such an experience was not to be forgotten. Clemens felt humiliated. At the end of his life he looked at the speech again. He found that there was not "a suggestion of coarseness or vulgarity in it anywhere." But only a few days later he called it "gross, coarse." Four months later he gave it what he called "a final and vigorous reading—aloud—and dropped straight back to my former admiration of it."[52] The Whittier Birthday Speech demonstrates that it was not always easy for Samuel Clemens to be Mark Twain. But he was in a bind. His very profitable success as a writer and as a lecturer rested on the literary personality he had created, and on that success he had built a life, complete with family, servants, and an elegant home in a cultured New England city. Living in Hartford, where genteel standards were high, if not so high as Boston's, was not always comfortable, for some members of the community always regarded him as a vulgarian who did not belong, a tramp printer, a Civil War deserter, and from the Confederate side at that. By the end of 1877 he had good cause to question how solid his standing was. How, one wonders, would he have answered the miner's query? Was "Mark Twain" an impostor? His future was highly uncertain. He had quite as many failures as successes: two disastrously bad plays and at least five books he had not been able to complete: "English Notes," "Orion's Autobiography," "The Mysterious Chamber," "Old Times," "Huck Finn's Autobiography," and soon there would be the novel version of *Simon Wheeler, Detective*. His one complete novel, *Tom Sawyer*, had brought him thin profits. His most recent book publication was very slight, a little book containing "A True Story" and "The Carnival of Crime"; and in 1878 there was to be only a pamphlet with the "Rambling Notes" and seven other pieces. He wrote to Howells a week after the Whittier dinner fiasco, "I feel that my misfortune has injured me all over the country; therefore it will be best that I retire from before the public at present." He was not defeated but was ready to retreat in order to reorganize his career, even if it meant leaving his Hartford home for a time. Fortunately he had planned such a move even before the Whittier speech, for he had written to Mrs. Fairbanks in September: "Our plan for the spring is thus: to leave, the first of May, & settle down in some good old city in Germany & never stir again for 6 months."[53] Living in Europe would reduce living expenses. The trip was in fact to last seventeen months, and the author was to complete very little during that time.

There are some indications of how Clemens felt about himself and his career at this time. He wrote, revealingly, to his mother in February 1878: "Life has come to be a very serious matter with me. I have a badgered, harassed feeling, a good part of my time." His "projects" were defeated. "I have about made up my mind to take my tribe & fly to some little corner of Europe & budge no more until I shall have completed one of the half dozen books that lie begun, upstairs."[54] His feeling of harassment showed publicly when he was unable to deliver the speech he had prepared for a dinner in April honoring Bayard Taylor, who was going to Germany to serve as U.S. minister. The speech itself survives, and though it was intended to be amusing, this time the speaker does not appear as Mark Twain. He paid tribute to Taylor's "character, scholarship, and distinguished literary service." He ended with a platitude. "In so honoring him, our country has conspicuously honored itself."[55] "Mark Twain" had been a long time a-borning. For several years after the publication of *Tom Sawyer* he was not often in evidence on the American scene and was soon for a time to disappear.[56]

CHAPTER FIVE

The Disappearance of Mark Twain

MARK Twain's many incomplete manuscripts, including that of "Huck Finn's Autobiography," were to collect dust for a good while. On March 8, 1878, the author signed a contract to write a subscription book about European travels, and the composition of that book now became the justification for the trip to Germany. Once again, his intention was to write a sequel to *The Innocents Abroad*. A secondary purpose was to make purchases for the Hartford house, which can be seen today restored to the ornate splendor that the Clemenses gave it. Along with a friend and a nursemaid, the family left New York in early April, and in May they were settled in Heidelberg, with a room away from the family rented specifically for the writer's task. Clemens made notes of the trip for the book he had in mind, but at first he had no plan other than to compose a travel diary of what he and his family were doing, as his notebook entries suggest. At the end of May he wrote to Howells that he was about to go to work. Olivia too was informed that the great day was about to arrive; she wrote to her mother, "Tomorrow Mr Clemens goes to work[;] he has been making notes since we left home, so he has a great deal of material to work from—"[1] Clemens kept up his notebook, where he recorded comments on the opera, current events, the family's dealings with their landlord, and other small adventures. The first drafts, made from these notes but later discarded from the book, do not stray far into fiction.

The earliest begins, "Towards the middle of April I sailed, with some friends & assistants, in the Holsatia, Capt. Brandt—& presently we had a very pleasant trip indeed." Soon the narrative took the form of a diary with dated entries, and the assistants and friends now prove to be Mrs. Clemens, the children, a nurse, and a courier. The diarist describes how after they arrived in Heidelberg, Mrs. Clemens's friend Clara Spaulding, he, and his wife were waited on at supper by two attendants, "two thirds of a waiter to each of us. This was a larger amount than necessary. But there was no way of reducing the style, since Heinrich [the courier], the children, & the nurse, were to feed elsewhere." Other excerpts that survive include diary entries, elaborately written-up descriptions, for April 25–30, the earliest days in Germany.[2]

But the manuscript still had no focus. He had written about fifty thousand words by mid-July, but "it is in disconnected form," he recognized, "and cannot be used until joined together by the writing of a dozen intermediate chapters," which he did not think he could write until fall.[3] But in early August an event occurred that made a significant difference: the arrival of his Bermuda traveling companion, Joseph Twichell, for a five-week visit. The two men walked together, then took two excursions. The writer was shaken out of his lethargy, began to make notes, and even discovered a plan for the book. He later wrote to Twichell that whereas he had feared "his interest in the tour" was "so slender that I couldn't gouge matter enough out of it to make a book," he now realized that it wasn't materials he needed but the right mood: "The mood is everything."[4] The plan, which he described as "new and better"[5] (better, apparently, than nothing) was to "appear,—casually and without stress,—that I am over here to make the tour of Europe *on foot*. I am in pedestrian costume, as a general thing," he explained to Howells in January 1879, "& *start* on pedestrian tours, but mount the first conveyance that offers, making but slight explanation or excuse, & endeavoring to seem unconscious that this is not legitimate pedestrianizing." He thought that assigning himself such a role, a kind of innocent, was enough to hang the book on. The "joke" was to be kept secret but was to be underscored by a preface, later discarded. The little joke remains at the beginning of the first chapter in the published version, where the author explains that he had decided to furnish mankind with "the spectacle of a man adventurous enough to undertake a journey through Europe on foot." Either way, the "joke" is slight—insufficient to provide a focal point for the book.

From Twichell's visit another idea occurred to the still-struggling author. When he found by December that he had not "gathered any matter" before or since Twichell's visit "that was worth writing up,"[6] he began to collect notes on an imaginary traveling companion, based on Twichell but without much personality—nothing like the old Mr. Brown. His notebook records attitudes and adventures with this character, first called Haggerty, then Harris. When in early January he had a frustrating adventure, trying to find a sock in the dark, he wrote up an elaborate account of it, first in his journal, and assigned it to the time of his travels with Twichell, or rather Harris. This new character is introduced at the beginning of the book, but his presence is insignificant—usually he is invisible—until halfway through, at the point corresponding to the time when Twichell arrived in Europe. Though he is unimportant as a character, the pages in which Harris appears are more nearly comic than the early ones, in which mostly commonplace travel adventures are interrupted by painfully obvious efforts to introduce humor.

Continuing to search for materials after Twichell's visit, Clemens led his family to Italy, then settled down in Munich for three months. In January 1879 he described himself as "yoked down to the grinding out of a 600-page 8 vo book," the phrase of the contract for a subscription book. By this time he knew that the book would lack unity and that there would be only some good "spots." He would have liked, he wrote regretfully, to follow a suggestion from Howells that he write "sharp satires of European life," but he was not, he told his friend, "in a good enough humor with ANYTHING to satirize it: no, I want to stand up before it & *curse* it, & foam at the mouth, or take a club and pound it to rags & pulp." He was clearly in no mood to be the easygoing Mark Twain. At the end of February the entourage moved to Paris, where Clemens intended at last to finish his book. But there he was ill for a month, and afterward his violent dislike of France and the French made him even more incapacitated to write the book he intended. He prepared several chapters highly critical of the French, including their habits of courtship and marriage (based not on personal knowledge but on a book); none of this material was included in the final version, though some pages were published elsewhere. The brief "Paris Notes" appeared in *The Stolen White Elephant, Etc.* (1882), and Bernard DeVoto published in *Letters from the Earth* (1962) "The French and the Comanches," wherein Mark Twain celebrates the ability of the French to execute massacres. He mentions several, but concludes that "none of these are half such matters of pride to the French as their peerless St. Bartholomew's." Presumably other portions of the voluminous remaining materials will one day be published, including a long description of the Grand Prix race. In Paris, Clemens finally came to a stop; he decided to enjoy himself for a while and to finish the book after his return to the United States. On July 20 the Clemenses left Paris, having enjoyed visits there from many American friends. They traveled through Belgium and Holland and then spent a month in England. Significantly, the writer now found England less satisfactory than he had earlier. He wrote in his notebook: "For some years a custom has been growing up in our literature to praise everything English, & do it affectionately. This is not met half-way & so it will cease. English individuals like & respect American individuals; but the English nation despises America & the Americans. But this does not sting us as it did when we were smaller. We shall presently be indifferent to being looked down upon by a nation no bigger & no better than our own."

Early in September the Clemenses arrived in New York. In an interview Mark Twain described his new book as being "about this trip I've taken . . . like the 'Innocents Abroad.'"[7] At Quarry Farm he continued his writing efforts. In all he wrote an immense amount, nearly half again as much as he needed, but he was not satisfied with his work, and for good reason. We can see what he rejected, for he saved most of the unused pages, even though he frequently referred to having thrown out or torn up quantities of material. In his papers can be found chapters on European dwelling houses, the purchase of a music box, a comparison of public transportation in Europe and America; an "art-lesson 'from the nude'" in Rome; a commentary on a French book on courtship; a discussion of German university requirements, intended to follow the account of dueling but squeezed out by the need to go on to something funny. Some other parts of the book, in addition to the aforementioned pieces on France, were salvaged and published elsewhere, such as "The Stolen White Elephant" and "The Invalid's Story," which appeared in *Merry Tales* (1892). This latter piece, which Mark Twain described as "the yarn about the Limburger cheese and the box of guns,"[8] he had heard from Twichell. It is derived from a kind of frontier humor about smells that he had always liked and was originally written for "Some Rambling Notes"; Howells recommended that it not be included in the *Tramp*.

In October, Clemens wrote to Twichell, "I have been knocking out early chapters for more than a year, now—not because they had not merit, but merely because they hindered the flow of the narrative."[9] During the autumn, despite interruptions (such as a visit to a Civil War reunion) he continued to write on what he now called "that most lagging and hated book."[10] Finally he decided in January that he had done enough. As an account of his trip the book ends abruptly (though few readers would have the book longer) with a telescoped account of the visit to France and England by way of Holland and Belgium. Before he had finished the last part, the early part of the book was already in print, and in March *A Tramp Abroad* was published. As with *Roughing It*, completing the book was a painful, exhausting experience.

The title *A Tramp Abroad* was intended to recall *The Innocents Abroad*. Unlike the earlier book, it has no plan, but such plan as the earlier book has was determined mostly by circumstance, not literary art. The *Tramp* is a series of chapters about the author's experiences while traveling with Mr. Harris in Germany, Switzerland, and—more briefly—Italy, but frequently interrupted by digressions. What could not be worked in, even as a digression, appears in six appendixes. Though nothing holds the book together except the binding, three themes were intended to provide some unity: the aforementioned idea of a journey through Europe on foot; Mark Twain's intention to study art; and his desire to learn the German language. The three are identified in the first chapter, but even there one finds a digression, the first of many retellings of German legends. Some of the best parts are unrelated to the account of the tour: Jim Baker's Blue Jay Yarn, which Clemens had reminded himself about at the beginning of his trip; the futile efforts to torment Nicodemus Dodge, Clemens's fellow apprentice back in the Hannibal printshop—even by placing Jimmy Finn's skeleton in his bed; a reminiscence of the winter of 1867, when Clemens and Riley were Washington newspaper correspondents; Mark Twain's forty-seven-mile tour of his bedroom floor in the dark to find a missing sock. Somewhat less far afield is the amusing legend of Sir Wissenschaft, a predecessor of the Connecticut Yankee: he kills a dragon with the fire extinguisher he has invented.

Neither the narrative account nor the digressions of *A Tramp Abroad* are spontaneously funny. Instead, the author seems to recall every few chapters that he has a reputation as a humorist. For example, in chapter 44 he and Harris "climb" Mont Blanc by telescope and observe the view: "the grand professional summits of the Cisalpine Cordillera, drowned in a sensuous haze; to the east loomed the colossal masses of the Yodelhorn, the Fuddlehorn, and the Dinnerhorn. . . ." The passage continues, too long. The most common techniques for creating amusement are burlesque and other forms of exaggeration. Mark Twain's attitude toward what he had written is shown by his comment to Twichell: "I have made the burlesque of Alp-climbing prodigiously loud, but I guess I will leave it so."[11]

As Twichell's journal shows, some of Harris's comments came from him. But while interaction between Harris and the narrator is of some interest, the book makes almost as slow reading as it did writing. The last part of the book leans heavily on the writings of the English Alpinist Edward Whymper; he—not Mark Twain—wrote chapter 41. Those who read an early printing, with 328 illustrations, may find the book more appealing. But the self-assured though often victimized Mark Twain is too seldom present. Even his idolizing biographer Albert Bigelow Paine admitted that in *A Tramp Abroad* "very often he does not laugh heartily and sincerely at all, but finds his humor in extravagant burlesque."[12]

Appendix D, "The Awful German Language," proves that Mark Twain was still alive. As a student of the language, he is regularly defeated. He is naturally sympathetic with the Californian who said that "he would rather decline two drinks than one German adjective," as he is with the student who found "the only word in the whole language whose sound was sweet and precious to his lacerated spirit": *damit*. But when "he learned that the emphasis was not on the first syllable, his only stay and support was gone, and he faded away and died." Mark Twain heroically volunteers to reform the language, to trim it down and repair it, though he is satisfied that a gifted person *could* learn the language—in only thirty years.

The high point of the book is the Blue Jay Yarn, which has been called a masterpiece of the same order as *Huckleberry Finn*. Just as in that novel and in the Jumping Frog story, Mark Twain employs a narrator. The story had been told by Clemens's friend Jim Gillis but is now assigned to one Jim Baker, a lonely California miner. A good part of the pleasure that the yarn provides is in the characterization of the narrator, who describes himself, unintentionally, in a long preface. Baker has a reverence for blue jays, their vocabulary and their grammar, but he notes also other, less appealing aspects of their "humanity": their lack of principles, their deviousness, and their interest in gossip. What Baker has to say on behalf of the jays' grammar is qualified by his own occasional lapses, and his appreciation of their "out and out book-talk" by his own remoteness from literature. He proves, however, to be an excellent storyteller, fond of wonderfully concrete details. He is fascinated with the blue jay who tries to fill a hole with acorns—dropping in "enough to keep the family for years," in the jay's opinion. Baker would have his listeners believe all jays have human characteristics.

Jim understands this jay, though *why* the bird dropped the acorns into the hole, Jim does not say. It was, the bird judged, a "perfectly elegant hole," and the anticipation of hearing a nut fall, hearing it *hit*, put the "heavenliest smile" on his face. His frustration when that sound is denied him makes him determined to fill the hole. The nub of the story is the exposure of the absurdity of this effort, when his fellow jays discover that he's been trying to fill a *house* with acorns by dropping them through a knothole in the roof. The spectator jays are vastly amused. Every summer for three years thereafter, jay after jay enjoys the absurdity. The story is skillfully told, with the stress shifting from the jay's humiliation, which is implied but not stated, to the other jays' glorious sense of humor, in order to avoid emphasizing the embarrassment of the nut dropper. "Jim Baker's Blue Jay Yarn" is the story of an unintentional practical joke, played on the joker, and his own naive gratifications. It is the perfect story for Mark Twain to tell, because from the earlier stories he had told about himself one sees that he and the jay had much in common.

Despite its shapelessness and the silliness of many of its burlesques, *A Tramp Abroad* sold well: sixty-two thousand copies in the first year in America, and in England, where he was very popular, it was the best selling of all Mark Twain's books during his lifetime. William Ernest Henley, who reviewed it, called the *Tramp* "a worthy sequel" to *Roughing It* and judged that many parts are "equal to the funniest of those that have gone before." [13] But the book is probably best seen as a break, though not a clean one, with Mark Twain's past and an indication of what kind of writer he conceived himself to be as he moved toward *The Prince and the Pauper*. The young Sam Clemens had much in common with Mark Twain, but the now middle-aged man was someone quite different. Nearly two years in Europe and ten years in Buffalo, Elmira, and Hartford were having their effect, as was Olivia Langdon Clemens.

The difficult gestation of the *Tramp* was in striking contrast to the composition of its successor. *The Prince and the Pauper* had its origins in Samuel Clemens's reading, not his experience. He read, probably in 1874, William E. H. Lecky's *History of European Morals from Augustus to Charlemagne* (1869), a book that was to arouse his interest both in early European history and in the sources of morality. (Its influence on "The Carnival of Crime" has already been noted.) In a copy of Lecky's history, Clemens wrote, "It is so noble a book, & so beautiful, that I don't wish to have even trivial faults in it." [14] Now his latent interest in history was heightened. It came to include the history of the English language, especially early Modern English, and in the summer of 1876 he compiled "Middle Age phrases for a historical study" and wrote "1601." The next summer he read books on England in the sixteenth century: James Anthony Froude's *History of England*, and the portion of David Hume's history on Henry VII and Henry VIII. He now had a title for his historical fiction but, still interested in the theater, what he planned was a play. He recorded in his notebook in July, "Write Prince and Pauper in 4 acts and eight changes."

The immediate sources for the book were two. First, the Westerner who had come east was much interested in the notion of role-exchanging. The earliest version of his plot takes place in Victorian England, with Albert Edward, heir to the throne, exchanging identities with a London slum dweller. Then he judged his purposes would be better served by moving further back into English history. Second, he read Charlotte M. Yonge's *The Little Duke*, which tells of how Richard, duke of Normandy, profits from his experiences at the corrupt court of Louis IV to become a just and merciful ruler. In November 1877 he recorded in his notebook the basic plot: "Edward VI and a little pauper exchange places by accident a day or so before Henry VIII^s death. The prince wanders in rags & hardships & the pauper suffers the (to him) horrible miseries of princedom, up to the moment of crowning, in Westminster Abbey, when proof is brought & the mistake rectified."

In February 1878, Mark Twain was writing what he now called "A historical tale, of 300 years ago," and unlike the *Tramp*, which was soon to occupy him, he was writing "simply for the love of it." He called his work "grave & stately" and thus "considered by the world to be beneath my proper level." Enough had already been written to permit Clemens to read portions to the Saturday Club or "Young Girls' Club" he had founded earlier, hardly the audience Mark Twain was accustomed to addressing.[15] But then plans for his European trip intervened, and he seems not to have touched the manuscript for about two years. He returned to it with "jubilant delight" early in 1880. His interest amounted to "intemperance," he told his brother.[16] In a letter to Howells he implies a strong distinction between his current book and the one he had been writing. His pleasure was so great, he declared, that he was not concerned whether the book sold or not, and he was enjoying the act of creation so much that he was trying not to rush for fear he would finish and end his pleasure. Mrs. Clemens liked what he was writing far more than his earlier work. In early September he thought he had completed the book, or so he wrote Thomas Bailey Aldrich, and by early December Howells had read and admired it, though he had some substantial suggestions for revision, which Clemens in part accepted. He dropped the "whipping-boy story," to which Howells objected, and he "added over 130 new pages of MS to the prince's adventures in the rural districts." These additions were made at least in part to give the novel the proper heft for a subscription book. "The number of pages before," the author explained, "was 734—the number is 870, now—fully as bulky a book as Tom Sawyer, I think." [17] (But buyers had judged *Tom* not big enough.) After a few final revisions on February 1, 1881, the book was finished. The author expressed his pleasure: "I like this tale better than *Tom Sawyer*—because I haven't put any fun in it. I *think* that is why I like it better. You know a body always enjoys seeing himself attempting something out of his line." [18] Mrs. Clemens was eager to have the book "elegantly gotten up," [19] and it was. Howells both read proof and reviewed the novel, anonymously, well before its publication in December 1881, when it appeared simultaneously in England, Canada, and the United States.

The Prince and the Pauper was indeed out of Mark Twain's line, and his friend Joe Goodman from Virginia City days told him so: "What could have sent you groping among the driftwood of the Deluge for a topic when you could have been so much more at home in the wash of today?" [20] What sent him was a need to write a book of the sort that Mrs. Clemens and his daughters (a third, Jean, was born in July 1880) would approve. And there were others pushing too. Mrs. Fairbanks had told him to write "another book in an entirely different style." "The time has come for your *best book*, your best contribution to American Literature." [21] The Hartford clergyman Edwin P. Parker had asked him to do himself "vast honor" and his friends "vast pleasure" by writing a book with "a sober character." [22] Clemens did exactly as he had been encouraged to do. Dedicated to "those well mannered and amiable children Susy and Clara Clemens," and subtitled "A Tale for Young People of All Ages," *The Prince and the Pauper* is well mannered and amiable. Susy was delighted. She recorded in her biography of her father (much of which years later Clemens inserted into his autobiography) that it was "unquestionably the best book he has ever written." She objected to people thinking of him as "a humorist joking at everything." In her eyes the new book was "perfect." [23] Mrs. Fairbanks rewarded her child—Clemens always addressed her as "Mother"—with the highest compliments. "The book is your masterpiece in fineness."[24] The December 28 Hartford *Courant* congratulated the author for "writing a book which has other and higher merits than can possibly belong to the most artistic expression of mere humor." His neighbor Harriet Beecher Stowe told him it was "the best book for young folks that was ever written."[25] Only Joe Goodman is recorded as thinking otherwise. He thought the book was a mistake.[26]

In what ways *The Prince and the Pauper* is a book designed to satisfy the genteel readers of Hartford and elsewhere is not hard to understand. It is a historical tale, laden with learning about the past and set in England. Thus it appealed to those burdened by a need to learn from a novel as well as be entertained, especially those Americans whose model was English gentility. Clemens himself had become its ardent admirer (though before he finished the book his admiration had cooled). He was well acquainted with England and had broken bread with many of its aristocrats. Having dredged up historical material from books, he was able to show off, like Tom Sawyer, even if his learning sat precariously balanced. His notebook contains a list of over seventy people to whom he proudly sent copies of his book, among them Holmes, Emerson, Whittier, and Longfellow, whom it must have been particularly gratifying to address after the humiliation of the Whittier birthday dinner; the Scottish clergyman-poet George MacDonald; Charlotte M. Yonge, whose *The Little Duke* had contributed to his book; Rose Terry Cooke. Specially printed and bound copies went to the amiable Susy and Clara. He had done something special—what *had been* out of his line—and he wanted the world to know.

Compared with Mark Twain's other books, fictional and otherwise, *The Prince and the Pauper* is well plotted and unmarred by wild burlesques. The experiences of the prince and the pauper after they exchange roles are neatly parallel: each boy finds that his "father" believes him to be mad; each is befriended by his "sister," and each wakes from sleep thinking that his trying experiences have been just a bad dream. But the novel lacks nearly every quality that one associates with Mark Twain. There is little humor. With a setting in the mid-sixteenth century, the time of Edward VI, so remote from Clemens's own experience that he documents it with footnotes citing various authorities, the book provides no sense of being present at the events it describes. The master of the colloquial style here writes dialogue that is a labored attempt at Elizabethan English. "Searched you well—but it boots not to ask that. It doth seem passing strange." A few metaphors reveal the writer's background. If the guardians of Tom Canty, the pauper who by mischance becomes the prince, "felt much as if they were piloting a great ship through a dangerous channel," for Tom himself, according to chapter 6, "Time wore on pleasantly, and likewise smoothly, on the whole. Snags and sand bars grew less and less frequent." Just below the surface there is much that reflects the author's interests and concerns. The courtly ceremonies of Europe had attracted him as early as his first visit, when he saw Napoleon II and met the czar of Russia, as well as later when he covered the shah's tour. Increased financial pressures on Clemens are reflected in Tom's worried comments in chapter 14 on royal expenditures: "We be going to the dogs, 'tis plain. 'Tis meet and necessary that we take a smaller house and set the servants at large." Like Tom Sawyer (and Samuel Clemens), Tom Canty yearns for excitement and is bored by routine, and—like the hero of the earlier novel—both boys are basically good-hearted, innocent. Their goodness is underscored by the cruelty of the society in which they live, an interest soon to become a major preoccupation. Clemens had always been sensitive to suffering, as his writings about the Chinese in California show. Now his reading in historical works had shown him, as he told Howells in March 1881 while writing the novel, "the exceeding severity of laws of that day." He was moreover disenchanted with monarchy if not with its trappings. What the prince learns of suffering and oppression makes him a merciful king when the two boys change places a second time. The education that the prince receives is more than an indictment of a system of government or a historical epoch. Unlike *The Little Duke*, *The Prince and the Pauper* depicts man's cruelty as part of his nature. Though a book for children, it is the first of the author's works to castigate the damned human race, as he was to call it. Like Huck and later King Arthur, the prince is educated and learns the facts of life through his travels, and like them he is encouraged by a companion, one Miles Hendon. The tone, however, is far more optimistic, though the reader may see that the lessons the prince learns will have little effect, because his reign as Edward VI was brief.

In *The Prince and the Pauper* an important theme is the mystery of identity. The switch of roles that forms the basis of the plot permitted Clemens to demonstrate what was becoming one of his pet ideas, later set forth simply: "Training is everything." The differences between the prince and the pauper are only skin-deep, for they are still young. The pauper in time learns to play the role of prince, as a result of his training. Later Clemens would perform a more fundamental experiment by switching a "black" slave and the son of a white aristocrat while they are still babies. But *The Prince and the Pauper* looks backward too. Like the tenderfoot narrator in *Roughing It*, both boys at the beginning of their adventures have their vision distorted by romanticism; their experiences serve as educational correctives.

The Prince and the Pauper was not published by the American Publishing Company, for on the death of Elisha Bliss, its president, in 1880, Clemens turned to James R. Osgood of Boston, formerly a partner in the firm of Ticknor and Fields. Osgood was to publish just three books by Mark Twain; he proved to be inexperienced in subscription publishing. Because of his ambitions, encouraged by those of Mrs. Clemens, production costs of the books, especially this historical novel, were high. These expenses were borne by the author, who thought he could increase his profits by such a financial arrangement. But because his readers did not expect him to write such a work and because of Osgood's lack of publishing knowledge, *The Prince and the Pauper* was a financial failure. The book, as might be expected, was given bad reviews in England—one writer called it "a ponderous fantasia on English history."[27] It fared better among American reviewers. Joel Chandler Harris welcomed its author as a "true literary artist."[28] What Howells wrote was doubtless most important, for it contributed to Clemens's view of himself as a writer. Howells called the new novel "a manual of republicanism which might fitly be introduced into the schools."[29] While he could not become the polite *littérateur* his Hartford friends were encouraging him to become, Mark Twain could and would be a serious social critic.

During the fall of 1881, when he had finished a version of *The Prince and the Pauper*, Clemens wrote to an old friend from his Western years who was then living in Hawaii. With "the house full of carpenters and decorators," he complained that he got little done in Hartford, not even adding a chapter to one of his incomplete books. He kept "three or four in the stocks all the time," he wrote;[30] this was to be his usual practice hereafter. With few exceptions, he wrote only during his summer stay at Quarry Farm. His explanation in 1881 was that he was kept busy answering letters from strangers. Another possible reason was that he was frequently without inspiration or ideas.

One project that he kept in the stocks for many years, adding to it as ideas occurred to him, was "Captain Stormfield's Visit to Heaven." Originating in what Captain Ned Wakeman told him in 1868 about a dream, the story was begun soon after. As he told his brother, he was at first unhappy with the results, tried again later, and talked it over with Howells. He continued to make notes about what he might include, then returned to it in the fall of 1881, about the time he was protesting that he could not write in Hartford. But now he judged that it could never be published, apparently because of Mrs. Clemens's objections. Since he liked the piece very much, he was, he explained in 1906, "never willing to destroy it."[31] Even in his last years he added to it from time to time. Eventually he published an "Extract" from it in *Harper's Magazine* in 1907 and 1908. But it was never finished. A version with two chapters that precede the 1907 extract appeared in 1952 and another edition with added materials in 1970.

Despite its fragmentary character, "Captain Stormfield's Visit to Heaven" is one of Mark Twain's best pieces. It had several sources: Wakeman's story, whatever it was; an 1868 novel about heaven that Clemens had read; a joke he seems to have found in a collection such as *Old Abe's Jokes* (1864); his desire to make fun of some Christian ideas, especially the concept of heaven; and his continuing pleasure in satirizing human nature, especially its pretensions. Because of the circumstances of composition, the story cannot be readily placed in Clemens's literary career. The author himself said he wrote it "a month or two" after he heard the story in 1868, but the comment was made nearly forty years later, in 1906.[32] Its themes are those that Mark Twain was drawn to in the 1870s, and it anticipates *Huckleberry Finn*.

One version has a title page, in Albert Bigelow Paine's hand, which reads:

> Travels of Capt. Eli Stormfield, Mariner, in Heaven
> Taken from his own Lips by
> Rev. George H. Peters, of Marysville, Calif.[33]

Rev. Mr. Peters, to whom the story is told, is the name given to Joseph Twichell in "Rambling Notes," and in a portion of his autobiography composed in 1906, Clemens refers to Twichell as "(alias Peters)."[34] Clemens had met Twichell in 1868, but it is doubtful that he would have introduced him, however indirectly, into the story until a good deal later. The word "visit" probably had its origin in the joke about a man who apparently died but later returned to life, reported that he had been to heaven, and described what he had experienced. The early chapters that Clemens did not publish tell of Stormfield's death and subsequent immense trip through space to his unknown destination. The character of the narrator Stormfield resembles the literary personality of Mark Twain. He is frank, forthright, irrepressible, authentic—though at times fooled by his own expectations. Speaking a slangy, colloquial English, he tells his story with obvious relish. During the long journey (it takes thirty years) Stormfield meets several people, much as Huck was to in his trip down the river. His experiences with Solomon Goldstein cause him to lose his anti-Semitism. He has already learned a good deal about Negroes, for when he meets one named Sam he notes that "he was a good chap, and like his race: I have seen but few niggers that hadn't their hearts in the right place."[35]

After the trip, which includes a steamboat-like race between Stormfield and a comet, he arrives in a heaven quite different from the traditional Christian one. In it creatures from all over the universe gather, including those from earth, known in heaven as "the Wart." In the Christian corner of this vast place men and women of the *Quaker City* variety of Christians discover that their vision of heaven is a bore, and that human nature remains what it was—to Stormfield's great relief. While the story has some of the appeal of fantasy, with a little science fiction added, it is also a thoughtful exploration of the human condition. For instance, the dead soon know how undesirable it is to reexperience the "awkward, diffident, sentimental immaturities of nineteen."[36] People are granted their wishes in heaven, such as to be young again, only to discover how vain they are. (In one of his very last works, Mark Twain would have more to say about what joys in heaven are most satisfying.) Those with ability, such as the unknown poet Billings from Tennessee, are royally received, for heaven is a natural aristocracy where talent is justly recognized. "Captain Stormfield" is a satire, perhaps Mark Twain's most successful one.

The fact that he was unable to complete the work deserves comment. His method of composition rested heavily on the unpredictable nature of inspiration: he supposed that he *might* be able to finish a work if he found just the right moment to return to it. As a consequence many novels and stories remained unfinished, and some that were finished, such as *Tom Sawyer, Huckleberry Finn*, and *A Connecticut Yankee in King Arthur's Court*, have endings that are unsatisfactory to many readers. Chopping off the beginning and breaking off without supplying an ending, Mark Twain called his Stormfield story an "Extract." The technique works beautifully, and one wonders if some similar method could be found to make palatable to more readers other attractive fragments, especially from Mark Twain's last years.

The publication of "Captain Stormfield's Visit" in 1907–8 was remunerative enough to provide Clemens with the money for the loggia of his last house, at Redding, Connecticut, and after trying other names, the owner chose "Stormfield" for his cold and remote hilltop dwelling.

Olivia Clemens had kept the story from being published during her lifetime; she was her husband's censor, appointed by him. When she was too ill to edit his work, he wrote to a correspondent, "I have been—in literary matters—helpless all these weeks. I have no editor—no censor." [37] After her death he commented, "She edited all my manuscripts, beginning the labor of love before we were married, continuing it 36 years. [38]" He told Archibald Henderson a slightly different version: "After my marriage, she edited everything I wrote, And what is more—she not only edited my works, she edited *me*." [39] Because his editor was the epitome of the genteel society of her time, Van Wyck Brooks found her the chief culprit in what he called the tragic ordeal of Mark Twain. In 1920 Brooks wrote, "Mark Twain had thrown himself into the hands of his wife; she, in turn, was merely the echo of her environment." [40]

Mrs. Clemens was in a position of power and authority for several reasons. Her husband's attitude was, in his own words, "a reverent & conscious worship. Perhaps it was nearly like a subject's feeling for his sovereign." [41] Clemens was often uncertain of his own taste and so sought her judgment. His daughter Susy tells of his leaving parts of a manuscript with Mrs. Clemens for her to "expergate." [42] Sometimes, however, he was more confident of his own judgment. Beside a speech he had written for Jim in *Huckleberry Finn*, he noted emphatically, "This expression shall not be changed." [43] What Mrs. Clemens did to her husband's manuscripts seems to have been on a much smaller scale than what Howells did. Also she was an expert proofreader, though she was a very bad speller.

Olivia Clemens's most important role was to encourage her husband to write the sort of book she approved, such as *The Prince and the Pauper*. Therein she was not often successful. Her attitude is shown in an undated note probably of about 1902: "Think of the side I know, the sweet dear tender side—that I love so. Why not show this more to the world?" [44] She was especially concerned about her husband's public image. He wrote in 1899 to his nephew Samuel Moffett, "Oh, yes, write as many articles about me as you please. I am not afraid of you." Mrs. Clemens added, "It is better however to submit the articles," to her or to Clemens. [45] Howells, who knew both husband and wife, probably had the truest understanding of the relationship. He told Paine that he greatly admired Mrs. Clemens's "wonderful tact with a man who was in some respects, and wished to be, the most outrageous creature that ever breathed."[46] But insofar as he also wished to share a lifestyle with the gentility, there were major losses for "Mark Twain" when Clemens married Olivia. A houseguest of the Clemenses recorded in her diary during an 1876 visit that her host "was always bringing the blood to his wife's face by his bad behavior. . . . His whole life was one long apology. His wife had told him how well we behaved (poor we!) and he knew he had everything to learn."[47] Olivia Clemens edited the man far more drastically than she edited the author.

The long-delayed "Captain Stormfield's Visit" occupied Mark Twain for only a few days in 1881. It is instructive to see what else he wrote during that year, following the completion of the *Tramp* and *The Prince and the Pauper*. In March, Howells encouraged him to write a small "burlesque book of etiquette." Pleased with the idea, Clemens gathered a collection of etiquette books and began his satire. Perhaps Howells, and Clemens, thought of the project as a way for the author to accommodate his reservations about genteel manners. Before he gave up the project, he completed nearly a hundred pages, some few pieces of which were published posthumously. He devoted three days of hard work to another burlesque that he was much taken with: a version of *Hamlet* with a new character added, Basil Stockmar, a subscription-book agent. Commenting on the play, Stockmar finds its characters to be "the oddest lot of lunatics outside the asylum."[48] The adapter did not return to this project after he reached Act II, scene 2. In May he sold "A Curious Experience" to the *Century Magazine*. This longish piece, over ten thousand words, is simply Clemens's retelling, without much personality or art, of a Civil War story that had been told to him. It wholly lacks originality. At least one reader who bought the *Century* issue in order to read a contribution by an admired writer felt that he had been cheated. Mark Twain was for the moment barren of original ideas, except bad ones.

Mark Twain was not, however, ever to lose altogether his talent for humor. Undeservedly forgotten, for example, are the captions he composed for the "Rations" provided at the twelfth annual reunion, in Hartford, of the Army of the Potomac, on June 8. They seem never to have been reproduced.

SALMON A LA PARISIENNE

The difference between a salmon and morality is wide, heaven knows; yet there be better ways of honoring the Creator than by seeming to notice it. —*Sir Thomas Browne.*

FRICANDEAU OF VEAL A LA JARDINIERE

In time, augmenteth a Veal and becometh a Bullock, and after, in time, perfecteth he himself and becometh a Bull, which is the noblest work of God. —*Jay Gould's Henry VIII.*

BEEF TONGUE A L'ECARLATE

Quo' she, though I be flayed, give me but beef tongue to my supper once in the day, and I'll content me; rest ye easy as to that, Mary. —*Recollections of Lady Jane Grey.*

BONED TURKEY EN BELLEVUE

The King saith, though you be even as a boned turkey in the potter's hands, yet shall you not escape calumny, for the evil is to him who evil thinks, death cometh unto us all alike, and they that dance the same shall pay the fiddler; and this is why it hath been said of old, he that betteth upon a pair and a jack knoweth his own sorrow. —*Thomas Carlyle.*

GALANTINE OF CAPON A LA PERIGORD

Sir, as to angels, I cannot speak, being ignorant; but this I do say, that barring them, there is not else that weareth feathers that can bide comparison with a capon. —*Doctor Samuel Johnson.*

MAYONNAISE OF CHICKEN AND LOBSTER SALAD

I can never look upon a mayonnaise of chicken without the solemn thought that the same Power which enabled me to eat and enjoy a mayonnaise of chicken could have enabled the mayonnaise of chicken to eat and enjoy me: and how humbly, and unceasingly and prayerfully grateful we ought to be that it was changed around to the way it is now. —*Brer Talmadge.*

STRAWBERRIES WITH CREAM

Give me my choice between New England breakfast-pie and liver and I should take strawberries and cream every time. —*John Milton.*

VANILLA AND NEAPOLITAN ICE CREAM, WATER ICES, &c.

General Benjamin F. Butler, in his "Thoughts on Holy Living," has the honorable observation: Better the humble gum-drop and contentment, than the lordly ice cream with a constant disposition to raise . . .

But here the menu, at least in the surviving copy, breaks off.[49]

Instead of his usual practice of heading for Quarry Farm and a summer of creativity, Clemens vacationed during June and July on the Connecticut coast, at Branford. Toward the end of June he described himself as "having a luxuriously lazy & comfortable time."[50] Only in August did the Clemenses visit Elmira. There the author was ill in bed for a time with lumbago. He was not even writing letters. With some determination he wrote to a correspondent, "I'm going to lay this pen entirely aside for a week or more."[51] Thereafter Clemens was to be ill with some frequency, but whether his illnesses prevented his writing or whether he protected himself with them from the knowledge that he could not write is unclear. He was able to complete an essay on "Mental Telegraphy" that he had begun in 1878, but he was unable to find a publisher that would accept something quite so out of his line, and the essay was pigeonholed until 1891, when it was published. In the fall he read some volumes of Francis Parkman's history, which provided information useful to him in his next major project. On a visit to Montreal in November to secure British copyright for *The Prince and the Pauper*, he made quantities of notes for a sketch on Canada. He considered making a burlesque of Jacob Abbott's moralistic *Rollo's Tour of Europe*, but nothing came of the idea. Both would seem to have been unpromising, but the writer needed to find *something* to do. Possibly Mark Twain returned to *Huckleberry Finn* in 1881, though it is more likely that he did not take it up either in this year or the following one. Instead of writing, Clemens was devoting much of his time to investments, mostly bad, and editing books, such as a "Cyclopedia of Humor," not writing them.

This year, according to Paine, saw Clemens's expenditures to be over the $100,000 mark, with some $45,000 being poured into bad investments and $30,000 on his house and additional adjacent land. For a while he could afford to be extravagant, for he grossed $250,000 in the same year, from books, lectures, and plays. He was also edging his way into the publishing business. Believing that he had been cheated by the American Publishing Company, he contracted with Osgood to take a large role in the preparation of *The Prince and the Pauper*. This meant, for example, that the illustrations had to meet with his approval. His excuse for not attending a St. Louis "River Convention" in the fall of 1881 was: "I am putting a book through the press, and this sort of work requires not merely daily but hourly attention."[52] The publication of the new book was a major preoccupation during much of 1881. At the end of this highly uncreative year and into 1882, he devoted weeks to preparing a "biography" of Whitelaw Reid, a project that came to nothing. He had mistakenly supposed that Reid, editor of the New York *Tribune*, had been attacking him; the biography was to have been revenge.

The year 1882 did see the publication of a book by Mark Twain. In March he asked his publisher James R. Osgood to look over the files of the *Atlantic Monthly* and combine what he found by Mark Twain there with selections, to be made in consultation with Howells, from some unpublished pieces he had collected—the writer abdicating any responsibility for either selection or ordering. The result was *The Stolen White Elephant, Etc.* Much of the volume merely reprints the contents of *Punch, Brothers, Punch!* (1878). The rest of its eighteen pieces are very slight: a witty speech on babies (delivered at the Grand Army reunion in Chicago), another on the weather of New England; a rather silly sketch, "An Encounter with an Interviewer"; many ephemera, such as "On the Decay of the Art of Lying"; leftovers from the *Tramp*. Of all Mark Twain's books it is the least distinguished. The most interesting pieces are probably the brilliant "Carnival of Crime" and two more "McWilliams" pieces derived from the experiences of the Clemens family, with lightning and the burglar alarm.

Investments, business, editing, even seeing a book through the press were activities of a sort that Clemens's lifestyle could accommodate; it could *not* accommodate the daily application required for literary composition, for there were *always* houseguests while the Clemenses were in Hartford. Olivia Clemens suggests the atmosphere in an undated letter: "The house has been full of company, and I have been 'whirled around.' How can a body help it? Oh, I cannot help sighing for the peace and quiet of the farm. . . . Sometimes it seems as if the very sight of people would drive me *mad*."[53]

Something better was soon to come, for the author if not for his wife. In the back of Clemens's mind was the long-delayed trip to the Mississippi River to find materials for a book. In July 1881 he had written to the Louisiana novelist George Washington Cable, "Howells is still in the mind to go to New Orleans with me in November for the Mississippi trip."[54] But Howells was not to go, and by December the plan was for Osgood to go instead. In February, Clemens began to make notes on steamboating. Very much aware of his ignorance, he recorded: "I am so indolent, & all forms of study are so hateful to me, that although I was several years living constantly on steamboats, I never learned all the parts of a steamboat. Names of parts were in my ear daily whose office & locality I was ignorant of, & I think I never saw the day that I could describe the marks on a lead line. I never knew what 'in the run' meant—I couldn't find the run in a boat today, & be *sure* I was right." These notes suggest that Mark Twain was planning—not more of the kind of personal story he told in "Old

Times," but to augment his earlier pieces with an authoritative, factual account of the river, with personalities and anecdotes introduced to enliven the account. He reminds himself: "Throw in incidents from many lands." "At Memphis get facts about the pilot who stood at wheel & was burned." "Get notable steamer explosions." "Find Ab Grimes" (whom he had known in his piloting days).

On April 10, Clemens signed a contract for a Mississippi book with Osgood; he agreed to have the book finished by October 1, 1882, less than seven months from then. On April 17, well prepared, Clemens left for the river. Besides Osgood, Roswell Phelps made the trip; a Hartford stenographer and former schoolteacher, he kept notes for the writer. The three took the train to St. Louis, then a steamboat to New Orleans. On April 22, Clemens wrote to his wife, "We are having a powerful good time & picking up & setting down volumes of literary stuff."[55] Two sets of notes survive: Phelps's full collection of notes, transcriptions he made of his shorthand, and some notes by Clemens. Unlike the notes made for *A Tramp Abroad*, these show the writer's excited interest in returning to what he had known long ago. In New Orleans he visited George Washington Cable and Joel Chandler Harris; the latter had come from Atlanta for the meeting. On a ten-mile harbor tour the former pilot was permitted to steer. Then Osgood, Phelps, and Clemens traveled back up the river on the boat of the old master pilot, Horace Bixby, celebrated in "Old Times." After reaching St. Louis, Clemens and Phelps went to Hannibal for a three-day visit, and then Phelps left to return home. Clemens had been away from Hannibal since 1867. He recorded in his notebook: "Alas! everything has changed in Hannibal—but when I reached third or fourth sts the tears burst forth, for I recognize the mud. *It*, at least, was the same—the same old mud." Ending his trip, Clemens went up the river, was rejoined by Osgood, and finally reached St. Paul. He was so tired that he went directly home, on May 22. The trip had lasted little more than a month.

But the visit was not wholly a success for Clemens, since he had managed to collect much less information than he had hoped. For example, when he wrote his account he admitted that "the main purpose of my visit [to New Orleans] was but lamely accomplished. I had hoped to hunt up and talk with a hundred steamboatmen, but got so pleasantly involved in the social life of the town that I got nothing more than mere five-minute talks with a couple of dozen of the craft" (chapter 51).

In Hartford the writer began the book as he intended, by adding to the account of his days as a cub pilot the story of his experiences with the pilot Brown and the death of his brother Henry. These chapters were in keeping with his plans sketched in his notebook: "Tell, now, in full, the events preceding & following the Pennsylvania's explosion, the fight with Brown; the boat steaming down Bend of 601 with nobody at the wheel—the white-aproned servants & passengers on deck applauding the fight—the prophetic talk on the levee between Henry & me that night in N. O. before Pa. [the *Pennsylvania*] sailed on her fatal voyage. Make exhaustive picture of pilot Brown & his snarling ways & meannesses." He next built his account around his 1882 trip, which begins with chapter 22, where Osgood is described as a poet. At first he planned to use his two companions, whom he labeled Thompson and Rogers, much as he had used Brown and Harris, and he recorded in his notebook. "'Harris' is along, as usual." Thompson and Rogers are introduced, but only casually, in chapter 22; they are not really significant until chapter 32, where they serve to integrate Karl Ritter's narrative, which Mark Twain had drafted years before, into the story. Thereafter the two companions are nearly forgotten, except for an occasional reference to the "poet." At one place Mark Twain needed a Brown-like character to cry over the quality of the drinking water. "Rogers was not his name," the author admits, "neither was Jones, Brown, Dexter, Ferguson, Bascom, nor Thompson, but he answered to any of these that a body found handy in an emergency; or to any other name, in fact, if he perceived you meant him" (chapter 22).

When he returned to his old haunts, Clemens seems to have planned to make use of himself in his account as the innocent victim once more. Since he had much experience as a pilot, this time he would have to use an assumed name to play the role of tenderfoot. He chose the name of C. L. Samuels of New York. If successful, the use of a naive narrator would have permitted the introduction of more humor, as it had in *Roughing It*, and if the naiveté was shown to be only a pose, it would have been easy to incorporate information, a desirable commodity in a subscription book, into the account. All these plans had soon evaporated, for Clemens was immediately recognized just as soon as he arrived in St. Louis, according to chapter 22, and recognized again just six hours below St. Louis soon after he encouraged the pilot to invent tall tales of the river to entertain his innocence. "Thus ended the fictitious-name business." Thereafter the narrator is simply Samuel Clemens, as he had been twenty years before. The explosion of his incognito, as he called it, meant the abandonment of a fictional narrator and therefore the simplification of the book and its writing.

The Clemens family's trip to Quarry Farm for the summer was delayed by the illnesses of Jean and Susy, and Mark Twain was prevented for a time from writing. Before they left in mid-July, the writer had nonetheless composed more than fourteen chapters. As these were to be augmented by "Old Times on the Mississippi," he had therefore finished nearly half the book. Soon after he arrived in Elmira, Clemens wrote to Osgood, "I wish you would set a cheap expert to work to collect local histories of Mississippi towns & a lot of other books relating to the river to me. Meantime all those people who promised to send such things to us ain't doing it, dern them."[56] This letter indicates that this book was to reflect his reading as well as his experiences. Another indication is his subscribing to the New Orleans *Times-Democrat*, which he had been receiving in Hartford and now had sent to Elmira. He also borrowed books from George Washington Cable.

At Quarry Farm, Mark Twain next composed the famous chapter "The House Beautiful," borrowed from his own description of the Grangerfords' parlor in the incomplete manuscript of *Huckleberry Finn*, as well as several bits from Clarence C. Cooke's *The House Beautiful: Essays on Beds and Tables, Stools and Candlesticks* (1877), and something from Charles Dickens's *American Notes* (he refers to Dickens by name). The borrowings are well integrated in this chapter into a powerful piece of satire. Soon the books from Osgood's agent arrived, twenty-five volumes in all. He then requested additional books, this time by name. Later he was also supplied with a series of magazine articles about New Orleans, the Mississippi, and St. Louis. Besides drawing on these sources here and there, he based chapters 27 and 29 specifically on them. In addition, he wrote two more chapters chiefly devoted to a picture of "departed America" as it had been seen by English travel writers of the early nineteenth century; theirs he called "a most strange and unreal-seeming world."[57] Intended to follow chapter 40, these chapters were later dropped at Osgood's suggestion and were not published until 1944. At the end of the two deleted chapters, Mark Twain wrote apologetically, "I dredged through all those old books, mainly to find out what the procession of foreign tourists thought of the river towns of the Mississippi. But as a general thing, they forgot to say" (p. 411).

In the deleted chapters, especially the second, Mark Twain found much to criticize in the America of the past: the severity of its laws, its chauvinism, the vulgarity of its newspapers. Of the disappearance of such features, he observes, "We mourn, of course, as filial duty requires—yet it was good rotten material for burial." But he finds, "The most noticeable features of that departed America are not all gone from us. A few remain; some as bulkily prominent as ever, others more or less reduced in size and significance" (p. 407). When he returned from the historical account to the narrative of the Mississippi trip, he began to introduce this new concern with social criticism into the account. This theme was encouraged by a chain of events as well as by his reading in travel books. In June, Howells had shown Clemens his essay "Mark Twain," which was to be published in the September issue of the *Century Magazine*. There Howells warns the reader that if "he leaves out of the account an indignant sense of right and wrong, a scorn of all affectation and pretense, an ardent hate of meanness and injustice, he will come infinitely short of knowing Mark Twain." This essay in turn prompted Robert Underwood Johnson, an editor of the *Century Magazine*, to write to Clemens on August 9 to request that he write a series of articles on "Permanent Sources of Corruption in Our Government," "the lobbying, logrolling, running primaries and conventions, R.R. pass system, establishment of newspapers to form public opinion, &c., &c., &c. We mean a serious exposition of the ways that are dark. . . ."[58] Though Clemens did not accept the proposal, he now had reason to think that America was ready to listen to what he might write about its social imperfections. Specifically, he began to organize his account around the principle of progress, so much so that the work has been called a hymn to progress. "From St. Louis northward there are all the enlivening signs of the presence of active, energetic, intelligent, prosperous nineteenth-century populations" (chapter 57). To underscore the point, he made much of the South's backwardness. The problem, he declared, was that the region was tied to outdated ideas, symbolized by the Louisiana state capitol in Baton Rouge, an "imitation castle," and by Sir Walter Scott's brand of medievalism, so popular in the South. Mark Twain hyperbolically argues that Scott was "in great measure responsible" for the Civil War because of his encouragement of both the South's system of rank and caste and its reverence for them. Mark Twain seems to have seen himself as a kind of Cervantes on a crusade to rescue the South from decadent romanticism. (He would assume the same role, and define it better, in *A Connecticut Yankee*.)

On September 19, Clemens wrote to a correspondent that he was "not well, & my book drags like the very devil."[59] Several illnesses slowed him down. But by the end of his stay at Quarry Farm, he had added to his manuscript twenty-three chapters. He had incorporated "The Professor's Yarn," left over from *A Tramp Abroad*, though he admitted, "I insert it in this place merely because it is a good story, not because it belongs here—for it doesn't." He had written an introduction based largely on Francis Parkman's history, and he had decided to illustrate "keelboat talk and manners" by stealing a chapter from his *Huckleberry Finn* manuscript, which at this time he must have supposed he might never complete, for chapter 31. He was thus about five-sixths done. He was, however, unable to meet the October 1 date for completion named in the contract with Osgood for several reasons. He had given himself too little time; he had illnesses to cope with, his own and of family members; and he had not found what he expected in the books he had been sent.

Sometime in the fall Clemens sent Osgood what he had written and asked him to edit it, since Howells was in Switzerland. Osgood's memo to Clemens survives, with the author's annotations and responses. Once again he was docile, ready to accept uncritically what was proposed.[60] The consequences of Osgood's editing, and of Mark Twain's submissiveness, were of real significance. Among the parts dropped are some in which Mark Twain's literary personality is most in evidence. Without them, the familiar narrator—irreverent, spontaneous, and humorous—and the vernacular narrators he introduces are largely absent, though Uncle Mumford survives. Omitted, for example, is this passage, which occurs at the point where the tall-tale-telling Rob Styles is questioned by the narrator in chapter 24.

"Have you ever been blown up on a steamboat?"
"Nine times."
"It is a large experience."
"Yes. I was flung through the roof of the same cabin in Walnut Bend three times in five years."
"That seems very remarkable."
"It was considered so. Yes, three times through the same roof. The third time, the man moved away."
"He moved away?"
"Yes. He was a nervous, sedentary, student-sort of a man, trying to cipher out the Development business, and Survival of the Fittest, and one thing or another, and he said he would rather move than be always being interrupted and bothered so. Repairs took a good deal of time, too."
"Yes, and expense, of course."

"Well, no; not expense; I paid that. I always do. But this third time, I fetched the cook along; and I reckon if the truth was told, he didn't altogether like it. He never said so; but I judged, from his coolish way, that he thought I was making too free. He had always been cordial before. I may be wrong; but you know you can always tell a good deal by the way a man acts. He appeared constrained—that was the thing that struck my notice, not anything that he said. He never once looked at the cook, and he didn't ask me to sit down—he had always asked me to sit down, before. Well, it was a pretty chilly atmosphere, take it by and large, and we didn't stay long. When we were leaving, he did make shift to ask me to drop in again when I was passing—nothing very hearty about it, though—but I just gave him a stiff bow, and remarked in just about as cutting a style of cold politeness as I knew how to handle, that I wasn't in the habit of shoving in where I couldn't fetch a friend along who was going my way and there wasn't time to organize and put the thing through according to the gilt-edged requirements of Walnut Bend society. I had him, there! He couldn't say a word. So I just shouldered my wheel and meandered away."

"You had your wheel along, too?"

"Happened to have it that time—didn't usually take it. But you don't take *anything*, purposely, you know. You don't *think* of anything. There isn't time." (Pp. 389–90)

The story is Mark Twain's invention, not Styles's; in his notebook the author simply recorded: "Had a great deal of talk about the river and the steam boat men, most of whom are dead now. He [the pilot] located a dozen for me who were still alive."

Another tall tale, one of Mark Twain's very best, was deleted from chapter 39, "Tough Tales." It is told by a resident of Arkansas City, "an austere man" with "a reputation of being singularly unworldly, for a river man." In addition to his comments about remarkable mosquitoes preserved and published in the book, he tells a longer wild yarn about a balloonist who reaches a belt of dead air and is stranded there. Eventually he is joined by a fleet of other balloons, inhabited by an international gathering of fifty-four corpses "and a lot of dried animals of one sort and another," a kind of Sargasso Sea of the air (p. 398). Had this tale been published in 1883 instead of appearing for the first time as an appendix to a Limited Editions Club book sixty years later, it might well be celebrated.

A good deal of the old Mark Twain is present in a deleted passage about a group of California miners that were criticized by a San Francisco religious paper for giving "the sublimest mountain gateway upreared by the hand of the creator in all that majestic region" the profane name of "The Devil's Gorge." The humiliated and disgraced

miners "hadn't meant the least harm," and to make amends they re-
named the spot "Jehovah Gap," Mark Twain comments, "A religious
editor must be hard to please, indeed, who would find a flaw with
that" (pp. 390–91).

That Mark Twain should appear—or rather reappear—in a book
about a revisit to the Mississippi is hardly surprising, especially since
he had traveled without his wife and family. He was, however, constantly reminded of the passing of time from 1858, when he became a
riverboat man, to the present 1882. He had described the change,
movingly, in a letter to Olivia Clemens: "That world which I knew
in its blossomy youth is old & bowed & melancholy, now; its soft
cheeks are leathery & wrinkled, the fire is gone out in its eyes, & the
spring from its step. It will be dust and ashes when I come again."[61]
Samuel Clemens too had changed: now he was a celebrity. Once in a
while a short passage in his account recalls the attitude of the earlier
writer, as in chapter 22, where he explains with pretended innocence,
"The first time I ever saw St. Louis, I could have bought it for six
million dollars, and it was the mistake of my life that I did not do it."
In a deleted passage, he continued, "I was young and heedless, and
naturally more given to pleasure-seeking than to providing for the
future; it was impossible to foresee that out of that smutty village
would grow the imperial city of today; and besides, I had only thirty-
five dollars, anyway. Still, if I had known then what I know now, I
would have borrowed" (p. 389). Here is the familiar voice.

Finishing *Life on the Mississippi* was difficult for Mark Twain. In
November and December he wrote the last chapters, but he was still
revising in mid-January. Then he wrote to Osgood, *"No I don't want
to read proof of the old Atlantic matter—but I want it read almighty
carefully in Boston, and no improvements attempted."* He was much
less particular about new material: "There will be 20 to 25,000 more
words than necessary; so the scissors can be freely used."[62] Despite his
comments, the author appears to have read proof of "Old Times," for
a comparison reveals that he made forty-five changes in these fourteen
chapters, and while all were small, many are distinct improvements.

Life on the Mississippi became a classic largely because of the *Atlantic* papers, important chapters in "Mark Twain's autobiography."
The rest of the book, despite what seems like padding and some dul-
lish sections, is what Mark Twain was aiming for: a memorable study
of the great river and of the process of change in American life. But it
disappoints those who look for Mark Twain in it. An edition that
restores the deleted passages, at least those mentioned here, would

give the book increased appeal. But Osgood was not the chief culprit. The author himself, it may be argued, misconceived the book. His original plan of 1871 was to "spend 2 months on the river & take notes," and, he told his wife, "I bet you I will make a standard work."[63] This conception seems to have remained with him and led to his wide reading and to his neglect of fictionalizing that had gone into *The Innocents Abroad* and *Roughing It*. The experience of writing *A Tramp Abroad*, not long before, also shaped the Mississippi book. Having slaved over the *Tramp* for a long time, the author was quite ready to flesh out his new book by citing authorities.

Life on the Mississippi was not commercially successful, at least from Clemens's point of view. The failing, the author believed, lay with the publisher Osgood. His company was still not an experienced subscription publisher. After three disappointing books, Clemens left Osgood, whose firm failed in 1885. Reviewers read *Life on the Mississippi* as "a graphic account teeming with solid information, occasionally alleviated by mirth-provoking oddities of thought and expression."[64] Lafcadio Hearn called it "in some respects . . . the most solid book that Mark Twain has written."[65] An English reviewer decribed the second half of the book as "mere reportage."[66] There seems to have been no reviewer to protest the disappearance of Mark Twain from the last thirty-eight chapters.[67]

CHAPTER SIX

A New Voice for Samuel Clemens

IN 1877 Samuel Clemens prepared a form letter that read:

> Dear ———
>   I have the honor to reply to your letter just received, that it is my purpose to write a continuation of Tom Sawyer's history, but I am not able at this time to determine when I shall begin the work.
>   You will excuse the printed form, in consideration of the fact that the inquiry which you have made recurs with sufficient frequency to warrant this method of replying.
> Yours truly,
Mark Twain[1]

A continuation of Tom Sawyer's history? There were to be many, all of them told by Tom's companion Huckleberry Finn, who would often steal the spotlight. When he finished *Tom Sawyer*, Mark Twain recalled that his first intention was to continue the story into adulthood, but he had thought better of it. In July 1875 he wrote to Howells, "By & by I shall take a boy of twelve & run him on through life (in the first person) but not Tom Sawyer—he would not be good for that." When Howells read *Tom Sawyer* he recommended dropping the last chapter; a revised version of it may well have developed as chapter 1 of the new novel, in which Huckleberry Finn introduces himself by explaining, "YOU don't know about me, without you have read a book by the name of 'The Adventures of Tom Sawyer,' but that ain't no matter. That book was made by Mr. Mark Twain, and he told the truth, mainly."

As he came toward the ending of *Tom Sawyer*, Mark Twain must have seen the possibilities that would be open to him if he made Huck his narrator. In chapter 30, he let Huck speak at some length, and immediately the story comes alive, for Mark Twain endows what Huck tells with a most distinctive personality. As was to become his habit, Huck invents a story to get himself out of a tight spot.

> Well, you see, I'm kind of a hard lot—least everybody says so, and I don't see nothing agin it—and sometimes I can't sleep much on accounts of thinking about it and sort of trying to strike out a new way of doing. That was the way of it last night. I couldn't sleep, and so I come along up street 'bout midnight, a-turning it all over, and when I got to that old shackly brick store by the Temperance Tavern, I backed up agin the wall to have another think. Well, just then along comes these two chaps slipping along close by me, with something under their arm and I reckoned they'd stole it. One was a-smoking, and t'other wanted a light; so they stopped right before me and the cigars lit up their faces and I see that the big one was the deaf and dumb Spaniard, by his white whiskers and the patch on his eye, and t'other one was a rusty, ragged-looking devil.

In the new book Huck's voice is even stronger and clearer, and he is now far more of a rebel than Tom had been. Thus the decision to adopt Huck as his narrator had important implications. Any discomfort, resistance, or resentment that Samuel Clemens felt from the "civilizing" he had been undergoing could be readily expressed in Huck's attitude. Telling the story with Huck's voice released tons of psychic energy.

By the time he began *Huckleberry Finn*, Mark Twain was experienced in using vernacular narrators, such as Simon Wheeler of the Jumping Frog story, and during the years between 1876, when he began the new novel, and 1884, when he finished it, Mark Twain continued to make use of such storytellers: Jim Baker, who tells the Blue Jay Yarn, Rob Styles and Uncle Mumford of *Life on the Mississippi*. But he was now using less and less frequently the voice of Mark Twain of the West, presumably because the author was now a different person. Using Huckleberry Finn as a narrator permitted the writer to return to his old values and attitudes of irreverence, skepticism, and outspokenness, with the consequence that the book when published offended genteel readers, such as the public library committee of Concord, Massachusetts, who found the book "the veriest trash," "rough, coarse, and inelegant."[2]

As Howells recognized, Mark Twain enjoyed being outrageous. But his entrance into polite Eastern society had inhibited him from playing the authentic Mark Twain. The use of Huck's pen permitted more complete liberation from the conventions than Mark Twain had ever permitted himself before. His literary personality in *The Prince and the Pauper, A Tramp Abroad,* and the 1882 portions of *Life on the Mississippi* was most of the time restrained, even tame. Huck's quite distinctive voice—he differs from Mark Twain in being quite without a sense of humor and is even melancholy in temperament—permitted the writer to celebrate what he still valued, or at least what one side of him did: freedom, self-indulgence, the pleasure principle, laziness, skepticism, but charity (caring), and decency too.

Adventures of Huckleberry Finn was begun even before *Tom Sawyer* was published. In the summer of 1876, Mark Twain wrote chapters 1–16, except for a substantial insert about the steamboat *Walter Scott* that would constitute the bulk of chapter 12 and the whole of chapters 13 and 14. The new book begins exactly where the previous one had stopped; it is therefore helpful, if not necessary, to read the sequel with Tom's story in mind. Huck is now a victim of the Widow Douglas's attempts to give him what he had never known: discipline, manners, life on a regular schedule. He sees it all as a restriction of his freedom; he finds uncomfortable what Clemens himself had sought when he married Olivia. He wrote to her in January 1869, "You will break up all my irregularities when we are married, and civilize me . . . won't you?" Huck cherishes his liberty so much that he cannot take very seriously the widow's warnings that his resistance will send him to hell. At first he turns almost desperately to Tom Sawyer for relief. But in chapter 2 Tom proves quite as rigid in his way as the widow is in hers; whereas in the earlier novel Tom had been an adventurous leader, now he insists that everything be done "regular.' "Don't you reckon that the people that made the books knows what's the correct thing to do? Do you reckon *you* can learn 'em anything? not by a good deal." At this point Huck does not object, though the reader suspects that he is sympathetic with Ben Rogers, who pronounces Tom's plan "a fool way." As Huck might, Ben qualifies his acceptance of Tom's plan by proclaiming, "I don't take no stock in it."

The boys do agree that they cannot desecrate Sundays with their games, and in the next chapter Huck explores his own religious attitude. Prayer, he finds from a survey of his experience, doesn't work. Huck's pragmatic skepticism permits Mark Twain to express his own amused attitude toward conventional religion, as Mrs. Clemens prevented her husband from doing in "Captain Stormfield's Visit" by prohibiting its publication. Perhaps Huck's philosophizing is intended to suggest the growth of a questioning spirit, for soon he shows little respect for Tom's schemes; he describes them simply as "lies."

The early chapters of the book consistently show St. Petersburg to be a false, dishonest, hypocritical community, much less attractive than the town described in *Tom Sawyer*. In chapter 4, Judge Thatcher, a pillar of society in the earlier book, is ready to bilk gullible Huck. Restrictive, rigid, regulated by arbitrary rules, the town is an uncomfortable place for a free spirit such as Huck. Whereas slavery is not a significant element in the world of *Tom Sawyer*, it is now at the heart of the society and is symbolic of what is wrong with it. Tom is very much identified with this conventional, respectable society, and to underscore the orientation of his sequel, Mark Twain characterizes him from the very beginning as an unattractive figure. In *Tom Sawyer* the author had described approvingly Tom's gradual socialization; now he has sold out, and as an instrument of conformity he explains to Huck what *must* be done. In the former book, Tom had looked at Huck's freedom with envy; now he calls Huck a numbskull, a "perfect saphead." Tom is now cruel and aggressive; he has had to develop techniques for controlling others, since he has nothing of value to offer. He is an egotist and a hypocrite.

This characterization of Tom implies that Huck will have to go his own way. In this serious world Huck is to have an adult to accompany him, the slave Jim, who makes two separate appearances in these early chapters. On both occasions he is seen rather comically, full of Negro superstitions of the sort Clemens had learned from a former slave at Quarry Farm. The first real indication that the story is to have a serious aspect comes not with Jim's appearance but through the introduction of Huck's Pap, who immediately becomes—and throughout the book remains—a threatening figure in Huck's consciousness.

Though Mark Twain presumably did not yet know it, Pap's mistreatment of Huck is the occasion for the action of the book: Huck's flight and his educational adventures on the river. At this point Pap serves chiefly as a means of defining Huck's situation. If the boy is an outsider, he is not a leech, or an aggressively antisocial outcast like his father. Significantly, Pap's chief complaint against society is the place it has given to black men. The existence of slavery at the bottom of society gives poor white trash like Pap some sense of dignity. The Negro that Pap finds objectionable is educated, a professor who can vote in his home state. "'It was 'lection day,'" Pap tells Huck in chapter 6, "'and I was just about to go and vote, myself, if I warn't too drunk to get there; but when they told me there was a State in this country where they'd let that nigger vote, I drawed out. I says I'll never vote again. Them's the very words I said; they all heard me; and the country may rot for all me—I'll never vote again as long as I live.'" There is a comic side to Pap, but there is nothing funny in his attempt to kill Huck in a fit of delirium tremens.

Huck's subsequent ingenious escape and his teaming up with Jim, who has fled slavery to avoid being sold down the river, lead to their journey southward by raft to the Ohio River at Cairo, from whence Jim intends to head northward among the free states. They cannot simply cross to free territory, since Pap has obtained money from Judge Thatcher to hunt Jim "all over Illinois." What Mark Twain had in mind to develop as a plot while he was writing this part is not clear. Perhaps he merely hoped something would occur to him. Perhaps it was to be a burlesque murder-detective story, like *Simon Wheeler, Detective*, with Jim put on trial for murdering Huck, who had covered his tracks by creating the impression that he had been killed. In chapter 16, Huck and Jim discover that they have passed Cairo, Illinois, where the Ohio River joins the Mississippi. Jim had conceived of the Ohio as his route to freedom, but Mark Twain, who—typically—was improvising his story, did not know the Ohio: the destruction of the raft at the end of the chapter was simply a way of stopping the trip down the river and away from Jim's access to freedom.

This first installment of the book that Mark Twain wrote in 1876 included the "Raft Passage" that he later stole for inclusion in *Life on the Mississippi*; it belongs after the second paragraph of chapter 16 and was included in the completed manuscript of *Huckleberry Finn* that the author submitted in 1884 to Charles L. Webster, his nephew, whom he had established as president of a new publishing house. Webster wrote, "The book is so *much* larger than *Tom Sawyer*, would in [it] not be better to omit that old Mississippi matter? I think it would improve it." Mark Twain agreed.[3] The passage thus was dropped only for reasons of space; it should be reestablished, as it has been in some editions such as in DeVoto's *The Portable Mark Twain*, because without it there is a gap in the novel and vital information is omitted. In this episode Huck swims to a big raft to learn where he and Jim are in relation to Cairo, Illinois, their first destination in their escape to the free states. There he overhears a good deal of remarkable conversation and learns how Cairo can be located. There the Mississippi is joined by the Ohio, and the water of the latter is distinguishable as "a wide band of clear water all the way down the east side of the Mississippi for a hundred miles or more." Soon Huck uses this information, in chapter 16, when he sees "the clear Ohio water in shore, sure enough, and outside was the old regular Muddy!" This observation causes him to acknowledge, "So it was all up with Cairo."

In the 1876 portion of the book two episodes show Huck's growing recognition of Jim's worth. Both begin as Huck's practical jokes on Jim. After the first badly misfires, Huck guiltily hides the evidence that would show Jim to have been bitten by a rattlesnake as a result of "some fun" Huck had attempted. In the second, Huck makes a dramatic apology for the trick he has played on Jim in having pretended that their separation in the fog was only something Jim had dreamed.★

When Mark Twain stopped writing this first section of the book, he was at an impasse, and when he did return to the story, he still had no idea, it appears, of how to continue, and, as we shall see, good reason not to value the manuscript highly. Sometime between mid-November 1879 and mid-June 1880 he composed chapters 17 and 18, at the time when he was finishing the *Tramp* and returning to *The Prince and the Pauper*. These chapters provide Huck with adventures on shore, with the Grangerfords and their feud with the Shepherdsons. Jim is now absent; movement in the story is suspended. Nevertheless, the chapters are masterly. Mark Twain makes fun of Victorian interior decoration through Huck's description of the Grangerfords' parlor and of Victorian sentimental poetry in Huck's description of Emmeline Grangerford's funeral verse. His admiration for both is humorously misplaced, but the effect is to create a warm picture of the family into which Huck has been received. The dignified Colonel Grangerford himself seems to be based on Clemens's memory of his father. In these courtly Southern aristocrats Huck all but finds himself a family—until he discovers the violence of their feud with the Shepherdsons and then witnesses the death of his friend Buck. Whereas Emmeline had sentimentalized her poetic accounts of death, in chapter 18 Huck tells of the deaths he observes with restraint. He explains how he *felt*, "so sick I almost fell out of the tree," then adds, "I ain't agoing to tell *all* that happened—it would make me sick again if I was to do that. I wished I hadn't ever come ashore that night, to see such things. I ain't ever going to get shut of them—lots of times I dream about them."

★This episode was derived from the author's friend Dan De Quille's book, *History of the Big Bonanza*, which Clemens arranged for the American Publishing Company to issue in 1877.

While writing chapter 18, Mark Twain decided that he should continue Huck's adventures by raft and wrote himself a note: "Back a little. CHANGE—raft only crippled by steamer."[4] But instead of revising, he has Jim tell Huck that the raft had only been damaged. He apparently wanted to continue his story of Huck and Jim together on the raft, if he could ever decide what his book was going to be about. At this time, presumably, he drew up a long list of possible activities for the two. They include:

> Negro campmeeting and sermon—"See dat sinner how he run."
> The scow with theatre aboard
> A house-raising
> Village school—they haze Huck, the first day
> The country cotillions
> The horse trade
> Candy-pulling
> Dinner manners at the tavern with a crowd.[5]

What he wrote next determined what he would *not* take up: Jim's escape to freedom. Soon after the feud chapters, probably in the summer of 1880, he wrote chapters 19, 20, and 21. Paine writes, "Clemens varied his work that summer, writing alternately on *The Prince and the Pauper* and on the story of Huck Finn."[6]

Having passed Cairo, Huck and Jim decide in chapter 16 that they must continue south until they find "a chance to buy a canoe to go back in." The two return to the raft after the feud episode and after Jim has got it "all fixed up again mos' as good as new, en we's got a new lot o' stuff, too, in de place o' what 'uz los'." They do not now discuss their need for a canoe, probably because Mark Twain has forgotten about it, and when Huck finds one in chapter 19, instead of planning how to transfer their stuff to it from the raft, preparatory to heading north, he uses it merely to try to pick some berries. To replace the motivation of Jim's search for freedom, assisted by Huck, the author introduces two new characters who provide a rationale for a journey southward into the area he had known as a pilot. The Duke and the King become uninvited guests on the raft. When in chapter 20 they ask if Jim is a runaway slave, Huck takes advantage of their being on a raft that follows the current to protect Jim by asking, "Goodness sakes, would a runaway nigger run *south*?" With the Duke and the King aboard, Jim and Huck are now more concerned about Jim being sold or seized as a runaway than with being headed northward in their new canoe. They naturally head south, and Mark Twain now has an excuse to describe life in the river towns as the four stop here and there for the two charlatans to pick up a few dishonest dollars. These con artists know how to take advantage of the gullible townsmen they meet, who seem eager to be deceived. The author's familiarity with their kind goes back at least as far as the stranger who loaded Jim Smiley's jumping frog with shot. The roles the two assume on the raft—"the rightful Duke of Bridgewater" (which soon becomes Bilgewater) and "the wanderin', exiled, trampled-on and sufferin' rightful King of France"—allow the writer to spread his net wider, almost to make *Huckleberry Finn* an international novel.

Mark Twain had been fascinated by pretenders to titles and estates, including two of his own relatives, one claiming to be the rightful Earl of Durham; later the author would write *The American Claimant* on the subject. (Soon he would read much about the lost dauphin, Louis XVII, in a book purchased in 1882, Horace Fuller's *Noted French Trials: Impostors and Adventurers*.) All the reading he had done in preparing himself to write *The Prince and the Pauper* could be put to better use in giving Huck the opportunity in chapter 23 to make an assessment based on *his* reading and experience.

> Look at Henry the Eight; this'n 's a Sunday-School Superintendent to *him*. And look at Charles Second, and Louis Fourteen, and Louis Fifteen, and James Second, and Edward Second, and Richard Third, and forty more; besides all them Saxon heptarchies that used to rip around so in old times and raise Cain. My, you ought to seen old Henry the Eight when he was in bloom. He *was* a blossom. He used to marry a new wife every day, and chop off her head next morning. And he would do it just as indifferent as if he was ordering up eggs. "Fetch up Nell Gwyn," he says. They fetch her up. Next morning, "Chop off her head"—and they chop it off. "Fetch up Jane Shore," he says; and up she comes, Next morning "Chop off her head"—and they chop it off. "Ring up Fair Rosamun." Fair Rosamun answers the bell. Next morning, "Chop off her head."

Now he put his manuscript away for three years. Encouraged to believe that he should be a genteel man of letters, Mark Twain would naturally find it difficult to suppose he ought to value a book celebrating freedom from civilized restraints, especially one whose hero is poor white trash. But with the effort of writing *Life on the Mississippi* behind him, he indulged himself by returning to the Huck Finn manuscript in the summer of 1883, when he judged that he had reached the end. The return to the river in 1882 probably gave him incentive to finish the book. He may have been encouraged by a sense that his story was topical, for much attention was being given at the time to the "Southern Question," and books realistically describing the South were popular. Clemens had read George Washington Cable's books, and on his Mississippi tour had talked with the writer at length in New Orleans. Cable's enlightened view of the black race probably influenced Clemens. As a result, when *Huckleberry Finn* appeared, it was read as a contribution to an understanding of the South.

Whatever the reason, Mark Twain now found he was able to write freely, as he reported to Howells in July from Elmira.

> I haven't piled up MS so in years as I have done since we came here to the farm three weeks and a half ago. Why, it's like old times, to step straight into the study, damp from the breakfast table, & sail right in & sail right on, the whole day long, without thought of running short of stuff or words. I wrote 4000 words to-day & touch 3000 & upwards pretty often, & don't fall below 2600 on any working day. And when I get fagged out, I lie abed a couple of days & read & smoke, & then go at it again for 6 or 7 days.

Perhaps because he had not valued the book, he apparently had not discussed this story with Howells recently, for he went on to write, "And *I* shall like it, whether anybody else does or not. It's a kind of companion to Tom Sawyer." By late August he could say to Howells, "I've done two seasons' work in one, & haven't anything left do do, now, but revise." The revisions were to be unusually extensive, and the book was not completely done until well into 1884.

The last phase of composition, under the revivifying sense of the Mississippi River and its environs resulting from the 1882 trip, takes Huck and Jim southward to Arkansas and Louisiana. But the book does not purport to present what Clemens had seen the year before; on its title page *Adventures of Huckleberry Finn* is dated "FORTY TO FIFTY YEARS AGO," or 1835–45. Mark Twain could write about the ugliness of "civilization" in America's heartland at that time because of his familiarity with the travelers' accounts he had recently read for *Life on the Mississippi*. There he wrote admiringly of Mrs. Trollope's account, of her justifiable indignation at the "rowdyism, 'chivalrous' assassinations, sham godliness, and several other devilishnesses."[7] The civilization that Huck observes is similarly disgusting, and the latter part of the book suggests the author's disenchantment with the South and its backwardness. As Brander Matthews observed in his 1885 review, the observations are so telling because his use of

Huck as narrator permits Mark Twain to "set down, without any comment at all, scenes which would have afforded the ordinary writer matter for endless moral and political and sociological disquisition."[8] Because Huck is the storyteller, he cannot serve Mark Twain as a satirist: as a boy he doesn't know enough to denounce what he sees, though he can be appalled. The satiric technique of the book is subtly ironic and much more effective than comparable parts of *Life on the Mississippi*.

The last part of the book includes some of the best passages—and some of the worst. The best feature is an unexpected one. As Huck and Jim travel down the river in the company of the Duke and the King, the reader is reminded of earlier events that now take on new meaning. When Jim and Huck were on the river by themselves, they were "free and easy," as Huck points out in chapter 18. At the end of chapter 29 the two believe that they are "free again and all by ourselves on the river and nobody to bother us." This image of Huck and Jim's earlier freedom becomes more and more meaningful and attractive as Mark Twain shows the Duke and the King tricking the people along the shore successfully. The behavior of the gullible victims becomes predictable, as in the response to the "thrilling Tragedy of The King's Camelopard or The Royal Nonesuch" with its tag line "Ladies and Children Not Admitted." The Duke observes astutely that "if that line don't fetch them, I dont know Arkansaw!" In the Tennessee town of the Wilkses, only two people are for a time skeptical enough to escape victimization. Mark Twain had observed the "decay of independent thought" in the South on his *Life on the Mississippi* trip. In the 1880s, freedom from society and its conformist pressures was a more vital theme to him than the chiefly historical one of freedom from slavery, the focal concern in the earlier chapters on the river.

Why is *Huckleberry Finn* far and away Mark Twain's greatest book? One way of answering is that the writing of the book was a liberating experience for its author, freeing for a time the man whose "whole life was one long apology" from both the inhibitions of the culture one side of him had chosen to embrace and the requirements of the subscription book. Now he wrote neither as Samuel L. Clemens nor as the almost relinquished Mark Twain but as the outsider Huck Finn. Through Huck the novelist who has been civilized escapes for a time to the river of his youth, escapes more completely and out of greater need than young Sam Clemens ever had. The exhilaration that the author felt is the energy behind the book, energy seldom so sustained in the writer's other books. The greatness of *Huckleberry Finn* is found, not surprisingly, in the character of Huckleberry Finn.

Huck is Mark Twain's most richly conceived fictional creation, and his situation too is complex. He is an innocent, but with the exception of a few blind spots he is shrewd, far from naive. His creative imagination helps him to survive even though he has as his companion an escaping slave. He has fundamental convictions, which deepen as the book continues, in opposition to those of the society in which he is placed. His own most meaningful attitudes are based on his acute moral imagination. Because Huck is intelligent, quick, and inventive, he is able to survive, but because he is lower-class, without education or status, he is powerless, able to accomplish very little. (Mark Twain's later hero, the Connecticut Yankee, shows what a hero *with* power could do.) Huck's age is, as Mark Twain might say, slippery. He is fourteen but prepubescent, capable beyond his years, though sometimes he seems much younger than fourteen. He has no family—or worse than none, since his father is at best a parasite, at worst a sinister and sadistic alcoholic. But Huck's imagination is full of sentimental stories in which he describes himself as a member of a close-knit family. He is ungrammatical, but he can spell. Like his creator, who took part in amateur playacting, Huck can take on a role with some skill and great satisfaction. He is a nonconformist, an outsider, partly by inclination, partly by ignorance. At the beginning of the book he is just beginning to learn, and largely to dislike, the ways of civilization. He is a pleasure-seeker who makes tough moral decisions. He has wide-open eyes; he is always alert, aware. Perhaps most attractively, he is profoundly obtuse about his own worth—not modest or self-effacing, simply obtuse.

In *Huckleberry Finn*, Mark Twain makes extensive use of a technique he had developed early: telling not so much what happens as what was experienced, by the ear, the eye, all the senses. Now the technique functions to characterize Huck. In chapter 19, for instance, Huck tells of the lonesomeness of the river:

. . .and maybe see a steamboat, coughing along up stream, so far off towards the other side you couldn't tell nothing about her only whether she was stern-wheel or side-wheel; then for about an hour there wouldn't be nothing to hear nor nothing to see—just solid lonesomeness. Next you'd see a raft sliding by, away off yonder, and maybe a galoot on it chopping, because they're most always doing it on a raft; you'd see the ax flash, and come down—you don't hear nothing; you see that ax go up agin, and by the time it's above the man's head, then you hear the k'chunk!—it had took all that time to come over the water.

Sometimes Huck addresses the reader intimately, telling him almost privately not what he senses but how what he senses makes him feel. These characteristics make Huck seem thoroughly authentic.

Huck's skill as a storyteller and his attractive personality serve as a backdrop for the central conflict of the book, which is not between Huck and his society but between Huck and himself (though the latter pair is a version of the former). During the course of his adventures, Huck has a struggle that recalls the physical one between Mark Twain and his conscience in "The Carnival of Crime." Huck has been brought up in a slaveholding society that reinforced the basis of its peculiar institution by appeals to religious authority, especially that of the Bible. Victimized by this training, the thorough indoctrination that his society has given him, Huck is able to help his friend Jim escape from slavery only by believing himself to be depraved. In chapter 31, Huck states his belief that "if I was to ever see anybody from that town [St. Petersburg] again, I'd be ready to get down and lick his boots for shame." In a notebook entry of 1895, Mark Twain refers to *Huckleberry Finn* in such a way as to suggest the centrality of Huck's struggle. Here the author writes of his belief in "the proposition that in a crucial moral emergency, a sound heart is a safer guide than an ill-trained conscience. I sh'd support this doctrine from a book of mine where a sound heart & a deformed conscience come into collision & conscience suffers defeat."[9] Though Mark Twain may overdramatize Huck's decision to help Jim when he declares that it means "All right, then, I'll *go* to hell," his conflict is nonetheless a painful and serious one and is central in both the characterization of Huck and the thematic focus of the book.

Huck Finn is not Mark Twain, but he resembles both the "before" and the "after" versions of the author's pen personality: he is the innocent *and* the veteran. Huck shows his innocence when he is (painlessly) victimized. He visits a circus and is taken in by a horseback rider whose cavortings give him a real scare. But mostly his creator implies that Huck is a version of his better self, despite the character's youth and ignorance. Through him the writer was able to explore two intertwined themes that engage him fully: the relationship of the individual to society, and the meaning of freedom. (In a late fragment, "Indiantown" [1899], he was to suggest strongly that he had a bad conscience over his having won a place—albeit a sometimes insecure one—in Eastern society by becoming a hypocrite.) Although he assigns Huck (like Melville's Confidence Man), a variety of masks to wear, identities to assume, in order to survive, he never permits him to sacrifice his fundamental honesty. Huck skillfully copes with society, even that of the feudal and feuding Grangerfords, without losing his humanity; in fact, he becomes more human and achieves a stronger identity. Huck's outlook and his attitudes are highly individualistic; he—and Jim—are most fully themselves on the raft, away from society's oppressions, as Huck notes at the end of chapter 18: "Other places do seem so cramped up and smothery, but a raft don't. You feel mighty free and easy and comfortable on a raft." The reader, and the writer, know that one day the raft will have to tie up, and Huck and Jim will have to return to some less isolated condition. But the writer, and the reader, approve of Huck's being an outsider, apart from a society dominated by sentimentalism, vulgarity, cruelty, and dying religion. The fact that Huck feels obliged to look up to Tom as an authority figure is powerfully ironic, since Huck's own attitude and behavior provide a severe judgment on Tom. The best parts of the book are devoted to Huck's liberation from Tom and his artificial ways, Huck and Jim's comradeship on the raft, and Huck's celebration of freedom and nature.

Though Huck is a fully realized character whose tale is masterfully told, the seriousness of his continuing debate with his conscience concerning what to do with Jim is undercut by the fact that Mark Twain used Huck as a deadpan comic mask, as in the circus episode. Moreover, if Huck is to be understood as an innocent hero confronting evil, then his inner life is too simple for him to play a tragic role. Lacking self-awareness and an inner self that he is free to realize, Huck is free, but has no place to go. He cannot grow up. Although he finally plans to "light out for the territory," in none of the sequels can Mark Twain show Huck in the significant exercise of his freedom: he is back once again with Tom, and again looking up to him. There is no way for him to achieve self-fulfillment, for his creator was unable to imagine a setting that would permit the expansion of his consciousness.

In the creation of his masterpiece, Mark Twain was able to utilize his beliefs, his feelings, experiences from his past and more recent ones— and also his reading. The shooting of Boggs by Sherburn, for example, is based on an incident of Clemens's boyhood in Hannibal. He recounted the story on four separate occasions in addition to the account in *Huckleberry Finn*. In his autobiography he described the event this way: "The shooting down of poor old Smarr in the main street at noonday supplied me with some more dreams: and in them I always saw again the grotesque closing picture—the great family Bible spread open on the profane old man's breast by some thoughtful idiot, and rising and sinking to the labored breathings, and adding the torture of its leaden weight to the dying struggles."[10] Colonel Sherburn's address to the lynch mob that comes after him seems to have been written specifically to illustrate an idea that Mark Twain had picked up from Thomas Carlyle's *The French Revolution, A History*, where after describing scenes involving Mirabeau, Marat, Robespierre, and Danton, Carlyle comments, "Is it not miraculous how one man moves hundreds of thousands?" Mark Twain's favorite Dickens novel, *A Tale of Two Cities*, had suggested to him how powerful the presentation of mob scenes in fiction could be. What is most remarkable is Mark Twain's skill in translating into the Mississippi River valley events that he had witnessed only in books. (Admittedly, Huck as narrator is almost forgotten in the scenes in which Sherburn faces down the crowd.) Also contributing to the mob scene is the author's distress at Southern violence and the tendency to resort to lynch mobs, as he indicated in a chapter written for *Life on the Mississippi* but deleted from it.

Another episode probably inspired by his reading is the one in which the Duke and the King assume the identities of the brothers of Peter Wilks, recently deceased, only to be confronted in chapter 29 with the real brothers. The scene resembles one in Horace Fuller's aforementioned book, wherein the real Martin Guerre, who has assumed the place of a lost husband, returns just as the impostor has almost convinced everyone that he is legitimate. Mark Twain, however, goes far beyond Fuller; not only does he provide *two* impostors but he brilliantly characterizes the people with whom they deal, especially Mary Jane Wilks and the undertaker. Another demonstration of the writer's inventiveness is Huck's struggles with Joanna Wilks as he plays the role of "valley" to the fake Englishmen. Huck is far more skillful when he is allowed to select his own roles. But the whole episode is full of delightful inventions, as when the King defends with elaborate etymologies his use of the term "orgies" to refer to funerals.

The book also reflects some of the author's many ambivalences. These are especially evident—and troublesome—in the ending. The much-discussed "evasion" chapters are the result of the writer's dilemma. What could he do to resolve the conflicts of the plot? What is to become of Huck in the face of the fallen condition of society? Were Huck to succeed in his plans, almost forgotten during the episodes with the Duke and the King, he would be a social outcast. To prevent that outcome, Mark Twain made elaborate plans to restore Huck to the community even though earlier he had shown Huck to be superior to its values. He reintroduces Tom, then has Huck abandon the sense of identity he has achieved by subordinating himself to Tom once more. When Miss Watson frees Jim, society is transformed into a more decent-seeming institution. Now Huck does not have to undertake any action that would threaten it and thereby face ostracism or life as an outlaw, and his earlier decisions to help the slave escape are proved to be without meaning. Jim, who is loyal to Tom as well as to Huck, is placated for the suffering inflicted on him by forty dollars that Tom gives him, an act that might be read as symbolic of the author's own terms of submission. John Seelye's *The True Adventures of Huckleberry Finn* provides an intelligent alternative with Jim's death and Huck's profound depression; J. D. Salinger's rather similar hero ends up in the hands of a psychiatrist. Mark Twain ended his book by escaping into fantasy.

Mark Twain took unusual care to revise his manuscript instead of giving it to Howells for editing or shipping it right off to be published. The manuscript and surviving notes by the author addressed to himself show his great care. For example, he wrote, "Back yonder, Huck reads & tells about monarchy & kings &c."[11] Jim needs to know something about royalty and nobility before the Duke and the King arrive. So Mark Twain wrote a long insert consisting of most of chapter 12 and all of chapters 13 and 14. Here Huck goes aboard the wrecked steamboat *Walter Scott* and obtains the loot that a group of thieves have collected so that he can "read considerable to Jim about kings and dukes, and earls, and such, how gaudy they dressed, and how much style they put on, and called each other your majesty, and your grace, and your lordship, and so on, 'stead of mister. . . .'" But not satisfied merely to prepare for a later scene, Mark Twain identified Scott as the guilty purveyor of corrupt romanticism, as he had in *Life on the Mississippi*. The incident also helped emphasize both Huck's charity and the contrast between the good life on the raft and the rascality of life on the land.

While the surviving manuscript at the Buffalo Public Library is not complete (it consists of about three-fifths of the text), it indicates the scope of the author's revisions. There were over nine hundred textual changes, including the deletion and addition of whole paragraphs, and extensive rewriting, especially of the account of Huck's final struggles with his conscience. One telling change is the transfer of the speech of the King over Peter Wilks's coffin in chapter 25 from direct quotation to indirect reporting; Huck's reaction to the hypocrisy now becomes as significant as what the King said, though most of the King's words are preserved. The original version reads:

> "Friends—good friends of the diseased, & ourn too, I trust—it's indeed a sore trial to lose him, & a sore trial to miss seeing of him alive, after the wearisome long journey of four thousand mile; but it's a trial that's sweetened & sanctified to us by this dear sympathy & these holy tears; & so, out of our hearts we thank you, for out of our mouths we cannot, words being too weak & cold. May you find sech friends & sech sympathy yourselves, when your own time of trial comes, & may this affliction be softened to you as ourn is to-day, by the soothing ba'm of earthly love & the healing of heavenly grace. Amen."[12]

This version is almost too good for the King. In the published version Huck renders what the King said in the boy's own language, which has no place for sentimentality.

> Well, by-and-by the king he gets up and comes forward a little, and works himself up and slobbers out a speech, all full of tears and flapdoodle about its being a sore trial for him and his poor brother to lose the diseased, and to miss seeing diseased alive, after the long journey of four thousand mile, but its a trial that's sweetened and sanctified to us by this dear sympathy and these holy tears, and so he thanks them out of his heart and out of his brother's heart, because out of their mouths they can't, words being too weak and cold, and all that kind of rot and slush, till it was just sickening; and then he blubbers out a pious goody-goody Amen, and turns himself loose and goes to crying fit to bust.

Like this one, most of the changes result in a real improvement; few are softenings of the sort usually identified with Mrs. Clemens and Howells.

Huckleberry Finn is addressed to readers who are much better educated than Huck, ones familiar with what Huck knows imperfectly, if at all: Shakespeare, the Bible, history (especially English and French) and geography. Some of the pleasures that the book provides come through an understanding of what Huck does not comprehend. But unlike most "classics," *Huckleberry Finn* offers few real roadblocks to understanding, and the ready accessibility of the book is one of its most striking virtues. As an American writer who had lived in Europe for more than two years, had traveled widely there, and had read a good deal of European literature and historical writing, Mark Twain brought much more to this book than he had to bring to *Tom Sawyer*, and whereas he had ransacked books either to give his writings authority or to stretch them out, in *Huckleberry Finn* Mark Twain's knowledge was put to more natural—and more artistic—use. One reason is the plotlessness of the book. It is sufficiently unified by the personality of the narrator, by theme, by the centrality of the voyage down the river, and by the omnipresence of the river itself. What Mark Twain was unable to do in *Life on the Mississippi* he was able to achieve magnificently in *Huckleberry Finn*: to capture the majesty, the power, the magnitude of the Mississippi. T. S. Eliot rightly called the book the only one in which Mark Twain's genius was completely realized; he was writing about matters with which he had intense associations, and he was writing freely, without the rigidities of a preconceived plot and the requirements of a six-hundred-page octavo subscription book.

Huckleberry Finn is idyll, satire, comedy, epic; it includes burlesque and it has many features of the picaresque. It is Mark Twain's celebration of innocence and a reflection of his growing pessimism. Whereas the earlier Mark Twain may have introduced violence into his writings for the sake of excitement, now it is dramatized to indicate man's inhumanity to man, as in the feud episodes. When Huck sees the tarred and feathered Duke and King being ridden on a rail by a mob in chapter 33, he seems to speak for the author when he concludes, "Human beings *can* be awful cruel to one another." The death of Boggs, Pap's violent death (offstage), and finally the selling of Jim for what Huck calls "forty dirty dollars"—all reflect this pessimism. Duplicity, one of the most prominent themes of the book, is a more subtle indication.

Adventures of Huckleberry Finn was "officially" published in the United States in December 1884 but was not actually available until the following February. During the period between completion and book publication, it was given extensive advanced publicity. Chapters appeared in the *Century Magazine* in December, January, and February—revised to suit the genteel taste of its editor, Richard Watson Gilder. Clemens read portions of it on a reading tour he made with George Washington Cable from November to February. Parts were published in February in New York and Chicago newspapers. The publisher of the book was Clemens himself, though technically Charles L. Webster and Company, headed by Clemens's nephew, who had for some time been his business agent; the author was the financier of the company. Since at first the book was to be sold by subscription, time was required to set up an organization. Later, copies were "dumped"— sold to retailers.

Few reviews of the book appeared in America; among them are an unfavorable one in the March 19 Boston *Transcript*, the voice of genteel Boston; a review in *Life* that emphasized the incongruity of the violence and the humor of the book; the aforementioned generally favorable one by Perry in the May 1885 *Century*; and a recently discovered one by Joel Chandler Harris which argues that though the life pictured in the book is itself coarse and vulgar, the writing is not.[13] In the British press there were favorable reviews in the *British Quarterly Review* and the *Westminster Review* and an enthusiastic one in the *Saturday Review* by the American Brander Matthews, who delighted in the fact that "we see everything" through Huck's eyes, "and they are his eyes and not a pair of Mark Twain's spectacles."[14] More striking than the reviews were the negative, even hostile, comments that appeared here and there and indicated that the genteel were offended by Mark Twain's irreverence. The Boston *Advertiser* was one such; the Springfield *Republican* referred to the author's "low" moral level; and even the Arkansaw *Traveler* found Mark Twain's "vulgar humor" out-of-date.[15] The book nonetheless sold well; 51,000 copies in the first fourteen months. How Clemens regarded the book is uncertain; perhaps he felt *uncertain*. He judged that its rejection by the Concord Public Library was "a rattling tip-top puff" that would "sell 25,000 copies sure."[16] He wrote to his sister, "Those idiots in Concord are not a court of last resort, and I am not disturbed by their moral gymnastics."[17] He must have found it less easy to ignore his family's opinion. Susy Clemens complained that it was a reversion to her father's "old style" after the much more satisfactory—to her eyes—*The Prince and the Pauper*.[18] The best evidence of what the author was thinking may well be the fact that he returned to Huck when next he reached Quarry Farm.

But now business became a major distraction from writing; it would continue to interfere for many years. Not only publishing but inventions and investments took time, even with helpers such as Webster and his assistant, Fred J. Hall. As early as 1881 Clemens had begun to put money into the Paige typesetting machine, which was to be his greatest disappointment. Even while he was writing *Huckleberry Finn* he invented a game to teach his children history, taking time out because he had "struck a dull place" in the book.[19] Soon the game and variations of it, along with their commercial possibilities, became a major preoccupation that lasted into the next year.

In the summer of 1883 Mark Twain completed another story, in addition to *Huckleberry Finn*. This one, "1002[d] Arabian Night," he intended to publish anonymously, even though Howells, who read it for him, reported in September that he was "bound to say that I think its burlesque falls short of being amusing." The long story, only recently published, is interesting chiefly because of its theme. Two babies, one the child of the sultan of the Indies, the other the child of the grand vizier, are exchanged: the boy is brought up as "Fatima" and the girl as Selim. The comic possibilities fascinated the author, but more serious ones were to occur to him a few years later when the theme was revamped and the setting changed to Missouri, where it became part of *Pudd'nhead Wilson*. Though his 1883 tale burlesques Scheherazade's tales, Mark Twain was a great admirer of the *Arabian Nights*. He drew from this work more than any other except the Bible and Shakespeare. Nearly fifty references to it have been identified. His Tom and Huck show that they too have read it.

The fact that these three undertakings—the completion of his masterpiece *Huckleberry Finn*, the invention of a history game, and the composition of a farcical burlesque—all occupied Mark Twain's mind at the same time is a frightening demonstration of how the pressures on him to be genteel and to make money caused him to resist, almost to betray his genius. His perspective, if it may be so dignified, is shown by a report he sent his former publisher, James R. Osgood, who remained his friend. "The thing I am grinding at, now," he wrote on September 1, "is my long series of history games, the which I *caveated* in the patent office the other day. *They'll* go, I judge." He valued the games for the dollars they might produce. Then, to complete his account of his activities, the inventor-author added, "I've finished '1002' (Arabian Nights Tale) & likewise 'the Adventures of Huckleberry Finn'; had written 50,000 words on it before; & this summer it took 70,000 to complete it."[20]

Another work that proved to be useful only when revamped was a play. In September 1881, Clemens had proposed to Howells that the latter write a play entitled "Col. Mulberry Sellers in Age." It would feature Mark Twain's colorful character from *The Gilded Age* and the dramatized version that followed it, with Sellers at seventy-five and Lafayette Hawkins (based on Orion Clemens) at fifty. The plot would focus on Sellers's delusion that he was the rightful Earl of Durham (much as the Duke pretends that he is the rightful heir in *Huckleberry Finn*), as well as on Sellers's "Impossible Inventions." Clemens wanted Howells to do the writing, though he intended to "re-write the Colonel's speeches" himself. In due time Howells explored the possibilities of such a play with some New York theater men, who encouraged him. Finally in the fall of 1883 Howells and Clemens went to work and wrote the play, together. Later they returned to it again and again. "No dramatists ever got greater joy out of their creation," Howells later wrote.[21] The protagonist of *The American Claimant, or Mulberry Sellers Ten Years Later* is obviously a lunatic, and after being given several trial performances, in 1877 the play died.

In January 1884, Mark Twain began a novel about Bill Ragsdale, a half-caste interpreter he had met in the Hawaiian Islands. It was to be a serious work, and for it the author "saturated" himself "with knowledge of that unimaginably beautiful land & that most strange & fascinating people," as he wrote to Howells. Ragsdale's successful career had ended with the discovery that he had contracted leprosy and his subsequent self-exile to the leper colony on Molokai, where he died. That Mark Twain chose to write such a serious story was possibly an act of atonement for having written the most ungenteel *Huckleberry Finn*. So much is suggested by his comment to Mrs. Fairbanks, whom he especially wanted to see what he had done. On January 24, 1884, he wrote to her: "I finished a book last week, & am shirking all other duties in order to give the whole remnant of my mind to a most painstaking revision of it—for this work is not a humorous but a serious work, & may damn me, tho' Livy says *No*. I do wish you would come & read it in MS & judge it, before it goes to the printers. Will you? You shall have till March 1st—5 weeks."[22] A few days later he wrote again, emphasizing the seriousness of the novel. Of what he wrote that January very little survives, only a few pages of description, though he referred to it as finished. Nothing more is said about it even in surviving correspondence.

The play and the lost novel were only two of the many literary activities that occupied Clemens during the year following the completion of *Huck Finn*. In January he finished a dramatization of *Tom Sawyer* that he had begun in 1875. He wrote to his business agent, Charles Webster, that it was "a *good* play, a good *acting* play."[23] But it has nothing of the atmosphere of the novel, no Jackson's Island episode, and Tom is insufficiently characterized. Instead the dramatist emphasized comedy. Not as bad as *Mulberry Sellers Ten Years Later*, its chief interest is a scene he "forgot" to include in the novel:[24] a school session with lessons on history, grammar, arithmetic, and spelling. The whole of Act IV, the last, is in the cave, where Tom and Huck save Amy and Becky from the threatening Injun Joe. Tom shows no signs of maturation. Told by Aunt Polly to kneel in repentance for his outrageous behavior, instead he stands on his head. Obviously written for money, the play was rejected on the grounds that adults could not represent the dozens of children required for the cast. Another effort at dramatization, this time of *The Prince and the Pauper*, likewise found no producer. The text does not survive. (Later, in 1890, two rival productions of the play were produced in New York.) Clemens's motives are clear from his letters to Howells, written in early 1884, full of calculations of dramatic royalties.

One odd item of early 1884 was written by request. Clemens's friend of Virginia City days, Joseph Goodman, requested a contribution for a new literary weekly he was editing, *The San Franciscan*. At first Clemens turned him down, then perhaps inspired by an item about a Nevada fossil in the January 5, 1884, Hartford *Courant*, he dashed off a sketch called "The Carson Fossil-Footprints," published in Goodman's journal of February 16, 1884. A tall tale described as a reminiscence, it purports to tell of events of 1861, when Clemens was clerk to his brother, the secretary of the territory of Nevada. The theme is repeated throughout: "I was there." The most amusing aspect of the essay, which is full of forced humor, is the author's presentation of himself. Before the audience that he seems to have conceived of as old friends, he is willing to let himself be victimized again; he is indeed his own victim. Pretending to be a learned archeologist, he lets his mask slip when he falls into the idiom of poker to explain himself.[25] The achievement was not much, but to find even second-rate Mark Twain is a pleasure to those who have watched him disappear.

In the spring of 1884 Clemens and his friend Twichell undertook to learn to ride the bicycle, and soon the author was writing up his experiences. He was following, as he had not always, a doctrine set forth a few months later: "Whatever you have *lived*, you can write— & by hard work and genuine apprenticeship, you can learn to write well; but what you have not lived you cannot write, you can only pretend to write."[26] The bicycle essay is characterized by a return to Mark Twain's earlier manner, as he reports with very good humor his disasters and catastrophes. The "Expert" who teaches him notes that he is not in good physical condition: he describes Mark Twain's biceps as "pulpy, and soft, and yielding, and rounded; it evades pressure, and glides from under the fingers; in the dark a body might think it was an oyster in a rag." The finished essay is the result of much labor; Mark Twain wrote to Webster that he had "revised, & doctored, & worked at the bicycle article," but ended not liking it.[27] Paine liked "Taming the Bicycle" better and placed it in a collection he published in 1917. Another adventure, this time with a dentist, led the author to write "Happy Memories of the Dental Chair," incomplete and published only in part.

The work of the summer at Quarry Farm was also to lead nowhere, though it was more ambitious. Early in July, Clemens wrote for copies of Richard Dodge's book *The Plains of the Great West* and "several other personal narratives of life & adventure out yonder in the Plains & in the Mountains . . . especially life *among the Indians*." He needed these books because he intended "to take Huck Finn out there."[28] He had promised as much at the end of Huck's earlier story. The author made extensive use of Dodge's book on the plains and also his *Our Wild Indians*, as well as other sources—and his own experience, for he had Huck and Tom take the Oregon Trail through Nebraska to Wyoming, the route he himself had taken in 1861. What he wrote is an informed account fo the plains experience, but the treatment of the Indians, against whom Clemens had a long-standing prejudice, is much less effective. Before he stopped, Mark Twain composed most of nine chapters. Then he put the work aside and did not return to it, as he had Huck's first story. The fragment, "Huck Finn and Tom Sawyer Among the Indians," was published in a 1968 collection.

Its beginning shows that the work was intended to be a sequel to *Huck Finn*: "That other book which I made before, was named 'Adventures of Huckleberry Finn.'" As a sequel, the fragment explores new territory, both literally and figuratively. The boys leave civilization behind and head west. Though the adventuresome orientation of Tom Sawyer dominates the first chapter and part of the second, the book soon becomes more serious. Huck's experience on the prairie in chapter 4 is a discovery of his need for people, for civilization. "It was the biggest, widest, levelest world—and all dead, dead and still; not a sound. The lonesomest place that ever was; enough to break a body's heart, just to listen to the awful stillness of it. We [Tom is with Huck] talked a little sometimes—once an hour, maybe; but mostly we took up the time thinking, and looking, because it was hard to talk against such solemnness." Even Tom becomes sober, somber. But Huck has still more to learn, for after the Indians attack a family of emigrants that the boys have joined, he gradually discovers that the pretty girl the Indians take with them is the object of their sexuality. The fragment ends with the boys and the girl's sweetheart still looking for her, but knowing what she has suffered, a painful knowledge. The author's inability to continue the story was not, apparently, simply that his tank had run dry; rather, he seems to have been unable to continue the story as a result of Huck's loss of innocence. Despite what he learned in the first book of adventures he tells, Huck then had preserved his innocence. When Mark Twain let Huck tell another story after "Among the Indians," he made a point of avoiding such painful knowledge. The author himself blocked out his memory of what he had written when he wrote to Webster on September 1, "This is the first summer I have lost. I haven't a paragraph to show for my 3-months working season."[29] For the twelve months after completing *Huckleberry Finn* he had nothing to show except the revised manuscript. Otherwise there was only a series of misdirections and fragments.

Some of the sources of Mark Twain's difficulties can be determined. Often he was the victim of his own crossed purposes, as a consideration of writings on religion and philosophy shows. Probably during this period Mark Twain drafted three statements of religious belief. Not published until 1973, these few sheets are of interest for several reasons. First, they set forth clearly and without equivocation attitudes that the author reflects in the works he published, though he was—and would continue to be—determined not to let his readers know the extent of his heterodoxy, for he feared he would be roundly attacked and his sales reduced. Second, they suggest an attitude that in the face of misfortune could readily turn into bitter pessimism. Third, they show Mark Twain's latent interest in donning the robes of the sage: he would choose to play this role often during his later years.

The writer acknowledges the existence of God but not in special providences or divine intervention in man's world. The Scriptures, he states, were "imagined and written by man" and the moral laws created by human experience. There is no system of divine reward or punishment. Whether there is life after death he is uncertain and "wholly indifferent." He finds biblical injunctions frequently wrongheaded and inconsistent. Most of his criticism, which is restrained, Mark Twain levels at man's hypocrisy and tendency to be cruel. The Bible he calls "the strongly worded authority for all the religious atrocities of the Middle Ages."[30]

Mark Twain's aversion to traditional Christianity dates at least from his San Francisco days and was amplified by his *Quaker City* experiences. For a while it was reined in as he was joining a bourgeois society that embraced moderate Protestantism, the society of Olivia Clemens, Joseph Twichell, and Hartford. At that time he adopted a kind of deism, with a belief in a God whose "beneficent, exact, and changeless ordering of the machinery of his colossal universe is proof that he is at least steadfast in his purposes."[31] The more skeptical but still cautious attitudes expressed in the statements of the 1880s just described gave way in 1885 when in a diatribe later inserted into his autobiography Mark Twain attacked man's cruelty, malice, nastiness; he is "the buzzing, busy, trivial enemy of his race."[32]

The man who had established himself as a humorist was becoming more and more a man of moods. His anger was augmented by his fear of exposing it directly, to the detriment of his place as a successful commercial writer. He was a businessman who wanted to protect the value of his reputation. As he became more and more convinced of the validity of his opinions and wrote them down, they came closer to the surface of his consciousness when he wrote what he hoped would sell. This mixture of motives would make it more and more difficult for Mark Twain to write popular books of the sort that he had produced with such success. Students of Mark Twain's career might see something more. After *Huckleberry Finn* the author was never again to find a wholly satisfactory vehicle for the expression of those deep concerns that his admirers so identify with him: the joyous celebration of freedom and authenticity.[33]

CHAPTER SEVEN

A Swan Song—and a Resumption

THE period from the end of the summer of 1884 to early 1891, better than six years, was the least productive in Mark Twain's career. During those years he thought of himself as being on the verge of retirement. His output can be summarized: several essays on copyright, now his favorite cause; one slim story—a retelling, without much art or personality; two plays, one little more than a *jeu d'esprit* in English and German, a second that does not survive; two sketches, good but slight; a reminiscence/sketch; and a long novel. The author's explanation for such niggardly use of his talents when he was presumably in the middle of his career was that he thought he had written himself out: "Everyone who has ever written has been smitten with that superstition at about that age."[1] He was fifty. This account, however, was provided twenty years afterward. A better one, perhaps, is that other ways of making money looked easier and more effective. Paine quoted him as having said in his fiftieth year, "I am frightened at the proportions of my prosperity. It seems to me that whatever I touch turns to gold."[2] Mark Twain was not referring to the work of his pen.

In February 1885, Ulysses S. Grant, long one of Clemens's heroes, accepted a publication offer for his memoirs from the author-turned-publisher, on behalf of Charles L. Webster and Company, and from then until Grant's death the following July, Clemens was much occupied with Grant and the book. His daughter Susy recorded, "Mama and I have both been very much troubled of late because papa, since, he has been publishing General Grant's books, has seemed to forget his own books and works entirely."[3] Following Grant's death, Clemens busied himself over Grant's funeral, the question of where the ex-president was to be buried, and then the posthumous publication of Grant's *Memoirs*. It proved to be a best-seller: more than 300,000 sets of this two-volume work were sold. In 1885 there was thus little time for literary work at Quarry Farm, and the summer of 1886 was similarly unproductive, though by then Mark Twain had begun a novel. In November of that year he described it as his "holiday amusement for six days every summer for the rest of my life." He went on to say that he did not intend to publish it, "nor indeed any other book," and planned to write only two other books, one of which would be his autobiography.[4] In the summers of 1889 and 1890 he wrote nothing, for he had by then finished his "holiday amusement." Significantly, he was domiciled for only a month at his Elmira hideout in 1889, and in 1890 the family summered in the Catskills. (One reason for the change in 1890 was the death of Theodore Crane, who with his wife had owned Quarry Farm.)

Clemens expected that from the Paige typesetting machine, in which he invested large quantities of both money and time, he would become wealthy. Now on exhibit in the basement of Clemens's Hartford home, the fiendishly complicated machine seemed time and again to be perfected or on the verge. Even when the Mergenthaler linotype machine was a proven success, the investor's confidence continued. By Clemens's estimate the machine should have paid him $55 million a year! After pouring in nearly $200,000 he found himself unable to raise enough more to buy all rights to the machine and its manufacture, and in February 1891 he seemed to have nothing at all to show for his investments. Several literary plans, as well, came to nothing. His notebook for April through August 1885 shows that he was thinking about an essay on wit and humor as well as a book on "Picturesque Incidents in History and Tradition." In the summer of 1888 he made notes for a play on the Franco-German War of 1870–71, based on Alphonse Daudet's "Le Siege de Berlin." This he seems to have finished and intended to publish in the *Century Magazine*. But the play was not published and does not survive. A dramatization of *The Prince and the Pauper*, to which he contributed, produced no money for him, only frustration.

The first fully realized work of these years was one proposed by Robert Underwood Johnson of the *Century Magazine*. In October 1884 the magazine had begun the publication of a series of papers on "Battles and Leaders of the Civil War" with leaders such as Grant, McClellan, Longstreet, and Beauregard among the contributors. Shortly thereafter, Johnson and Clemens discussed the series, with the editor explaining his need for an essay, presumably a serious one, on the war beyond the Mississippi River. In a letter of May 11, 1885, Johnson described what he wanted as a "little article on your experiences in the Rebel Army, making it, as far as possible, characteristic of the state of things in Missouri early in the war." "We have some difficulty," wrote Johnson, "in covering that part of the field." The correspondence continued, with Mark Twain complaining that the paper was not going well and Johnson urging him on. Finally, in November, Johnson received "The Private History of a Campaign That Failed," which he called "excellent-uproarious."[5] The piece appeared in the December *Century*.

That Mark Twain remembered what Johnson had asked him to do is suggested by the ending of the essay, in which the author describes his piece as

> a not unfair picture of what went on in many and many a militia camp in the first years of the rebellion, when the green recruits were without discipline, without the steadying and heartening influence of trained leaders; when all their circumstances were new and strange, and charged with exaggerated terrors, and before the invaluable experience of actual collision in the field had turned them from rabbits into soldiers. If this side of the picture of that early day has not before been put into history, then history has been to that degree incomplete, for it had and has its rightful place there.

Likewise the beginning of the essay makes clear that the author expected it to be read in the context of the *Century* series: "You have heard from a great many people who did something in the war; is it not fair and right that you listen a little to one who started out to do something, but didn't?" Thereafter Mark Twain purports to tell of his experiences of June and July 1861 with the Marion County, Missouri, Rangers, a small group of disorganized volunteers. The truth of the matter was quite different from his account; the writer distorted his history both for amusement and in order to make an observation about warfare. At least to begin with, the "History" was intended to be funny, with the onetime volunteer mocking his old Hannibal friend John L. Robards, who called himself RoBards, by telling about a man named Dunlap who chose to be called d'Unlap. Most of the sketch is devoted to the boys and their adventures, somewhat in the style of

Tom Sawyer and his friends on an outing: trying to learn to ride a horse or a mule and to organize themselves, despite the lack of an effective leader. The situation next becomes more serious as a report reaches them one night that a stranger is approaching. They soon see him draw near, on horseback and—"I got hold of a gun in the dark, and pushed it through a crack between the logs, hardly knowing what I was doing, I was so dazed with fright. Somebody said 'Fire!' I pulled the trigger." At length and in some detail Mark Twain describes how he and his comrades face the fact of what they have done: killed a man. Thereafter retreating and retreating, Mark Twain and half of the fifteen men who made up the Marion Rangers found before long that they had been through enough and quit.

Besides providing a humorous sketch, Mark Twain seems to have had in mind two purposes when he wrote the "Private History." First, he had to provide his audience with an answer to the question, What did *you* do during the war? He had already told the rest of the story of his early years in his books: what his boyhood had been like, how he had become a pilot, had gone west, then visited Europe. To answer the question without embarrassment was not easy. He fell back on two techniques. He treated the events of the war, *his* war, in burlesque fashion; he made them into a joke. Then he emphasized his own innocence by exaggerating his youth. In the narrative he appears to be closer to sixteen than to twenty-five. In addition, he used the occasion to write not merely a reminiscence and a defense of his conduct but also an attack on the concept of war. The "Private History" shows how some men became identified with the Confederacy, some with the Union, neither for any very good reason. The random sample of the Marion Rangers that Mark Twain describes suggests that many participants in the war had no good reason for fighting. The one man killed in Mark Twain's war is Noman and Everyman, his death meaningless. The pacifism implied in the "Private History" is, however, not evident in his next major work, where indifference to bloodshed is characteristic of Mark Twain's spokesman; consistency was never the strong suit of this divided personality.

In the same month the "History" appeared, Mark Twain informed his agent Webster, "I am plotting out a new book, & am full of it."[6] The project was inspired by Clemens's reading of Sir Thomas Malory's *Le Morte d'Arthur* in late 1884. From his lecture tour with George Washington Cable he had written to his daughter Susy full of excitement at the book that Cable had encouraged him to read. "When I get home, you must take my Morte Arthur & read it. It is the quaintest and sweetest of all books. And it is full of the absolute english of 400 years ago."[7] Soon he had made notes on the comic situation of a "knight errant in the middle ages." Listing the problems of such an armored knight—such as the inability to scratch, to blow his nose, to dress or undress—he seems to have intended a burlesque. The next step, apparently, was to make the knight a "Hartford man waking up in King Arthur's time," as Howells put it in January 1886 while commending Clemens's idea. This Yankee was to combine special mechanical abilities and characteristics of both Clemens's current hero, General Grant, and the author himself.

What would eventually happen in the story is suggested by some of the notes that Clemens now made. An early one suggested violence of a sort that Mark Twain had not previously found occasion to depict in his fiction: "Have a battle between a modern army, with gatling guns—(automatic 600 shots a minute), torpedos, balloons, 100-ton cannons, iron-clad fleet, &c &c Prince de Joinville's Middle Age Crusaders." Another reads: "He mourns his lost land—has come to England & revisited it, but it is all changed & become so old, so old!— & it was so fresh & so new, so virgin before." This entry suggests that Mark Twain planned for his Hartford man to return to England in modern times. Another suggested what would bring about his misplaced Yankee's ultimate defeat: "Country placed under an interdict."

In February 1886, Mark Twain wrote to Webster that he had now "begun a book, whose scene is laid far back in the twilight of tradition. I have saturated myself with the atmosphere of the day & the subject, & got myself into the swing of the work. If I peg away for some weeks without a break, I am safe; if I stop now for a day I am unsafe, & may never get started right again."[8] Ten days later Susy recorded, "Yesterday evening [February 22] papa read to us the beginning of his new book, in manuscript, and we enjoyed it very much, it was founded on a New Englanders visit to England in the time of King Arthur and the Round Table."[9] But the author soon put the work aside—he must have thought himself "safe." He did not even take the manuscript with him to Elmira in the summer. At Quarry Farm he told an interviewer, "I made up my mind that I would loaf all summer," even though "the three summer months which I spend here are usually my working months."[10] He had not discarded the work, for in November he read parts of it, "A Word of Explanation" and the first four chapters of what he called "The Autobiography of Sir Robert Smith of Camelot," to the members of the Military Service Institute and their guests at Governor's Island, New York. He briefly described how the rest of the work continued the story, as he then anticipated. He also seems to have let reporters copy parts of his manuscript, which they quoted in their news accounts. At this point two plot elements were in reverse order from the way they were to appear in the final version: Sir Robert's killing of the king's opponents with gatling guns, then running the kingdom himself, with the Knights of the Round Table thereafter becoming members of a stock exchange. Mark Twain made the whole story sound amusing; later he would develop more serious purposes.

These early portions of the story provide the frame, including the introduction of the unnamed Hartford man now temporarily named Sir Robert Smith. He wakes up in King Arthur's Britain and supposes when he sees a medieval fortress that he must be in Bridgeport, where the showman P. T. Barnum had built such a house. The author begins "The Tale of the Lost Land," told by the Hartford man about his discovery that he had awakened on June 19, 528. It is an adventure story, with much borrowing from Malory and the narrator commenting on the frankness of the spoken language, an interest of Mark Twain's in his earlier "1601." This part of the story is heading toward an event scheduled for noon on June 21, when the narrator is supposed to be executed.

The narrator describes himself as "a Yankee of Yankees—and practical; yes, and nearly barren of sentiment, I suppose—or poetry in other words," but having given him an opportunity to describe his ancestry and an ability to construct or invent any kind of machine, Mark Twain thereafter makes little effort to distinguish the character from the author. The reader never looks through the Yankee, as he does through Huck, to see the author and his attitude, for the Yankee practically speaking *is* the author, Mark Twain. In some ways he resembles the early Mark Twain, but he is also Samuel Clemens of the late 1880s. Like Huck, the Yankee is not genteel, or at least was not intended to be, but unlike Huck, he has intellectual interests: in society, religion, politics, industry—in short, those of his creator. One almost expects the Yankee to discuss Lecky, Carlyle, and Clemens's other favorite writers; instead, the Yankee merely echoes them. His nineteenth-century technological skills prove to have as their most obvious function providing the author with an excuse to have the Yankee indulging in Tom Sawyer-like, Colonel Sellers-like fantasies—showing off. The Yankee's indulgences, however, have far more meaningful fictional consequences than do Tom's or the colonel's. After Huck's loss of innocence "Among the Indians," Mark Twain was now seeing himself as "a practical commercial mind"[11] and was ready to identify himself with a character who can make the world over if he chooses. The author's admiration for his Yankee—to rush ahead for a moment—is suggested by his description of him, after the book was finished, as "a natural gentleman" with "a good heart & high intent."[12] Despite the author's intention, few readers find the Yankee as attractive as earlier versions of Samuel Clemens.

In the summer of 1887, after more than a year's neglect, Mark Twain at last returned to his manuscript at Quarry Farm. There he described himself as working seven hours a day "in such a taut-string and excitable condition that everything that can worry me, does it." His book soon reflected his mental state. Presumably as a result of this sense of irritation, Mark Twain found himself no longer writing a comedy; instead, he explained, the work had "slumped into funereal seriousness."[13] His correspondence shows that he was discouraged by a disappointment over a series of difficulties at his publishing house. He was before long able to accept the new tone, even to take satisfaction from it, for he could see the change as having favorable consequences for sales. He called it "an uncommonly bully book," "a 100,000 copy book if Huck Finn was a 50,000 copy book."[14] The portion written in 1887 *before* the "slump" seems to have been chapters 5–12, with the exception of chapter 10, written later. Here the Yankee escapes execution by utilizing his knowledge that an eclipse of the sun is due. In chapter 5 he threatens that he "will blot out the sun, and he shall never shine again; the fruits of the earth shall rot for lack of light and warmth, and the peoples of the earth shall famish and die, to the last man." Then after becoming "the second personage in the Kingdom" after Arthur and winning the title of "the Boss," he begins to assert himself.

Already the Yankee's defeat at the end of the book was in the author's plan, for in chapter 8 he wrote: "Yes, in power I was equal to the king. At the same time there was another power that was a trifle stronger than both of us put together. That was the Church. I do not wish to disguise that fact. I couldn't, if I wanted to. But never mind about that, now; it will show up, in its proper place, later on. It didn't cause me any trouble in the beginning—at least of any consequence." Touches here and there in the "pre-slump" chapters may strike some readers as rather bitter attempts at humor, as when in chapter 9 after a tournament "the quacks detaching legs and arms from the day's cripples" ruin "an uncommon good old cross-cut saw for me." But mostly the early part of the book is entertaining, good-humored. Mark Twain cannot resist burlesquing tales of knighthood and chivalry in chapter 11 when the Yankee agrees to rescue the occupants of "a vast and gloomy castle," but such burlesque is in keeping with the plan to create comedy. Real troubles with consistency are most evident in the early chapters in the language, which is both genteel and vernacular. The Yankee describes the beginning of his rescue mission with Alisande (later Sandy), the damsel in distress, in chapter 11. Everyone was respectful,

> except some shabby little boys on the outskirts. They said:
> "Oh, what a guy!" And hove clods at us.
> In my experience boys are the same in all ages. They don't respect anything, they don't care for anything or anybody. They say, "Go up, baldhead" to the prophet going his unoffending way in the gray of antiquity; they sass me in the holy gloom of the Middle Ages; and I have seen them act the same way in Buchanan's administration; I remember because I was there and helped.

Who this Yankee was and what kind of tone his book was to have were already problematic, before the slump.

Though passages that are amusing or intended to be so continue to appear, it was in chapter 13 that the author led his hero into adventures that created a more serious tone. There the Yankee experiences the discomforts that first attracted Mark Twain to the idea of writing a story about a knight in armor. Trying to sleep without undressing before a lady, the knight is tormented by bugs, ants, and worms; he is frozen and "crippled with rheumatism." The discomforts are, however, not amusing. Then the Yankee and Sandy next meet a group of men repairing a road. The author now pauses to provide a long critical analysis of feudalism, hierarchy, monarchy, and the established church. Hereafter the Yankee's adventures frequently serve as the occasion for such analyses, with the head superintendent of the Connecticut arms factory even recalling "the ever memorable and blessed [French] Revolution" as part of the context from which he passes judgment on the value of ancient English institutions.

In *Huckleberry Finn* some of these same concerns are explored but with less intensity and in much better humor. There, however, they are always—or nearly always—subordinated to the story; any extended effort at philosophizing is made impossible by Huck's character and limitations. Whereas the earlier book was flavored by Clemens's reading in historians who wrote with a moral purpose, notably Carlyle and Lecky, now the author was aroused by a historian who was a polemicist. In 1886 and 1887 he had been reading *The People's History of the English Aristocracy*, by George Standring, an English radical polemicist. This book moved the creator of the Yankee, since it was in keeping with the sentiments that Mark Twain had been developing. Now supplied with ammunition he was eager for his fictional spokesman to use, he echoed Standring's discussions of the evils of primogeniture and entail and the British devotion to nobility. It was his old favorite Lecky, however, who taught him to believe that the chief villain behind medieval society's ills was the church. Such reading now ended his love affair with England, which had begun to fail with his 1879 visit. Mark Twain was soon thinking that his new book would help destroy remnants of medievalism that remained in England. The shift in direction of the Yankee's story came about when his hero's situation encouraged him to make the Yankee into a crusader for modern liberal causes. The old Mark Twain had no head for such systematic reform.

Before he left Elmira, the author had reached chapter 20, in which the Yankee completes his mission with Sandy—or supposes it is completed. This section includes their extended stay at Morgan le Fay's castle, where the Yankee is exposed to an exhibition of man's inhumanity to man in the queen's dungeon. A few touches of humor now make the narrator—or the author—into something of a sadist, as when in chapter 17 he gives Morgan le Fay permission to hang the band that plays "In the Sweet Bye and Bye"—whereas earlier the queen had ordered only the composer hung. In this episode the author was reverting to the extravagances of burlesque; they do not blend well with his new serious purposefulness.

Another significant influence was to be felt before the author returned to his manuscript. During the spring of 1888, Clemens was asked by L. S. Metcalf, editor of *Forum* magazine, to defend the United States against Matthew Arnold's condescending criticism in "Civilization in the United States." In the previous spring Clemens had himself been offended by Arnold's criticism of Grant's English in his *Memoirs* and had delivered a patriotic speech defending the general. Now he was eager to write what Metcalf wanted, but found that he could not produce a satisfactory manuscript. Since Arnold soon died, he could not direct a reply specifically to the Englishman. Instead he planned to write, eventually, a book on "English Critics on America, Letters to an English Friend," and in 1890 he did deliver a speech "On Foreign

Critics." But his more immediate task in 1888 was to finish his Yankee book. Some of what he wrote in response to Metcalf's request went into the novel, when he did return to the book in the summer, back in Elmira. Getting a late start, he wrote only chapters 21–24, though he made notes then on how to finish the story.

In these chapters the Yankee shows off by restoring the "holy fountain" by the use of gunpowder and fireworks. He sounds like Tom Sawyer in chapter 23 when he explains, "You can't throw too much style into a miracle." Throughout this episode and the next, the Yankee keeps "his trademark current," improving his reputation. Clemens's notebook suggests that he identified himself with the Yankee in such comments as these: "I make a peaceful revolution & introduce advanced civilization." "The first thing I want to teach is disloyalty till they get used to disusing the word loyalty as representing a virtue."

In October, after his short summer of writing in Elmira, Mark Twain took up his book again at Joseph Twichell's house in Hartford, where he went to avoid the usual interruptions that he often complained of at home. He now composed chapter 10, "Beginnings of Civilization," which is necessary to explain the introduction of the telephone, the telegraph, and other modern inventions. The treatment of slaves in chapters 24 and 25 is chiefly derived from a book on American slavery: *Slavery in the United States: A Narrative of the Life and Adventures of Charles Ball, A Black Man* (1837); Lecky's *European Morals* is another source. The presence of slavery here suggests that the novel is at one level a continuation of the author's critique of the South in *Life on the Mississippi*, with the Yankee out to reform the world that Samuel Clemens had known in his youth. Chapters 27–33, more than one-quarter of the book, describe the Yankee's adventures while traveling with King Arthur, the story being continued by the travels, as in *The Prince and the Pauper*, where Edward and Miles Hendon have a similar outing, and in *Huckleberry Finn*, where Huck and Jim's adventures on the river constitute the plot. In all three books the purpose is to educate—Huck, royalty, *and* the reader—by displays of injustice and inhumanity, though in the new book the writer was far more outspoken.

The remainder of the book hastily disposes of several of the author's earlier ideas for the plot, with the Yankee's killing of nine knights by revolver and the subsequent translation of the remaining knights into railway conductors, sewing-machine salesmen, and the like. Without any previous hint to prepare for the event, the reader is confronted with the fact of Sandy's marriage to Hank Morgan, the Yankee being given a name at last in chapter 39. Their marriage permits the author to remove Morgan from the country so that in his absence a whole series of events can take place. Consequently, in chapter 42, Morgan and the reader are provided with a telescoped account of the events, so abrupt as to cause Morgan to exclaim, "What changes! and in such a short while. It is inconceivable. What next, I wonder?" The reader's sentiments, exactly. The church's interdict against the Yankee and the complete destruction of the advanced civilization he had created leave him with just fifty-two boys as his loyal followers. The holocaust that the Yankee and his boys then create is Mark Twain's most terrific use of violence, shocking and disturbing to readers who know about mass destruction. The postscript returns the story to the nineteenth century, in a final meeting between the reader of the Yankee's manuscript, introduced in the preliminary "A Word of Explanation," but now probably all but forgotten, and the dying Yankee. In March 1889, three years after it was begun, the novel was completed.

Some readers find the Yankee's destructiveness prophetic of what technology would permit man to do against humanity, with Morgan an authoritarian villain, and the book as a whole an indictment of industrial progress. Mark Twain intended to say something different. To his English publisher he wrote, "I wanted to say a Yankee mechanic's say against monarchy and its several natural props. . . ."[15] When he selected chapters for magazine publication he offered a summary of parts of the story, to which he supplied an interpretation. "Meanwhile the Yankee is very busy; for he has privately set himself the task of introducing the great and beneficent civilization of the nineteenth century, and of peacefully replacing the twin despotisms of royalty and aristocratic privilege with a 'Republic on the American plan' when Arthur shall have passed to his rest."[16] The ultimate defeat of the Yankee was in Mark Twain's plans from the beginning, and of course there was no valid way he could end the book except with the complete destruction of the "beneficent civilization" the Yankee created. The defeat of the hero does not imply that his creator no longer believed in him or in progress. The mood of the "Final PS by MT" is indeed one of loss and even tragedy, as the dying Yankee grieves over his separation from his wife and child; but such domestic tragedy is only fitting and is without broad implication. The author's own comment was: "If any are inclined to rail at our present civilization, why— there is no hindering him; but he ought to sometimes contrast it with what went before, and take comfort—and hope, too."[17]

Despite the clarity with which the author saw his work, the novel is flawed at its center, for in it he raised issues beyond his grasp. The skeptical realism that had served him so well since his days in the West created contradictions when it was employed in a novel whose purposes had become polemical. Superficially *A Connecticut Yankee in King Arthur's Court* resembles *Huckleberry Finn* in that many of the inhabitants of each world are victims of deception. "There was never such a country for wandering liars," declares the Yankee in chapter 11. But few of those he meets willfully play the role of "con artist"—only Merlin is so characterized. Faced with such a situation, the Yankee sees as his primary mission in the early chapters the removal of the blinders from the eyes of the inhabitants of this strange, dreamlike world so that like him they can see with the eyes of common-sense realism. Such is the real purpose of the Yankee's mission with Sandy—ostensibly to rescue forty-four captive maidens. But the world of King Arthur is an imagined one, based on readings in Malory and elsewhere, a fact that the reader is unlikely to forget; it is far different from the world of Huck and the river, the outlines of which the author created from experience. That is to say, this Arthurian novel is not realistic but in fact a romance—even if its protagonist begins as a realist. The basic situation fades after the early chapters, since the Yankee soon proves not to be a realist but an idealist, a reformer determined to recreate the world he has accidentally entered into, according to his own prejudices. When he falls, he seeks to bring down Arthur's world with him. That this realist-turned-reformer also enjoys playing the role of comical entertainer whenever the occasion presents itself adds to the confusion the reader must face.

After the unfavorable comments on *Huckleberry Finn* and its creator, Mark Twain was determined that there was to be nothing in his new book that could be found offensive. He first submitted his already-revised manuscript to Edmund Clarence Stedman, a distinctly genteel poet and critic, who wrote a long response. Stedman found only a few objectionable passages, including some reversions to what he chastisingly called the author's "very early manner." He admired what his friend had done; he told Clemens, in sum, "You have let your whole nature loose in it, at the prime of your powers."[18] Still, Mrs. Clemens, who was unable to read the manuscript because of an eye problem, was afraid that there still remained "coarseness which ought to be rooted out, & blasts of opinion which are so strongly worded as to repel instead of persuade," he told Howells in August, while assuring him that the book had been scrubbed clean. He had indeed eliminated many touches that would have offended.

Among the passages deleted are some that *are* coarse—the coarsest, probably, ever to appear in a book Mark Twain was writing for publication, as well as passages that reflect the author's growing pessimism. Two passages, both amusing, would certainly have been considered vulgar by nineteenth-century readers. The first appears in what is now chapter 17 and describes the priest at Morgan le Fay's castle.

> He was the private chaplain, and the royal family were devoted to him, could not do too much for him, though they tried. That is, they married him to a comely young girl, one of the chambermaids, who enriched him with a ready-made family of royal origins, natives of the castle—a pleasant way of providing for the private chaplains of noble families which was to retain its popularity in England for eleven or twelve centuries yet—barring an interval between the abolition of Catholic priest-marriages and erection of the Protestant Established Church.[19]

The second explains a joke, implied in the published text, in chapter 21. The Yankee questions the need for "a fair great foundling asylum" built by the joint labors of nearby monks and nuns.

> "A foundling asylum! As I understand it, these were the only people in the valley: where was it to get its custom?"
> "They said heaven would provide."
> "And did it?"
> "Indeed ye may not doubt it. The nunnery and the monastery, taken the two together, do but cover six acres and a quarter, but the asylum covereth thirty."
> "This miracle lays over the other one, Sandy."
> "Ye say well, fair sir. And the one doth help belief in the other; whereso they shore up the faith of doubters, and none come there weak of faith but go in a manner whole away." (P. 670)

Other passages vividly describe strong smells associated with hermits and the use to which the Yankee put the bath water after it had been used to turn "all those sable nuns and monks into white people"; the water became an almost magically potent fertilizer (pp. 671–73).

Another deletion shows Mark Twain's developing misanthropy. In chapter 20, after Sandy flings herself upon the hogs she believes are distressed damsels, a long passage, absent from the published version, describes the Yankee's reaction. It reads, in part:

> Yes, we are just as pitiful and shabby as we can be, we human beings, in some of our aspects; but it is seldom that we are confronted with the fact

and forced to recognize it. All Beliefs that are not our Beliefs, are Superstitions; all Superstitions are Grotesque Absurdities. Why certainly—of course. It is a truism.

I despised Sandy for hugging the hogs, for it showed that she was the slave of a grotesque and absurd superstition that the apparent hogs were not hogs, but ladies. But I presently remembered that I had only recently sloughed off the Roman-Catholic-Presbyterian belief that a baby that does without some ecclesiastical mummeries over it, is burned in hellfire forever and ever because of that omission. So Sandy was but the mirrored reflection of my very recent self, after all—and of course no longer despicable. (Pp. 668–69)

The elimination of such passages as these was motivated by the author's belief that he was at the end of his career. In August 1889 he told Howells that the book was "my swansong, my retirement from literature permanently," and he used a self-dramatizing metaphor to suggest his determination to end his career in a way that would not distress his wife. "I wish to pass to the cemetery unclodded." Howells's efforts to purify the text further gave "peace to Mrs. Clemens's soul," her husband declared. Though Mark Twain was not yet on his way to the cemetery, he was to be far more heavily clodded for his *Yankee* than for *Huck*.

A Connecticut Yankee in King Arthur's Court is Mark Twain's only major work of a period when he was seeing himself in a new and different light. He was older; he had read much, especially in historical writings; he had traveled; he had entered the world of business and for a time experienced considerable success. In an America whose dominant values were shaped by the free-enterprise system, he could think of himself as being in the mainstream. Moreover, his opinions were being sought, respectfully, by journal editors; he was being asked to speak for America. In 1886 he had shown the breadth of his concerns by delivering an address advocating respect for the American wage-earner, a tribute to the Knights of Labor. While finishing his new book, Mark Twain drafted a series of prefaces that indicate his belief that he had written a book with major implications. His first concerns, he wrote, were the "odious laws which have been in vogue in the Christian countries within the past eight or ten centuries," and these he had illustrated "by the incidents of a story." His second concern was "human liberty," which he described as being just a hundred years old and even now just "for white people."[20] Profoundly influenced by reading

Lecky, he saw Christianity—or rather the powerful established church—as the chief opponent of more humane laws and of liberty, for the church inculcated the qualities of submission, passivity, and respect for the status quo. Thus the people of Arthur's England, from lowest to highest, cannot see the Yankee as a human being deserving respect and dignity. "Before the day of the Church's supremacy in the world," Mark Twain writes in chapter 7, "men were men and held their heads up, and had a man's pride and spirit and independence." The church "preached (to the commoner) humility, obedience to superiors, the beauty of self-sacrifice; she preached (to the commoner) patience, meanness of spirit, non-resistance under oppression. . . ." The Yankee's—and Mark Twain's—instruments of change are civilization and education, beginning with soap and ending with the "man factory."

The church's training was the source of all that was wrong with the society Mark Twain's time traveler visited, and in chapter 18 the author's philosophy, soon to be set forth even more didactically, is clearly anticipated:

> Training—training is everything; training is all there is *to* a person. We speak of nature; it is folly; there is no such thing as nature; what we call by that misleading name is merely heredity and training. We have no thoughts of our own, no opinions of our own; they are transmitted to us, trained into us. All that is original in us, and therefore fairly creditable or discreditable to us, can be covered by the point of a cambric needle, all the rest being atoms contributed by, and inherited from, a procession of ancestors that stretches back a billion years to the Adam-clam or grasshopper or monkey from whom our race has been so tediously and ostentatiously and unprofitably developed.

The idea came right out of Lecky.

A "laboratory novel," *A Connecticut Yankee* considers the question of whether men can be trained to become participants in responsible self-government. The answer is qualified. King Arthur shows that retraining can work, but the credulity, irrationality, and conformity of many of the king's subjects are too deeply dyed for reformation. The thesis suggested by the conclusion, along with the other ideas connected with the Yankee's experiment, is derived from Lecky, who developed the concept of reversion. Arthur's subjects have been so victimized by their earlier training that they revert to being mere animals when terrorized by the church's interdict.

How Mark Twain felt about the book as an expression of his feelings and his thoughts, however derivative, is suggested by a letter written in August 1889 to Howells, who had just sent the author a favorable report on his manuscript. Now, perhaps with a sigh, Mark Twain wrote: "Well, my book is written—let it go. But if it were only to write over again there wouldn't be so many things left out. They burn in me; & they keep multiplying & multiplying; but now they can't ever be said. And besides, they would require a library—& a pen warmed up in hell." These comments suggest an author not fully in control of his material.

While one cannot question Mark Twain's deep need to set forth his sentiments, *A Connecticut Yankee* has several disturbing weaknesses in addition to the lack of harmony between its realistic and romantic assumptions. The theories urged are insufficiently fictionalized, and when the ideas are illustrated by incidents, the result is too often sentimentality and melodrama. While slavery and oppression are powerfully described, Mark Twain was seldom able to suggest the consequences of the introduction of modern civilization and liberation. Instead, the Yankee's "improvements" are often laughable, as when Arthur and the Yankee are rescued in chapter 38 by "five hundred mailed and belted knights on bicycle." Throughout, the Yankee is the victim of the author's moodiness: there is a mixture of anger at cruelty, chauvinism, slapstick comedy, and distorted echoes of Malory, a combination that could not be blended.

The book was intended to appeal to both English and American readers, although to his English publisher Clemens had written that "the book was not written for America; it was written for England."[21] English readers were likely to find that the *Yankee* confirmed Matthew Arnold's view that Americans were materialists who lacked culture. One passage they might have pointed to is in chapter 16, when the Yankee meets one of his missionary knights who was "much depressed, for he had scored here the worst failure of his campaign."

> He had not worked off a cake [of soap]; yet he had tried all the tricks of his trade, even to the washing of a hermit; but the hermit had died. This was, indeed, a bad failure, for the animal would now be dubbed a martyr, and would take his place among the saints of the Roman calendar. Thus made he his moan, this poor Sir La Cote Male Taile, and sorrowing passing sore. And so my heart bled for him, and I was moved to comfort and stay him.

For American readers, prospective purchasers of another subscription book, the *Yankee* was described as an answer to "the Godly slurs that have been cast at us for generations by the titled gentry of

England. . . . Without knowing it the Yankee is constantly answering modern English criticism of America, and pointing out the weaknesses and injustice of a privileged class."[22]

Published in December 1889, *A Connecticut Yankee in King Arthur's Court* was much more widely reviewed than *Huckleberry Finn*; eleven American reviews, eleven British, and one Australian review have been identified. The range of reaction was considerable, from laurels to clods. The book was called offensive, laborious, vulgar; and delightful, clever, and delicious.[23] One extreme, perhaps, is the admiring reviewer who found it "impossible to read . . . without seeing that the great American humorist has been moved by the spirit of democracy." He identified as themes of the book "human equality, natural rights, unjust laws, class snobbery, the power of the rich and the dependence and oppression of the poor."[24] At the other end of the critical spectrum is the reviewer who found that Mark Twain "has turned didactic, and being ignorant is also misleading and offensive."[25] English readers were also offended because Mark Twain was dealing with what Lord Tennyson had all but sanctified in his *Idylls of the King*. They might, moreover, have noted that Mark Twain's illustrator, Daniel Beard, had designed Merlin to resemble Tennyson. Beard's illustrations appeared in both the American edition and the English, the latter being entitled *A Yankee at the Court of King Arthur*. Beard's satirical drawing, suggesting for example that the Slave Driver is a version of Jay Gould, gave the book a greater sense of contemporaneity. But the book sold only thirty-two thousand copies in the United States during the first year. The Webster Company was in such bad condition that it was unable to pay Clemens anything at all.

With two books in a row being described in some quarters as vulgar, Clemens wrote to an English friend and admirer, Andrew Lang. The surviving draft shows it to have been a long letter, in which the author defends himself from critics. They judge, he complains, by "the cultivated-class standard," while writers, such as himself, might choose to address "the mighty mass of the uncultivated," the class that, he contends, he had merely sought to entertain, since he was "not qualified" "to help cultivate the cultivated classes." He asked Lang for help in persuading critics to recognize what is written for "the Belly and the Members" as well as what is "written for the head."[26] Written in an excess of modesty, the letter is not to be taken as the author's serious view of himself, but it does suggest that he was painfully hurt by what had been written about his two most recent novels. He was particularly sensitive because he thought of them as marking the end of his career. Under the circumstances, it is hardly surprising that Mark Twain hereafter seldom returned to his earlier manner.

While the *Yankee* was still in the stocks, Mark Twain had written a "letter" from the "Office of the Recording Angel," a satire that he had tried unsuccessfully to work into his novel. The piece then remained unpublished until 1946, when Bernard DeVoto published it as "Letter from the Recording Angel" in *Harper's Magazine*. A short sketch that in some ways anticipates the more famous "War Prayer," the "Letter" is a satire specifically of Olivia Clemens's cousin, Andrew Langdon, a Buffalo coal dealer, and more generally of greedy businessmen. The angel demonstrates Langdon's hypocrisy by comparing on the one hand his "family worship" prayers and "prayer-meeting prayers" and on the other his "secret supplications of the heart," which by "rigid rule" in heaven are given precedence. Thus his prayer, "Be mercifully inclined towards all who would do us offense in our persons or our property" must be discounted because it conflicts with a prayer that the neighbor who threw a brick at a serenading family cat would suffer "some form of violent death." This skillfully aimed satire of "Christians" would be followed in time by equally bitter attacks on "Christianity."

The other writings of the *Connecticut Yankee* years are slight. For "English as She Is Taught" Mark Twain provided simply a framework and running commentary on schoolchildren's boners, most in vocabulary. He published it in the *Century Magazine* for April 1887; it may be found in the "Definitive Edition." "Meisterschaft," a play in English and German, was written for the young people who studied German at the Clemenses' home. (The title is from Richard S. Rosenthal's textbook, *The Meisterschaft System: A Short and Practical Method of Acquiring Complete Fluency of Speech in the German Language*.) It was published in the *Century Magazine* in January 1888, after someone improved Mark Twain's German. But he himself noted, "There is some tolerably rancid Geman here and there in this piece. It is attributable to the proof-reader." [27]

"A Majestic Literary Fossil" is a slight piece of journalism, composed in 1889 and published in *Harper's Magazine*. Here Mark Twain unearths a medical dictionary of 1745 and provides a commentary on quoted passages. Like the play, it helps fill the pages of the "Definitive

Edition." Another piece is far more original: "A Petition to the Queen of England," written in the fall of 1887 and published in *Harper's*. Informed that he owes income tax on his British royalties, Mark Twain petitions the queen, since the tax in question was granted to "Her Majesty." "My idea had been that it was for the government, but now I see that it was a private matter, a family matter, and that the proceeds went to yourself, not the government." Spinning the piece out with reminiscences of seeing the Prince of Wales, irrelevant details, and citations from the document he has received, Mark Twain adopts a version of his early manner, playing the sublime fool, a naive, simpleminded man from the country. The chief difference is that the author has now become a personage, a fact that he reflects in his petition, though with the utmost modesty. Whereas, in the *Yankee* Mark Twain is frequently angry, here he is calm, self-assured. He presents himself as altogether well-meaning but not very bright. He avoids several possible lapses into familiar comedy routines to maintain a wonderfully consistent, and charming, personality. The sketch, however slight, is a milestone worth attention, since the appearance of the authentic Mark Twain was a rare phenomenon in the late 1880s.

Sometime after the completion of the *Yankee*, perhaps late in 1890, Mark Twain began two articles, and while he finished neither, they suggest that he had reached another turning point, not in technique but in attitude. The earlier is entitled "Letters from a Dog to Another Dog Explaining & Accounting for Man: Translated from the Original Doggerel"; it is an anticipation of one of Mark Twain's last works, "Letters from the Earth." The letter-writer tries to explain that human beings are ridiculous, selfish, and cruel only because of their environment. All man's foibles, including his belief that he ascended from lower animals and his invention of heaven—which excludes all animals except himself—are explored. But the dog-narrator asks for generosity: "Give a man freedom of conscience, freedom of speech, freedom of action, & he is a Dog."[28] Though the piece is playful, it is Mark Twain's most severe indictment of humanity to date, more sweeping than the one inspired by Sandy's embracing the pigs. But before he completed the "Letters" (he never did) he began a kind of sequel, "A Defense of Royalty & Nobility." Here the author of the *Yankee* reverses the position he took in the novel by arguing that Americans who condemn monarchy and nobility are hypocritical since they revere millionaires and those whose membership in the Four Hundrd results from having the right ancestors: "ancient Dutch peddlers & barkeeps of the region." He then cites from chapter 6 on kingship and nobility of his own Dog Letters in order to argue that it is not environment but human nature that makes man both seize privileges and admire reverentially those who hold them.[29] This is a striking reversal. *A Connecticut Yankee* implies that real progress is possible for man, that he deserves better than he gets; training is everything. Now Mark Twain argues that human nature itself is the important *given*. These ideas would turn up in his next novel, and for many years Mark Twain would dwell on his low estimate of human nature. Personal misfortunes would later intensify this attitude. The most obvious sources of his pessimism were his financial disappointments and the various physical ailments that frequently incapacitated him.

In February 1891, Clemens realized that he could no longer devote thousands of dollars a month and much of his energies to the typesetting machine and that he would have to return to the pen as a means of making a living. His investments and his heavy living expenses required that he make some changes immediately. Already he had borrowed ten thousand dollars from his mother-in-law. "He dug out from his pigeonholes," according to Paine, "such material as he had in stock"[30] and arranged for the publication of "Mental Telegraphy," written fourteen years earlier, and "Luck," a thin and unoriginal story composed in 1886. Both were published in *Harper's Magazine*. Sometime in 1891, again according to Paine, he drafted a statement, perhaps a letter, in which he examined his life and his career, with emphasis on what he had learned from the varieties of work he had done, as printer, pilot, soldier, prospector, reporter, platform lecturer, financier, publisher, and author. He concluded, wisely, that "as the most valuable capital or culture or education usable in the building of novels is personal experience, I ought to be well equipped for that trade." The author was rededicating himself to his true career, though he had wandered into sixteenth-century England and King Arthur's court and would again wander very far from his personal experience. How could he believe, one wonders, what he wrote? "I confine myself to life with which I am familiar when pretending to portray life."[31]

As he returned to his career, his first effort began as a salvaging operation. He novelized the play that he and Howells had devoted so much time and affection to. (The idea of making a novel out of it dates from as early as 1884.) The new book was begun on February 20, and a few days later Clemens announced to Howells that his title was:

COLONEL MULBERRY SELLERS,
AMERICAN CLAIMANT
OF THE
GREAT EARLDOM OF ROSSMORE
IN THE
PEERAGE OF GREAT BRITAIN

As he began, the author was unusually elated. He wrote to his brother, "I think it will simply howl with fun. I wake up in the night laughing at its ridiculous situations."[32] He wrote to Fred J. Hall, "I have written 10,000 words on a book whose canvas [for orders] is to begin September 1, and issue December 10 with 75,000 orders—and not a single one short of that."[33] Soon crippled by rheumatism, he tried dictating into a phonograph, only to find as he told Howells in April, "it hasn't any ideas & it hasn't any gift for elaboration, or smartness of talk, or vigor of action, or felicity of expression, but it is just matter-of-fact, compressive, unornamental, & as grave & unsmiling as the devil." The manuscript contains Mark Twain's note at the end of chapter 11: "Here follows 6,000 or 8,000 words done on the phonograph. The cylinders will be found (uncorrected & execrably worded) in my billiard room, if wanted."[34] Presumably these words were later transcribed and typed for the author. Maybe the phonograph had something to do with the glaring faults of the novel. Maybe the explanation was what he told Joe Goodman: "I am at work again—on a book. Not with a great deal of spirit," then, bolstering himself, "but with enough, yes, plenty."[35] The novel was completed just seventy-one days after it was begun, and shortly thereafter the author sold the rights to subscription publication to the McClure syndicate, which published it in various American newspapers and, in England, in the *Idler Magazine*.

Clemens wrote Howells in May that from the play he had salvaged only half a day's writing. Because his inspiration was the play to begin with, he told his story largely by means of dialogue, with only a few comments from the author, mostly about the distinctively English characteristics of one of his two central characters. Instead, the author created a spokesman to express his sentiments in extended discussions with the Englishman. The story begins with two of the secondary elements of the play, Colonel Sellers's eagerness to become an earl and his conviction that the rightful heir, who falls in love with his daughter, is his "materialization" of a dead man. The basic idea of the claimant in both the play and the novel stemmed from the claims of Clemens's distant cousin, James M. Leathers, to be the rightful Earl of Durham. Leathers had even sought out Clemens as a financial backer and promised to split the profits if the author would provide him with legal expenses. The idea fascinated Clemens, who himself day-dreamed of discovering that he was the Earl of Durham. Mark Twain's original claimant has a name like Clemens's cousin, Simon Lathers. His death, just before the action of the novel begins, permits Colonel Sellers to take his place as the American Claimant. What had dominated the play, Sellers's preposterous scientific inventions, appear as well in the novel. The only dialogue that Mark Twain borrowed from the play concerned Sellers's invention of a cursing phonograph for timid sea captains.

One of Mark Twain's pet ideas, switching identities, appears in several forms. The actual heir, Viscount Berkeley, comes to America, where he is able to assume a new identity when he is thought to have died in a hotel fire. Now transformed into "Howard Tracy" and outfitted in cowboy clothes, the costume of a bank-robber who died in the fire, Berkeley falls in love with Sellers's daughter, and she reciprocates. Thereupon Berkeley wonders if he should be jealous of the dead "hero." "In a sense the dead man was himself; in that case compliments and affection lavished upon that corpse went into his own till and were clear profit. But in another case the dead man was not himself; and in that case all compliments and affection were wasted, and a sufficient basis for jealousy" (chapter 22). When Washington Hawkins argues that he knows Tracy to be an impostor whose correct name is Snodgrass, Sally Sellers responds, "Oh, now, Mr. Hawkins, you *can't* go that far. A body can't really know it, you know. It can't be *proved* that he's not what he says he is" (chapter 24). The disguises and role-playing have no real significance and are merely part of the farce, though some readers may look for meaning and significance.

More amusing is the identity switch of Sally Sellers. When Sellers becomes the American Claimant and calls himself Rossmore, he changes Sally's name to Gwendolen. The fact that Sally attends Rowena-Ivanhoe College, where her address is Kenilworth Keep, Redgauntlet Hall, suggests that Mark Twain had maintained his scorn for Sir Walter Scott, now augmented by his recognition (as in "Defense of Royalty & Nobility") that Americans can be as conscious of social rank as the British. According to her letter home in chapter 5, Gwendolen-Sally has suffered from the snobbery of her classmates because she could not show four generations of "American-Colonial-Dutch-Peddler-and Salt-Cod-McAllister Nobility." All the college students are painfully rank-conscious.

As if balancing criticism of America against his earlier criticism of England, Mark Twain extends his argument, significantly. In chapter 1, Viscount Berkeley's departure for America is occasioned by his conviction that across the water he will find that, since "all men are equal and have an equal chance," he will be able to make his own way. He has his chance when he loses his English identity in the fire. Then he can become, in the words of the author's summary, a "Freeman & radical."[36] His ideas are reinforced by a visit to the Mechanics Club in chapter 10. There a speaker attacks Matthew Arnold's criticism of the American press, and the speech, quoted at length in the novel, proves to be adapted from an unpublished and undelivered speech, "The American Press," which Mark Twain had himself written in reply to Arnold.[37] (The original manuscript does not contain the visit to the Mechanics Club, which seems to have been an afterthought.) Next Berkeley hears another speech treating a second subject that Mark Twain had recently discussed, admiringly: American industrial progress. Berkeley finds both speeches persuasive and exults in the limitless opportunities America has to offer. He is captured by the American Dream. Soon, however, he finds that clerkships are open only to those with political connections and that factory jobs are open only to union members. As a foreigner, Berkeley is refused union membership. His disenchantment is suggested by what he writes in his diary at the end of chapter 12: "It does look as if in a republic where all are free and equal, prosperity and position constitute rank." In time Berkeley's eyes are further opened by the author's spokesman, Barrow, who persuasively argues that, human nature being what it is, every man must be out for what he can get. If he is born to be an earl, he should thank his good fortune. At the end of the novel, Berkeley is prepared to accept a return to his original place in society.

Outwardly Berkeley resembles some of Mark Twain's earlier innocents who learn from their experience, but this time there is no place for humorous adventures. Except for some scenes in which he is introduced to the horrors of the boardinghouse (scenes that echo the experience of Dickens's Martin Chuzzlewit), much of Berkeley's initiation is by way of lecture and discussion, not incident. One adventure is promising: the only job that Berkeley can find is assisting a team of portrait painters whose work is designed to give their subjects a sense of dignity. The episode, unfortunately, is treated with a very heavy hand.

All that remains of Mark Twain's optimism in *The American Claimant* is the ridiculous figure of Colonel Sellers, who is "always keeping breast to breast with the drum-major in the great work of material civilization" (chapter 8). The novel ends with his describing his latest project: furnishing climates, for a fee, by controlling sunspots. It is as if Sellers is Mark Twain's Yankee with nothing left but dreams. He is contrasted with his daughter, who gladly gives up her aristocratic aspirations for real love.

The American Claimant is Mark Twain's response to his own *Yankee*. But whereas the earlier novel, despite its didacticisms and muddled thinking, has strong imaginative appeal, its successor is the writer's poorest novel—crowded with plot, theses, ideas, heavy-handed satire. Writing quickly, Mark Twain used his own serious social analysis of a few years as the object of his attack, for then he had been guilty, according to his spokesman, of leaving out "the factor of human nature" (chapter 14). For a variety of reasons, Mark Twain had become, at least temporarily, a pessimist. The tendency had been observable for some time, but the collapse of his dreams of great wealth and his other disappointments were contributory.

The most striking of the several changes in Clemens's life and writings at this time was an outward one. On June 6, 1891, the Clemenses went to Europe again, chiefly because of Mrs. Clemens's health—but because of her husband's too. They would soon discover another reason to live abroad: with a diminished income, they escaped the enormous costs of their Hartford home. But what began as a trip intended to last six months was to last ten years, and the family was never to live together again in Hartford. During these years Clemens visited America frequently, on business; in 1893–94 one visit lasted nine months. But his residence was in Europe, in Aix-les-Bains, Marienbad, Berlin, Bad Nauheim, Florence, Munich, Paris, London, Lucerne, Vienna, and elsewhere, with a full year being occupied with a round-the-world lecture tour. The retreat was symbolic of his state of mind. He was an American writer who had lost his focus.[38]

Mark Twain's closest literary friend and adviser was the novelist William Dean Howells, who edited the Atlantic Monthly *in the 1870s. There many of Mark Twain's best pieces appeared, such as "Old Times on the Mississippi." (Reproduced with permission of Mark Twain Memorial, Hartford, Connecticut)*

The Hartford house was home for Clara, Jean, and Susy Clemens, here shown on the ombra in 1885, with their parents. (Reproduced with permission of Mark Twain Memorial, Hartford, Connecticut)

As he gained in fame Mark Twain became one of the most photographed personages of the nineteenth century. This not very flattering picture was taken in a New York photographer's studio in 1886 or 1887. (Reproduced with permission of the Mark Twain Papers, the Bancroft Library)

In 1891 the Clemenses' financial situation caused them to leave Hartford and live in Europe. In 1895 in an attempt to pay his debts, Mark Twain made a world lecture tour. Here he is on the U.S.S. Mohican, ready to lecture in Seattle. (Reproduced with permission of Mark Twain Memorial, Hartford, Connecticut)

For nearly ten years the Clemenses lived in England, Germany, Austria, Italy, and elsewhere. During those years they suffered the loss of their daughter Susy, who died in 1896. Here is how Mark Twain looked in 1900, the year when he and his family finally returned to America. (Reproduced with permission of Mark Twain Memorial, Hartford, Connecticut)

In 1903 because of Olivia's failing health the Clemenses returned to Europe, and in 1904 "Livy" died in Florence. Thereafter Mark Twain lived in America except for a 1907 trip to England to receive an honorary doctorate from Oxford University. Here he is pictured at the House of Lords in London with Rudyard Kipling and Camille Saint-Saëns. (Reproduced with permission of Mark Twain Memorial, Hartford, Connecticut)

In 1908 Mark Twain once again built a house in Connecticut, this time in Redding. Here he is pictured in that year, in a white suit such as he regularly wore, winter and summer, in his last years. In his Redding house Mark Twain died in 1910. (Reproduced with permission of Mark Twain Memorial, Hartford, Connecticut)

CHAPTER EIGHT

European Wanderings

AS he began his European sojourn, the health of Mark Twain's literary career was unsatisfactory. Encouraged to take himself seriously, he had grown intellectually as the result of his reading, as well as from his interest in political liberalism and his religious and philosophical questioning. Though he had chosen to abandon his lucrative profession to undertake ventures that seemed more likely to be profitable, now that he needed money badly he had no ready resources except his pen. But if that strange mixture *The American Claimant* was a fair sample of what he could now produce, his literary career appeared to be over. Journalism was, however, still a possibility. Beyond that, his experience had shown that though he might suffer a few false starts, a likely literary idea would come along. If not, he could once again try some kind of sequel to what had worked before. But he no longer had the luxury of abandoning tasks that proved unsuitable, as he had with the English book of the early 1870s. He was obliged to cash in, if at all possible, on what he could produce. He would keep especially alert for novelties and current fads. Being across the sea from editors with whom he had to transact business might be difficult, but he had already learned to make concessions, as he had found himself doing in his dealings with James R. Osgood in the preparation of *Life on the Mississippi*.

During the summer of 1891, Clemens tried to combine health cures for his wife and himself with writing for much-needed money. For the McClure syndicate and the New York *Sun*, he had contracted to write six letters from Europe at one thousand dollars a piece, and by the end of August he had written four. The first was "Aix—The

Paradise of the Rheumatics," a pleasant piece of ephemeral journalism, such as they all turned out to be. Two passages are worth noting, however. The buildings of Aix alerted the author to the passing of time, especially to changes in man's ways. He was most interested in changes in man's conception of the deity. While the passage implies a belief in God, but not in special providences, it is chiefly the vastness of the universe and the insignificance of man's planet that engages Mark Twain. "To-day He is a Master of a universe made up of myriads of gigantic suns, and among them, lost in that limitless sea of light, floats that atom," the earth, "a mere cork adrift in the waters of a shoreless Atlantic." The writer's imaginative grasp of the dimensions of the universe was to augment his pessimism, with man perceived as all but insignificant.

Another side of his pessimism comes into focus in this essay: his notion of man as a seat of diseases, a theme he would explore fully in "Letters from the Earth." Here, however, his attitude is humorous. He meets a man who came to the baths to learn if he had any ailments. If he had any, he was told, the baths would make them appear. The doctor's prognosis proves valid as each day the baths cause more and more illnesses to appear, until after the fourth treatment he becomes "one vast, diversified, undulating continent of pain, with horizons to it, and zones, and parallels of latitude, and isothermal belts, and right up to the latest developments, you know. The doctor said it was inflammation of the soul, and just the very thing." Except for this amusing anecdote, there is, apparently, no fictionalizing, just description and report.

From Aix the Clemenses went to Bayreuth for ten days "At the Shrine of St. Wagner," as he called his account. When he attempted to arrange for the journey there, he had the material for an account of his ineptitude, "Playing Courier," good-natured but slight. The letter on Bayreuth mixes amazement at the reverence with which Wagner's operas are treated and some appreciation; it is on the whole a sober account. Next comes "Marienbad—A Health Factory," which describes the Clemenses' trip to Bohemia and the health treatments, all briskly but unremarkably described. One might have hoped that in getting his body in order, Mark Twain might have put his writing arm back in good working order, but the evidence shows no such thing. Another unremarkable essay resulted from the Clemens family's trip to "Switzerland, the Cradle of Liberty" in September. It features a story about a well-meaning American brewer who offered to help the king of Greece by making him a foreman at his American plant, without discovering the identity of the man.

To prepare for more ambitious travel writing, Clemens left his family to make a ten-day trip down the Rhone. Eventually he drafted 174 pages of "The Innocents Adrift," but though he was optimistic about the results for several years, he finally gave up the project. A version heavily edited by Paine appeared in *Europe and Elsewhere* (1923). In the fall the Clemenses settled in Berlin, where the writer devoted three days and nights to the translation of *Der Struwwelpeter*, which he called "the most celebrated child's book in Europe." He expected the Webster Company as well as Chatto and Windus of London to publish the translation, illustrated.[1] But the book did not appear until 1935, when Harper and Brothers published *Slovenly Peter*, a collection of verses about the fates of naughty children, with a preface by Clara Clemens, the translator's surviving daughter. In Berlin the family lived for a time at an unsavory location, innocently selected, with Mark Twain writing a sketch on the subject, which his family persuaded him not to publish. Instead he supplied a sixth and final letter on "The German Chicago," full of admiration for Berlin, written while the writer was recovering from pneumonia. Another piece written at this time, "Postal Service," exists only as an unpublished fragment. Both pieces are full of comparisons of American and European ways. Meanwhile, Fred J. Hall, who succeeded Charles Webster on his retirement, collected and published through the Webster Company a thin collection entitled *Merry Tales*. It consists of "The Private History," "Luck," "Meisterschaft," "Playing Courier," and two older pieces, "A Curious Experience" and "Mrs. McWilliams and the Lightning."

The authentic Mark Twain was, however, still alive, though shy about making public appearances. During that Berlin winter he appeared privately, a fact well hidden for almost eighty years. In a sketch entitled "A Singular Episode" but later referred to by the author as "The Late Reverend Sam Jones's Reception in Heaven," Mark Twain—who identifies himself by name—manages to obtain entrance into heaven by exchanging passes with the sleeping archbishop of Canterbury on the train to New Jerusalem and Sheol. This exchange leaves the archbishop with the damnable reputation of "a professional humorist," a person of "frivolous nature and profane instincts." The archbishop turns out to be satisfied to go on to Sheol when he learns that a fellow passenger, the Texas evangelist Sam Jones, has won admission to heaven. Despite his "special, illuminated, gilt-edged" pass, Mark Twain is soon in trouble for being what he describes as "a light speaker," in fact a blasphemer. The brief sketch ends quickly when all the inhabitants of heaven rush for the underworld after getting an earful of Jones's preaching.

In this unpretentious and charming story, Mark Twain takes obvious satisfaction in seeing himself as a highly questionable personage in the genteel circles of heaven. The manuscript bears this annotation: "Not published—forbidden by Mrs. Clemens.—S.L.C." But the author could read the story as after-dinner entertainment, as he also read "Captain Stormfield's Visit," and he reported to Mrs. Clemens the pleasure he took in an 1894 reading.[2] In November 1907 he commented, "I was ever so fond of the 'Reception' article, and dearly wanted to print it, but it was hilarious and extravagant to the very verge of impropriety, and I could not beguile my wife into consenting to its publication. In that day Sam Jones was sweeping the South like a cyclone with his revival meetings, and converting the unconverted here and there and everywhere with his thundering torrents of piety and slang. I represented him as approaching the New Jerusalem in the thorough express, and in the same pullman in which he and his feet together were occupying two chairs, sat his grace the Archbishop of Canterbury (Mr. Tait) and I."[3] The sketch was finally published, inconspicuously, in 1970.

"Sam Jones's Reception" was truly "a singular episode." In April 1892, unable to escape his health problems, Clemens wrote to Hall, "I do not expect to write any literature this year. The moment I take up a pen my rheumatism returns."[4] Perhaps his lack of inspiration had something to do with his physical problems. At any rate, soon his pen would be as busy as ever. The beginning of the deliverance seems to have come following a two-week visit to the United States on business in June. While on the return vessel, he wrote "About All Kinds of Ships," a formless piece that compares his 1892 ship with ones he has traveled in before, an imaginary interview in which Noah is questioned by a German ship inspector, a description of what sailing on Columbus's ship might have been like, or whatever occurred to the writer. On his return he wrote a letter about Bad Nauheim, where the Clemens family stayed until September. The former essay was collected and appears in the Definitive Edition; the latter has not survived.

In August 1892, Mark Twain at last found something that engaged him, a story that at first he called "Huck Finn in Africa." Only five days after he had begun it he reported to Fred Hall that he had written half, or twenty-six thousand words, of a book he was now calling "Huckleberry Finn and Tom Sawyer Abroad" or "Huckleberry Finn

Abroad." He thought of it as the first of a series, with Huck as narrator in each. Nigger Jim and his two young heroes would visit Germany, England, and elsewhere. By finding a way to stop the story and then start it up again, he thought he could write a novel (really a novella) in two parts. In this fashion he could have the first part soon ready for serial publication.[5] He did find a way, though an obviously contrived one, to stop the story, and this part, some thirty thousand words, was published as "Tom Sawyer Abroad" in *St. Nicholas Magazine*, a children's monthly, for the Clemens family insisted it was a story for girls and boys.

The history of the composition and publication of *Tom Sawyer Abroad* is instructive. The work had been begun as a means of using an unidentified plot idea that was not employed in the first half. But the first half was all there was to be, for the author held back from writing more to see if the first numbers should prove popular, then never returned to it. Though *Tom Sawyer Abroad* is a sequel to *Tom Sawyer*, not *Huckleberry Finn*, it deserved better than it received at the hands of the editor of the magazine in which it appeared, Mary Mapes Dodge, to whom the author sold the story for four thousand dollars. Mark Twain thought he knew what the editor of a children's magazine expected. He told Hall, "I tried to leave the improprieties all out; if I didn't, Mrs. Dodge can scissor them out."[6] Scissor she did. She made Huck's language more genteel and reduced references to bodily functions, alcohol, and death, to Negroes, and to church groups that might have been offended. In Mrs. Dodge's version, scabs became scars, sore places are tender spots, and Jim becomes a darky, not a nigger. A long passage—some eight hundred words—was cut from chapter 8, a discussion of the place of swearing in the Catholic church, based presumably on the anathema. Huck asks Tom, "Can a bishop curse, now, the way they useter?" To which Tom replies, "Yes, they learn it, because it's part of the polite learning that belongs to his lay-out—kind of bells letters as you may say—and although he ain't got no more use for it than Missouri girls has for French, he's got to learn it, same as they do, because a Missouri girl that can't polly-voo and a bishop that can't cuss ain't got no business in society."[7] Presumably the writer learned of Mrs. Dodge's alterations, for he wrote to Hall that he should use the original version, not the *St. Nicholas* printing, as the basis for *Tom Sawyer Abroad* in book form. Perhaps the letter arrived too late. At any rate, when the Webster Company published the story as a book in 1894, this edited *St. Nicholas* text was used as the basis of chapters 1–10 of the publication and the authoritative typescript only for the remainder. For what Mark Twain had written for publication—presumably after the work had been censored by Mrs. Clemens—one must go either to the English text, which seems to have been based on a copy of the original, or to the recent Iowa-California edition, published in the same volume as *Tom Sawyer*, based on the holograph manuscript.

Tom Sawyer Abroad begins as the next adventure of the boys after *Huckleberry Finn*, its mood being that of the final chapters of *Huck*. "Do you reckon," the voice of Huck asks, "Tom Sawyer was satisfied with all them adventures? I mean the adventures we had down the river, and the time we set the nigger Jim free and Tom got shot in the leg. No, he wasn't." The story takes Huck, Tom, and Jim in a navigable balloon from St. Louis to Africa. There they have a series of adventures, first in the Sahara, where they rescue a kidnapped child and experience a sandstorm. They discuss the possibility of importing Sahara sand to America, but decide against it when Tom shows a rather sophisticated familiarity with import duties. After Jim and a guide picked up in Egypt return to Missouri to fetch a corncob pipe for Tom, they come back with word that Aunt Polly insists on Tom's return. After Tom gets his pipe, the story abruptly breaks off, with this sentence: "So then we shoved for home, and not feeling very gay neither." Mark Twain wrote that the story, though he could continue it, "doesn't need another finish."[8] Few readers will agree.

Huck tells the story but the focus is on Tom, whose aggressive leadership makes Huck and Jim into Tom's straight men. Much of the story is devoted not to adventures but to conversations among the three, with Huck's and Jim's ignorance constantly frustrating Tom, soon in thoroughly predictable ways. The Huck who traveled by Mississippi raft is notable for his absence. The story is a disappointment, despite some amusing touches, for nothing is made of the trip—it is purposeless. One conjectures about what it might have been had Mark Twain delivered the episode that served as the genesis of the story: "Somewhere after that great voyage he [Huck] will work in the said episode in an effective (and at the same time apparently unintentional) way."[9] The absence of this episode or any other excuse for the balloon trip, except as a pleasant celebration of ballooning, severely limits the story.

The basic idea of the story, without the unrealized episode, had come to the author in 1868 when he recorded in his notebook, "Trip of a man in a balloon from Paris over India, China, Pacific Ocean, the Plains, to a prairie in Illinois, in a balloon." Soon after, he began writing this sketch in his notebook, but before he had finished it, he noted, "Jules Verne's 'Five Weeks in a Balloon' came out," and he dropped it. Later, in 1876, he used a version of the plot idea to take a man mysteriously to the prairie in "A Murder, a Mystery, and a Marriage," which is still unpublished; and in a deleted portion of *Life on the Mississippi* there is a tall tale of a balloon adventure. In *Tom Sawyer Abroad* the adventures of the three balloonists show definite borrowings from Jules Verne's story, and, strangely, Verne's three characters in fact resemble Mark Twain's three. Some of the adventures are borrowed: for instance, both groups see a lion at an oasis and see a mirage; both stories tell of hovering over a caravan buried in the sand, and in both stories one of the travelers jumps from the balloon into a lake.

After its serial publication, *Tom Sawyer Abroad* was published as the Webster Company's last book, copies arriving in Washington, D.C., for copyright the very day of the company's failure. Only the English edition, with a better text, received the attention of reviewers. Critics found it a disappointment to admirers of both Tom and Huck. Needless to say, the book publication was not sufficiently remunerative to Clemens. The author, the germ of the story, and the manuscript all deserved better than they got.

While revising *Tom Sawyer Abroad*, Mark Twain was on to a novel he had begun earlier in the summer of 1892. At first he called it "Those Extraordinary Twins." The story of its composition and reshaping is complicated, but the novel, much praised by such illustrious critics as F. R. Leavis and Leslie Fiedler, is hardly to be understood without some knowledge of its history. Inspired by an account of the Tocci Siamese twins, who had distinctly different personalities, the work was begun as a "howling farce," with the author supremely gratified by his achievement. "I think all sorts of folks will read it. It is clear out of the common order—it is a fresh idea—I don't think it resembles anything in literature."[10] Mark Twain had been fascinated by Siamese twins since 1869, when he had written about Chang and Eng, two separate individuals joined by a ligature. Later he would refer to his "crude attempt to work out the duality idea, which has puzzled and interested the world during so many ages."[11] The twins he now wrote about, Angelo and Luigi, had one body, two heads, four arms, and two legs. It was these "conglomerate twins," as he called them, whose comic possibilities so entertained the writer. They create a great sensation when they arrive in a small Missouri town. They are soon found to disagree about everything: the use of intoxicants, religion, politics. There is romance, with Angelo finding that he has a rival not in his brother but in Tom Driscoll, "nephew" of a local judge. As he continued the story, Mark Twain became interested in a plot for determining the responsibility of an act by one of the twins, with some "scientific" method, perhaps palmistry, put to use.

Then he was seized by a new idea. He would have Tom Driscoll's mother, a light-skinned member of the black community, identify herself to her son and explain that she had switched him while he was a baby with a white child who had been brought up as a slave, one Chambers. The mother, Roxana, would then use her information to blackmail Tom into stealing from Judge Driscoll, who at this stage was Tom's father—a fact he had kept from Tom. During the robbery, Tom kills the judge, who first identifies himself in order to attempt to prevent his murder. So much, at least, seems to be suggested by two manuscript notes in the Mark Twain Papers. One reads, in part:

> "Spare me!—I am your father!" (He was hesitating—had concluded that he couldn't do it.)
> "Now for *that*, you shall die."
> (Kills him) Tom (Chambers) is to be pardoned—he is glad—but when he finds he is a valuable slave, he commits suicide.

The second in its entirety reads:

> Shall we have baby foot-marks of Tom and Chambers taken at 10 months to prove legitimacy of Chambers after Tom's suicide & declaration of what Roxy told him?
> Yes.[12]

When he reached approximately this point, the Clemenses moved to Florence for a nine-month stay, and the author put his story aside. In mid-November, he picked it up again, excited by a new possibility. He had been reading Sir Francis Galton's just-published book, *Finger Prints*. He was fascinated by the newly discovered technique for crime detection. It gave him the idea of a murder trial, with a minor character, assigned the hobby of collecting fingerprints, now become a major character, or, as Mark Twain put it, "The minor character will now become the chiefest, and I will name the story after him, 'Pudd'nhead Wilson.'"[13] Later he told a correspondent that the accident of hitting on Galton's book "changed the whole plot & plan of my book."[14] Working long and hard now, as much as thirteen hours a day, he completed a story of sixty to eighty thousand words by December 20. What seized his imagination was the possibility of a sensational courtroom scene in which Wilson would reveal by means of fingerprints the true identity of the men who had been switched as babies. After completing this big scene, he then wrote early episodes in which Wilson fingerprints the babies, Roxy exchanges them, and then, after the passing of time, Tom torments the white boy, now considered black, with whom he had reversed roles. The Italian twins remain the focus of much attention, though they are not present in the best scenes.

This version of the story, which survives in manuscript form at the Morgan Library in New York, has three weaknesses. First, because Mark Twain wrote the ending before he composed many of the scenes for which it was intended to be the denouement, he gave too much attention to the showman Wilson, and too little attention to those most affected by the revelation, Tom and his mother, whose roles are slight in the manuscript. Second, since he not only created new scenes that involve Tom but also retained ones from his earlier version, Tom is inconsistently portrayed. The original Tom was white; the revised one is partly black. Thus in the published version in chapter 10 Tom is tormented by the discovery that he is, by Southern racial standards, black; in chapter 11 that obsession has disappeared, or rather it does not appear, the chapter having been written before chapter 10, before Mark Twain decided to give Tom black blood. Third, the book still contained farcical scenes involving the Siamese twins, quite out of keeping with the serious elements, the presence of which would later lead the writer to call his book *The Tragedy of Pudd'nhead Wilson*. But despite these flaws, he considered that he had finished. The introduction of the fingerprint notion had been exhausting. He had "to entirely re-cast and re-write the first two-thirds,"[15] and though the original composition "didn't cost me any fatigue," "revising it nearly killed me. Revising books is a mistake," the author sighed.[16]

In February 1893 he sent his manuscript, which he considered complete and good, to Fred Hall, "typewritered and ready for print."[17] About a month later, Clemens himself headed for America, and there, apparently, Hall discouraged him from publishing the story in its present form. After a brief visit he returned to Italy, with his manuscript. By late July he was in Germany, with a revision of the work complete. First, he had subordinated but not eliminated the twins, and separated them; they are no longer "conglomerate." But he failed to revise his manuscript thoroughly, and vestigial remains of the twins' former nature remain. For example, Angelo describes in chapter 6 how they had been "placed among the attractions of a cheap museum in Berlin," obviously in their status as freaks. Second, he pruned the story to focus it on the murder and the trial. He gave this emphasis because the fingerprints idea was "virgin ground—absolutely *fresh*, and mighty curious and interesting to everybody."[18] He did little rewriting, too little; mainly he deleted. Novelty and sensationalism would sell books; a serious, probing study of the race relations would not.

The pruning made the story acceptable; it was sold to the *Century Magazine* for $6,500 and was published in seven installments from December 1893 to June 1894. Later, a year after he had finished the final revision, Mark Twain salvaged what he had pruned about the twins to make it into a separate story, with the twins returning to their conglomerate state; he added some connecting links without troubling to hide the fact (he put them within brackets in reduced type), and wrote a self-denigrating preface in which he described some of the history of the story or stories. Since the Webster Company was no longer in business, the author arranged for publication of both stories by his old publishers, the American Publishing Company of Hartford. *The Tragedy of Pudd'nhead Wilson And the Comedy Those Extraordinary Twins* should be read together, complete with the author's preface to the latter.

Because of the impatience with which Mark Twain performed the "literary Caesarean operation," as he called it in his preface, *Pudd'nhead Wilson* is not a satisfactory story. Presumably much of the author's original literary and philosophical motivation stemmed from his interest in exploring favorite themes and ideas, such as the influence of training, the problem of identity, and the effect of role exchange. But in the revamping, all these matters became blurred. Specifically, the book appears to argue that race is insignificant and that training is all-important. The notion is set forth as a generalization in "Pudd'nhead Wilson's Calendar" at the beginning of chapter 5: "Training is everything. The peach was once a bitter almond; cauliflower is nothing but cabbage with a college education." This thesis is persuasively demonstrated by "Chambers," the real Tom Driscoll, brought up as a slave and permanently damaged by the experience. But what of the false Tom, brought up as an aristocrat? His mother says in chapter 14 that his weakness, his cowardice, is a result of his black blood: "It's de nigger in you, dat's what it is." Her comment is to be understood as the author's irony: slavery has made black people despise their own race. But not altogether ironic, for the false Tom seems truly bad by nature. If the source is not his blood, perhaps it is his training as a slave-master. But in this book aristocrats are honorable men, especially the most prominent, Judge Driscoll.

What Mark Twain wrote originally—and presumably what he meant to convey—was clear enough. In what is now chapter 10, just after Tom's recognition that because he is partly black he can be sold like a dog, the author provided the following explanation, later deleted.

> In his broodings in the solitudes, he searched himself for the reasons of certain things, & in toil & pain he worked out the answers:
> Why was he a coward? It was the "nigger" in him. The nigger *blood?* Yes, the nigger blood degraded from original courage to cowardice by decades & generations of insult & outrage inflicted in circumstances which forbade reprisals, & made mute & meek endurance the only refuge & defence.
> Whence came that in him which was high, & whence that which was base? That which was high came from either blood, & was the monopoly of neither color; but that which was base was the *white* blood in him debased by the brutalizing effects of a long-drawn heredity of slave-owning, with the habit of abuse which the possession of irresponsible power always creates & perpetuates, by a law of human nature. So he argued.[19]

It is training that has ruined "Tom"—inherited training. It is not his black blood, which is insignificant (one part in thirty-two), but his inherited submission (one part in two) that determines his character. This Lamarckian doctrine is what Mark Twain had offered as an explanation of Tom's behavior, though he chose to have Tom see it for himself, since the author restrained himself from comment. The passage was dropped, presumably, to give the story focus. As revised, "The whole story is centered on the murder and the trial," Mark Twain explained; "from the first chapter the movement is straight ahead without divergence or side-play to the murder and the trial; everything that is done or said or happens is a preparation for these events."[20] Mark Twain preferred Tom Sawyer-like sensations to philosophizing in fiction, though he was developing a taste for the latter. Expediency seems to have determined his attempt to get something published to sustain himself in a difficult financial pinch.

While Mark Twain's "literary Caesarean operation" was necessary, the problem of identity was more fully explored when the two stories were one. As conglomerates the twins have two personalities in one body, like Jekyl and Hyde, and "Tom" is searching for a father:

"his mind centered itself upon a single problem—how to find his father, in case he was still alive—& upon a single purpose: to kill him when he should find him. He said he would make this the whole business of his life, & allow nothing to stay or divert him until it was accomplished."[21] This passage was dropped. What does remain in *Pudd'nhead Wilson* is the author's sense of detachment, underscored by a consistently ironic vision of life. External and internal forces, not the author, seem to be manipulating the characters and their lives, with Wilson, according to the author, not a character but only "a piece of machinery—a button or a crank or a lever, with a useful function to perform in a machine, but with no dignity above that."[22] Among the manifold ironies are those in the entries of "Pudd'nhead Wilson's Calendar": "Why is it that we rejoice at a birth and grieve at a funeral? It is because we are not the person involved." Even if many of the calendar entries sound suspiciously like Mark Twain, they contribute to the tone of the book without authorial intrusion. Also central in the book is the ironic "fiction of law" that makes Roxana "black" though she appears to be white, the fact that the false Tom is really a slave and the real Tom becomes one, and the ending in which "Tom's" sentence of life imprisonment is changed to being sold down the river, since it would be unjust to the judge's estate for a slave to lose his commercial value.

These ironies are illustrations of the underlying philosophy of determinism, which is much more fully developed here than it was when the author wrote the *Yankee*. As in Clemens's recent personal experience, commercial values dominate, with powerful consequences. From Wilson's joke about dog ownership, which opens the book, to Roxy's suffering from the failure of a bank and her blackmailing Tom, the book stresses the dire results of the institution of slavery by the importance it gave to ownership. In the world of the novel, each person rigidly occupies a place in the hierarchical structure; each person's behavior is determined. The lives of the aristocrats, such as Judge Driscoll, are determined by laws that "could not be relaxed to accommodate religions or anything else. Honor stood first; and the laws defined what it was and wherein it differs in certain details from honor as defined by church creeds and by the social laws and customs" (chapter 12). When Roxy attempts to change the structure by removing her son from his place at the bottom of the social scale, her efforts almost immediately create unexpected results: her son, now her master, takes pleasure in abusing her. Wilson as an instrument of doom returns the switched identities to their original places.

Only recently has *Pudd'nhead Wilson* received much attention. A few reviews appeared when the book appeared in England, none in America. Several reviewers singled out for praise the portrayal of Roxana, one of the few women in Mark Twain's writings whose sexuality is given attention.[23] But like nearly everything else in the novel, there are inconsistencies in it. Her creator seems unable to decide whether she is a woman who looks white or one who acts black, and she is both a doting mammy and a black shrew. Her beauty, so stressed at the beginning of the books, soon fades or is forgotten.

Though "The Comedy of Those Extraordinary Twins" came to be little more than an appendage to *Puddn'head Wilson*, some of its pages on the relationship of the twins, here conglomerate, are not to be neglected by those interested in Mark Twain's growing concern with duality. In later works two personalities in Siamese twins are superseded by multiple personalities within one individual. Here Luigi tells Aunt Betsy that since both he and Angelo have "utter and indisputable command" of their joint body during alternate periods, "We are no more twins than you are." Aunt Betsy, who has no more idea of what to make of the remark than the reader, replies, "I know you ain't you don't *seem* so." When Judge Driscoll challenges Angelo to a duel, he refuses, and so Luigi accepts in his place. At the duel Luigi tells Angelo that he is there only by courtesy: "Officially you are not here at all; officially you don't exist." Just as Mark Twain had discovered his story of the Yankee becoming serious despite his wishes, so the "Twins" became serious, so serious that an operation was necessary. Had the writer kept to one of his earlier plans, the conglomerate "Twins" and *Wilson* story would have had an added dimension, for Tom and Chambers were to have been half-brothers, both sons of Judge Driscoll.

The summer of 1892 was the beginning of a period of intense literary activity for Mark Twain. Nearly everything was written to keep the pot boiling. Besides *Wilson* and the other pieces already mentioned, Mark Twain produced during this time five short stories, nine essays, and possibly a brief reminiscence, "Macfarlane," which Paine included in his edition of the autobiography. "A Cure for the Blues" is an essay that Mark Twain puffed as "the most delicious that has been offered to a magazine in thirty years."[24] It was written as the introduction to a short story, *The Enemy Conquered: or, Love Triumphant* (1843), by one Samuel W. Royster. In his appreciative essay Mark Twain expresses delight in the story of Major Elfonzo's love for Ambulinia Valeer; its dreadful eloquence and ridiculous artlessness proved utterly entertaining, to him. He proposed that Royster's story be reprinted, following his introduction, but *Harper's Magazine* turned them down; they were then published in the *Century*.

A little better is "The £1,000,000 Bank Note," a story probably inspired by the author's need for credit as he was facing bankruptcy. It tells of an experiment. Armed with a borrowed million-pound bank note, the narrator is able to rise to prosperity and marriage with a wealthy heiress merely by impressing people with the uncashed note. The story was published in a collection issued by the Webster Company in 1893 (before *Tom Sawyer Abroad*): *The £1,000,000 Bank Note and Other New Stories*, which was misleadingly named, since the banknote story was the *only* story in the collection. The others, essays or sketches, are "A Cure for the Blues" (with *The Enemy Conquered* to fatten the collection); two newspaper letters, "Playing Courier" and "The German Chicago"; the pieces on ships and the old medical book; "Mental Telegraphy" and "A Petition to the Queen," in all a lightweight collection.

Two other stories of this period show Mark Twain even more out of his element, as he attempted to write the kind of story he once satirized. "The Californian's Tale" is another of the pieces that Mark Twain had ready for Hall to place in the fall of 1892. Before it could appear in one of the collections Clemens and Hall were trying to make, the author lent it to Arthur Stedman for *The First Book of the Authors Club, Liber Scriptorum*, in 1893. Despite its name, "The Californian's Tale" is not told by one of Mark Twain's vernacular narrators, though it is a first-person narrative; it is sentimental in the manner of Bret Harte's California stories. The germ of the story is an experience Clemens had in his California days. In 1882 he had recorded in his notebook:

> That poor fellow at Tuttleville who entertained me on a long walk with enthusiastic talk about his wife, whom he was on his way to the next village to see, & who had been absent about a week, that I had the strongest desire to look upon a woman who could inspire such worship. And to my pain & astonishment I found that he was *always* making the weary journey & returning from it disappointed & marveling. His wife had been dead *23 years*. On her return from a week's absence, young & beautiful, the stage went over a precipice—& when he arrived, uninformed, expecting to take her in his arms, they lifted a sheet & showed him her corpse.

Changing the cause of the woman's death to her capture by Indians, Mark Twain told a tearjerker.

In "The Esquimaux Maiden's Romance," published in the *Cosmopolitan Magazine* at the end of 1893, Mark Twain's arctic companion tells of her disappointment at the loss of her lover, exiled for having stolen one of her father's highly prestigious fishhooks. The hook is eventually found in the girl's hair—too late. While the narrator was having a bit of fun at the expense of the girl's highly provincial sense of what wealth consists of, he and the author seem unable to decide whether the story is sentimental or satiric. Perhaps the story served its purpose when it provided the author with eight hundred dollars that he used for living expenses during a New York visit. More consistently satirical, but not funny, "Is He Living or Is He Dead?" tells of a group of starving artists who boost the prices of the works of one of their number, François Millet, by arranging for him to be "dead" and even arranging a funeral. It was also published in the *Cosmopolitan*. Later the writer used the plot for a full-length play.

Why was Mark Twain writing such stuff? He needed money. The soon-to-be-defunct Webster Company was more and more a liability. His manager Fred Hall found it "absolutely impossible" to send him money "with any regularity."[25] The pieces he published in the *Cosmopolitan*, the Eskimo and artists stories, were not very remunerative; the editor had offered him only five thousand dollars for *twelve* such pieces. One good story, of uncertain date, was published at this time, "Adam's Diary."

"Adam's Diary" appears to have been composed sometime before the spring of 1893. At that time Mark Twain was approached by two acquaintances, Charles and Irving Underhill, who sought from him something amusing for a publication they were preparing concerning Niagara Falls. At first he protested that he could not think of anything funny to write on the topic, but then he realized that his unpublished "Adam's Diary" could be adapted by placing the Garden of Eden at Niagara Falls. He is said to have become so enthusiastic that he declared, "Where else could it have been? Wasn't Niagara just made for the Garden of Eden? Of course it was the Garden of Eden."[26] By April 14, 1893, he was ready to mail off the revised version, for he had "worked at the Adam Diary until I have got it to suit me."[27] It then appeared in *The Niagara Book* (Buffalo: Underhill and Nichols, 1893), which contains ten essays, including one by William Dean Howells and "The Earliest Authentic Mention of Niagara Falls. Extracts from Adam's Diary. Translated from the Original Ms. By Mark Twain."

The diary made its next appearance in *Tom Sawyer, Detective* (London: Chatto and Windus, 1897). This text appears to be the pre–*Niagara Book* version, for it has no references to Niagara Falls, nor does it contain Mark Twain's joke about the Fall being caused not by an apple but by a chestnut, "an aged and moldy joke." But before this time, in 1895, Mark Twain had sent to Harper's a copy of *The Niagara Book* with this comment on the first page: "[Revised for use in Harper edition of my books. It is revised enough, now I think, but Alden can revise it some more if he likes. S.L.C.]" This text *is* heavily revised, with all the Niagara references removed. On the envelope is a comment from Frederick A. Duneka of Harper's: "J. 27/4 On finding that we had set Adam's Diary for book-form I brought this out. It was learned, however, that Mr. Clemens had sent a later copy than this condensed for the mag."[28]

The next publication, and the first by Harper, took place in 1904 in a separate edition of *Extracts from Adam's Diary*, with many illustrations. This text, however, is the same as that in *The Niagara Book*. In the summer of 1905, Mark Twain prepared, once more, a revision, this time by marking up the 1904 publication. He wrote to Duneka on July 16, 1905, to report what he was doing and to request "another Adam's Diary, so that I can make 2 revised copies."[29] In the Mark Twain Papers two photocopies survive.[30] One is from Clemens's own copy of the 1904 publication, annotated; it is now in the C. Waller Barrett Collection at the University of Virginia. The other is from a copy of the 1904 volume that belonged to Duneka. The former has corrections in Mark Twain's hand; the latter has the same corrections in Duneka's. Moreover, Duneka's copy includes a typescript of four pages that reproduces the five manuscript pages of additions (discussed below, p. 259) with a note as to their proper location in the revised work. Neither the 1895 nor the 1905 revisions were adopted in the 1906 Harper publication of "Adam's Diary" in *The $30,000 Bequest and Other Stories* or in subsequent American printings.

When "Eve's Diary" was published in *Harper's Magazine* in December 1905, it did not include any part of "Adam's Diary." Nor does the publication in *Their Husband's Wives*, edited by William Dean Howells and Henry Mills Alden (New York: Harper and Brothers, 1906). The 1905 addition to "Adam's Diary" first appeared in *Eve's Diary* (New York: Harper and Brothers, 1906), and this text appears in subsequent American printings.

The essays of this period are far more rewarding than the stories. Four are so alive and so successful that they suggest Mark Twain was able once more to present himself before the public. In each of the four he is witty, self-assured, and good-natured. The longest is "In Defense of Harriet Shelley," written in Italy in the fall of 1892 and published in the prestigious *North American Review* in July 1894. (Publication was delayed because the manuscript was mislaid by the author for some time.) An attack on Edward Dowden's life of Percy Bysshe Shelley, which Mark Twain calls "a literary cake walk," the essay is easily dismissed as Mark Twain's defense of the moral purity of Victorian woman. Rather, it is an unusually hard-hitting and fair-minded critique, with Mark Twain writing as an admirer of Shelley, an admirer too of good prose, and a detester of overwriting, as well as unwarranted calumny. Mark Twain is describing Dowden's book:

> This is perhaps the strangest book that has seen the light since Franken-stein. Indeed, it is a Frankenstein itself; a Frankenstein with the original infirmity supplemented by a new one; a Frankenstein with the reasoning faculty wanting. Yet it believes it can reason, and is always trying. It is not content to leave a mountain of fact standing in the clear sunshine, where the simplest reader can perceive its form, its details, and its relation to the rest of the landscape, but thinks it must help him examine it and understand it; so its drifting mind settles upon it with that intent, but always with one and the same result: there is a change of temperature and the mountain is hid in a fog. Every time it sets up a premise and starts to reason from it, there is a surprise in store for the reader. It is strangely near-sighted, cross-eyed, and purblind. Sometimes when a mastodon walks across the field of its vision it takes it for a rat; at other times it does not see it at all.

After this elaborate metaphor, the writer conducts an extended analysis of the relationship between Shelley and his first wife, Harriet. This time a love of exaggeration and digression did not get the best of him; he provides a strong, persuasive discussion, unmarred by distortions.

The other essays were written in the United States. At the end of August 1893, not long after completing the final version of *Pudd'nhead Wilson*, the author headed for America again, the second time that year. Now he would make an extended stay, with business and financial troubles keeping him too uneasy to permit him to return to his family until the following spring. The stock market had crashed in June, and with it went the chances of the Webster Company's survival. Fortunately for him, during this visit Clemens met Henry H. Rogers, a Standard Oil executive who soon became his financial adviser and later his agent and friend. When the Webster Company collapsed, Rogers supervised Clemens's entry, in April 1894, into voluntary bankruptcy proceedings. Rogers arranged for Olivia Clemens, who had invested her own money in the publishing company, to be awarded her husband's copyrights and royalties as a preferred creditor. Finally, in May, Clemens was able to settle down in Europe again, though it was not until the following January that the author-turned-businessman saw all his optimistic expectations disappointed; until then he still hoped to make money from the Paige typesetter. He, and more especially his wife, were determined to pay off all the debts of Webster (he owed about $80,000), but his analysis of that possibility was not hopeful. From Olivia Clemens's inheritance the family could expect $4,000 a year; from American Publishing Company royalties an additional $1,500; and from Chatto and Windus, his English publisher, about $2,000. From new writings he calculated he could bring in $5,000 a year. With so little coming in, he seems to have realized, it would be years before he could be debt-free.

During the winter of 1893–94, while living at the Players Club in New York City, Mark Twain managed to write three pieces, all nonfiction, this despite the fact that he said he was "so tuckered out with 5 months of daily and nightly fussing with business, that I shall not feel any interest in literature or anything else until I have had a half-year of rest and idleness to compensate that account."[31] "The Private History of the Jumping Frog Story" was written at the request of William H. Rideing, who was associated with the *North American Review*, where it was published in April 1894. It describes the writer's shock at being shown that his frog story was to be found in ancient Greek, with a wily Athenian as the stranger and a Boeotian in Jim Smiley's role. Mark Twain could only suppose that history repeats itself. He did not know what is now known, that the Greek text was based on Mark Twain's story and that the editor of the anthology had prepared it. In explaining how his story came to be written, Mark Twain shows particular interest in the manner in which the story was told to him so many years before in California. This interest in the manner of telling a story is the focus of "How to Tell a Story," written on February 8, 1894, and first published in the *Youth's Companion* in October 1895. Here Mark Twain explores the technique of the humorous story, as distinguished from the funny story and the witty story. The humorous story, which he identifies as American, has its basis in oral delivery. It should be told gravely, with the teller concealing the fact that his story is amusing. For Mark Twain the most important feature is the pause, and he demonstrates his technique by suggesting how he tells a Negro ghost story, "The Golden Arm."

The third of the essays of the New York winter is "Fenimore Cooper's Literary Offenses." Though Mark Twain never wrote an extended critique of his favorite literary whipping boy, Sir Walter Scott, this essay shows what he might have done. Unlike "A Cure for the Blues," this piece is gloriously funny, probably the author's funniest essay. He sets forth eighteen "rules governing literary art" that he contends Cooper violated in *The Deerslayer*. They include: "7. They require that when a personage talks like an illustrated, gilt-edged, tree-calf, hand-tooled, seven dollar Friendship's Offering in the beginning of a paragraph, he shall not talk like a negro minstrel in the end of it." Some of the "rules" Mark Twain regularly violated in his own fiction; others point up principles that he was seriously devoted to. "12. *Say what he is proposing to say, not merely come close to it. 13. Use the right word, not its second cousin.*" "17. Use good grammar. 18. Employ a simple and straightforward style." On these four, Mark Twain nearly always practiced what he preached. The analysis of the plot and representative episodes of Cooper's novel is often inaccurate and unfair, however, though Mark Twain wrote with such assurance and wit that many readers have found it difficult to take Cooper seriously thereafter. The essay appeared in *The North American Review* in July 1895. Fifty years later Bernard DeVoto published Mark Twain's sequel, "Cooper's Prose Style," which is less funny, and identified the two as being, according to the manuscript, by "Mark Twain, M.A., Professor of Belles Lettres in the Veterinary College of Arizona." (Clemens had received an honorary M.A. from Yale in 1888.) This second essay begins as an appreciation, though the professor soon finds a few blemishes. One, of course, is his longtime target, Cooper's Indians. Here he argues, "A Cooper Indian who has been washed is a poor thing, and commonplace; it is the Cooper Indian in his paint that thrills. Cooper's extra words are Cooper's paint—his paint, his feathers, his tomahawk, his warhoop."[32]

Two other essays are slight. "Traveling with a Reformer" was derived from trips Clemens had made to Chicago with Osgood in 1882 and with Fred J. Hall more recently to investigate the typesetter, again. Having discussed petty irritations that afflicted travelers, the author imagined, vividly, how they might be eliminated by a reformer with a talent for invention. The piece appeared in the *Cosmopolitan* in December 1893. "Mental Telegraphy Again" appeared in *Harper's* in September 1895. Since these publications are on topics very far from Mark Twain's literary competence, they suggest that his need for money from journalism and the increasing breadth of his interests were leading him to a role he would play with satisfaction, that of the sage, the wise old man.

After his long stay in the United States in 1893–94, Clemens joined his family in Paris. They summered in the south of France and later at Étretat in Normandy. Though the author made another trip across the water that summer (he was gone for six weeks), he managed to do a little writing, some of it on shipboard, during what had formerly been his writing season. Besides work on a major novel that he had begun early in 1893—of which more shortly—Mark Twain wrote "What Paul Bourget Thinks of Us," published in the *North American Review* in January 1895. The essay began as a means of putting some "odd time" to use, with the author "laughing," enjoying himself. He wrote three "malicious chapters" but was not satisfied, as he reported to Rogers in October 1894. He kept focused on the matter for three weeks before mailing the essay off. When Paul Blouet (under his pen name of Max O'Rell) attacked the essay, also in the pages of the *Review*, Mark Twain wrote "A Little Note to M. Paul Bourget," for he supposed, mistakenly, that Bourget had replied through Blouet. Neither of these essays is important. Bourget's *Outre Mer*, a journal that he had kept during a visit to the United States, had been critical of America, though hardly as severe as Mark Twain had been on several European countries in *The Innocents Abroad* or on France in pages he had written for *A Tramp Abroad*. Nevertheless, Mark Twain was offended by Bourget. While writing a novel set in France about one of its national heroes, he attacked the French, who supposed they understood the "American soul."

> There is only one expert who is qualified to examine the souls and the life of a people and make a valuable report—the native novelist. This expert is so rare that the most populous country can never have fifteen conspicuously and confessedly competent ones in stock at one time. This native specialist is not qualified to begin work until he has been absorbing during twenty-five years. How much of this competency is derived from conscious "observation"? The amount is so slight that it counts for next to nothing in the equipment. Almost the whole capital for the novelist is the slow accumulation of *unconscious* observation—absorption. . . . [The native novelist] lays plainly before you the ways and speech and life of a few people grouped in a certain place—his own place—and that is one book. . . .
>
> And when a thousand able novels have been written, *there* you have

the soul of the people, the life of the people, the speech of the people, and not anywhere else can they be had.

Seldom had Mark Twain been so pretentious.

The "native novelist" had long been fascinated by a figure from Bourget's homeland, Joan of Arc. According to his later account, as a boy in Hannibal, Clemens had picked up in the street a single leaf from a biography; it dealt with Joan in prison, insulted and mistreated.[33] This chance event began a lifelong interest. In the early 1880s he had someone compile a reading list, and by the time he reached Europe in 1891 he had read with care some accounts of France's saintly liberator, such as Janet Tuckey's romantic and popular *Joan of Arc*. Soon he made preliminary plans for a book. A notebook entry of September 1891 reads, "Chatto send me—Joan of Arc books/Sieur de Joinville's Louis IX," and one written later that fall reads, "Only one Burgundian in Domremy [Joan's village]. She would have liked to have him beheaded 'if it would please God.'"[34] Mark Twain's interest in Joan was not unusual, for in his time she was the subject of a cult in France, Germany, and England, as well as America. Susy Clemens and her mother had read Schiller's *Jungfrau von Orleans* in 1885; both were delighted. In the midst of a period devoted to potboilers, the book on Joan was Mark Twain's one serious effort to create literature.

The book was begun in Italy, three miles from Florence in the Villa Viviani, on August 1, 1892, after the completion of *Pudd'nhead Wilson* but before the Caesarean operation. Paine suggests that the ancient villa was an influence on the composition; at any rate the family lived there happily for nine months.[35] At first Mark Twain described the book—as he had the *Yankee*—as "private & not for print." It was "written for love, & not lucre, & to entertain the family with, around the lamp by the fire (the day's chapter of the tale, the day's product of 'work' as this sort of literary daydreaming has been miscalled)."[36] He thought of the book, for good reason, as "a companion to the Prince and the Pauper."[37] He wrote at first very rapidly and found himself well along by early February. Then he was quite ready to see the book published, but only "in handsome style, with many illustrations." At this point, thinking more about the dignity of his craft than of money, he supposed that his work would appear only as a book; he was not interested in magazine serialization.

Interruption came in March, when Clemens returned to America.

By that time he had reached the raising of the seige of Orleans in book 1, chapter 22, and he was not sure whether he would continue the story beyond that point.[38] A year later he still had written no more, though he then expressed great eagerness to "get to work at that book once more."[39] But much of the summer of 1894 Clemens spent in America. On the way there he was able to revise what he had written and make "some good corrections & reductions."[40] He seems to have judged he was finished, for soon he showed his manuscript to Henry M. Alden, editor of *Harper's Magazine*. But Alden left no doubt of his opinion. He commented, persuasively, "You have told the story of a success, and have abandoned it at the culminating point of the triumph. It is as if the story of the Saviour stopped with His entry into Jerusalem, amid the hosannas of the children."[41] Now recognizing that he had to continue his story, he was nonetheless interested in realizing some income from what he had written so far. He returned to the house of Harper, and after some delays managed to discuss with Harry Harper the possibility of publishing in his magazine what he had written—"the first part of Joan"—and reached an agreement on price. At this time the author was determined to publish the book anonymously; the agreement with Harper included a proviso that the price would go up substantially if the identity of the author became known and Mark Twain's name had to appear on the book.[42] Encouraged by this anticipation of income, Mark Twain returned to France and full-time work on the book. He told Olivia and Susy, "I shall never be accepted seriously over my own signature. People always want to laugh over what I write and are disappointed if they don't find a joke in it. This is to be a serious book. It means more to me than anything I have ever undertaken. I shall write it anonymously."[43]

The scope of the book continued to grow. As he told Henry Rogers—now a regular correspondent—in September, the author thought for a time that he would describe "Joan's childhood and military career alone." He was, he explained a week later to Rogers, trying to write the book "at my level best," with help from Olivia and Susy. Always taking satisfaction in his accomplishment, he made frequent reports to Rogers. The writing and the reading on which it was based were going on simultaneously in France throughout the fall of 1894, when the writer decided to tell the whole of Joan's dramatic story. The book became the longest of Mark Twain's novels, as long as his travel books, 125,000 words. When he reached Joan of Arc's death, he found himself exhausted. A few days later he wrote the remaining pages and finished on February 8, 1895, in Paris. Already the earlier chapters had been prepared for publication, which began in *Harper's* in March. There the publication was anonymous, as the author wished it to be. Soon, however, he instructed Harper to put his name on the story, in order to create publicity for an American lecture tour he was expecting to make (it was never to be), but then he found his wife vetoing the idea and had to cancel his instructions.[44] When the book was published in May 1896, Mark Twain's name appeared on both the spine and the cover but was missing from the title page, where the character who narrates the story is identified as the author. This arrangement did not please the real author, who wrote a rather confused letter to Harper in August in which he said that he wanted people to know that he was the author and that he deserved credit for the *writing*, whereas readers supposed that he was cashing in on another person's work. He wanted the title page to cite him as *author*, not editor.[45] Actually it was the English edition that cited the work as "Edited by Mark Twain."

Joan of Arc is not Mark Twain's book in the sense that *Huckleberry Finn* or *A Connecticut Yankee* is. For one thing, it is highly derivative. During the composition of the first two-thirds, the story of Joan's childhood and military leadership, Mark Twain made heavy use of Janet Tuckey's biography and Michelet's *Jeanne D'Arc*. He described this debt to Rogers: "I used for reference only one French history and one English one—and shoveled in as much fancy-work and invention on both sides of the historical road as I pleased." He wrote to Rogers in January 1895 that for the last third, the story of Joan's trial and death, he "constantly used five French sources and five English ones." These are the sources cited at the beginning of the book as "authorities examined in verification of the truthfulness of this narrative." Because of the author's reliance on his reading, *Joan* is best described as a fictionalized biography. It is, however, intended to be read as history insofar as the title page describes it as *Personal Recollections of Joan of Arc By The Sieur Louis de Conte (Her Page and Secretary) Freely Translated out of the Ancient French into Modern English from the Original Unpublished Manuscript in the National Archives of France by Jean François Alden.*

Sieur Louis de Conte, an actual historical personage, was selected as narrator, apparently, because he shared Clemens's initials. He writes from a position so close to Mark Twain's that the author could escape with little effort at characterization: an older man (he was eighty-two, Clemens sixty), he is Joan's ardent admirer. Since Mark Twain was now disillusioned with life, he was in a position to use more comfortably than ever the narrative technique he had employed successfully in *Roughing It* and "Old Times": emphasizing the difference between the person whose youthful experiences are being described and the mature veteran who is telling the story. A few touches suggest the difference, as when Conte describes his earlier self: "I was young and had not yet found out the littleness of the human race, which brags about itself so much, and thinks it is better and higher than the other animals" (part 2, chapter 27). But this distinction is seldom clear. Instead Mark Twain presents Conte as having simultaneously two attitudes, ones he himself shared: sentimentality and cynicism. Perhaps because he could indulge both attitudes, writing about this heroic young woman met the author's need. Cynical about mankind, seeing adulthood as a time of defeat, he still had something to hold dear, for to him youth continued to be appealing, and as the father of three daughters, he looked at young women, or more accurately girls, as symbols of purity such as he needed to believe in after the defeats he had recently experienced. Significantly, Mark Twain's Joan grows in beauty but experiences no sexual development. In his copy of Michelet he wrote, "The higher life absorbed her & suppressed her physical (sexual) development." [46]

Like the Yankee, Joan was a personage with power, but unlike that imagined character Joan influenced human history, as Mark Twain's narrator repeatedly observes. Joan's martyrdom serves the author's growing pessimism, as do the presence of many weaklings in the book. The one aspect of Joan's career that, predictably, gave the writer difficulty was her religious devotion and specifically her belief that she was guided by supernatural voices. As his *Yankee* shows, Mark Twain believed that the Catholic church was the greatest enemy to human freedom and progress. Even while reading for *Joan* he expressed his contempt for her religion. In the margin of the Countess de Charbannes's *La Vierge Lorraine, Jeanne d'Arc*, he commented that only her "base superstition could lift her to that fearless height." [47] But in his own book, he limited his skepticism severely; his interpretation of Joan is very close to that of his Catholic sources. One passage in which the narrator suggests reservations about Joan's voices was omitted from the manuscript:

> Privately, I myself never had a high opinion of Joan's Voices—I mean in some respects—but that they were devils I do not believe. I think they were saints, holy & pure & well meaning, but with the saint's natural incapacity for business. Whatever a saint is, he is not clever. There are acres of history to prove it. . . . The voices meant Joan nothing but good,

& I am sure they did the very best they could with their equipment; but I also feel sure that if they had let her alone her matters would sometimes have gone much better. Remember, these things I have been saying are privacies—let them go no further; for I have no more desire to be damned than another.[48]

The last sentiments sound exactly like the cautious Mark Twain, anxious lest his reputation be damaged by the revelation of his philosophy.

Joan of Arc was an unsuitable subject for Mark Twain's talents; few of the qualities that one looks for from a familiarity with his best work are here. What one misses most is his realistic point of view. Conte's unqualified admiration, even worship, of his heroine's perfection contrasts sharply with Huck's skepticism. Nonetheless, there are many evidences of Mark Twain's style, techniques, and interests. Sometimes a digression is required for the writer to indulge himself, as in Uncle Laxart's bull-ride story in chapter 37 of book 2, originally intended for *The Prince and the Pauper*. This story is rendered as repeated by Conte, unfortunately, for he does not understand why Joan found it hilariously funny; his rendering is in fact just what he calls it: "purely ridiculous." Scenes and characters just off the center of the stage, the fancywork that Mark Twain shoveled in, are drawn from the author's Western experiences. Of these the most important are the boastful but heroic Paladin, whom Mark Twain invented, and Joan's favorite general, La Hire. The Paladin's ability as a storyteller (he exaggerates more each time he repeats a story) reflects Mark Twain's continuing interest in the art of oral narrative. The figure that dominates the scene, the modest but confident Joan, is portrayed with more effectiveness than critics have usually been willing to grant, once the reader has passed some early mawkish sentimentality, especially that concerning the "fairy tree" of Joan's village. The trial scenes are potent melodrama, with Joan's goodness struggling against the archvillain Cauchon's deceitful malice. Joan talks too much in these scenes—the trial records that Mark Twain used are very full.

Besides her innocence and purity, Joan's work as liberator of France appealed strongly to Mark Twain because he was devoted to freedom, whether that of Huck on a raft or that of the prisoners released by the Yankee. So ignorant of the Middle Ages that he was unable to maintain even a pretense of a medieval point of view, he was deeply engaged by Joan's personality. Moreover, he was delighted to have as his protagonist a person whose innocence is not destroyed and whose dedication to liberty is powerfully sanctioned. Eventually Joan loses first her freedom, then her life, but she never loses her determination. Her story as Mark Twain tells it is not one of defeat but of qualified success. He believed that "Joan of Arc was not made as others are. Fidelity to principle, fidelity to truth, fidelity to her word, all these were in her bone and in her flesh—they were parts of her. She could not change, she could not cast them out. . . . Where she had taken her stand and planted her foot, there she would abide; hell itself could not move her from that place" (book 3, chapter 14).

In time Clemens looked back at *Joan* as his favorite book and his best, perhaps because he identified it with Susy, who liked it especially and who was a model for Joan; Susy had died soon after his book was published. In January 1902 Mark Twain wrote:

Susy at 17—Joan of Arc at 17. Secretly, I drew Joan's physical portrait from the Susy of that age, when I came to write that book. Apart from that, I had no formally-appointed model for Joan but her own historical self. [Yet there were several points of resemblance between the girls: such as vivacity, enthusiasm, precocious wisdom, wit, eloquence, penetration, nobility of character. In Joan the five latter qualities were of a measure that has not been paralleled in any person of like age in history; but I comprehended them in her all the better from comprehending them in their lesser measure in Susy.][49]

The bracketed part is deleted on this hitherto unpublished manuscript.

Surprisingly, *Joan* was well received in England. Andrew Lang described the book as "honest, spirited, and stirring." Sir Walter Besant found Mark Twain's Joan "more noble, more spiritual, of a loftier type than we could have conceived possible in the author of 'Huckleberry Finn.'" The London *Daily Chronicle* now found that Mark Twain was "far more than a mere man of letters . . . he is a great writer." The Glasgow *Herald* "doubted whether the Church's decree of beatification [of Joan] was as significant a compliment as is this tribute from the pen of Mark Twain."[50] The *Bookman* found *Joan* "much finer in texture than, we confess, we had expected from this writer."[51] Richard Le Gallienne reported that in *Joan* Mark Twain revealed "a great imagination" and "a great heart."[52] American reviewers, on the other hand, were unhappy. A review by William P. Trent entitled "Mark Twain as an Historical Novelist" found that Mark Twain had made his contribution elsewhere.[53] The historian James Westfall Thompson called *Joan* "a gorgeous failure."[54] Clemens's friend William Dean Howells was troubled chiefly when Mark Twain attempted "the supposed medieval thing." As an admirer of Mark Twain at his best, he found it "impossible for anyone who was not a prig to keep to the archaic attitude and parlance which the author attempts here and there." He provided an unusually apt comment, likely to be echoed by many readers, when he noted: "I wish he had frankly refused to attempt it at all. I wish his personal recollections of Joan could have been written by some Southwestern American, translated to Domremy by some mighty magic of imagination as launched the Connecticut Yankee into the streets of many-towered Camelot, but I make the most of the moments when Sieur Louis de Conte forgets himself into the sort of witness I could wish him to be."[55] In 1924, when George Bernard Shaw offered to the world his own *Saint Joan*, he complained in his preface that Mark Twain's theory of progress had obstructed his understanding of why Joan was burned and that his lack of appreciation of medieval churches and chivalry made him unqualified to deal with her epoch.

Just before Mark Twain finished *Joan of Arc*, he completed another work, a short novel or long story. During a business trip to America in April 1893 he began what he called "Tom Sawyer's Mystery."[56] But he had not yet located a mystery for Tom to solve. Nevertheless, he wrote several chapters that spring, for he was determined to take advantage of the interest in detective stories and in the possibilities of an exciting courtroom scene. During his career he wrote, or attempted to write, a number of stories that involve crime detection, or make fun of it: *Simon Wheeler, Detective*, "A Double-Barreled Detective Story," *Pudd'nhead Wilson*, and "The Chronicle of Young Satan." Courtroom dramas are features of several of these works, as well as *The Gilded Age* and *Joan of Arc*. An early idea for the plot of *Huckleberry Finn* may have included these elements.

While he was still looking for a plot, Mark Twain wrote some pages having to do with stolen diamonds; eventually he was able to make them part of Tom Sawyer's startling revelation in the courtroom. Then he found his plot. Late in 1894, Clemens attended a social gathering in Paris, where he met Lady Hegermann-Lindercrone, a Dane, who told him about a murder trial that had taken place in her country in the sixteenth century. The story had become well known because it serves as the basis of a novel, *The Minister of Veilby* (1824; English title), by Steen Steensen Bilcher. The writer seized on this story. He wrote Henry Rogers on January 2, a few days later, "I've got a first-rate subject for a book," and then decided instead to use the plot for the Tom Sawyer story he had already begun. He acknowledged his debt, somewhat inaccurately, with a footnote: "Strange as the incidents of this story are, they are not inventions, but facts—even to the public confession of the accused. I take them from an old-time Swedish criminal trial, change the actors, and transfer the scene to America. I have added some details, but only a couple of them are important ones." Because he did not know Bilcher's novel (not then available in English) and because the English edition of Mark Twain's story lacked this note, Danish writers have suggested from time to time that he was careless with his sources.

Once Mark Twain found his plot, he finished his 28,000–word story with haste; he was done by January 23, and sold it to Harper and Brothers. It was first published in *Harper's Magazine* in August and September 1896 and in the same year in a Harper collection, *Tom Sawyer Abroad, Tom Sawyer Detective, and Other Stories*. He was paid two thousand dollars for the serial rights, then royalties on the book. From the beginning, the story was conceived as a money-maker. It is the poorest of the stories of Huck and Tom. Jim is absent, and Huck serves simply as Tom's companion. Huck's narrative is personalized mainly by his unlimited respect for, almost adoration of, Tom, though at one point Huck justifies his own differences in outlook: "It was always nuts for Tom Sawyer—a mystery was. If you'd lay out a mystery and a pie before me and him, you wouldn't have to take your choice; it was a thing that would regulate itself. Because in my nature I have always run to pies, whilst in his nature he has always run to mystery. People are made different. And it is the best way" (chapter 2). Huck seems to have adopted some of his creator's determinism.

There is next to no pleasure to be derived from Huck's telling of the story, unless it is from his reference to the lawyer whose case Tom finally destroys as "the lawyer for the prostitution." (Olivia Clemens let that one through.) Yet not long before Mark Twain had written "How to Tell a Story" and in a letter of 1888 had expressed a belief that would seem to have been quite fitting in his situation as plot-borrower: "There is no merit in 99 stories out of a hundred except the merit put into them by the teller's *art*; as a rule, nothing about a story is 'original,' and entitled to be regarded as private property and valuable, except the art which the teller puts into the telling of it. . . . One should always begin a story by saying he got it from somebody else."[57] There is too little of the storyteller's art in *Tom Sawyer, Detective*. Painfully plot-ridden, the story itself is more complicatd than Mark Twain's source. The chief new ingredient is Jake Dunlap, who returns home after a seven-year absence. The discovery of his dead body before he is known to have arrived leads the community to believe that his identical twin, Jubiter, has been murdered by his employer, Tom's uncle Silas Phelps, who had appeared in *Huckleberry Finn*. Tom Sawyer establishes Silas's innocence at a sensational trial. In Mark Twain's source, the innocence of the minister is proven twenty-one years after he had been found guilty and executed by beheading, when the supposed victim returns and tells how he had been forced to leave town. Otherwise, resemblances are striking. For example, in both the villain disguises himself by wearing the minister's *green* gown; in both, the minister mistakenly admits his guilt. The story has a few Mark Twain touches, such as Jubiter disguising himself as a deaf-mute, like the Duke in *Huckleberry Finn*, and the confusion resulting from the introduction of identical twins.

The first four years of Clemens's long European exile saw him experiencing illness and bankruptcy, making a half-dozen trips back to the United States on business, and residing in houses, villas, hotels, and apartments in Switzerland, Germany, Italy, and France. The writer managed to produce a great deal, but nearly all of it is flawed (*Pudd'nhead Wilson* and *Tom Sawyer Abroad* being the most striking instances), or too remote from the native novelist's best abilities to be distinguished—*Joan of Arc* being the obvious case in point. Mark Twain's career had, however, been marked by similarly infertile periods in both the 1870s and 1880s; he had always written both badly and well, switching from *Huckleberry Finn* to "The 1002^d Arabian Night" at will. Whether he could return, at age sixty, to his former brilliance must have seemed to a close and sympathetic observer entirely possible. One threat, perhaps, was his developing pessimism. But as *Joan* had shown, he could still see the bright as well as the dark, and beneath the laughter of *Huckleberry Finn* there was already a dark strain in Mark Twain's imagination.[58]

CHAPTER NINE

Despair

ALL through 1894 Clemens had managed to persuade himself that he would somehow, despite the most obvious evidence, succeed in cashing in on his Paige typesetting investments so that he and his family could return to America and live there prosperously ever after. Only in December, just before Christmas, did his financial adviser Henry H. Rogers manage to break through his defenses and force him to face the truth. His reply to Rogers tells what had happened. "I *seemed* to be entirely expecting your letter, and also prepared and resigned; but Lord, it shows how little we know ourselves and how easily we can deceive ourselves. It hit me like a thunderclap. It knocked every rag of sense out of my head, and I went flying here and there and yonder, not knowing what I was doing, and only one clearly defined thought standing up visible out of the crazy storm drift—that my dream of ten years was in desperate peril." From this dream Clemens slowly awoke. The trauma heavily stamped itself on him, and from the experience, augmented by further disasters, he would repeatedly write, or attempt to write, a story of a man whose happy life was completely destroyed.

He was able to finish both *Tom Sawyer, Detective* and *Joan* before he thought of a way to make a dramatic change in his life. In early February he told Rogers that he was planning "to go around the world on a lecture trip . . . not for money but to get Mrs. Clemens and myself away from the phantoms and out of the nervous strain for a few months." A year before in New York, Mark Twain had done a reading with James Whitcomb Riley at $250 a night and with some success. After his recent financial defeats, he now needed some more successes. The tour was soon designed to produce income as well, for Clemens began to realize that *Pudd'nhead Wilson* would not provide him with the funds he expected. He wrote to Rogers in February, "Apparently I've got to mount the platform or starve; therefore I am examining the thing seriously." Just two weeks later he made a quick trip to New York to arrange for the tour. James Pond, who had directed his tour with Cable, was to be in charge of the American aspects; R. S. Smythe, an Australian agent, arranged for engagements in Hawaii, Australia, New Zealand, Ceylon, India, Mauritius, South Africa, and England. Several of these, however, were never to be.

In May the Clemens family returned to Quarry Farm for their first visit there since 1888. They seem to have viewed the upcoming tour as a symbolic act, a kind of campaign, not unlike Joan's. Jean and Susy Clemens stayed behind, in America; Clara accompanied her parents. The year-long trip began in July; by late August the travelers were crossing the Pacific. Unable to land in Hawaii because of a cholera epidemic, to his great disappointment, Mark Twain spoke first in Australia during five weeks in September and October, then five weeks in New Zealand, despite persistent troubles with a carbuncle. After additional readings in Australia, he went to sea again in January 1896. Two months were given over to India, though he was ill there for two weeks. All of May and June and half of July were devoted to South Africa readings and touring. By the end of July the Clemenses were settling in England, at Guildford in Surrey.

The trip was not a great financial success. Clemens cleared only about $30,000, with $5,000 of that coming from the American phase; expenses for the rest of the trip were high. In 1884–85 a fifteen-week tour with Cable had netted him $15,000. But other profit was anticipated: he had taken many notes and intended to begin work in England on another travel book. He would forego further lectures, in England, since he had presented himself well over a hundred times during the previous twelve months. Now Susy and Jean Clemens were expected to join the travelers in England, but when word reached them that Susy was ill, Olivia and Clara hurriedly returned to the United States—too late, for Susy died of meningitis on August 18. The Clemenses, who had been devoted to Susy (though she and her father had not been close in recent years), were deeply bereaved, and the writer's pessimism was strongly augmented.

Even before the news had arrived, Mark Twain had begun a description of how he viewed "Man's Place in the Animal World"; he completed it two months later. Here Mark Twain argues that man *descended* from the animals, not ascended from them. To man alone he ascribed revenge, indecency, vulgarity, obscenity, cruelty, slavery, patriotism, religion, and the Moral Sense. "Since the Moral Sense had but the one office, the one capacity—to enable man to do wrong—it is plainly without value to him. In fact it manifestly is a disease." The curse of the Moral Sense would be a theme of some of the author's best late fiction. Perhaps because of his recent illnesses, another theme of the essay is man's physical infirmities: "The mere names of the agents appointed to keep this shackly machine out of repair would hide him from sight if printed on his body in the smallest type of the founder's art." Only in his intelligence is man in any way superior to animals.

Perhaps because he had aired his grievances so fully in this essay, which he did not publish, Mark Twain was able to restrain himself while writing what he called for a time "Around the World," an account of his trip. The writing, undertaken while the Clemenses lived in the Chelsea district of London, was therapeutic, as the writer himself recognized. "I work all the days, and trouble vanishes away when I use that magic."[1] In time he became, he wrote to Howells in February, indifferent—"Indifferent to nearly everything but work; I like that; I enjoy it; I stick to it." He began the new book on October 24, 1896. Just as he had in writing *Life on the Mississippi*, in 1882, he made heavy use of published authorities in composing his account of the trip, about fifty in all. (Some passages that borrowed from his sources were trimmed, especialy from the English version of the book.) Although many of these citations seem like padding, Mark Twain could justify them on the grounds that he was dealing with remote areas, concerning which he was no expert. He intended to balance his subjective comments with other writers' more objective ones.

As usual, he changed his plans several times. The first five chapters, describing the American phase of the tour, were later dropped, though a few pieces, such as "A Delicately Improper Tale," were salvaged. At one time he planned to write about only the first half of the tour, leaving India and Africa for a sequel. Then he decided he would "end with India—there will be room for nothing more. At a later date I can make a book about South Africa if there is material enough in that rather uninteresting country to make the job worthwhile."[2] By March 28 the book appeared to be about ready for revision; Mrs. Clemens was then giving the manuscript a second reading, and by April 13 he judged the work was finished. Then he announced, "I have changed my plans & am extending the book to take in South

Africa—a big addition to the job, I can tell you, after I supposed I was done."[3] He finally finished, for the second time, on May 18. He had felt obliged to write, as he had told Rogers in January 1897, "7 days in the week, 31 in the month." The author noted that this book was the only one "I have ever confined myself to from title page to Finis without relief of shifting to another work meantime."[4] Chapters of the book appeared in November 1897 in *McClure's Magazine*, the publication being arranged by the author's publisher (the American Publishing Company!), but without his permission.

The title of the new book created some difficulty. The author considered "Imitating the Equator," "Another Innocent Abroad," "The Latest Innocent Abroad," and "The Surviving Innocent Abroad," suggesting that the book was a belated sequel to his first. Finally the book had two titles. In England it was *More Tramps Abroad*, in America *Following the Equator*. Although on this occasion, as with *Tom Sawyer Abroad*, the English text is far better, Mark Twain wrote the book as an American subscription book. He aimed to make it quite as good as the *Innocents*, and he wrote to Rogers to ask for the number of words in *Roughing It*, since he wished to make the new book of the same length; actually it is longer, despite the publisher's trimming. In arguing for publication through subscription sales, Mark Twain noted that whereas most readers had been saturated with travel books, he would be able to appeal to factory hands and farmers who never visit a bookstore.[5]

Following the Equator is the most elegant of Mark Twain's books, with an elephant in color on the cover and over two hundred illustrations, many of them full-page photographs, with "plate" paper used throughout to display them properly. But Frank Bliss, Elisha's son and now head of the American Pulbishing Company, pruned severely and arbitrarily. He cut off the ends of chapters and trimmed anti-British remarks and much that he found boring. In appearance *More Tramps Abroad* is much more ordinary, but Chatto and Windus made fewer cuts. Fortunately Mark Twain's manuscript survives, in the Berg Collection of the New York Public Library, and one can see what kinds of editing the book was given—by the author, his wife, and the two publishers.

In the first place, the author consciously revised his text with an eye to the image of himself that he wished to project. He wanted to portray himself as humble but clever, and physically vigorous (though he was not). On occasion, he deleted sardonic remarks, as when he wrote about an irritating woman he had met on a ship in New Zealand. Eventually he softened his feelings toward her, he explained, "softened them infinitely; & so, when by & by she started ashore & slipped & fell in the water, I saw her fished out without regret."[6] He dropped comments on his health problems and removed remarks that showed both bragging and self-pity. Two long sections written for the book were cut at an early point: "The Enchanted Sea-Wilderness," an incomplete narrative published in 1966 in the collection *Which Was the Dream?* and a short story, "Newhouse's Jew Story," published in 1972 in *Fables of Man*. After the author finished his editing, his wife took her turn. A full record of Olivia Clemens's responses survives. She acted mostly as a proofreader who wanted her husband to get his facts straight (she had been with him much of the time), but she also attempted to restrain her husband's irreverence. Van Wyck Brooks made much of her criticisms, some of which Paine had quoted in his biography, but in fact the author was by no means ready to accept her suggestions uncritically when it was his turn again to review the manuscript. Next the work went to the two publishers. What Bliss did was far more destructive than anything Olivia Clemens did; moreover, many of his changes were made at proof stage, without the author's approval. An unenthusiastic reader, Bliss marred the book by cuts that create incoherence. More than any of Mark Twain's books, this one needs a new edition that would restore passages that the author had no intention of deleting.

Compared with his earlier travel accounts, this last one is much less uneven, though it has no such glories as "Jim Baker's Blue Jay Yarn" of *A Tramp Abroad*. One passage does, however, echo Baker's comments on the jay. Of the Indian crow, which he labeled an "Indian sham Quaker," Mark Twain remarked that he is "just a rowdy, and is always noisy when awake—always chaffing, scolding, scoffing, laughing, ripping, and cursing, and carrying on about something or other. I never saw such a bird for delivering opinions. Nothing escapes him; he notices everything that happens, and brings out his opinion about it, particularly if it is a matter that is none of his business. And it is never a mild opinion but always violent—violent and profane—the presence of ladies does not affect him" (chapter 38, or part 2, chapter 2). Here Mark Twain sees in the bird an exaggerated version of his earlier, authentic self. This travel book, whatever it is to be called, has very little of the forced humor and burlesque that mars the account of Mark Twain's European adventures, and it has some beautiful purple prose, such as the famous description of an ice storm. The weakest pages are those written last. The author leaned heavily there on his notes, and even went so far as to place pages from his notebook directly into his manuscript.

Just as *Joan* was written to meet the author's need, so was this book. But now he was more desperate: he needed to believe he could live again after the loss of both his daughter Susy and his dreams of wealth. As he wrote, memories of India, its teeming life and its color, did much to comfort him: it was "the one sole country under the sun that is endowed with an imperishable interest for alien prince and alien peasant, for lettered and ignorant, wise and fool, rich and poor, bond and free, the one land that *all* men desire to see, and having seen once, by even a glimpse, would not give that glimpse for the shows of all the rest of the globe combined" (chapter 38; or part 2, chapter 2). Memories of India brightened his last years.

Clemens realized far more from the book than from his lectures. His American royalties were 12.5 percent, and he was given a ten-thousand-dollar advance. Published in November 1897, the book along with the tour and other income, permitted Rogers to pay off all Clemens's debts by the end of January 1898. The final payments were given wide publicity, and Mark Twain was considered a hero for his strenuous efforts. In both America and Great Britain the book sold well, with 28,500 copies sold in the first five months in the United States. Most American reviews were favorable; readers praised the author's poetic feelings as well as his humor. Some English reviews found the book padded, labored, and disappointing; others called it "a first-class book of travel," marked by "humor, good sense, good nature, shrewd observation."[7]

Henry Rogers had been attempting to stabilize the writer's finances by arranging for the publication of a "Uniform Edition" of Mark Twain's books. Harper's announced such an edition, and in 1896 the first five volumes appeared. Clemens was much pleased at the scheme because of both the prestige and the income it would provide, but the difficulties in creating a collected edition were great. The American Publishing Company owned the rights to the five books it had published and was now planning a rival edition of the author's works. This edition appeared in twenty-two volumes in 1898 and 1899, and six more volumes between 1899 and 1907; it is called the "Autograph Edition." Not until 1904 was Rogers able to negotiate an agreement by which Harper's took over all Mark Twain's copyrights (mostly held by Mrs. Clemens) and became his exclusive American publisher. The result was that the Clemenses were guaranteed an annual income of twenty-five thousand dollars.

Even though Mark Twain had managed with some success to make the account of his round-the-world tour a sunny book, the disasters he had experienced were beginning to have a powerful effect on his imagination. The narrative fragment he had written for the book toward the end of 1896, "The Enchanted Sea-Wilderness," is an indication of his mental state. It tells of a ship's being becalmed in a region between the South Pole and the Cape of Good Hope called the Devil's Race Track, eventually at its center, the Everlasting Sunday. The plight of the voyagers seems to have been Mark Twain's dramatization of his own situation—of his perception of his situation. He had written of Susy's death to old family friend, Joseph Twichell: "You have seen our whole voyage. You have seen us go to sea, a cloud of sail, and the flag at the peak, and you see us now, chartless, adrift—derelicts; battered, water-logged, our sails a ruck of rags, our pride gone. For it is gone. And there is nothing in its place. The vanity of life was all we had, and there is no vanity left in us."[8] The description matches that in the story, with the voyagers seeing only death around them. An early part of the "Sea-Wilderness" fragment is also analogous to Clemens's situation, as he felt it. An unusually intelligent dog, "just a darling," saves the crew of a ship by rousing the sleeping captain when the ship catches fire. The sailors flee the ship, with the captain insisting that the dog be left behind to die rather than being permitted to escape in the lifeboat.[9] The writer seems to have been describing his own sense of guilt in leaving Susy behind as he circled the globe; she had died, feverishly, in the Clemenses' Hartford home. The fragment was only one of a whole series of disaster stories that Mark Twain was to write over the next several years; he finished none.

Even before he had finished the book about his trip, Mark Twain was planning other stories and books, as his notebook indicates. He wrote to Rogers in January 1897, "I've got a new book in my head—3 or 4 of them, for that matter. . . . I shall write *ALL* of them, a whole dam library." The first of these he had intended to begin after finishing *Joan* in 1895, but illness and tour plans intervened. The plot idea was based on Clemens's own experience; he had had a dream that made him question the reality of his own life. "I dreamed I was born & grew up & was a pilot on the Mississippi, & a miner & journalist in Nevada, & a pilgrim in the Quaker City, & had a wife & children & went to live in a Villa out of Florence—& this dream goes on and *on*, & sometimes seems so real that I almost believe it *is* real. I wonder if it is? But there is no way to tell; for if one applies tests, *they* would be part of the dream, too, & so would simply aid the deceit. I wish I knew whether it is a dream or real." [10] As noted earlier, when the Paige machine had finally proved to be valueless, Clemens described himself as shocked at finding that his "ten-year dream" had dissolved, and when he visited his Hartford house while in America planning his world tour, he wrote to his wife that it "seemed as if I had burst out of a hellish dream & had never been away." [11] The death of Susy had augmented his sense that his happy life in Hartford had been only a dream. Afterward the Clemenses felt that they could never go back there, especially since Susy had died in their old home. In his autobiography Mark Twain described the death of Susy as analogous to the burning down of a man's house.

> The smoking wreckage represents only a ruined home that was dear through the years of use and pleasant associations. By and by, as the years go on, first he misses this, then that, then the essential thing. And when he casts about he finds that it was in that house. And always it is an *essential*—there was but one of its kind. It cannot be replaced. It was in that house. It is irrevocably lost. He did not realize that it was an essential when he had it; he only discovers it now when he finds himself balked, hampered, by its absence. It will be years before the tale of lost essentials is complete, and not till then can he truly know the magnitude of his disaster. [12]

These dream images and that of the house that burned appealed so powerfully to the author that they remained vivid in his consciousness.

On May 23, 1897, just five days after the story of the round-the-world trip was finished, Mark Twain began "Which Was the Dream?" Though inspired by his own disaster, the author draws on the experiences of his hero General Ulysses Grant, as described in some pages Mark Twain had written in 1885. The protagonist and narrator of the story, Major General X, is a successful politician who first experiences the loss of his house to fire, then bankruptcy when his wife's cousin swindles him. In the stress of the situation, the general loses consciousness, to awaken eighteen months later, in California, in poverty. An important character of the fragment is the general's daughter Bessie, who is modeled after Susy Clemens. In his autobiography, Mark Twain tells how when Susy was told as a child not to cry over little things, she questioned, "Mama, what is 'little things'?" [13] Bessie asks the same question. Other parallels abound. But Bessie, unlike Susy, survives the disaster: Mark Twain was *trying* to write fiction. Notes for the continuation of the story show that it involved the family's traveling toward Australia, into the Devil's Race Track of "The Enchanted Sea-Wilderness."[14] They also suggest that the story was to be a long and complicated one. What may not be clear from the surviving text is that after describing his own life and the charming ways of young Bessie—in a narrative written for her birthday—the general, falling asleep, *dreams* his disasters. Mark Twain had tried to suggest that the narrator was dreaming by adding a prefatory entry from the diary of the general's wife, in which she reports seeing him drowse while trying to write his narrative. This part, the beginning of the story, was added during the summer. Why Mark Twain abandoned the manuscript is not clear. Though the story is interesting, the section on Bessie is too long and mars the focus badly.

Still in mourning, Mark Twain agreed before he left England to write an account of Queen Victoria's jubilee for some American newspapers. June 22, 1897, was the day chosen to celebrate her sixty-year reign. His account is a pleasant piece of journalism, with a few humorous touches. Paine put it into the volume he called *Europe and Elsewhere*. Later, during the summer, the Clemenses moved back to the Continent, to Weggis in Switzerland. Returning to his old pattern, the writer devoted the summer to composition. On the anniversary of Susy's death her father wrote a poem, "In Memoriam Olivia Susan Clemens," later published in *Harper's Magazine*, and a statement (which he himself called "blaspheming") entitled "In My Bitterness." It was not published until 1973. Here he attacked the God who "gives you a wife and children you adore, only that through the spectacle of the wanton shame and miseries which He will inflect upon them He may tear the palpitating heart out of your breast and slap you in the face with it."[15]

After this outburst, it is comforting to find Mark Twain returning to his earlier humorous manner, if only briefly. In Switzerland he fictionalized slightly his own recent experiences—without reference to Susy—in England and on his way to Switzerland in "Letters to Satan." But he wrote only one letter, which Paine published in 1923. Without a follow-through, this piece simply indicates that Mark Twain could still do what he had done, under the proper conditions. A better indication is a nearly complete novelette of some thirty thousand words, "Tom Sawyer's Conspiracy." Notebook entries of 1896 and 1897 suggest plot ideas "For New Huck Finn," one of which was adopted: "Tom is disguised as a negro and sold in Ark[ansas] for $10, then he

& Huck help hunt for him after the disguise is removed."[16] Mark Twain wrote four chapters in Switzerland, then ran out of ideas. In these chapters, Tom plans the adventure, and he and Huck undertake the elaborate scheme. The setting once again is the author's hometown; St. Petersburg, Missouri, is vividly sketched, and an incident from the author's childhood is effectively introduced when Tom chooses to catch the measles, which turns out to be scarlet fever, by getting into bed with Joe Harper. Later the author found a way to go on with the story, and over the next several years he returned to it several times, as he had with *Huckleberry Finn*. Instead of Tom's invented "conspiracy," the boys contend with a murder, and Jim is the suspect. This development permits a dramatic courtroom scene, with Tom in a very difficult situation as his plans backfire and Jim seems likely to be found guilty. The Duke and the King appear briefly too, but within a few pages of the ending toward which the story is clearly headed, Mark Twain broke off, and by 1902 he was referring to "the discarded Conspiracy."[17] The story is nonetheless the best of the Huck Finn sequels, far better than *Tom Sawyer, Detective*, the author's most recent effort to resurrect Huck and Tom. "Tom Sawyer's Conspiracy," which ought to be better known, was first published in 1969.

Huck Finn's narrative style is almost up to that of the book that made him famous. The story begins with summer just coming on and Huck explaining, "Winter is plenty lovely enough if it *is* winter and the river is froze over and there's hail and sleet and bitter cold and booming storms and all that, but spring is no good—just rainy and slushy and sloppy and dismal and ornery and uncomfortable, and ought to be stopped. Tom Sawyer he says the same." Combining humor and suspense with unusual skill, the story creates vividly the pre–Civil War atmosphere of the border town whose citizens are deeply fearful of abolitionists. This time the narrator is telling his story after the war. He tells how Tom himself had invented plans for a civil war but gave them up, "and it was one of the brightest things to his credit. And he could a had it easy enough if he had sejested it, anybody can see it now. Harriet Beacher Stow and all of them other secondhanders gets all the credit of starting that war and you never hear Tom Sawyer mentioned in the histories ransack them how you will, and yet he was the first that thought of it. Yes, and years and years before ever they had the idea."[18] Less satisfying is Mark Twain's attitude toward detectives; he both glamorizes and satirizes detective work. He may have become more sympathetic from his recent reading of Conan Doyle stories of Sherlock Holmes, from which he derived some ideas. Readers of *Huckleberry Finn* may also be troubled by the degeneration of Jim; the explanation seems to be not that Mark Twain was less sympathetic with Afro-Americans but that he was more aware of the psychological effects of slavery.

Mark Twain's accomplishment in this fragment seems the greater because in another piece written about the same time, "Villagers of 1840–3," he looks at his fellow Hannibal townsfolk of his youth with what is mostly a cynical attitude. The sordid and seamy side of life in the village is emphasized in this remarkable catalog, with its commentary on 168 people. The manuscript, which is a document, not literature, may have been longer; it breaks off in the midst of a description of Orion Clemens, who died on December 11, 1897. Perhaps the author destroyed the pages that followed after he heard of his brother's death.

Two fictional fragments, begun in Switzerland in the summer of 1897, explore sexual identity. One also features Orion, here called Oscar and nicknamed "Thug" for his gentleness. The story begins by making much of Orion's short-lived religious enthusiasms, a trait that seemed to obsess Mark Twain: he returned to it often. Employing Dawson's Landing as a setting, with Pudd'nhead Wilson as a minor chorus character, the author found his attention drawn more and more to another, to whom he gave some Susy-like qualities. Her name was given to the story: "Hellfire" (properly Rachel) Hotchkiss, a tomboy. She and Thug have one thing in common: both are hampered by their "misplaced sexes." "Pudd'nhead Wilson says Hellfire Hotchkiss is the only genuwyne male man in town and Thug Carpenter's the only genuwyne female girl, if you leave out sex and just consider the business facts. . . ."[19] But neither this idea, which recalls the plot of "The 1002ᵈ Night," nor any other remains in focus. Oscar's mother, who is introduced at the beginning of the story in a long dialogue with his father, becomes a dominant figure before the story breaks off; she is based on Jane Lampton Clemens, the author's mother. Like "Which Was the Dream?" "Hellfire Hotchkiss" is marred by Mark Twain's obsessive memories of his family. The fragment was published in *Satires & Burlesques* (1967).

A thematically related piece begun during that same summer in Weggis is "Wapping Alice." Based on an incident of the Clemenses' household of 1877, when the author forced the lover of one of his housemaids to marry her, the story began as autobiography, though set in London. In an autumn revision, however, Mark Twain changed the name of the narrator from Clemens to Jackson and tried to publish it as fiction. He had made one significant change, a twist—which had never happened in Hartford. After the marriage has been performed, "Alice" is discovered to be a man, who had invented the romance as entertainment. The story is interesting chiefly because of its curious treatment, again, of sexual identity. The author's attitude toward this piece is both curious and amusing. After it had failed to find acceptance, he wrote to Rogers, "I perceive that a part of Alice needs re-writing—so *she* isn't publishable as she stands. She'll never get that re-writing. She should have applied when I was interested in her— and she didn't. I wash *my* hands of the business."[20] And so "Alice" remained unpublished until 1981. Another piece attempted in this busy summer was a historical novel based on the life of Wilhelmina, Mar-gravine of Bayreuth. Mark Twain drafted a chapter and pages of notes, then gave it up.[21]

The summer of 1897 was in retrospect an unsuccessful one—so the author thought when he wrote to Howells in August 1898. "I started 16 things wrong—3 books and 13 mag. articles—& could make only 2 little wee things, 1500 words altogether, succeed—only that out of piles & stacks of diligently-wrought MS., the labor of 6 weeks' unremitting effort." But he dismissed all of them as unimportant except one, "Which Was the Dream?" One of the completed pieces appears to be merely an obituary for a Hartford friend, J. Hammond Trumbull, who had provided learned chapter headings for *The Gilded Age*. Back in New York, Harper published a collection of Mark Twain's nonfiction, *How to Tell a Story and Other Essays*.

For several years Mark Twain had been interested in writing an auto-biography. Inspired by the example of Grant's dictating his memoirs in 1885, Mark Twain had dictated an account of his dealings with Grant during the same year, and in 1890 he wrote a brief account of his dealings with James W. Paige, the inventor of the typesetter. But he did not make a real beginning until the fall of 1897, when the Clemenses settled in Vienna for a stay that lasted over a year and a half. (In the summer of 1898 they resided at nearby Kaltenleutgeben.) In Vienna, Mark Twain wrote seven autobiographical pieces. One of them, "Early Days," is a triumph. Perhaps because of his recent fail-ures and disappointments, the writer sees his own past with a good deal of nostalgia, but he is never sentimental, never pauses too long over incidents or persons. Among the high spots are the sketch of James Lampton, the original of Colonel Sellers, and the description of the Quarles farm where he spent his boyhood summers before he went to work. His memories cause image after image to spill forth.

> I know the taste of the watermelon which has been honestly come by, and I know the taste of the watermelon that has been acquired by art. Both taste good, but the experienced know which tastes best. I know the look of green apples and peaches and pears on the trees, and I know how entertaining they are when they are inside a person. I know how ripe ones look when they are piled in pyramids under the trees, and how pretty they are and how vivid their colors. I know how a frozen apple looks, in a barrel down cellar in the wintertime, and how hard it is to bite, and how the frost makes the teeth ache, and yet how good it is, notwithstanding. I know the disposition of elderly people to select the specked apples for the children, and I once knew ways to beat the game.[22]

Later, when Mark Twain began to dictate his autobiography on a regular basis, he indulged himself by taking up whatever suited his fancy. In "Early Days," there are only brief digressions. It is the best of the autobiography. Despite its virtues, Mark Twain told Rogers in November that he would "never write the Autobiography" until he was "in a hole."

About the same time that he wrote the pages on his youth, Mark Twain began a story set in Huck's and Tom's St. Petersburg, but later, perhaps because he still had hopes for "Tom Sawyer's Conspiracy," he decided to add some variety to his fiction by changing the setting to the Austrian village of Eseldorf and the time from the 1840s to 1702. He called the new work "The Chronicle of Young Satan." This fragment forms the basis of the much-admired book that Albert Bigelow Paine and Frederick A. Duneka (of Harper and Brothers) edited and published in 1916 as *The Mysterious Stranger*. Since the composition took place over a period of years in 1897, 1898, 1899, and 1900, the work is discussed later in this chapter.

Now an admired celebrity, Mark Twain very much enjoyed his stay in Vienna. Finding the complicated politics of the Austro-Hungarian Empire fascinating, he wrote a long essay about his visits to the Austrian parliament, "Stirring Times in Austria," published in *Harper's* in August 1898. A remark in this essay prompted an inquirer to question his opinion of the Jews. In time he responded with another essay, "Concerning the Jews," also published in *Harper's*, in September 1899. The former is an excellent piece of topical journalism; in the latter

Mark Twain parades his good will but shows no real insight into anti-Semitism. He was, however, very proud of the essay and told Rogers in July 1898 that it was a "gem."

In January 1898, Mark Twain "resolved to stop book writing and go at something else." Once again he returned to play-writing and devoted months to several projects. He told Rogers in February that he was learning the play-writing trade "pretty fast" and would "stick to the business" until he found out whether or not he could succeed at it. He was less optimistic with Howells, to whom he had written a few days earlier: "I have made a change lately—into dramatic work—& I find it absorbingly entertaining. I don't know that I can write a play that will play; but no matter, I'll write half a dozen that won't anyway." The prediction was not much off the mark. He translated Ernst Gottke and Georg Engel's play *Bartel Turaser* and Philip Langmann's *Im Gegefeuer (In Purgatory)*. Both were soon rejected by New York theater men. He also dramatized his own short story, "Is He Dead?" Though not so bad as some of Mark Twain's plays, it too was rejected. The translations have not survived; "Is He Dead?" has not been published. Indeed, Mark Twain wrote to Rogers in August with instructions: "*Put 'Is He Dead' in the fire.* God will bless you. I too." The nature of Mark Twain's interest in the theater at this time is suggested by his essay "About Play Acting," written around this time and published in *Forum* magazine in October 1898. Here the would-be dramatist expresses his admiration for Adolf von Wilbrandt's very popular play *The Master of Palmyra*, in which a person discovers in several reincarnations that life has nothing to offer. Such serious drama greatly appealed to the aging Mark Twain, who was becoming more and more interested in philosophical literature, both as reader and as writer.

Also early in 1898, Mark Twain wrote a sketch and a short story inspired by Jan Szczepanik, a Polish inventor who had developed a precursor of television. Both "The Austrian Edison Keeping School Again" and "From the 'London Times' of 1904" were published in the *Century Magazine* in 1898; they are slight and merely show that the author retained his ability to produce what he could sell. A little of the author's outlook is suggested by the surprising, and unconvincing, ending of the "London Times" piece, which is bitter: an innocent man is executed. (The reader is expected to find an analogue to the Dreyfus Affair.) Later he tried a more serious piece of fiction, which he called "An Adventure in Remote Seas." The surviving fragment of just two chapters again deals with the area toward the South Pole that had fascinated him since his trip to Australia. The story has a theme—that nothing has value apart from use—and demonstrates it when a group of sailors discover, first, sixty million dollars' worth of gold coins, and second, that they have been left stranded with no way to escape. The author too found himself with nowhere to go and gave up the story.

In 1897 Mark Twain drafted a dialogue on "The Moral Sense." In the following year, between April and July, he gave serious attention to what he later called his "gospel": a dialogue between a young man and an old man on moral and ethical issues. Originally he called it "Selfishness" or "What Is the Real Character of Conscience?" Elaborated, edited, and reorganized over the next seven years, it was privately printed for the author in 1906 in 250 copies as *What Is Man?* with no indication of the author's identity. Some copies were distributed, but not until April 23, 1910, two days after Clemens's death, was the work given any public attention. Then the New York *Tribune* published excerpts in a feature article, and other periodicals, English and American, gave the piece further publicity. The first American trade edition was published in 1917 in *What Is Man? and Other Essays*. Thereafter it was included in editions of Mark Twain's works.

The dialogue and the care the author gave it show that he took himself seriously as a thinker, though he limited his concern to a few topics. In the 1906 edition the dialogue—of some thirty thousand words—is divided into six chapters. These discuss determinism, personal merit, human motivation, training, instinct, thought, and free will. Other portions, including a long one on God, were not included in the 1906 version but were finally published in 1973. Though a whole area of Mark Twain's developing intellectual interest—his tentative belief in the powers of the mind and even in an immortal self—is neglected, *What Is Man?* does usefully sum up ideas that Mark Twain had been developing, organizing, and occasionally expressing for twenty years or more. Even in the anonymous version of 1906, which appeared only after all traces of Mark Twain and Samuel Clemens had been removed, the author expressed fear of the "disapproval of the people" around him, as he explained in the preface.

The dialogue argues that man is a machine whose performance is determined by training. Man is "moved, directed, COMMANDED, by *exterior* influences—*solely.*" Everything he does is done in order to secure his own approval and that of his neighbors and the public.

Many examples are cited, including some drawn from a novel, Florence Wilkinson's *The Strength of the Hills*. The effect of outside influences in training is explored, with the old man offering, with much ado, a plan for man's betterment. "Diligently train your ideals *upward* and *still upward* toward a summit where you will find your chiefest pleasure in conduct which, while contenting you, will be sure to confer benefits upon your neighbor and the community" (chapter 4). There is of course no free will, and man has absolutely no reason to be proud. (The early versions of the dialogue stress this last argument.) But man can be happy, *if* he is born with a happy temperament. The work itself is not gloomy, and some of the examples cited are interesting.

The deterministic side of Mark Twain found in *What Is Man?* has often been ascribed to his need not to be held responsible for his failures. But his reading over many years seems like a far more important source, especially his favorite Lecky's *History of European Morals*, Darwin (whom he cites in the dialogue), and other recent scientists such as Huxley and William James. He had been heading toward determinism since the early 1880s, and in 1883 he discussed some of his ideas in a talk on "What Is Happiness?" before the Monday Evening Club of Hartford. Of little value as literature, even less as philosophy, *What Is Man?* offers to those interested in Mark Twain a careful statement of one side of his philosophy during his later years.

Much more personal than *What Is Man?* is the long poem, some fifty quatrains, that Mark Twain wrote in the same year, 1898; it is entitled "Omar's Old Age" and echoes a work that the author had read as early as 1876, the "Rubáiyát" of Omar Khayyám. Only portions survive, some of which were published in 1966. The poem deals with the enfeeblements of old age and complains of the effectiveness of germs and the failure of both control over bodily functions and sexual ability. One stanza declares, "Behold! The Penis mightier than the sword!" The "poet" went so far as to urge his English publisher to make a book of the verses, a limited edition, with the aim of making money. Not surprisingly, Andrew Chatto opposed the idea. In all Mark Twain wrote over 120 poems in his lifetime. Of those identified, ninety-five are comic, thirty-one are serious. A thin volume of the more interesting ones was published as *On the Poetry of Mark Twain*.

Another highly personal statement is "My Platonic Sweetheart," written in late July 1898 and rejected by three periodicals. It was published only after the author's death, in an abbreviated version edited by Paine. Originally entitled "My Lost Sweetheart," this autobiographical piece tells of the author's recurring dream of his childhood sweetheart (actually Laura M. Wright). He dreamed of being with her in a Missouri village, then in a magnolia forest in Natchez, in an Hawaiian valley, in Athens, in India. Always he is seventeen, she fifteen. The experiences are so powerful that they persuade the writer that dreams are true and the dreamers immortal. The more interesting part of the sketch does not appear in the published version. This part is a revision of a passage recorded in the author's notebook, dated January 7, 1898, while he was still in London. (Paine published this original version, misdated, in 1935, when he edited selections from Mark Twain's notebooks.) Here the writer describes his continuing interest in "the duality idea," which he had taken up many years before in "The Carnival of Crime in Connecticut." He tells how from a conversation with his conscience he had learned "he was not *me*, nor a part of me, but merely resided in me." Then the author was further enlightened, first by Robert Louis Stevenson's *Dr. Jekyll and Mr. Hyde,* then by French experiments with hypnosis and the work of William James. He concluded that he consists of a "waking self," a "somnambulic self," and a "dream self." This last self especially interested Mark Twain. He is a

> spiritualized self who nightly or daily, at home or church or wherever the chance offers, takes a holiday for a couple of seconds and goes larking about the world for hours during those seconds, has adventures, sees wonderful things, makes love, falls over precipices, gets lost in mazes, is pursued by shrouded corpses and other horrors and cannot make headway for fright, gets mixed up in quarrels while doing his best to avoid them, enlists for the war and retreats from the field in front of the first volley, gets run away with by scared horses, tries to deliver lectures without any subject, appears in crowded drawing rooms with nothing on but a shirt; in a word, does a thousand rash and foolish things which nothing could ever persuade my workaday "me" to do—then comes back home and remembers it all, re-sees it all, with a memory for form, color and detail compared to which mine is as blank paper to a printed book, and I get up in the morning and innocently tell the family what *I* have been seeing and doing! I—who can't shut my eyes this minute and reproduce the family's faces nor any but a vague single detail of the woodsy picture which is stretched before me in front of this window![23]

This idea of the three selves would soon form the basis of a long, uncompleted novel, "No. 44, The Mysterious Stranger."

That "My Platonic Sweetheart" was written so soon after the first draft of *What Is Man?* shows clearly that Mark Twain's deterministic philosophy and his bitter pessimism and misanthropy were to some extent counterbalanced by his delighted fascination with the mysteries of identity and multiple personality and even by a readiness to believe in an immortal self. (Other evidence, explored below, supports this notion.) The cheerfulness of "My Platonic Sweetheart" even includes a joke the author calls "much the best I ever made in a dream." He found himself in his dream to be the seven-year-old son of a fashionably dressed couple in Paris—Adam and Eve. He was an impertinent child, calling his father "Ad." "Eve was shocked at my abbreviating my father's name in that irreverent way, and told me to say it again and put on the rest of it. I refused, and said 'Ad' again. She told me to get under the table and stay there until I was willing to obey that order. I was under the table a while, then I had an idea, and crawled out and stood by her knee and said—'Dam!'"[24]

In August 1898, Mark Twain recorded in his notebook: "Last night dreamed of a whaling cruise in a drop of water. Not by microscope, but *actually*. This would mean a reduction of the participants to a minuteness which would make them nearly invisible to God, & he wouldn't be interested in them any longer."[25] The dream led him to try another version of the dream-disaster story. This time he thought he had found a good plan, which he said was to make the first half or two-thirds comedy. He now wrote to Howells, "I think I can carry the reader a long way before he suspects I am laying a tragedy-trap." The new story was called by DeVoto, who edited it for publication, "The Great Dark." In it the narrator, Mr. Edwards, and his family have been examining a drop of polluted water under a microscope, when Edwards takes a nap. Before he falls asleep, he discusses with the "Superintendent of Dreams" his wish to explore the world of a drop of water with his family in a comfortable ship. Soon his wish is realized: he finds himself on an eerie, frightening, nightmare-like voyage, in perpetual night. There are some light touches, but whatever the author intended, the mood is by no means comic. The superintendent is along, but when he and Edwards have a small falling-out, the latter tells him that he can end the dream if he wants—to which the superintendent replies: "The dream? *Are you sure it is a dream?*" and he continues, "You have spent your whole life in this ship. And this is *real* life. Your other life was the dream!"[26] Soon Edwards realizes that his wife and family know no other life than the one on shipboard and have no memories to correspond with his, except memories of dreams. "And now another past began to rise, dim and spiritual before me and stretch down and down and down into dreaming remoteness of by-gone years—a past spent in a ship!"[27] The dream comes to suggest the horror that lurks within the human psyche, below consciousness. The discussion of the difference between dreams and reality is decidedly engaging. (In a related fragment Mark Twain explains how in one of the countries of "Dreamland" there are "no exact equivalents for our words *modesty, immodesty, decency, indecency, right, wrong, sin.*"[28])

Soon the narrator and the reader are plunged deeper into nightmare as the ship is attacked by a giant squid. Though blinded, the creature remains threateningly nearby. Mutiny adds to the terror, even after the ship's captain, based on Mark Twain's old hero Ned Wakeman, is able to put it down. (For some of these events the author drew on the materials of the article he was writing at the time, "My Debut as a Literary Person," on the *Hornet* disaster at sea.) At this point, unfortunately, the writer interrupted the story. Notes suggest how he might have continued, with horror piled on horror: the crew going crazy, the narrator's son and the captain's daughter being taken to another ship, the seas drying up. Finally the narrator "Looks up—is at home—his wife & the children coming to say goodnight. His hair is white."[29] Despite some burlesque elements and a story about a seaman who takes the temperance pledge, the dominant mood of this 35,000-word fragment is black; it is the best of the dream–disaster story attempts.

Another product of the summer of 1898 is entirely different—different in atmosphere and theme, different in that it was completed, published (in *Harper's*, December 1899), and proved profitable. Mark Twain made two thousand dollars. "The Man That Corrupted Hadleyburg" is his most effectively plotted story, highly economical and suspenseful, rich in implications. What strikes most readers is the pessimism of its biting satire: all nineteen of the town's leading citizens are corrupted by greed as the result of a hoax. Part of the reason for their failing is that "through the formative years temptations were kept out of the way of young people"; consequently, at the end of the story the inhabitants of Hadleyburg change the town motto by dropping the word *not*: "Lead us into temptation." But the story is not consistently deterministic. Instead, a presupposition of freedom, albeit of a somewhat limited version, is the basis of the plot. The story focuses, almost clinically, on the mental processes of the two main characters, Mary and Edward Richards, who rationalize themselves into dishonesty, even by arguing for determinism. Richards declares that their action "was ordered. *All* things are ordered." The moral degeneration of the Richardses leads them first to fear of humiliating exposure, then to delirium; even their confession and misdirected self-righteousness are damning. They are not villains in a conventional sense, but they are thoroughly reprehensible. Unlike *What Is Man?* "Hadleyburg" implies man's responsibility for his actions.

The central scene of the story is the kind Mark Twain liked best to create: a public meeting, with a large crowd gathered; unfolding, sensational revelations that excite the audience and lead it to act like a single person, even joining to sing improvised verses to a Gilbert and Sullivan tune. It surpasses all the courtroom scenes that so often provide a climax in Mark Twain's stories. In it, as well as in the private episodes intimately focused on the Richardses, what Mark Twain emphasizes most is embarrassment, a profoundly painful experience that he treats with special skill and understanding here—as well as earlier, in *Roughing It*, "Old Times on the Mississippi," and *Huckleberry Finn*.

The year 1898 was truly a strange one in Mark Twain's career. A play, translations, serious and commercial fiction, philosophy, and autobiography are among the forms that his writing took. He even took advantage of his summer experience "At the Appetite Cure" to write, and publish, a piece on the subject; it is ordinary journalism. Perhaps the most unlikely of his writings was the piece he began writing after completing "Hadleyburg" and continued to work on until the following spring. When published in the *Cosmopolitan Magazine* in October, the piece was entitled "Christian Science and the Book of Mrs. Eddy." At the time Christian Science was a highly controversial, much discussed topic, one suitable for journalistic exploitation. Moreover, Mark Twain had long been interested in the subject of mental healing. That his daughter Susy had been a devotee was a source of his interest; Clemens had written to her during his world tour, "I am perfectly certain that the exasperating colds and carbuncles came from a diseased mind, and that your mental science could drive them away, if we only had you here to apply it." [30] But admiration of the principle, which he called "Humanity's boon," was not the same, he told a correspondent, as admiration for the founder of Christian Science, Mary Baker Eddy, whom he called in 1903 "the monumental sarcasm of the Ages." He continued, "It seems to me that when we contemplate her & what she has achieved, it is blasphemy to longer deny the Supreme Being the possession of a sense of humor." To Mark Twain she was "the queen of frauds and hypocrites." [31] His interest in both Mrs. Eddy and Christian Science was to continue; the first piece he wrote became, somewhat revised, chapters 1–4 of book 1 of Mark Twain's book, *Christian Science*. (The revised text is quoted below.)

The specific occasion for the composition of "Christian Science and the Book of Mrs. Eddy" was the author's experience with an American practitioner of Christian Science in Austria in the summer of 1898, when he had a bad fall. In the sketch Mark Twain returns to one of his most attractive roles, that of victim, as he tries to contend first with the resolute woman who lectures him on metaphysics, then with a horse doctor whom he calls in when he finds his recovery slow. In his conversation with Mrs. Fuller, the practitioner, Mark Twain is eager to submit and be rid of his pains, which he has been informed are unreal.

> "I am full of imaginary tortures," I said, "but I do not think I could be any more uncomfortable if they were real ones. What must I do to get rid of them?"
> "There is no occasion to get rid of them, since they do not exist. They are illusions propagated by matter, and matter has no existence; there is no such thing as matter."
> "It sounds right and clear, but yet it seems in a degree elusive; it seems to slip through, just when you think you are getting a grip on it." (Chapter 2)

On her departure Mrs. Fuller leaves behind a copy of Mrs. Eddy's *Science and Health*, a book that Mark Twain finds more amusing than Fenimore Cooper's *Deerslayer*. His experiences as a reader are vividly described. "When you read it you seem to be listening to a lively and aggressive and oracular speech delivered in an unknown tongue, a speech whose spirit you get but not the particulars; or, to change the figure, you seem to be listening to a vigorous instrument which is making a noise which it thinks is a tune, but which, to persons not members of the band, is only the martial tooting of a trombone, and merely stirs the soul through the noise, but does not convey a meaning" (chapter 3). This wholly successful, richly varied essay was well received; Twichell wrote to his friend, "Some judge it the best you ever did."[32] The editor of the *Cosmopolitan* was so pleased with the attention that the essay received that he increased his payment by two hundred dollars, to one thousand dollars. Much less good are some pages on Christian Science also written in 1899 but not published in America for several years; they did appear, however, in England and Germany in 1900 in *The Man That Corrupted Hadleyburg and Other Stories and Sketches*.

In November 1898 Mark Twain recorded a long note for a story. It begins: "Story of little Satan, jr., who came to [Petersburg Hannibal] went to school, was popular and greatly liked by [Huck and Tom] who knew his secret. The others were jealous, and the girls didn't like him because he smelt of brimstone."[33] (The bracketed words were deleted.) The story fragment of sixteen thousand words entitled "Schoolhouse Hill" combines the world of Huck and Tom with another portrait of Orion Clemens, here Oliver Hotchkiss, along with a charming portrait of the miracle-working, amoral Number Forty-four, the son of Satan. Because his father erroneously tempted Adam and Eve and thereby "*poisoned* the men of this planet—poisoned them in mind and body,"[34] Number Forty-four aims to improve man's lot. The author intended to subvert this plan, ironically, by converting him to Christianity. According to the very full notes, he was to fall in love with Hotchkiss's niece Annie Fleming, who is a version of Hellfire Hotchkiss, heroine of an earlier fragment.[35] Despite its lack of focus, "Schoolhouse Hill" is a fascinating return to St. Petersburg, Mark Twain's last, since a final account does not survive.

The writer's interest in Satan was long-standing. His mother, he recounts, prayed for Satan, who she felt was especially in need of such help.[36] According to the late essay "Is Shakespeare Dead?" Clemens's own interest originated during his school days, when he planned to write Satan's biography "and was grieved to find that there were no materials." In "Concerning the Jews," written in the summer of 1898, the author had written, "Of course Satan has some kind of case, it goes without saying. . . . As soon as I can get at the facts I will undertake his rehabilitation myself, if I can find an unpolitic publisher." One source of this interest and sympathy was that Satan was both an underdog and a rebel against the God that Mark Twain was more and more considering his personal enemy. And he had at least begun "Letters to Satan" in 1897.

In May 1899, Mark Twain returned to "The Chronicle of Young Satan," mentioned earlier. He had abandoned it in early 1898 because he thought he had not started it right. But now he believed he had found the way to do what he intended, and he was so happy that he called his writing "an intellectual drunk." What he was up to, he told Howells in a very important revelation, was crucial to his career.

> For several years I have been intending to stop writing for print as soon as I could afford it. At last I can afford it, & have put the pot-boiler pen away. What I have been wanting was a chance to write a book without reservations—a book which should take account of no one's feelings, no one's prejudices, opinions, beliefs, hopes, illusions, delusions; a book which should say my say, right out of my heart, in the plainest language &

without limitations of any sort. I judged that that would be an unimaginable luxury, heaven on earth. There was no condition but one under which the writing of such a book could be possible; only one—the consciousness that it would not see print.

At last he was writing it.

> It is in tale-form. I believe I can make it tell what I think of Man, & how he is constructed, & what a shabby poor ridiculous thing he is, & how mistaken he is in his estimate of his character & powers & qualities & his place among the animals.*

Mrs. Clemens, he reported, found the tale "perfectly horrible—and perfectly beautiful."

When he returned to his manuscript of the previous year just before writing to Howells, he discovered that in "The Chronicle of Young Satan" he had telescoped the story by coming too soon to the trial scene that serves as a climax. He therefore began to insert new philosophic materials between two blocks that he had already written: what are now chapters 1, 2, and the beginning of 3, and the trial scene that would become part of chapter 10. These he wrote mostly in London, where the Clemenses moved in May, and in Sanna, Sweden, where Jean Clemens was treated for epilepsy during the summer. At that time he wrote the rest of chapter 3, then 4, 5, and the early part of chapter 6. All the rest that he finished—chapters 6, 7, 8, 9, and part of 10 and what was written of chapter 11, were composed between June and August of 1900, outside London at Dollis Hill.

The germ of this story is a notebook entry made at the end of June 1897: "Satan's boyhood—going around with other boys & surprising them with devilish miracles."[37] As he developed the story, the author suggested that this young Satan is a dream such as those he had described in "My Platonic Sweetheart": Satan gives himself the name of Philip Traum (dream). Mark Twain's reading of a book on psychic phenomena, *Phantasms of the Living*, may have contributed to

---

*Mark Twain may have been referring to this desire to write a book right out of his heart in a notebook entry made on his world tour, in late 1895: "It is the strangest thing that the world is not full of books that scoff at the pitiful world, and the whole human race—books that laugh at the whole paltry scheme and deride it. Curious, for millions of men die every year with these feelings in their hearts. Why don't *I* write such a book? Because I have a family. There is no other reason. Was this other people's reason?" (*MTN*, p. 256)

the story; the book deals with materialization, dematerialization, and dream experiences. Almost like a wish fulfillment, Satan is introduced into Mark Twain's story the day after the boys to whom he appears have heard an old man's tale of "actual angels out of heaven" who "have no wings, and wore clothes, and talked and looked and acted like any natural person." The boys have "stretched out on the grass in the shade to rest . . . and talk over strange things" when an unfamiliar boy appears, to their great pleasure, in chapter 2.

Even as a fragment, "The Chronicle of Young Satan" is a masterpiece, horrible *and* beautiful, as Olivia Clemens said. In forty-five thousand words Mark Twain creates a world of both fantasy and reality, with a transcendent hero, Young Satan, nephew of the famous one. He resembles the boy Jesus of the apocryphal gospels, with which the writer had long been familiar. In 1867 he had quoted a description: "Jesus and other boys play together and make clay figures of animals. Jesus causes them to walk; also clay birds which he causes to fly, and eat and drink. The children's parents are alarmed and take Jesus for a sorcerer."[38] Mark Twain's narrator, Theodor Fischer, looks back at his youth from the vantage point of maturity, the same technique that the author had used successfully in the 1870s, but ineffectively, in *Joan of Arc*. One sign here of the narrator's double point of view is that he remembers his own identification with his community, Eseldorf (Donkeyville), which was and has presumably remained naive and deluded. The story begins with this emphasis:

> It was 1702—May. Austria was far away from the world, and asleep; it was still the Middle Ages in Austria, and promised to remain so forever. Some even set it away back centuries after centuries and said that by the mental and spiritual clock it was still the Age of Faith in Austria. But they meant it as a compliment, not a slur, and it was so taken, and we were all proud of it. I remember it well, although I was only a boy; and I remember, too, the pleasure it gave me.[39]

Theodor remembers his boyhood identification with Catholicism, ignorant Catholicism. He and his friends "were trained to be good Catholics; to revere the Virgin, the Church and the saints above everything. . . . Beyond these matters we were not required to know much; and in fact not allowed to. The priests said that knowledge was not good for the common people." The "Chronicle" is a *bildungsroman*, the story of Theodor's initiation and education at the hands of Mark Twain's spokesman, who disguises himself as the boy Philip Traum. The backdrop of plot serves as an unobtrusive structure and helps Satan teach important lessons about what life offers. Satan educates Theodor by sharing with him the truth about the Moral Sense, the fact that man is not free, and the impossibility of human happiness. He teaches skillfully, far better than the Old Man of *What Is Man?* for nearly always he finds examples, or creates them, in the boys' lives. Many of these are charming and dreadful, as when Satan, like the apocryphal Jesus, makes miniature living creatures, then casually destroys them. The incidents that occur in Theodor's world, such as Nikolaus's death, are more effectively told than the later ones, when Mark Twain has Satan take Theodor far from home, to China, and when he provides a quick glance at history from Adam and Eve to the Inquisition. The reader is frequently reminded of Theodor's double perspective, as when he finds fault with Satan for depriving Father Peter of his reason: Satan "didn't seem to know any way to do a person a favor except by killing him or making a lunatic out of him. I apologized, as well as I could; but privately I did not think much of his processes. At that time" (chapter 10).

Mark Twain's exuberant joy in depicting spectacle and showmanship (demonstrated by Tom Sawyer, the Yankee, and Pudd'nhead Wilson) reaches its most effective use in the "Chronicle." Like the bored boys of Hannibal, roused by the arrival of a steamboat, the boys of Eseldorf are charmed by Satan's miracles as they learn from him and from them. No dull lessons here. Ironically, Satan's most effective revelation is that the seemingly youthful innocence of the boys is not what it appears to be, and that it is Satan, despite his name, who is unfallen, and not the boys, for they are the victims of the Moral Sense. Satan explains:

> No brute ever does a cruel thing—that is the monopoly of the snob with the Moral Sense. When a brute inflicts pain he does it innocently; it is not wrong; for him there is no such thing as wrong. And when he does not inflict pain for the pleasure of inflicting it—only man does that. Inspired by that mongrel Moral Sense of his! A Sense whose function is to distinguish between right and wrong, with liberty to choose which of them he will do. Now what advantage can he get out of that? He is always choosing, and in nine cases out of ten he prefers the wrong. There shouldn't *be* any wrong; and without the Moral Sense there *couldn't* be any. And yet he is such an unreasonable creature that he is not able to perceive that the Moral Sense degrades him to the bottom layer of animated beings and is a shameful possession. (Chapter 3)

Satan's own lack of grief and guilt—since he is not burdened with a moral sense—emphasizes the pathetic absurdity of man.

The creator of "The Chronicle of Young Satan" had written to Howells in April 1899 that "man is not to me the respect-worthy person he was before" and therefore he could not "write gaily nor praisefully about him any more." To which he added, "And I don't intend to try." But "Young Satan" is marked by much good humor and youthful vitality as well as pessimism and misanthropy. Above all, the story is almost magically imagined. Satan speaks in praise of the power the author has given him:

> I *think* a poem—music—the record of a game of chess—anything—and it is there. This is the immortal mind—nothing is beyond its reach. Nothing can obstruct my vision—the rocks are transparent to me, and darkness is daylight. I do not need to open a book; I take the whole of its contents into my mind at a single glance, through its cover; and in a million years I could not forget a single word of it, or its place in the volume. Nothing goes on in the skull of any man, bird, fish, insect or other creature which can be hidden from me. I pierce the learned man's brain with a single glance, and the treasures which cost him three-score years to accumulate are mine; he can forget, and he does forget, but I retain. (Chapter 6)

Perhaps the most memorable passage is Mark Twain's encomium of humor. He argues, through Satan, that mankind "has unquestionably one really effective weapon—laughter. Power, Money, Persuasion, Supplication, Persecution—these can lift at a colossal humbug,— push it a little—crowd it a little, century by century: but only Laughter can blow it to rags and atoms at a blast. Against the assault of laughter nothing can stand" (chapter 10). The author describes his technique of balancing off his celebration of humor and the imagination against his pessimistic philosophy when in the same chapter he has Theodor describe Satan's ways: "He liked to rough a person up, but he liked to smooth him down again just as well." The last episode that Mark Twain wrote (he stopped in the middle of it) takes Theodor to India and Ceylon, where the author had recently visited. As he abandoned Theodor's village to display Satan's mastery over time and distance, he developed a "centrifugal tendency" that led everywhere and nowhere.

Before he stopped writing "The Chronicle of Young Satan," Mark Twain started—and dropped—another novel. This one he seems to have conceived of as written for publication, though whether he would call it a potboiler is not clear. "Indiantown" occupied him for only a short time, perhaps two weeks, during the summer of 1899. While only three chapters were written (less than ten thousand words), the setting these pages sketch was used in a longer fragment, "Which Was It?" discussed in the next chapter. A Mississippi River town well south of St. Louis, in cotton-growing country, Indiantown is viewed from an adult's perspective. More unexpectedly, the narrator is genial, kindly, leisurely. He sketches in characters based on Orion Clemens (again!) and Joseph Twichell. By far the most interesting are David Gridley, a self-portrait of the author, and his wife Susan, who is recognizably based on Olivia Clemens. Described as flawless, Susan devotes herself to the manufacture of an "elaborate sham" to replace the man she had married: "As far as his outside was concerned she made a masterwork of it that would have deceived the elect."[40] She went so far as to try to cure David of swearing by quoting him; this incident is parallel to one that Mark Twain describes in his autobiography.[41] Both Susan Gridley and Olivia Clemens made a practice of "dusting off" their husbands, to their children's great satisfaction, and both allowed their husbands to blow off steam at home. "Otherwise there would have been explosions in public."[42] A long passage, too long to quote, sketches the duplicity of David Gridley, and one is tempted to see in it the origins of Mark Twain's interest in identity and multiple personalities as well as a suggestion that the original Sam Clemens of Hannibal, the river, and Washoe somehow survived, though hidden, despite his wife's efforts, and Clemens's own, to make him genteel. Did Clemens create in Gridley a version of himself? Gridley remained in his own eyes "just a piece of honest kitchen furniture transferred to the drawing-room and glorified and masked from view in gorgeous cloth of gold."[43]

Joseph Twichell would have understood what his longtime friend was saying. He told Isabel Lyon, who became Clemens's secretary, "how much Mrs. Clemens had done towards remodelling Mr. Clemens. . . . Of course there couldn't be anybody who could train him so that he wouldn't drop a little back to his wildnesses, and his strengths. But Mrs. Clemens did more than anybody else in the world could have done."[44] Why did the writer sketch this self-portrait? From what is known, one can only answer: to relieve by a kind of confession his guilt at being what in "Indiantown" he called "a comprehensive, complete and symmetrical humbug."[45]

In Sweden, Mark Twain wrote "My Boyhood Dreams," which discusses the author's youthful ambitions as well as those of his friends Thomas Bailey Aldrich and John Hay. In London, where the Clemenses returned in October, he wrote some slight but publishable pieces that show that his disdain for writing for money was not complete. "Two Little Tales," "The Death Disk," and "My First Lie and How I Got Out of It" represent a step backward. Some time was given over to preparing *The Man That Corrupted Hadleyburg and Other Stories and Essays*, published by Harper in 1900; some days were wasted on notes for an edition of the trial records of Joan of Arc and some on "Proposition for a Postal Check," a dialogue that went unpublished. But until he returned to "The Chronicle of Young Satan" in the summer (he continued to think of summer as a time for writing) the remainder of Mark Twain's European decade was not fruitful. He expected to return at last to America, even to a position as magazine editor, an idea he soon abandoned. He indicated a developing interest in international affairs by writing "The Missionary in World Politics," in which he attacked Christian missionaries in China. He intended to publish this piece anonymously in the London *Times*, ever fearful of hurting the selling power of his name, then decided not to send it off. The year was 1900, and Mark Twain, who had reached the end of ten years without a home, told a correspondent that he was "getting heartbreakingly anxious to get home—to get home and never budge again." [46]

Perhaps one reason for Mark Twain's homesickness was that he had been reminiscing again, for his autobiography. "Playing 'Bear'—Herrings—Jim Wolf and the Cats" was published in the *Autobiography* in 1924, when Paine dated it "about 1898." But the holograph manuscript, in the Mark Twain Papers, is marked with both Paine's dating and a later correction to "1900." These vivid reminiscences have in common their focus on youthful embarrassment. "Jim Wolf and the Cats" retells the story that Mark Twain had published in 1867 and goes on to describe how later writers appropriated it and published it as their own. The other sketch is one of the best parts of the autobiography, almost on a par with "Early Times." It begins by telling of the author's acute distress at age twelve on discovering that while donning a bear costume for an entertainment he had unknowingly undressed in front of two young women in hiding. They revealed their presence when the black boy accompanying young Sam asked:

> "Mars Sam, has you ever seed a dried herring?"
> "No. What is that?"
> "It's a fish."
> "Well, what of it? Anything peculiar about it?"
> "Yes, suh, you bet dey is. *Dey* eats 'em innards and all!" [47]

[The manuscript originally read "guts and all."] After telling of meeting in Calcutta one of the young women whose "burst of feminine snickers" was heard from behind the screen (only in India did she identify herself, by means of the slave boy's description of how herrings are eaten), Mark Twain then sketches, in seven paragraphs, his experiences with violence during his boyhood. The strength of these pages suggests the strength of feeling behind the author's boy books. "There was the slave man who was struck down with a chunk of slag for some small offense; I saw him die. And the young Californian emigrant who was stabbed with a bowie knife by a drunken comrade; I saw the red life gush from his breast."[48]

For Mark Twain, the second half of the 1890s was far more productive than the first. As the result of an act of will, he had finished his account of his world tour. It proved if nothing more that he could give readers of his earlier travel books what they seemed to want. (Earlier, *Joan of Arc* had proved that the writer even in his fifties could do something entirely different, a correlative to his own hopes *and* disappointments.) After his daughter's death he tried to find adequate expression of his sense of the human condition—and his own, with some success.★ Perhaps most important, he had discovered that he could return to his youth through autobiography. Though much of what he wrote was never finished, he proved that he could abandon the strictly commercial spirit he had shown in writing *Tom Sawyer, Detective* and adopt in its place a truly original and experimental approach to the writing of fiction, most successfully in "The Great Dark" and "The Chronicle of Young Satan." But while there was an occasional solid achievement, notably "The Man That Corrupted Hadleyburg," the writer's increasing indifference to publication meant that while he was writing a great deal, his contemporary readers were getting only a few samples, often mere journalism.[49]

★Mark Twain's outlook had not changed as much as it may appear; mainly he had become more preoccupied by his need to express his attitudes. As early as 1882 he had written: "All 'civilizations' are legitimate matter for (private, but not public) jeering & laughter, because they are so conspicuously made up of about three tenths of reality & sincerity, & seven tenths of wind & humbug." But the passage, written for *Life on the Mississippi*, was canceled. (MS *Life on the Mississippi*, Pierpont Morgan Library, II, 713; quoted in Horst H. Kruse, *Mark Twain and "Life on the Mississippi"* [Amherst: University of Massachusetts Press, 1981], p. 55.)

CHAPTER TEN

Citizen of the World

WHEN the Clemenses returned home on October 15, 1900, Mark Twain soon discovered that he had managed to create a new image of himself. As the result of having succeeded in paying his debts, he was greeted as "one who has borne great burdens with manliness and courage."[1] As the result of such recent serious writing as "The Man That Corrupted Hadleyburg," he was hailed as a "critic and censor" who had become "more philosophical" and was now dedicated to "justice, absolute democracy, and humanity."[2] If his readers had been given access to what Mark Twain had just been writing, they would have found that he had indeed developed a strong interest in justice, democracy, and humanity—all over the world. He had become especially interested in conflicts involving Western nations outside their natural sphere of influence: the Boer War, the Boxer Rebellion, the war between the United States and Spain over possessions in the Pacific and the Caribbean. In "The Chronicle of Young Satan," he had Satan prophesy in chapter 8: "The Christian missionary will exasperate the Chinese; they will kill him in a riot. They will have to pay for him, in territory, cash, and churches, sixty-two million times his value. They will exasperate the Chinese still more, and they will injudiciously rise in revolt against the insults and oppressions of the intruder. This will be Europe's chance to interfere and swallow China, and her band of royal Christian pirates will not waste it." To his friend Twichell, Clemens had written that he hoped the Chinese "will drive all foreigners out and keep them out for good."[3]

On his return to America, more than a dozen newspapers published accounts of Mark Twain's comments. He described how he had become an anti-imperialist as a result of his travels: "I left these shores, at Vancouver [in 1895], a red-hot imperialist. I wanted the American eagle to go screaming over the Pacific." But since then his eyes had been opened. "And so I am an anti-imperialist. I am opposed to having the eagle put his talons on any other land."[4] The Clemenses settled down in New York City; they would make the city and its suburbs their home for three years, with summers as usual, in the country. After Vienna, Paris, and London, the writer needed to be close to the center of American cultural and political life. During the autumn of 1900 he was frequently invited to make speeches, and on several occasions he criticized both British and American imperialism. At the end of the year he wrote for newspaper publication "A salutation speech from the Nineteenth Century to the Twentieth, taken down in shorthand by Mark Twain." It is short but clear: "I bring you the stately matron named Christendom, returning bedraggled, besmirched and dishonored from pirate-raids in Kiao-Chou, Manchuria, South Africa & the Philippines, with her soul full of meanness, her pocket full of boodle, and her mouth full of pious hypocrisies. Give her soap and a towel, but hide the looking glass."[5] Here spoke a citizen of the world.

Though he expected the result would be "a diminution of my bread and butter,"[6] Mark Twain soon published his strongest statement and one of his best polemical pieces, "To the Person Sitting in Darkness," which appeared in the February 1901 *North American Review*. The title is an ironic reference to Matthew 4:16: "The people which sat in darkness saw great light." The light of Christian civilization had become, according to Mark Twain, "an outside cover, gay and pretty and attractive, displaying the special patterns of our Civilization which we reserve for Home Consumption, while *inside* the bale is the Actual Thing that the Customer Sitting in Darkness buys with his blood and tears and land and liberty." Pretending to defend the actions of Western nations in South Africa, China, and particularly the Philippines, he writes:

> There have been lies; yes, but they where told in a good cause. We have been treacherous; but that was only in order that real good might come out of apparent evil. True, we have crushed a deceived and confiding people; we have turned against the weak and the friendless who trusted us; we have stamped out a just and intelligent and well-ordered republic; we have stabbed an ally in the back and slapped the face of a guest; . . . we have debauched America's honor and blackened her face before the world; but every detail was for the best. . . . Give yourself no uneasiness; it is all right.

The commentator feels obliged to examine atrocities with care in order to avoid being unfair to the perpetrators. If the irony is obvious, the explanation is too: Mark Twain would not be misunderstood. His special target is the Rev. William Ament of the American Board of Foreign Missionaries, who required the Chinese to pay inordinate fines for damages suffered by his converts during the Boxer Rebellion.

After the magazine publication, the Anti-Imperialist League of New York published the essay as a pamphlet and seems to have distributed as many as 125,000 copies; despite the author's fears, the essay was mostly well received. He was encouraged to continue writing such criticism. Even before the verdict was in, he had begun another piece, "The Stupendous Procession." Here he imagines a version of the funeral procession for Queen Victoria, who had died on January 22, 1901. Among the marchers are such mourners as "THE TWEN-TIETH CENTURY, a fair young creature, drunk and disorderly, borne in the arms of Satan"; Christendom, in flowing robes drenched in blood; England, Spain, Russia, France, Germania, and America, all guilty of blood crimes; the Statue of Liberty, with torch extinguished.[7] Here the author's anger is less controlled, and perhaps as a result the piece remained unpublished until 1972.

Probably in February 1901, Mark Twain wrote a brief, much more modest essay, "Corn-Pone Opinions." Based on a text the author says he heard in his youth from a slave ("You tell me where a man gets his corn-pone, en I'll tell you what his 'pinions are") the essay takes up the philosopher's now-favorite subject, the effect of outside influences and the need for self-approval on human behavior. Through this essay he revealed his understanding of his own situation: he was writing social and political criticism because he had been encouraged to think he was a writer whose opinions were widely respected. He liked the attention he was getting, too, and wrote to a correspondent that he was in "hot water with the clergy and other goody-goody people, but I am enjoying it more than I have ever enjoyed hot water before."[8] Instead of dropping the subject when he was attacked by clergymen, he wrote "To My Missionary Critics," which offered no apologies, though it ends by suggesting that missionaries no doubt mean well. The essay, originally entitled "The Case of Rev. Dr. Ament, Missionary," was published in the *North American Review* in April. Mostly a recapitulation of the criticisms made in the original essay, it provides specific details from newspaper stories instead of effective literary argument.

In early February 1901, Mark Twain recorded in his notebook: "Write Introduction to 100-Year Book." Three days later he recorded, "Introduction 100-year. Gov't in hands of Xn Sci, or R. Catholic? *Whole* suffrage introduced to save Protestantism in 1950, but too late; RC and XC^c ahead—got the field."⁹ These notes about the future dominance of Christian Scientists and Roman Catholics suggest the revival of an idea Mark Twain had jotted down in 1883 or 1884: "For a play: America in 1985: The Pope here & an Inquisition. The age of darkness back again. Pope is temporal despot too." Now he was fascinated by Mary Baker Eddy and planned a work in which Christian Science would dominate America, "The Secret History of Eddypus, the World Empire." He wrote twenty thousand words before he stopped, probably in March, then began again in February 1902 after reading Andrew D. White's *History of the Warfare of Science with Theology.* Then he added only five thousand words before giving up the notion. While his interest was still hot, he described the work as "a mine of learning . . . a little distorted, a trifle out of focus, recognizably drunk. But interesting, & don't you forget it!"¹⁰ Much of "Eddypus" is interesting, even fascinating, but also self-indulgent, and it is eventually dull.

In the "Secret History" (published in 1972 in *Fables of Man*), Mark Twain looks at both an imagined future and the past he himself has experienced. The future is the year 2901, here dated A.M. 1001—the "Year of Our Mother," for Mary Baker Eddy has replaced Christ, just as Eddy-mania has replaced Christianity. In the preface to book 1, she is described as "Fourth Person of the Godhead and Second Person in Rank." The ruler of the church-state that she founded uses her name as a title, even though since the consolidation of the Christian Science Church and the Roman Catholic Church all popes have been men. As usual, Mark Twain delights in sex confusion; here he explains how following the death of M. B. G. Eddy XXIV the last Catholic pope "relinquished his title, abolished his Papacy and his Church, put on the late [Christian Science] Pope's clothes, and became Mistress of the World and of Christian Sciencedom, under the name and style of Her Divine Grace Mary Baker G. Eddy XXV, and went to demonstrating over things like an Old Hand. She (that is, he) was English, and in his boyhood her name was Thomas Atkins. She (that is, he) reigned sixteen years; and when she died she left the cards most competently stacked, and secure in the hands of such as knew the Game."¹¹ Early in the new era, even before the consolidation, all libraries were destroyed, and "intellectual night followed" (p. 325). Indeed, history is now a jumble. It is known, however, that "Louis XIV, King of England, . . . was beheaded by his own subjects for marrying the Lady Mary Ann Bullion when he already had wives sufficient. He was succeeded by his son, William the Conqueror, called the Young Pretender, who became embroiled in the War of the Roses, and fell gallantly fighting for his crown at Bunker Hill." One of the most valuable pieces of preserved historical information has to do with a strange kind of holy war, known as the crusades and "undertaken for the introduction and enforcement of what was known as the Golden Rule" (p. 326).

For book 2 of the "History" the chief authority is "his Grace Mark Twain, Bishop of New Jersey in the noonday glory of the Great Civilization." The bishop's chief work is "Old Comrades," which seems to be a kind of autobiography. In the "Author's Introduction" to that work, reproduced in the "History," he speaks from the grave and tells of his dear friends Thomas Bailey Aldrich and Howells. Another of his works, "The Gospel of Self," was powerfully influential, but nevertheless it led to the bishop's death, by hanging. He seems to have had many offspring, two of them being Huck Finn and Tom Sawyer. One of his interests was books, his favorites being several ones of unknown authorship, among them "Innocents Abroad; Roughing It; Tramp Abroad; Pudd'nhead Wilson; Joan of Arc; Prince and Pauper." The father of history had one great failing: no sense of humor.

In chapter 3, drawing presumably on the great bishop's writings, the unidentified author describes the primitive ways of life in the early nineteenth century (A.D.), recognizably in America. But then the "creators of the Great Civilization" began their work, the burden of chapters 4 and 5. One such hero is Sir Isaac Walton, who "discovered the law of the Attraction of Gravitation, or the Gravitation of Attraction, which is the same thing," and another is John Calvin Galileo. The work of astronomers had an especially great impact. With their discoveries, "the lid had been taken off the universe, so to speak, there was vastness, emptiness, vacancy all around everywhere, the snug cosiness was gone, the world was a homeless little vagrant, a bewildered little orphan left out in the cold, a long way from any place and nowhere to go." This comically, and painfully, distorted history may indicate the author's belief that history was another joke played on man, or that he was letting his imagination have free play. "Eddypus" deserves the attention of readers, who will, however, discover that just as Mark Twain's interest in the work dulled, so does theirs.

In June the Clemenses began a summer at Saranac Lake, New York, where the author received from someone at the *Century Magazine* a batch of newspaper clippings about lynchings that had recently occurred. As a result, he planned "a large subscription book to be called 'History of Lynching' or 'Rise and Progress of Lynching' or some such title," as he told Frank Bliss of the American Publishing Company.[12] But then Mark Twain, who seems to have been motivated as much by a desire for money as by social concern, had second thoughts. He decided that his identification with a book on lynching would hurt his Southern sales. Only a few days after sending his proposal to Hartford, he wrote again: "I shouldn't have even half a dozen friends left, after it issued from the press." He had already written an essay, perhaps to serve as an introduction, for he told Bliss, "I shan't destroy the article I have written, but I see it won't do to print it."[13] "The United States of Lyncherdom" did not appear in Mark Twain's lifetime; it was first published in Paine's collection, *Europe and Elsewhere*, in 1923. Using as the occasion for his angry reaction a lynching in his home state of Missouri, Mark Twain examines mob violence in the context that he had so solidly established in his mind: the power of public opinion. He sees lynching as a fashion that spreads like a disease. As early as 1883, when he composed the account of the efforts to lynch Colonel Sherburn in *Huckleberry Finn*, he had argued this position. (In this essay he refers to his personal experience from which the Sherburn episode was created.) Despite its striking title, which is itself a powerful indictment, "The United States of Lyncherdom" is not the statement one might expect from a man ready to prepare a history of lynching in America. Though the lynchings that are his subject all involved Negroes, Mark Twain apparently did not recognize that a major purpose of this form of violence was to keep Negroes in a place of subservience. Indeed, not only is the racial basis disregarded, the polemicist even accepts the notion that mob violence results from provocation. His suggestion that American missionaries be brought home from China to stop the "bloody insanities" shows that the writer was still glorying in his earlier essays, of whose authorship Mark Twain reminds his readers, none too subtly.

Another undertaking of the summer of 1901 shows that Mark Twain continued to entertain the self-indulgent mood that marks "Eddypus." "A Double-Barreled Detective Story" is probably the worst story that Mark Twain ever wrote, yet he published it in two installments in *Harper's Magazine* in early 1902. The first chapters appear to be painfully serious, with cruelty, even sadism, a theme. With chapter 4 (the second barrel) the story seems to start again, beginning with a long description of an October morning, obviously a parody of someone's purple prose, and now the story becomes a farcical burlesque, featuring Sherlock Holmes as an incompetent detective, and no explanation provided. Mark Twain was apparently inspired by the first installment of A. Conan Doyle's *The Hound of the Baskervilles* to attempt a burlesque of Conan Doyle, using both his new novel and the earlier *A Study in Scarlet* (1887) as his targets. The latter has a similar break in the narrative, followed by a long descriptive passage. But the fact that the whole story is meant to be a burlesque of the Sherlock Holmes stories is not clear unless one has just read the objects of Mark Twain's attack; otherwise it is merely confusing. In a letter to Twichell, who had loaned him *A Study in Scarlet*, Clemens describes his story as a "condensed novel" satirizing Conan Doyle's "pompous sentimental 'extraordinary man' with his cheap & ineffectual ingenuities."[14] Perhaps because even the author recognized in time that the satirical purpose is not clear enough, he inserted—when the story was included in a book—a lengthy footnote at the beginning of chapter 4 that includes letters he had received in response to the story, and comments about it as "the most elaborate of burlesques of detective fiction."

Mark Twain's literary output had always been uneven, with good and inferior works coming one after the other. Now most of what he wrote was either inferior or seriously flawed, if not botched. Perhaps the prize specimen of his unevenness in the early years of the twentieth century is the longest of his novel fragments, *Which Was It?* Begun in the summer of 1899, this story—another version of "Which Was the Dream?"—occupied the writer at Saranac Lake in the summer and later in the house at Riverdale, at the north boundary of New York City, the Clemenses' home for two years beginning in the autumn of 1901. With some exceptions these pages are tedious, especially the early ones. In the following summer, when the Clemenses were at York Harbor, Maine, the author added to it and brought it close to an ending. Then he thought he could publish it, first "serialized in a *weekly* only."[15] It was never finished, and it remains a 100,000-word fragment. In the summer of 1906 he looked back at it in an autobiographical dictation. Then he was sure he could finish the book, ". . . but I shan't do it. The pen is irksome to me. I was born lazy, and dictating [the autobiography] has spoiled me." And so he decided that "the book will remain unfinished."[16]

This novel is the story of George Harrison, who, like General X in "Which Was the Dream?" falls asleep and dreams catastrophes, "fifteen bleak years." Before the narrative begins, his house burns, killing his wife and daughters. But this time the story is not about disasters but about the protagonist's failings, or apparent failings, and their effect on his conscience. Harrison begins his story by explaining that he cannot tell it as *his* story: "I could not say, 'I did such things,' it would revolt me, and the pen would refuse." So he writes his story in the third person. Harrison is, or appears to be, a hypocrite. Tempted like the Richardses of Hadleyburg, he becomes a robber and a murderer, then finds that he must live with his guilt, for he is too cowardly to confess it. In the manuscript, Mark Twain sketched a tree, labeled "disaster," with its base in false pride and its fruits seven distinct crimes. Since Harrison corresponds to General X and to David Gridley of "Indiantown," earlier efforts to tell the dream-disaster story, he thus represents in some sense the author. One wonders if the story was Mark Twain's way of dealing with his own sense of guilt, originating either in the hypocrisy he emphasized so fiercely in "Indiantown" or in the combination of his bankruptcy and the death of Susy, for which he felt responsible. It is perhaps significant that Harrison loses his mask at the time of the robbery and murder and that it is later used to blackmail him. Throughout the story Harrison's guilt is emphasized by the counterfeit theme—counterfeit money, Mrs. Gunning's mail-investment swindle, forged letters.

By far the most interesting feature of the narrative, which is alternately too leisurely told and too condensed, is the role taken by Jasper, the mulatto blackmailer, who forces Harrison to become his servant. Victimized again and again by whites, forced to purchase his freedom three times, beaten for being out at night without a pass, he takes all his grievances out on Harrison and shows no compassion. The episode has been read by A. G. Pettit as a turning point in Mark Twain's response to Negroes and the South, with Huck's genial friend Jim now being replaced by a vengeful mulatto and the onetime humorist urging the punishment of white sins. (There is evidence that as early as the 1880s Mark Twain was imagining that in 1985 Negroes would be on the verge of supremacy in America.[17]) But at least as engaging is the fact that it is Harrison who is being tyrannized. It appears that he needs some form of punishment to help atone for his crimes. Though the story breaks off before anything can be made of the matter, the original idea was for Harrison to have dreamed both his disaster and his crimes. A related fragment even suggests that Harrison's guilt is misplaced since his father was the real criminal. Both these pieces of evidence imply that Mark Twain was most interested in showing that Harrison's suffering from his guilt was unwarranted—that he was in fact not guilty. But such subtleties as misplaced masochism were beyond the skills of the author. Reading *Which Was*

It? is embarrassing to anyone who has enjoyed the best of Mark Twain's writing, for the story is patently his—warts and all.

In the fall of 1901, Clemens was awarded an honorary degree from Yale. Since the degree increased his sense of responsibility to the public, his chief concern for a time was politics, and his opponent Richard Croker and his Tammany Hall gang. For once in his life, he became thoroughly engaged in politics. He gave speeches and marched in a political parade. When Tammany lost, one newspaper identified Mark Twain as the responsible force.

> Who killed Croker?
> I, said Mark Twain,
> I killed Croker,
> I, the Jolly Joker.[18]

At least privately, he did in fact claim credit.[19] Whatever the status of his career, Samuel Clemens was feeling good about himself. At the end of 1901 he wrote to his friend Aldrich: "I am having a noble good time—the best I have ever had. All my days are my own—all of them: & I spend them in my study. It comes of wisdom; of establishing a rational rule & then sticking to it: to take no engagement outside the city, & not more than 2 per month. They can't improve on this happiness in heaven."[20]

In early 1902, Mark Twain continued his role as social philosopher with two pieces. To the question "Does the race of man love a lord?" Mark Twain volunteered an emphatic *yes* in an essay in the April *North American Review*. The next month a more timely piece appeared in the same journal, an ironic "Defense of General Funston," in which Mark Twain castigated the man who captured, through trickery, the Philippine patriotic leader Aguinaldo.* Here the writing is very much under control, though one may wonder whether the author's displacement of blame from the man to his disposition—which had "a native predilection for unsavory conduct"[21]—is effective. The expression of determinism in this essay suggests the author's new willingness to share his thoughts and feelings with the world more fully than he had. A little sketch published in the summer of 1902 is similarly frank, this

---

*Mark Twain also drafted a review of Edwin Wildman's biography of Aguinaldo, which he had used in the "Defense." In the long but incomplete review, he compared Aguinaldo to Joan of Arc (Paine no. 89, MTP).

time in expressing pessimism. The piece names "the five boons of life": fame, love, riches, pleasure, and death. They are, from time to time, offered to a man who eagerly selects first one, then another, always to be disappointed. Finally he would have the one boon he had avoided: but death is now no longer available to him—he has waited too long and now must experience "the wanton insult of Old Age." "The Five Boons of Life," which Paine calls "that beautiful fairy tale," should be put beside the recently published sketch that Paine identified as being written the same year, "The Victims." Among the philosophical, religious, and historical fantasies published in 1972, this one stands out because of its imaginative treatment both of man's vulnerability to disease and of the native disposition of animals to behave according to their kind, two of the old man's favorite themes. Only a skeleton, this children's fable tells of a picnic attended by "all the nicest creatures." Among those who went were these four:

> Little Dora sparrow begged
> So little Dora went to the picnic and mamma Sparrow went out to hunt
> little Sammy Pinch-Bug and harpooned him with her beak
> Little Harry Weasel begged
> So little Harry went to the picnic, and mamma Weasel went out to hunt
> and joined her teeth together in the person of little Dora Sparrow
> Little Jacky Fox begged
> So little Jacky went to the picnic and mamma Fox went out to hunt
> and bit little Harry Weasel in two.[22]

Perhaps this fable was inspired by one of the major events of 1902 for Clemens, his last return to his boyhood home. In June he traveled to Missouri to receive an honorary degree from the University of Missouri, before which he made a five-day visit to Hannibal. He found his mind swarming with images of his youth. He took up, apparently as a result of the trip, an idea he had recorded in his notebook in 1891: then he pictured the reunion of Huck and Tom at the age of sixty, by which time their experiences have proved to be as bitter as those of the youth of "The Five Boons": "Life has been a failure, all that was lovable, all that was beautiful is under the mound. They die together." Now, in 1902, he made more notes on what he called "the final Huck Finn book," to which he gave the name "50 Years Later."[23] A notebook entry suggests that the story was to have two parts, the first ending in a "moonlight parting on the hill—the entire gang. 'Say, let's all come back in 50 years and talk over old times.'"[24] Mark Twain began his story during the summer, when the Clemenses were vacationing in Maine, and by October he seems to have completed the first part and sent it to Howells. Then, apparently, he gave the idea up. In 1906 he said, "I carried it as far as thirty-eight thousand words four years ago, then destroyed it for fear I might someday finish it."[25] Unlike other manuscripts he said he destroyed, this one does seem not to have survived.

During the summer of 1902, Mark Twain did manage to finish two short stories, soon published: "The Belated Russian Passport" is an O. Henry kind of story, seemingly pathetic, but with a comic twist at the end. It put Mark Twain's talents to no good purpose. Better but painfully sentimental is "Was It Heaven? or Hell?" Based on a true story that Howells had told him earlier in the summer, it tells of the successful efforts of two elderly women to protect their dying niece from knowledge of her daughter's illness and subsequent death. Soon the author found himself in a painfully similar situation. In August, Olivia Clemens had a severe heart attack; she was left an invalid. (Her health had never been good.) With difficulty she was moved in October to Riverside, and when Jean became seriously ill of pneumonia in December, the family had to protect Mrs. Clemens from knowing, exactly as in the story. At this time a new important member was added to the Clemens household, Isabel Lyon. She was expected to serve as Olivia Clemens's secretary, but soon she became the author's assistant, a function that grew until 1909, when she was discharged.

Sometime in the summer or fall of 1902, Mark Twain returned to his 1899 Christian Science writings (the ones not yet published in the United States) and revised them for publication in the *North American Review*, where they appeared in December and January. Soon after he added a new one, on the growth of the religion, published in February, and another, a rejoinder to Mrs. Eddy's comments on the writer's criticism, appeared in April, again in the *North American Review*. This piece is a discussion of the title "Mother" used as a form for addressing Mrs. Eddy. In the meantime, the humorist-novelist-social critic had decided to put together an entire book on the subject, and Harper agreed to such a publication. Soon the author was pressured to finish his book as early as possible. In mid-February, Frederick A. Duneka of Harper's wrote: "There should be an interval of six weeks between the receipt of a manuscript and the publication of the book. This can be cut down, of course, but not very much. It is our wish to issue the Christian Science volume not later than the last of April. Will this impose too great a burden on you."[26] (Was it a slip that the question mark was omitted?) Under such prodding the author finished the manuscript, the book was set in type, and publication was announced as forthcoming. Then perhaps fearful of antagonizing Christian Scientists, the Harper editors changed their minds and the publication was indefinitely postponed. After waiting three years, Mark Twain tried unsuccessfully to retrieve the manuscript. Finally, in February 1907, Harper published the work as *Christian Science* (a better title might have been *Mary Baker Eddy*) when the new religion was being attacked in the newspapers.

The bulk of the post-1899 material was written under difficult circumstances. The author was staying close to his ailing wife and was working quickly. Perhaps as a result, he took the easiest way he could find to produce a book. The new parts are chiefly an examination of various Christian Science publications. Throughout the work, Mark Twain's target is Mrs. Eddy's dictatorial rule, which he refers to as "The New Infallibility." Little is said about the practice of Christian Science, and much of that little is favorable. But unlike the early chapters, the last two-thirds of the book is uninteresting. The reader must wade through Mark Twain's excessively thorough analysis of the organizational structure of the church, with extended quotations from documents, followed by appendixes—padding—of quoted documents. The good-humored tone of the early chapters is entirely different from that of book 2, which was written, doggedly, to supplement sufficiently the pieces written four years earlier to make a book. While no reader could wish it longer, it is far shorter than the writer's earlier books. Moreover, since the author was of two minds about Christian Science, a reader does not know how to respond to Mark Twain's book.

Even a summer at Quarry Farm, where Mark Twain might have been inspired by memories of his best periods of productivity, was not fruitful in 1903. He was preoccupied with business and his plans to move to Italy, to Florence, in the autumn, for Olivia Clemens's health. The author did manage to complete one short story, "A Dog's Tale," soon published in *Harper's Magazine*. Intended for Jean Clemens, who was strongly opposed to vivisection, the little story is told by a heroic dog who saves a baby from a fire but dies of a broken heart after her offspring is destroyed by curious scientists, led by the baby's father. The onetime archfoe of sentimentalism had drifted over to the enemy's camp with "The Californian's Tale" and "Was It Heaven? or Hell?" This most determinedly softhearted—and contrived—tale showed that Mark Twain had given up his aim of authenticity, though circumstances permitted an occasional return.

In October the Clemenses moved to Florence; Howells thought the move was probably permanent. The writer did settle down to business early, and despite Olivia's illness and his own, the stay was remarkably productive. Clemens was eager to invest ten thousand dollars, which he expected to realize from what he could publish, and he was able to achieve his goal in just a month of writing. The first of his pieces, "Italian Without a Master," begins: "It is almost a fortnight now that I am domiciled in a medieval villa in the country, a mile or two from Florence." In this pleasant return to his earlier manner, Mark Twain reveals his amusing ignorance of Italian as he confidently attempts to cope with terms in Italian newspapers. Even better is "Italian with Grammar," in which he tells of his efforts to master the fifty-seven forms of the Italian verb system. It is a highly imaginative, good-humored sketch. The original was too long; only the first half was published.

A third piece is a story, "The $30,000 Bequest." Like "Hadleyburg," it is an analysis of the destructive consequences of greed, a subject on which the author might well have considered himself an authority; he took it up repeatedly. As the story opens, an unusually honorable couple, Mr. and Mrs. Foster, have established a rewarding life by dint of hard work and economy. They are, however, soon victimized by their romantic dreams of "comrading with kings and princes and stately lords and ladies" when they hear that Foster's uncle is intending to bequeath them $30,000—"Not for love," he explains, "but because money had given him most of his troubles and exasperations," and he wishes to place his wealth "where there was hope that it would continue its malignant work." The money never comes, but the expectation itself proves malignant and destructive. The story, like "Indiantown," is partly autobiographical. The couple of the story seems to resemble the Clemenses, with Mr. Foster's bad temper, rashness, and eventual dishonesty not much restrained by Mrs. Foster's intense interest in speculation. Here, at least by implication, the author assumed responsibility for the disaster that had resulted from his preoccupation during the late 1880s with wealth. But he also suggests that he was provoked by circumstances and encouraged by his wife.

Mark Twain was still a commercial writer, for he still needed money. The need presumably explains the preoccupation with money in these three stories. Early in 1904, in a letter to Twichell, he described his "sort of half promise to Harpers magazines to supply 30,000 words each year" to augment what he would receive from the collected edition Harper was issuing. To his surprise and pleasure, in "25 working days" he was not only able to produce 37,000 words of "magazining," but found that both he and his wife judged them publishable. With these done, he could now declare with satisfaction, "No more magazine work hanging over my head."[27]

Thereafter in Florence, Mark Twain devoted himself to two works that remained unpublished until after his death—portions are yet to appear. One was the autobiography, his off-and-on project over the years. Now he was so pleased with a new method that he thought he might destroy his earlier efforts. (He did not.) Less than two weeks after his letter to Twichell, he wrote to Howells:

> I've struck it! And I will give it away—to you. You will never know how much enjoyment you have lost until you get to dictating your auto-biography; then you will realize, with a pang, that you might have been doing it all your life if you had only the luck to think of it. And you will be astonished (& charmed) to see how like *talk* it is, & how real it sounds, & how well & compactly & sequentially it constructs itself, & what a dewy & breezy & woodsy freshness it has, & what a darling & worship-ful absence of the signs of starch, & flatiron, & labor & fuss & the other artificialities!

His purpose at this time, he told Howells, was to provide "notes" to the books he had already written, in order to add to their copyright life. He dictated two hours or so a day, about fifteen hundred words each time, but was soon interrupted by illness and did not start up again for two months. Only about eighteen thousand words of these dictations, supplemented by some written portions, have been published—rather uninteresting despite the author's enthusiasm: pages about the Clemenses' Florence residences of 1892–93 and 1903–4, a few pages on John Hay and some on Henry Rogers, some interesting ones on the writing of *The Innocents Abroad*. Unpublished portions, at the Mark Twain Papers, describe the writer's study at the time he was dictating and his problems with the owner of the house he occupied. What he had written earlier was far better. For the moment this return to a version of the vernacular mode had disappointing results.

The most remarkable portion of the autobiography composed at Florence is the "Preface. As from the Grave." It reads, in part: "In this Autobiography I shall keep in mind the fact that I am speaking from the grave. I am literally speaking from the grave, because I shall be dead when the book issues from the press." A similar preface, it may be recalled, was attached to the work of the Father of History, "Old Comrades," on which "Eddypus" was said to be based. But here Mark Twain went on, cautiously: "It has seemed to me that I could be as frank and free and even unembarrassed as a love letter if I knew that what I was writing would be exposed to no eye until I was dead, and unawares, and indifferent."[28] He *intended* to ignore whatever restrictions he had felt earlier: his wife's censorship or Howells's, his concern with his reputation and its effect on the sale of his books. He needed to be frank and free, as did Gridley of "Indiantown." But it was never to be, in Florence or elsewhere. In time he himself would recognize that he would always feel inhibited. Though he aimed at frankness, even the presence of a stenographer, "that petrified audience-person" who is always there, was enough, he told Howells in April 1909, "to block that game." Perhaps the spirit of his wife lived on.

On January 5, 1904, Mark Twain wrote to Duneka to report that having trimmed "Italian with Grammar" and written, revised, and re-revised "Sold to Satan," he had supplied Harper with all that was expected and could therefore "dig out one of my unfinished novels—a couple of them. Not for issue as single books, & not serially, but only to be added to the Complete Subscription Set."[29] The novel he turned to was the one that Mark Twain was to refer to in 1906 as "the book I wrote in Florence."[30] This is the work that supplied the attractive title for what Paine and Duneka published in 1916, though their heavily edited *The Mysterious Stranger* includes only the last chapter of the Florence book. Mark Twain called the story "No. 44, The Mysterious Stranger." It belongs to no one period of the author's last years. The first chapter is a revision of "The Chronicle of Young Satan" of 1897–98. Chapters 2–7 were written sometime between November 1902 and October 1903, before the move to Florence. There Mark Twain wrote chapters 8–25, as well as a good deal more, but in 1905 he destroyed at least 125 manuscript pages of what he had written in Florence. He also wrote in 1904 the six-page "Conclusion of the Book," published as chapter 34 when the whole surviving manuscript was published in 1969. Next in 1905 he returned to the manuscript, and after destroying part and then expecting to finish the story, he managed to produce only chapters 26–32. Then in order to ready something else for publication, he put it aside. In the following summer he said in his autobiography that he would then "dearly love" to finish the story, but would not because he was "tired of the pen."[31] Nonetheless, at the end of the summer of 1908 he wrote one additional chapter, published as chapter 33. Both it and chapter 34 serve as conclusions, though they have quite different implications. The whole of the story does not quite fit together, but it is more than a fragment, if less than a finished whole. The last of the long fictions composed after Susy's death, it was not clearly identified until the publication in 1963 of John Tuckey's *Mark Twain and Little Satan*, because before that date attention had been given exclusively to the 1916 publication, *The Mysterious Stranger*. In 1942 Bernard DeVoto, who had succeeded Paine as custodian of the Mark Twain Papers, wrote of it only that "this story includes a print-shop such as young Sam Clemens worked in." He added, "I will say nothing except that it led directly to the one that came through to triumph at last, the book which, after it had been painfully written over and changed and adjusted and transformed, was to achieve the completion denied its many predecessors, the book we know as *The Mysterious Stranger*."[32] Regrettably, DeVoto was mistaken on several counts. The print-shop story was begun four years *after* Mark Twain had last contributed to "The Chronicle of Young Satan," the one DeVoto identifies as the work that came to triumph at last. The latter, which Paine and here DeVoto call *The Mysterious Stranger*, is misnamed, for the "Satan" figure is mysterious about his identity only in the print-shop story. Finally, the print-shop story is more nearly complete than "Young Satan."

While "No. 44" lacks the special blend of fairy-tale whimsy and pessimistic determinism of "The Chronicle of Young Satan," it has its own merits. It is highly, even wildly, imaginative, at the same time that its basic setting, the print shop, is based vividly on the author's memories of his first occupation. More fully than any other of Mark Twain's stories, it takes up what the author liked, even relished: food (especially that described in chapter 22: hot corn pone, fried spring chicken, "cream-smothered strawberries, with the prairie dew still on them," "coffee from Vienna, fluffed cream"), cats (including the charming Mary Florence Fortescue Baker G. Nightingale), and a minstrel show, complete with the singing of "Buffalo Gals, Can't You Come Out Tonight?" What seems like mere self-indulgence in other late stories here enriches the central fantasy of the story and makes the story authentic despite its shapelessness. Thoroughly liberated from the demands of commercial book publication, Mark Twain is even able to provide for the first time an effective portrayal of romantic, even passionate, love.

Despite an undercurrent of seriousness, which is doubly underscored by the two endings, "No. 44" shows the old author returning to the motif that makes *Huckleberry Finn* so memorable: the celebration of freedom. What he had played with in the unpublished part of "My Platonic Sweetheart" becomes the focus of this story and is taken up with great imaginative zest. Like young Satan of "The Chronicle,"

No. 44 serves as the *raissonneur* of the novel; he opens the eyes of August Feldner, the narrator, to the author's more than half-serious ideas. The central one is that

> each human being contains not merely two independent entities, but three—the Waking-Self, the Dream-Self, and the Soul. This last is immortal, the others are functioned by the brain and the nerves, and are physical and mortal; they are not functionable when the brain and nerves are paralyzed by a temporary hurt or stupefied by narcotics; and when the man dies *they* die, since their life, their energy and their existence depend solely upon physical sustenance, and they cannot get that from dead nerves and a dead brain. When [Feldner explains] I was invisible the whole of my physical make-up was gone, nothing connected with it or depending upon it was left. My soul—my immortal soul—alone remained. Freed from the encumbering flesh, it was able to exhibit forces, passions and emotions of a quite tremendously effective character.[33]

Here Mark Twain posits a higher form of freedom. But the story is as much fun as philosophy: the several entities referred to take part in the story. No. 44 puts flesh on August's dream-self, who is devoted to "romance and excursions and adventure" (p. 315). This "fleshing" of the dream-self is both mysterious and comic in an imaginative episode in which the various selves of August and Marget, whom he loves, interact. It is also highly serious when August's dream-self, Emil Schwarz, tells him of the burden of being in the flesh and of his desire for liberation for himself and the fleshed version of Marget. Like Ariel in Shakespeare's *The Tempest*, Schwarz implores:

> "It is these bonds"—stretching his arms aloft—"oh, free me from *them*; these bonds of flesh—this decaying vile matter, this foul weight, and clog, and burden, this loathsome sack of corruption in which my spirit is imprisoned, her white wings bruised and soiled—oh, be merciful and set her free . . . say you will be my friend, as well as brother! for brothers indeed we are; the same womb was mother to us both, I live by you, I perish when you die—brother, be my friend! . . . Oh, this human life, this earthly life, this weary life! It is so groveling, and so mean; its ambitions are so paltry, its prides so trivial, its vanities so childish and the glories that it values and applauds—lord, how empty!" (P. 369)

The fleshed dream-selves of this story are Mark Twain's final and most fascinating rendering of the notion of the double that had interested him so long. Based partly on his reading, partly on imaginative speculation, the account of the selves originated as well in Mark Twain's sense of the conflicting needs of the human, the desire to be "a person who wants the earth, and cannot be satisfied unless he can have the whole of it" (p. 344) as well as to be liberated, free from the deterministic forces painfully described in *What Is Man?* What is not clear but seems to be implied is that No. 44 is a symbol of the whole self, both conscious and unconscious, and that his purpose is to help August Feldner, an ordinary mortal, discover powers that mankind has neglected. The continuing process of educating August, not fully described since the story is incomplete, was to lead to the conclusion, chapter 34, in which No. 44 disappears after announcing to August that he has "revealed you to yourself and set you free."

Mark Twain's productive Florence sojourn ended when on June 5, 1904, Olivia Clemens died. Her death was much less of a shock than that of Susy, but it deepened, at least for a time, the author's pessimism. The ending to "No. 44," which he wrote in 1904 (though he was still far from bringing his story to that ending) seems to have been written under the influence of his loss, and it suggests a further step beyond the "dream-disaster" ideas he had been fictionalizing. The lessons that 44 teaches to August are very similar to those Clemens set forth in a letter to Joseph Twichell written in July 1904. But in the letter Clemens wrote that the vision he expressed was how life and the world appeared a "part of each day—or night" since the death of his daughter.[34] In the story, the ideas are presented without such qualification.

> "*Life itself is only a vision, a dream.* . . . . *Nothing exists save empty space—and you!* . . . you will remain a *Thought*, the only existent Thought, and by your nature inextinguishable, indestructible. . . . Strange, indeed, that you should not have suspected that your universe and its contents were only dreams, visions, fictions! Strange, because they are so frankly and hysterically insane—like all dreams: a God who could make good children as easily as bad, yet preferred to make bad ones; who could have made every one of them happy, yet never made a single happy one; who made them prize their bitter life, yet stingily cut it short." (Pp. 404–5)

No. 44's long speech is not fully prepared for, since the ending was not attached to the chapters that go before it, but it is nonetheless deeply moving.

The death of Olivia Clemens did not make a great difference in the literary career of Mark Twain, though the burden on his finances was now less great. At the age of sixty-nine, he had established his ways, eccentric though they were. While his daughter Clara now acted for a time as censor, he felt free to publish, at last, an extract from the never-finished "Captain Stormfield's Visit to Heaven" in 1907. But he was rapidly losing his interest in writing, especially as he found out how much easier it was to dictate his autobiography. He was not, however, losing his interest in marketing his writings, as shown by his eagerness to publish even the inferior *Christian Science*. That was Mark Twain's last completed book—as distinguished from collections of shorter pieces, booklets, pamphlets—and his only one after his book about his world tour. But he had made more than ten attempts to write another: three stories about Satan figures, two on Huck and Tom, at least five on the dream-disaster theme, and the "Eddypus" history. Despite his reluctance to take pen in hand, there were to be still more aborted efforts.

Why so many failures—if failures they are? All of them, except "Eddypus," were to have been novels, and each of the novels that Mark Twain wrote had a strange history. *The Gilded Age* was a partnership novel. *Tom Sawyer* was planned as a much longer book; the author found himself with a book that could be considered complete literally before he knew it. *Huckleberry Finn*, *The Prince and the Pauper*, and *A Connecticut Yankee* all were written over a period of several years and completed only after several interruptions. *The American Claimant* was derived from a farce co-authored by Howells, and *Pudd'nhead Wilson* was the result of major recasting and a not wholly successful Caesarean operation. (Only a mixed metaphor can describe *Wilson*.) Other novels were abandoned earlier: "Simon Wheeler" and the Hawaiian novel, among others. Had Mark Twain not tired of the pen, as he put it, some of these later novels might well have been finished, even if not given a satisfactory ending.* Some of the unpublished fictional fragments, though tantalizing, have no place to go. One such is entitled "The Girl Who Was Ostensibly a Man."[35]

*Would Mark Twain have approved of the edited version of *The Mysterious Stranger*? Since it has proved popular, the answer, probably, is yes, though he might have resisted Paine's and Duneka's elimination of an evil priest—for he might have suspected that Duneka's being a Roman Catholic might have had something to do with the decision.

CHAPTER ELEVEN

Final Soliloquies

IN 1900, Mark Twain's triumphant return had quickly led to his involvement with both international affairs and local politics. In 1904, when he returned from abroad after the death of his wife, he was repelled by politics. He told Joseph Twichell, "Oh, dear! get out of that sewer—party politics." He added, echoing the language of his gospel, "I wish I could learn to pity the human race instead of censuring it and laughing at it; and I could, if the outside influences of old habits were not so strong upon my machine."[1] After a quiet summer in the Berkshires and at Quarry Farm, the remaining Clemenses settled again in New York City, this time at 21 Fifth Avenue, at Ninth Street. Following a seige of illness, the old habits, aroused by contemporary events, stirred Mark Twain into writing. On January 22, the Russian czar's guards in St. Petersburg fired on strikers, and within a few days Mark Twain composed "The Czar's Soliloquy," published in the *North American Review* in March. In twenty-five hundred words he takes up once again a theme looked at in an 1899 piece, "Diplomatic Pay and Clothes," in which he argues that clothes make the diplomat. Standing naked before a mirror (as a newspaper story reported he regularly did), the czar declares emphatically, "There is no power without clothes." (Mark Twain acknowledged his debt to Thomas Carlyle's *Sartor Resartus* by using the expression "As Teufelsdröckh says.") In his nakedness the czar accepts responsibility for his actions, some of which are described from his collection of newspaper clippings. The czar fears the growth of genuine patriotism; "*loyalty to the Nation* ALL *the time, loyalty to the government when it deserves it.*"[2] This time Mark Twain's personal philosophy is not permitted to intrude: nothing is said about the czar's training or his disposition. The soliloquy is a forceful attack on a cruel tyrant.

The brief gibe at the end of the "Soliloquy" ("Is the human race a joke?") is developed in a continuation, "Flies and Russians," which extends the czar's remarks. Here his ruminations lead him to conclude that Nature made a mistake in creating both flies and Russians and that "the grotesque nature of the result was not clearly foreseen."[3] It is an amusing piece, but the illusion that the czar is speaking is not maintained. Perhaps for that reason the piece remained unpublished until 1972, when it appeared in *Fables of Man*.

The real sequel to "The Czar's Soliloquy" is *King Leopold's Soliloquy: A Defence of His Congo Rule*, begun in February. The history of this piece is complex but interesting. In October 1904 the founder of the English Congo Reform Association sought out Clemens and asked him to work for his cause. The Belgians were squeezing profits out of the newly acquired Congo and committing atrocities in the process. He won from Clemens a promise that the Congo would receive his attention. The "Soliloquy" that resulted was turned down by the *North American Review* and then was issued as a pamphlet in September 1905 by the Congo Reform Association, with proceeds going to the association. Published in England as well, the "Soliloquy" was successful enough that *An Answer to Mark Twain* was published for distribution in England.

King Leopold's Soliloquy is four times as long as its predecessor and more ambitious. This time the characterization of the speaker is much fuller, and the gradual shift from a pose of wounded innocence to outright cynicism is skillful. The piece is the occasion for the presentation of an extended case against the Belgian king, based on quotations from newspaper accounts and reports from missionaries about the atrocities committed by greedy imperialists. Unfortunately, in this essay Mark Twain made a mistake by assuming that the U.S. government had endorsed Leopold's rule in the Congo. Because of that false assumption, he especially criticized American support. The soliloquy labors under other difficulties as well. Though missionaries were among the supporters of the Congo Reform Movement, the piece has a strenuously antireligious bias. (Later the author himself made tentative plans for a campaign to enlist the support of Protestant clergymen.) Moreover, the soliloquy presents a definitely pessimistic attitude toward the possibility of reform. Thus three errors of fact and strategy mar the pamphlet.

In November 1905, despite these problems, Clemens became vice-president of the American Congo Reform Association and took up his pen again for the cause, but neither of the pieces he wrote, "A Thanksgiving Sentiment" and another without a name, was published. In his capacity as reform leader, Clemens made three visits to Washington, D.C., to confer with the president and State Department authorities before he learned what the position of the United States really was. Vexed and discomforted, he then thought that he should withdraw his soliloquy, but though he did not, he became disillusioned about reformist activities and resigned his office. Ironically, the "Soliloquy" proved to be a significant contribution to the effort to stop abuses in the Congo. Improvements in Belgian practices were effected. Although Clemens never realized what he had done, this last and most complete commitment to reform was Mark Twain's most successful.

A third and quite different kind of soliloquy, though apparently generated by the interest in the genre he had taken up, is "Adam's Soliloquy." The piece itself is negligible, but it seems to have revived Mark Twain's interest in Adam and Eve, for whom soon after he wrote diaries and an autobiography. But for the moment he continued his interest in social and political criticism with what is usually considered his best such piece, "The War Prayer," written in February or March 1905. Basing his sketch on a story he had heard in 1862 and recorded in *Life on the Mississippi* (chapter 57), he describes a wartime scene—any war will do, since one of the virtues of the piece is its timelessness, as was discovered during the Vietnam War. Patriotism at the time is rampant, opposition a very risky business. At a church service, God is invoked to "watch over our noble young soldiers, and aid, comfort, and encourage them in the day of battle and the hour of peril, bear them in His mighty hand, make them strong and confident, invincible in the bloody onset; help them to crush the foe, grant to them and to their flag and country imperishable honor and glory. . . ."

A longtime disbeliever in special providences, Mark Twain might be expected to question such a plea. Instead, perhaps remembering the satiric technique of "Letter from the Recording Angel" (1887), he introduces an "aged stranger" who announces that God has heard the prayer and has interpreted it literally. Here is what God heard:

> O Lord our God, help us to tear their soldiers to bloody shreds with our shells; help us to cover their smiling fields with the pale forms of their patriot dead; help us to drown the thunder of the guns with the shrieks of their wounded, writhing in pain; help us to lay waste their humble homes with a hurricane of fire; help us to wring the hearts of their unoffending widows with unavailing grief; help us to turn them out roofless

with their little children to wander unfriended the wastes of their deso-
lated lands in rags and hunger and thirst, sports of the sun flames of
summer and the icy winds of winter, broken in spirit, worn with travail,
imploring Thee for the refuge of the grave and denied it—for our sakes
who adore Thee, Lord, blast their hopes, blight their lives, protract their
bitter pilgrimage, make heavy their steps, water their way with their
tears, stain the white snow with the blood of their wounded feet! We ask
it, in the spirit of love, of Him Who is the Source of Love, and who is
the ever-faithful refuge and friend of all that are sore beset and seek His
aid with humble and contrite hearts. Amen.

Mark Twain ends the piece with the appropriate comment "It was
believed that the man was a lunatic, because there was no sense in
what he said." After it was rejected by *Harper's Bazaar* as "not quite
suited to a woman's magazine,"[4] it was filed away until posthumous
publication in *Europe and Elsewhere* in 1923.

Throughout 1905 and into 1906, Mark Twain regularly took up
his pen to contribute short pieces, many of them in the form of letters,
to several periodicals, especialy *Harper's Weekly*—ten in all, all slight.
They show that the author was a man of rapidly changing moods,
sometimes playing the part of philosophical observer but too often
haunted by his past and his continuing need to make sense out of life
and to render his vision in an apt and extended fiction. He had not
altogether lost his sense of humor and his enjoyment, even delight in
life's daily offerings, as his letters to Henry Rogers' daughter-in-law
show. But the blend of humor and tragedy that would reflect his impression of the human condition was beyond his ability. Even his
shorter, less ambitious but nonetheless substantial pieces (more fully
engaged than the *Harper's Weekly* pieces) gave him trouble, chiefly in
the structural demands of a beginning and an ending. Had he developed a more serious interest in the art of fiction, perhaps he could
have seen, as modernist writers have, new and more suitable struc-
tures. But he never recognized the new fictional possibilities being
created by his contemporaries, for his ambition to express complex
relationships and personalities was never balanced by an interest in
structure. He was, as he described himself in the prefatory note to
"Those Extraordinary Twins," a man "not born with the novel-writing
gift," or so he chose to think.

The first of Mark Twain's two remaining efforts at extended fiction
was begun at the end of the winter of 1904–5, nine months after the

death of Olivia Clemens. The chief interest of "The Refuge of the Derelicts" (also called the "Adam Monument") is that it reveals how the writer's literary imagination was working late in his life. He created a fictional vehicle for the presentation of his philosophy, using the idea of a monument to Adam. He then introduced figures that haunted his memory and imagination. It was old wine in a new but not very attractive bottle. Isabel Lyon's journal for March 17 records that the author had read the beginning of a new story of a "poet who had a marvelous idea of erecting a statue to Adam, & he tells a friend of the project. He had no money & so would have to interest other people in the idea. The first person he goes to is an old Admiral. . . ."[5] The focus of the fragmentary novel then becomes reports in the poet's diary (with little revealed about the personality of the diarist) dealing with Admiral Stormfield, based on Captain Ned Wakeman (again) as well as Clemens's old friend and adviser Henry H. Rogers, along with Stormfield's collection of failed and defeated derelicts. (Mark Twain told Paine that there is "no such figure for the storm-beaten drift as the derelict."[6]) The structure of the fragment is loose; the slight plot supplied by the poet's efforts to induce the admiral to contribute to the monument fund serves as a peg on which the author hangs philosophy, anecdotes, and portraits.

At the end of March, Mark Twain read to his household a newly composed essay on William Dean Howells. It was published in *Harper's Magazine*, but not until June 1906. Deeply in Howells's debt because of his friend's support and helpful criticism, private and public, Mark Twain here celebrates literary ideals that he and Howells shared: choice of the right word, graceful and unbroken meters, compactness, and especially effective but unobtrusive stage directions, "those articles which authors employ to throw a kind of human naturalness around a scene and a conversation." These are Mark Twain's stylistic views, though compactness is a virtue found more commonly in his sentences than in his larger units.

On May 18, 1905, Clemens and his household, including Isabel Lyon and Jean, began the first of two long summers at Dublin, New Hampshire, near Mount Monadnock. Almost as soon as he arrived he began his last effort at a novel, "Three Thousand Years Among the Microbes." He was soon delighted both with his productivity and with the story itself, which he said yielded more enjoyment than any book he had undertaken in twenty years. Though he hoped he could work on it all summer, his inspiration lagged after a little over a month. "Microbes" differs from the other late fragments in being chiefly a satire. It is based on an idea he had recorded in his notebook in 1884 and later dreamed: that humans and "other creatures are the microbes that charge with multitudinous life the corpuscles" in God's veins. Paine published selections from this work in his 1912 biography; a complete edition appears in *Which Was the Dream?* (1968). The fragment is about fifty thousand words long.

Unlike "The Refuge of the Derelicts," this last long story is original in conception and up to a point interesting and provocative. It tells the story of a scientist who has been magically transformed into a cholera germ in the body of an aged and malicious tramp named Blitzowski. There he finds that a whole world exists, a world of microbes analogous to man's world, though more densely populated. Measurements there are naturally on a different scale, with three thousand years amounting to three earthly weeks. The scientist-narrator is named Bkshp, but he is familiarly known as "Huck," an abbreviation for his American middle name, Huxley. (Bkshp appears to be an abbreviation for the name of Huckleberry Finn's real-life model, Tom Blankenship.) Because of his previous human experience, Huck is able to tell his adventures from a double point of view. Happy in the germ world, he is, according to chapter 1, "the germiest of the germs"; and so he can observe the germs from their point of view as well as from his human memories. Though wildly imaginative, the story he tells is for a time kept under control through the author's controlling satiric purpose. The United States is satirized as GRQ, Getrichquick, and Christian Science is another object of satire. The style too is effective, at first. In a preface the "translator" describes the style of the original microbic as that of a stevedore in short sleeves and overalls, but he is by no means a grown-up Huck Finn. Here and there one finds touches of the early exuberance of Mark Twain, for the first half is told with considerable zest, but eventually the effort at ingenuity comes to dominate the narrative, and the interest of the work falters much as it does in "Eddypus."

Mark Twain's explanation for dropping "Microbes" was that he wanted to finish "No. 44,"[7] and as already noted he did work on the book in June and July. In June he also wrote "As Concerns Interpreting the Deity," not published until 1917, when Paine included it in *What Is Man? and Other Essays*—minus the last 750 words that seem to have been the excuse for writing the piece. A complete version appears in *What Is Man? and Other Philosophical Writings* (1973). This delightful and quite successful hoax begins with what appears to be a learned discussion of Egyptian and Dighton Rock inscriptions, but the real purpose was to mock the pastor of the Plymouth Church of Brooklyn, who had interpreted the Russo-Japanese War of 1904–5 as God's work. A June 12, 1905, New York *Times* story on the minister's interpretation of the deity was the occasion of this good essay, which had of course only contemporary relevance.

On July 12, Mark Twain felt obliged to meet requests from Duneka for contributions to *Harper's Magazine* and turned from "No. 44" to "Eve's Diary." His technique, he explained to Duneka, was for Eve to use "Extracts from Adam's Diary," written some dozen years before, as "her unwitting and un[con]scious text, since to use any other text would have been an imbecility."[8] As a kind of tribute to Olivia Clemens, the diary emphasizes what the author believed to be distinctively female characteristics: love of beauty and nature, affection, reliance on intuition, curiosity. Eve is a young girl, full of wonder at the creation and at herself. She considers herself an experiment, and when she sees Adam, she calls him the other Experiment. Since she is very soon much attracted to him, her efforts to win his love apparently lead to the Fall. "I tried to get him some of those apples, but I cannot learn to throw straight. I failed, but I think the good intentions pleased him. They are forbidden, and he says I shall come to harm; but so I come to harm through pleasing him, why shall I care for that harm?" She does not report the event of the Fall, but afterward she records, "The Garden is lost, but I have found *him*, and am content." A long examination of *why* she loves him concludes, "*Merely because he is masculine, I think.*" "Eve's Diary" ends with an epitaph for Eve—and Olivia Clemens. Adam records, "Wherever she was, *there* was Eden." The diary is good-humored and so full of Eve's delightful naiveté that its sentimentality is never offensive; one welcomes Mark Twain's return to a portrayal of youthful innocence. Of his Eve, Mark Twain wrote, she "has no refinements, either of conduct or speech, & I think she is charming."[9] The "Diary" was published in the Christmas issue of *Harper's Magazine* and made into a book in 1906, with many illustrations.

Thereafter Mark Twain revised "Adam's Diary," which he judged "not literature." "I have struck out 700 words," he wrote Duneka, "and inserted 5 MS pages of new matter (650 words) and now Adam's Diary is dam good—sixty times as good as it was." He added, "I hate

to have the old Adam go out any more—*don't* put it on the presses
again, let's put the new one in place of it. . . ."[10] What happened next
is strange; it suggests either that Duneka had a casual attitude toward
his responsibilities as editor or that the writer had a change of heart,
for when "Adam's Diary" next appeared, it was the same old Adam
that his creator had rejected. Duneka had received the revised manuscript and written to Clemens, "Thank you ever so much for the corrections of 'Adam's Diary,' which I shall have made at once. . . ."[11]
The five new pages, extant at the Mark Twain Papers,[12] *were* published, but not in "Adam's Diary"—they appear toward the end of
Eve's, where they are introduced as "Extract from Adam's Diary,"
though they do not belong there.

While Eve is a man's view of a woman, Adam is almost a comic
character; Paine says, "Mark Twain created Adam in his own image"[13]—
he should have said "in the image of the earlier Mark Twain." Adam
first sees Eve as competition; she is preempting his territory. His comments are full of delicious anachronisms: "The new creature eats too
much fruit. We are going to run short, most likely." In the original
version it was not an apple but a chestnut, a moldy joke, that caused
the Fall. In both Adam's diary and Eve's, the Fall is treated in a wholly
human context.

One charming passage written for "Adam's Diary" remains unpublished. The fragment is probably the one mentioned in a letter
written by Duneka to Clemens in September 1905: "Replying to your
letter of yesterday suggesting that it might be well to supplement 'Eve's
Diary' with a new chapter for 'Adam's Diary,' I am sorry to say that
the Christmas number is already made up and it would entail a very
great deal of expense and delay to make any changes at this time."[14]
The passage reads:

> *Saturday.* The Voice says he made this property in six consecutive days,
> and is resting to-day. (Consecutive—a good word; will set it down and
> use it again.) He says he made me yesterday. Also the creature with the
> long hair, that follows me about, and calls herself Eve and says she is a
> Woman—whatever that may be. Seems bent upon living with me—*is*
> bent upon living with me, in fact. This will not answer; it would be
> irregular. I hinted as much, but she lacks delicacy, and was not disturbed.
> I said it would cause remark. She said there was nobody but the animals
> to take notice of it. I reminded her that there was herself, and also me,
> and added that the true basis of right living is principle, not expediency;
> that an upright life uprightly lived for show would be a sham, and val-
> ueless. She tossed her head and sniffed at that, and said "I wouldn't be as
> goody-goody as you for wages." I reminded her, coldly, that such a speech

was hardly proper, from one mere acquaintance to another; that I had had no formal introduction to her, knew nothing about her character and antecedents, that she had intruded upon the estate unasked, and that I must be excused if I regarded her ways as somewhat too familiar, in the circumstances. She retorted that I was as much as intimating that she was an adventuress. This being the truth, I was not willing to deny it, therefore an uncomfortable silence supervened. Then she said that if all respectability was lodged in me, some share could hardly be denied her, since out of a rib of my body she had been made. This was too much. I had not missed any rib, and said so. She said I was asleep at the time. It could not be profitable to dispute with a person who stopped not at inventing history when argument failed; wherefore I turned my back and went my way, leaving her to entertain herself with the animals, a thing much to her liking and theirs, apparently.[15]

Read in the context of a knowledge of Mark Twain's literary career, the passage has a great deal to offer. Here he returns to his amused attitude toward gentility by creating the ultimate snob, the first one. (This Adam and the Adam of the rest of the diary are quite different.) It is further evidence that the social graces that Clemens adopted under his wife's tutelage were a veneer, that he was after all *not* veneer clear through.

The longest of the several pieces on man's earliest ancestors is "Eve's Autobiography." Here Eve looks back at her nine hundred years of life and quotes at length from her diary record of the years before the Fall. This begins at her creation. She records how she found that all the creatures except herself had mates. A talking parrot that for a time she thinks might serve soon proves inadequate. Only after a year's strenuous search does she find Adam. This sketch, unlike the other ones, is both humorous and bitter—mostly humorous. This time Adam and Eve are both scientists, with dictionary-making as an avocation. Though uneven, the piece has some delightful touches. Here is a passage from Eve's diary for the year 15: "The children promise well. . . . Cain is the cleverest of all. He is really an expert at making the simpler kind of fossils, and will soon be taking the most of that work off our hands, I think. He has invented one fossil, all by himself—the planning and arranging of prehistoric deposits."[16]

During the summer of 1905 one more piece came from Mark Twain's pen. In April, Jean Clemens had published in *Harper's Weekly* "A Word for the Horses," on the evils of checkreins and martingales. Perhaps as a result, in mid-September Mark Twain received a letter encouraging him "to write a story of an old horse that is finally given over to the bull-ring." The letter-writer was campaigning to put a stop to bullfighting in Spain. The obliging author replied that he would try.[17] After a good deal of effort, he finished the story later that month, pleased because he had been able to draw on his memories of Susy in the portrait of Cathy, the little girl who is devoted to Soldier Boy, the horse killed in the bullring. A long story, over seventeen thousand words, "A Horse's Tale" was published in two installments in *Harper's Magazine*, in August and September of 1906, and in 1907 as an illustrated book. Mark Twain's last story to be published in his lifetime might well have been written as the basis for a Shirley Temple movie. Told in part by the horse himself, in part through letters, interspersed with chapters wholly in dialogue—one between Soldier Boy and a Mexican Plug—the story is interesting, but with two objects of sentimental interest, the girl and her horse (both of whom are killed in the bull ring), it is distinctly overdone, though exactly what had been requested of him. In a 1906 autobiographical dictation, Mark Twain included a letter he had received complaining about his "heart-rendering stories," especially "A Horse's Tale." He replied that the story was a response to a request and "was not written for publication here, but in Spain."[18] There seems to be, however, no record of its publication in Spain.

After leaving New Hampshire in October, Clemens returned to New York. At the time, his life was largely devoted to social engagements, the most monumental of which was a seventieth-birthday celebration. Then, as if to illustrate the writer's theory concerning the force of "outside influences," early in 1906 Albert Bigelow Paine entered Clemens's life and soon arranged to become the author's biographer. On January 9 work began on Paine's collection of materials when Mark Twain once more returned to his autobiography, now with an added motive. The task was to be enormous but easy. On the first day the writer stated his plans to Paine. The stenographer present for this auspicious occasion recorded:

> The only thing possible for me is to talk about the thing that something suggests at the moment—something in the middle of my life, perhaps, or something that happened only a few months ago. It is my purpose to extend these notes to 600,000 words, and possibly more. But that is going to take a long time—a long time.
>
> My idea is this—that I write an autobiography. When that autobiography is finished—or before it is finished—then you take the man-

uscript and decide on how much of a biography to make. But this is no holiday excursion—it is a journey.[19]

It was to be a long journey. Thereafter dictations became a regular, often daily event. Though Mark Twain made much of the dangerously frank character of what he dictated, those closest to him soon knew that his comments had distinct limitations. He himself told Isabel Lyon that he would tell the truth about himself but with one reservation: "There were the Rousseau confessions, but I am going to leave that kind alone, for Rousseau seems to have looked after that end."[20] Paine soon found that as source materials the dictations had to be checked, for "these marvelous reminiscences bore only an atmospheric relation to history."[21]

Beginning with twelve dictations in January, Mark Twain continued for three years. Until June in the first year, there were each month from seven to seventeen sessions; then there was a short break. Of this early group, a month was devoted to comments inspired by Susy's biography of her father, which she had begun in 1885 when she was fourteen. Often he proceeded by process of association. Sometimes he worked from obituaries. In June, back in Dublin, New Hampshire, he dictated for five days not reminiscences but chapters that he promised Howells "will get my heirs & assigns burnt alive" if they are published "this side of 2006 A.D.," his reflections on religion. By this time he was describing the dictations as "already perfectly outrageous in spots." He liked what he said. "I don't care for my other books, now, but I dote on this one. . . ." He described "the law of the book: the newest & hottest interest takes precedence of *anything* I may be talking about."

After another break in late June and July, he continued throughout 1906, when a total of 134 dictations were recorded. In 1907 as interest cooled there were fewer, seventy in all, with only four during November and December. In 1908 there were just thirty-four. The last dictations were made in early 1909, the very last being dated April 16. Dictations averaged about 1,500 words each, making the total (including undated dictations) about 450,000 words, to which should be added some 60,000 words written or dictated before 1906. But what could be done with such a huge and shapeless mass of material?

Though Mark Twain referred to the autobiography as a work intended to be published posthumously, a first step toward publication was taken in August 1906, less than nine months after the project was conceived, when Mark Twain arranged with George Harvey, president of Harper's and editor of the *North American Review*, to publish selections in the *Review*. These appeared in what was for a time a fortnightly, from September 7, 1906, until December, then in monthly installments from January through October 1907, twenty-five installments in all, and all these only from the dictations of winter and spring 1906. For them, the author received thirty thousand dollars, which he eventually used to build a house at Redding, Connecticut. In 1909 he used materials from dictations to publish *Is Shakespeare Dead?* After Mark Twain's death, Paine published a few pages and a good many passages in his 1912 three-volume work, *Mark Twain: A Biography*. In 1922 Paine published a few more pages in *Harper's Magazine*, and a little in 1923 on the Whittier birthday speech in his collection *Mark Twain's Speeches*. Finally in 1924 he published a two-volume edition, including much of the pre-1906 material but selections only from the dictations through April 11, 1906; he thus drew on only 71 of 252. These he published in the order of composition, "in accordance with the author's wishes," according to Paine. He did not include in these volumes all that had been published in the earlier periodical selections. Apparently he intended to publish at least another volume from dictations following those of April 1906, but perhaps because the reviews of the first two volumes were not enthusiastic, he prepared no more. Paine's successor as literary editor, Bernard DeVoto, published another volume of selections, chiefly from dictations later than those Paine had used. He called it *Mark Twain in Eruption: Hitherto Unpublished Pages About Men and Events*. Whereas Paine's selection had emphasized the author's life, DeVoto presented his volume as "kind of table talk." Besides selections on Hannibal and Mark Twain's comments on his own work, DeVoto published many discussions of political figures, especially Theodore Roosevelt. His arrangement is not biographical but topical.

In 1959 Charles Neider made use of unpublished manuscripts as well as the published parts to prepare what he called *The Autobiography of Mark Twain*. His arrangement is intended to show Mark Twain telling the story of his life in chronological order, a difficult task for an editor since in a single dictation the author discussed both early events and much later ones. Neider chose to include little of the social and political criticism that DeVoto had published, but he did provide some thirty thousand words of previously unpublished material. For the serious reader, this edition labors under an additional difficulty: since the selections in it from the dictations are not dated, unlike those in Paine's and DeVoto's volumes, it is hard to locate the source of a given passage. Neider had hoped to include in his version the reflections on religion that were dictated in June 1906—though they are not autobiographical and thus do not fit into his scheme, but Clara Clemens Samossoud denied permission to publish them until 1963, when they appeared in the autumn issue of the *Hudson Review*. Tentative plans to publish a more complete edition of the autobiography were made by Frederick Anderson in his position as literary editor of the Mark Twain estate, but his death in 1979 interrupted the effort, which may be taken up in time by Dr. Robert Hirst, the current editor.

The rationale for Mark Twain's autobiography was best stated when in 1907 Mark Twain wrote, "Dictated things are talk, and talk is all the better and all the more natural when it stumbles a little here and there." [22] This principle reminds one of the talk of Mark Twain's vernacular narrators, such as Simon Wheeler and Captain Stormfield, or even Huckleberry Finn, though Huck signs his report "Yours truly," as if it were a letter. Many of the dictations are natural, easy, comfortable, and informal, and some are also vituperative, unfocused, egotistical, and trivial. Unlike the other long pieces of the author's last years, they are not burdened by expectations—the author's or the reader's—of structure or even coherence. But the author was laboring under the mistaken notion that he was at last telling the whole truth. In a letter to Clemens in February 1904, Howells wisely questioned whether anyone could tell the truth about himself: "The black truth, which we all know of ourselves in our hearts, or only the whity-brown truth of the pericardium, or the nice, whitened truth of the shirtfront?" It is the whity-brown truth that Mark Twain tells, at best. For example, when Clara debuted as a singer at Norfolk, Connecticut, he said that he had urged her to publicize herself as "Mark Twain's daughter." "This was vinegar for Clara, but saccharine for me." After she sang, he "made a plunge for the stage . . . to congratulate her and . . . to show off and get my share of the glory." [23] He admitted his egotism: "I like compliments, praises, flatteries, I cordially enjoy all such things, and am grieved and disappointed when what I call a 'barren mail' arrives—a mail that hasn't any compliments in it." [24] The "Reflections on Religion" are outspoken, but not much more so than some other of the author's late comments. He calls God hard names here:

> In His destitution of one and all of the qualities which could grace a God and invite respect for Him and reverence and worship, the real God, the genuine God, the Maker of the mighty universe is just like all the other

gods in the list. He proves every day that he takes no interest in man, nor in the other animals, further than to torture them, slay them, and get out of this pastime such entertainment as it may afford—and do what he can not to get weary of the eternal and changeless monotony of it.[25]

There are no real revelations in the autobiography. Too often the habits of a lifetime of lecturing and after-dinner speaking betrayed the author and he became an entertainer once again. However edited and organized, the autobiography is not a great book, if it can be called a book at all. Mark Twain made far better use of his memories in *Tom Sawyer, Huckleberry Finn,* and "Old Times on the Mississippi," for there they are shaped, filtered through nostalgia, and refined with art. "Narrative *writing,*" he said, "is always disappointing. The moment you pick up a pen you begin to lose the spontaneity of the personal relation, which contains the very essence of interest. With shorthand dictation one can talk as if he were at his own dinner-table—always a most inspiring place."[26] No doubt dictating his memoirs was interesting to the speaker; though full of spontaneity, the results are not always interesting to the reader.

Moreover, large aspects of the literary and personal life were ignored, for Mark Twain used his autobiography not to provide a record of his life but for entertainment—his own chiefly—and to continue his career as a writer for profit, profits to both himself and his descendants. He used it, too, for therapy, to relieve himself of guilt over the deaths of his brother Henry and his son Langdon. When he had finished his account of another source of guilt, his bankruptcy, he said: "There—Thanks be! A hundred times I have tried to tell this intolerable story with a pen, but I never could do it. It always made me sick before I got half-way to the middle of it. But this time I have held my grip and walked the floor and emptied it all out of my system, and I hope never to hear of it again."[27] Similarly, he wrote to Howells in June 1906 about the relief of getting some things "out of my system, where they have been festering for years—& that was the main thing," more important apparently than communicating what he had to say to posterity. "I feel better, now," he sighed.

Sometimes Mark Twain simply editorialized on news events: clippings are attached to the dictations. Sometimes he inserted unpublished manuscripts, such as that of "Wapping Alice," part of the dictation of April 9, 1907. When he was awarded an honorary doctorate from Oxford University in 1907 and went to receive it, he was acclaimed as a national hero in Britain. From this trip he had materials for nineteen days of dictation at Tuxedo Park, New York, where he summered that year. Some amusing and valuable remarks are scattered through the unpublished materials, in the midst of opinions he had been volunteering for years. It took him a long time to tire of hearing his own voice.

In the year when Mark Twain began his autobiographical dictations, 1906, he took up his pen long enough to begin a substantial essay that is also autobiographical. Begun as a commemorative essay on his dead daughter ten years after her death, it was later broadened to include extensive and highly amusing descriptions of the people who had influenced Susy and her sisters, such as accounts of George Griffin and Patrick McAleer, two long-time Clemens servants, and a funny portrait of the "Egyptian volcano," the most productive of Clara's many wet nurses, whose proper name was Maria McLaughlin and whose ability to consume food and drink was enormous. During the year's shortest month she drank, he reported, 256 pints of beer, though she by no means restricted her liquid intake to that beverage. "A Family Sketch," some twelve thousand words, deserves publication more than any of the unpublished autobiographical dictations.[28]

The decision to dictate his autobiography had a significant effect on the remainder of Mark Twain's career: it all but stopped him from writing anything for some time. His letters of early 1906 are full of expressions of satisfaction in the dictations, both the process and the product, the medium and the message. Both seem to have encouraged his egotism and his love of showing off. Perhaps as a consequence, late in 1906 at copyright hearings in Washington, D.C., Clemens made his first winter public appearance in the white suit that was to become habitual. After receiving his honorary degree from Oxford, he found occasions to wear his scarlet Oxford gown over his white suit, for example at Clara's wedding in 1909. The fact that Paine was preparing notes for the biography he was to write and was traveling to Europe and the American West for materials and that his letters were being prepared for publication must have made the author feel that he had now been admitted to the Writers' Pantheon and could enjoy himself. Toward that end in 1908 the author created the Mark Twain Company, to relieve himself of the task of overseeing his estate and "to keep the earnings of Mr. Clemens's books continually in the family, even after the copyright on the books themselves expires," as the New York *Times* reported.[29] The company survived until 1978, when by the terms of the will of Clara Clemens Samossoud it was succeeded by the Mark Twain Foundation, which still collects the author's royalties.

Writings by Mark Twain besides the autobiography (he revised and corrected the dictation transcripts in pen) continued to appear in print during his last years. As noted, "Eve's Diary" and "A Horse's Tale" were published as books in 1906 and 1907. The author finally released, somewhat reluctantly, an extract from Captain Stormfield's story of his visit to heaven; it appeared first in two issues of *Harper's Magazine*, then in 1909 as a book. It had been held back so long that Mark Twain was surprised when it was found to be inoffensive. What would have been found offensive, though some readers might well have judged it one of Mark Twain's best short pieces of his last years, is "Little Bessie," which he began on a yachting trip with Rogers in early 1908. It opens with the question that Susy Clemens had asked so plaintively years before: "Mama, why is there so much pain and sorrow and suffering? What is it all for?" In the series of dialogues that follow, little Bessie, almost three, persistently asks her mother probing questions about God's justice, the virgin birth, and the Trinity; she finds it difficult to accept the pious, Sunday school answers. Bessie's charming naiveté makes these few pages amusing. The skeptical attitude Mark Twain had shown in his Western sketches survived for over forty years, becoming deeper dyed. Paine published a selection of "Little Bessie" in his biography; the complete dialogues are in *Fables of Man.*

In the late spring of 1908 the Clemenses moved into the Connecticut house built with earnings from the autobiography; it was now called Stormfield, after the recently published sketch. There was, however, not much time remaining for life there. The death of Clemens's sister's son, Samuel Moffett, in the summer shook the author badly. Perhaps that death and the author's resulting depression and illness had something to do with what he wrote in September, for inclusion in "No. 44"—a chapter in which 44 teaches August Feldner another lesson by providing a historical pageant of the dead, biblical figures, Caesars, King Arthur, even the Missing Link. This serves as chapter 33 of the published version (1969) and may have been an effort to connect what he had written earlier to the "Conclusion of the Book," in which 44 disappears.

For a while Stormfield was too full of guests for its illustrious occupant to undertake any writing. But early in 1909, after receiving proofs of a book on Sir Francis Bacon, George Greenwood's *The Shakespeare Problem Restated*, he began the series of dictations that became a little book, *Is Shakespeare Dead?* Here Mark Twain describes the paucity of biographical information on Shakespeare and suggests that Bacon is the most likely candidate for authorship of the great plays. Some interesting pages recall the author's piloting days, when he first became familiar with the plays, but when Mark Twain compares his Hannibal reputation with Shakespeare's Stratford one, the results are not gratifying. Moreover, Mark Twain inserted into his work twenty-two pages of Greenwood's work, without permission— hardly appropriate behavior for an advocate of copyright laws. Whereas Harper was contracted to publish whatever Mark Twain wrote, the editors now were eager to shut Mark Twain off. The writer's career had fallen on evil days; he was a failing old man.

The complicated jealousies of his household—involving conflicts among Clemens's manager, Ralph Ashcroft, his secretary Isabel Lyon, his daughter Clara, and his biographer Paine resulted in Clemens's firing members of his entourage on whom he had intimately depended. Subsequently he composed a long account of what he conceived of as their treachery. This "Ashcroft-Lyon Manuscript" (unpublished) is a "letter" to Howells, since the autobiographer was now substituting a new plan for recording his meditations—"to write letters to friends & *not send them*," as he wrote Howells in April 1909. There are over four hundred pages of manuscript, to which are attached clippings, accounts, and whatever the old man could suppose might be part of the case against the two. It is a sad story.

Sometime in 1909, Mark Twain showed that he was still capable of turning out perfectly competent, if undistinguished, commercial fiction. "The International Lightning Trust" is a rather amusing satire on business practices, with greed being treated sympathetically this time. Two young men offer insurance against being struck by lightning; they reap huge profits. The story was in the hands of a Harper editor when Clemens died in 1910. It remained unpublished until its 1972 appearance in *Fables of Man*.

In the fall of 1909, Mark Twain wrote for *Harper's Bazaar* an essay on "The Turning Point of My Life." It was to have been part of a series by literary figures on the topic. Mark Twain's original version began with what Paine called "one of his impossible burlesque fancies," but Paine's—and Jean Clemens's—disapproval seems to have brought on not only a revision but also an attack of angina pectoris. (Clemens had been diagnosed as suffering from the disease in June.) The burlesque tells of the fortunes of two apples, Tom Crab and William Greening. At first the latter seems to have all the luck, but Crab is selected by Luther Burbank and is so nurtured that he produces "a great spray of hitherto unimaginable roses." Later revised in Bermuda, with the apple adventure dropped, it was published in February 1910. In "The Turning Point" Mark Twain set forth his deterministic philosophy by explaining how he came to be a writer. The account is a not altogether accurate survey of a chain of circumstances that led to Mark Twain's career, beginning with the illness Clemens had suffered when he was a boy. "I can say with truth that the reason I am in the literary profession is because I had the measles when I was twelve years old." The essay is a polished, interesting piece of prose that shows Mark Twain could still be a craftsman at age seventy-four.

In October 1909 Mark Twain returned once more to "dangerous" writings, and this time he produced something that would have shocked his readers far more than "Little Bessie" had it been published at the time. In August, Mark Twain had warmed up for this work by writing a letter (first published in a 1973 collection) on God as the author of evil. It concludes that "if our Maker is all powerful for good or evil, He is not in His right mind."[30] The thirteen "Letters from the Earth," some seventeen thousand words written in October and later, begin as reports from Satan to Saint Michael and Saint Gabriel from the earth, where Satan is suffering a temporary banishment. He is shocked and bewildered by man's strange Christianity. Soon the fiction is largely forgotten, and Mark Twain expresses his mature opinions on the folly of man's worship of God and the hypocrisy of Christianity; the ignorance of the writers of the Bible, with the story of Noah receiving extended treatment; the stupidity of the Bible's teachings; and God as the author of illness. Though the letters begin by attacking man for his crazy theology, they soon shift, subtly, to attacks on the "real" God, as Mark Twain had called Him in his 1906 dictations. While the work is not finished or polished, the writing is exceptionally vital and brisk. Topics he had taken up elsewhere in a bitterly pessimistic, even angry, mood here are treated with good-humored detachment, perhaps because of the fictional pose taken in the early letters.

In his autobiography, Mark Twain devoted one dictation to an account of his conversation with Elinor Glyn, an English novelist, with whom he had talked about sex. In the dictation he expresses surprise at his own frankness but describes himself as a servant of convention, without which mankind would be plunged into "confusion and disorder and anarchy."[31] But at the very end of his life, he cast aside his inhibitions—he was writing now, not dictating to a stenographer—and in "Letters from the Earth," hiding behind only a thin fiction, he describes sexual pleasure as one of his chief concerns. Intercourse is described as the greatest delight of heaven. The writer stresses repeatedly the superiority of woman's sexuality. She is "competent every day, competent every night." On the other hand, man

> is competent from the age of sixteen or seventeen thenceforward for thirty-five years. After 50 his performance is of poor quality, the intervals between are wide, and its satisfactions of no great value to either party; whereas his great-grandmother is as good as new. There is nothing the matter with her plant. Her candlestick is as firm as ever, whereas his candle is increasingly softened by the weather of age, as years go by, until at last it can no longer stand, and it is mournfully laid to rest in the hope of a blessed resurrection which is never to come.[32]

One can only wonder if this zesty report is not the result of Mark Twain's liberation from the inhibitions that he had uncomfortably lived with during his years with Olivia Clemens—literary inhibitions, that is. Obviously he was in good spirits when he began these letters; only in the last of them does the humor fade and personal grievances begin to take over. A long but self-sufficient fragment, "Letters from the Earth" was not released until 1962. (Bernard DeVoto tried to publish it in 1939 but was prevented by Clara Clemens Samossoud's objection.) The publication drew wide attention. A much better text was published in *What Is Man? and Other Philosophical Writings* (1973).

At the end of 1909, after a month in Bermuda, Clemens returned home to celebrate Christmas with Jean, at Stormfield. (Clara, now Mrs. Ossip Gabrilowitsch, was abroad.) On the night of December 23, Jean died, drowned in the bathtub during an epileptic fit. Her father called her death "this final disaster."[33] And in an effort to control his reaction he wrote a last essay. He told Paine, who published "The Death of Jean" in *Harper's Magazine* in December 1910, that it might serve as the "final chapter" of his autobiography. The essay looks back at the author's griefs, the losses of Susy and Mrs. Clemens, and of friends too. It describes the circumstances of Jean's death and his recent happy talks with her. It is a sentimental essay, a kind of farewell to life.

Early in 1910, Clemens visited Bermuda once again, now in poor health. There he wrote one more sketch, "Advice to Paine," suggestions on deportment on arriving at heaven's gates or the "other place."

Significantly, it is a last attempt at humor, and remarkably successful. Paine published a few selections in his biography, but the whole of this amusing piece deserves publication. It begins: "In hell it is not good form to refer, even unostentatiously, to your relatives in heaven, if persons are present who have none there." Some other suggestions: "Do not show off. St. Peter dislikes it. The simpler you are dressed, the better it will please him. He cannot abide showy costumes. Above all things, avoid over-dressing. A pair of spurs & a fig-leaf is a plenty." "Be careful about etiquette when invited to dinner. For evening dress, leave off your spurs."[34] With these instructions, the writer faced the next world, finished with this one.

On March 25, Clemens knew from chest pains that he had little time left. He returned to New York, then to Stormfield, where within a week he died, talking at the last of dual personality, of Jekyll and Hyde. Mark Twain was harder to kill, and lives on. Since April 20, 1910, a whole library of previously unpublished works has appeared. That omnium gatherum, the autobiography, still requires years of somebody's attention before it can be said to be published.[35]

CHAPTER TWELVE

A Backward Glance

"**E**XPERIENCE has taught me long ago that if *I* tell a boy's story or anybody else's it is never worth printing; it comes from the head not the heart, and always goes into the wastebasket."[1] So said Mark Twain in 1906. To this a reader might reply, "Not quite always, Mark, though in your *best* fiction—which is what you were discussing in this dictation—you nearly always did employ an imagined storyteller, Huck Finn being of course your best. Some of your 'boys' are men who tell of their youthful adventures, like Joan of Arc's friend Conte; your Yankee seems like an adult only in years. But you have a good point still. It is probably no accident that your least successful novels, such as *The American Claimant*, are narrated by you as the omniscient novelist. *The Prince and the Pauper* would have been less pretentious had you decided to have a character tell that story. Your notion seems especially sound for your short pieces. While you created some disasters, such as the unspeakable 'The Invalid's Story' and your pathetic dog's and horse's tales, most of your failures seem to have resulted from your lack of interest in the teller and his telling, and most of your successes from the creation of memorable narrators, from Simon Wheeler and Jim Baker to Stormfield and Adam and Eve."

But probably Mark Twain is not listening. What the reminiscing author chose to forget back in 1906 are his great early triumphs, created when *he* told his stories as "Mark Twain." In the early years of that wonderful voice, the author created a character whose personality is bigger than the books in which he appears, perhaps because the books themselves—*The Innocents Abroad, Roughing It, Life on the Mississippi*—are so uneven. Then that old Mark Twain went away, too soon. By the end of 1884 Clemens would write that he used only his pen name when he appeared before the public.[2] He was no longer making a distinction between his eccentric narrator and Samuel Clemens. The individualistic quality was disappearing, especially after the Whittier birthday speech disaster. This old, original, and authentic Mark Twain was a humorist, but under the influence of his wife and his Hartford neighbors, as well as friends such as Howells, he came to regard the humorist's role as beneath his dignity. In his 1884–85 lecture tour he broke down after a highly successful performance and told Cable, "I am demeaning myself, I am allowing myself to be a mere buffoon. I can't endure it any longer."[3]

The writer retained a fondness for his old creation. During his round-the-world tour he included many pieces told either by a vernacular narrator or by the Mark Twain of old, such as Baker's bluejay yarn and the Mexican Plug story from *Roughing It*. He continued to find pleasure in reading aloud such stories as "Captain Stormfield's Visit" and the one about the Reverend Sam Jones entering heaven. (After reading "Stormfield" at a dinner party in New York in 1894, he wrote to Olivia, "It is a raging pity that that book has never been printed."[4])

Though the writer ceased to be "Mark Twain" and became Mark Twain, he remained by temperament and talent a humorist even while he judged himself more and more worthy to play the role of sage or even philosopher. Eventually he felt obliged to defend his earlier identity as a humorist, long after he had taken steps to abandon it. In 1888 he called his work "a worthy calling: that with all the lightness and frivolity it has one serious purpose, one aim, one specialty, and it is constant to it—the deriding of shams, the exposure of pretentious falsities, the laughing of stupid superstitions out of existence. . . ."[5]

His identification as humorist and as author of subscription books has misled many of those who think they know Samuel Clemens, or Mark Twain, or both. The writer himself was largely responsible for myths about himself. He appeared, for example, to be not much of a reader; presumably he thought that he would be more acceptable to his audience if he appeared less sophisticated than he was. He was, it is now known, a very bookish man, devoted to reading. His decision to appear otherwise no doubt contributed to his popularity, but it has made him seem far more limited than he was.

Mark Twain's native and developed abilities as storyteller and humorist were shaped by his commercial bent. After undirected early years, his great success with *The Innocents Abroad* and his marriage to a woman accustomed to wealth did much to determine what he would write, first subscription books, then in addition magazine pieces to be collected for book publication. His view of magazine-writing—and indirectly of his wife's censorship—is expressed in a letter to the publisher of the *Ladies' Home Journal*, who had requested portions of his autobiography for publication in 1898. He explained that what he had written "would not answer for your magazine. Indeed a great deal of it is written in too independent a fashion for any magazine. One may publish a *book* and print whatever his family shall approve and allow to pass, but it is the Public that edits a Magazine, and so by the sheer necessities of the case a magazine's liberties are rather limited."[6] Striking to find a writer explaining to an editor his responsibilities; striking too that Mark Twain supposed that the general rule was that a writer's *family* decided what he might be permitted to publish.

Because he began his career as a book author by writing long subscription books, Mark Twain always measured his creativity by quantity. His work went well when he "piled up manuscript." One finds him writing to Howells about his autobiography in June 1906: "I've dictated (from Jan. 9) 210,000 words, & the 'fat' adds about 50,000 more. The 'fat' is old pigeon-holed things of the years gone by, which I or the editors dasn't print." In the author's eyes, much of the virtue of the autobiography was found in its spectacular dimensions.

Perhaps quantity was emphasized so much because Mark Twain was uncertain about his ability to judge quality. His attitude toward his own artistic principles was frequently modest, and for good reason. In a letter of 1888, published in *The Art of Authorship* (1890), he wrote, "Upon consideration, I am not sure that I have methods in composition. I do suppose I have—but they somehow refuse to take shape in my mind; their details refuse to separate and submit to classification and description; they remain a jumble."[7] Perhaps this modesty was responsible for his willingness to permit editors and publishers to make a jumble of such works as *Life on the Mississippi*, *Tom Sawyer Abroad*, and *Following the Equator*, though what he originally put into *A Connecticut Yankee* demonstrates how ill-equipped he was to be a critic of his own creation. Moreover, the huge collection of unpublished, mostly unfinished works that he left at his death reinforces one's sense that in his last years he was an uncertain, often fumbling artist, painfully uncertain of how to use his genius. He attempted to write sequels or to adopt current fads, such as the detective story, and presented once again his fixed philosophical ideas or, almost obsessively, another fictional portrait of his brother Orion.

An important factor in Mark Twain's career is what he called in 1896 "my stupid notion that I could do no work at home," a notion that dominated him "for many years," including his best ones. He told an interviewer:

> The fact of it is that for many years while at home, in America, I have written little or nothing on account of social calls upon my time. There is too much social life in my city for a literary man, and so for twenty years I gave up the attempt to do anything during nine months of twelve I am at home. It has only been during the three months that I have annually been on vacation and have been supposed to be holiday-making that I have written anything. It has been the same during the five years that I have been away from America. I have done little or no work. I wish now that I had done differently and had persisted in writing when at home. I could easily have done it, although I thought I could not. I seemed to think then that I was never going to grow old, but I know better than that now.[8]

This statement suggests a belated recognition of an ill-spent life. Though he was exaggerating, it is true that during long periods he let his attention be distracted, not only by social calls but by both ill-conceived literary ideas, especially his belief that he could reap rich profits as a dramatist, an idea that died hard, and by business ambitions that not only wasted his time but led to traumatic disappointment.

But Mark Twain's greatest problem as a writer may have been trying to cope with himself. In 1906 he referred to "periodical and sudden changes in me, from deep melancholy to half insane tempests and cyclones of humor" that were "among the curiosities of my life."[9] This tendency toward the manic-depressive may help explain the unevenness in tone of his writings—and their unevenness in quality as well. It may be another source of the author's abiding interest in doubles and multiple personalities, an interest that troubled even his deathbed.

That Mark Twain failed frequently to utilize his abilities in the creation of imaginative literature is an understatement. He was prodigal of his talents. He poured himself out brilliantly at times, even in unsent letters. Many of these, as well as a remarkable quantity of letters he sent, have survived and are now being published. Such collections as the two-volume selection that Paine edited in 1917 and the correspondence with Howells published in 1960 suggest what is there. Some letters are as good as his best sketches.[10] Angry, funny, more revealing than his autobiography—these tell the story of the life of Samuel Clemens and reveal his mind and heart.[11]

One fact about Mark Twain's literary career that has been given too little attention is that he flourished during an undistinguished period in the history of American literature. Some of the other notable writers of his day, such as Emily Dickinson and Walt Whitman, were not permitted to contribute much to contemporary cultural life; another, Henry James, left America for more congenial surroundings in England. Mark Twain's years abroad were valuable to him intellectually, no doubt, but they had little effect on *how* he wrote. In America his was an age when genteel and sentimental novelists were creating a new audience of middlebrows, with serious writers threatened thereby with a loss of their public. Mark Twain contributed to this milieu, but it victimized him as well. He was very close to William Dean Howells, who was useful to him as editor and literary friend, but the other editors and writers with whom Clemens associated were distinctly limited. Henry M. Alden, Thomas Bailey Aldrich, Frederick Duneka, Richard Watson Gilder, Edmund Clarence Stedman, Charles Dudley Warner, and their like were all minor talents, but these friends and associates helped create a literary epoch that was tame, thin, genteel, and essentially uninteresting. Uncertain of his own gifts, Mark Twain was not the man to improve the standards of his day. That he was not affected by them more adversely than he was is amazing. While it is difficult to separate Mark Twain from his times, since he was very much a part of them, it is obvious that he thrived despite, not because of, his literary environment. He might have compensated for this fortune through reading, but while he read avidly and widely, he read chiefly for content, for ideas and information. He borrowed episodes rather than techniques, though the example of Robert Browning seems to have influenced him in the writing of the soliloquies of the czar and King Leopold.

On the credit side of the ledger, the long life of Samuel Clemens was one that brought him close to his country's history and the character of its regions. He knew the Border South, the Deep South, and the Frontier West; in Boston he met Emerson, Longfellow, Holmes, and Whittier, writers from an earlier age; he knew Grant and the Standard Oil chief Henry H. Rogers; he was familiar with slavery and the political corruptions of the post–Civil War years, the "Gilded Age"; he loaned his pen to attacks on turn-of-the-century imperialism. Moreover, he knew the world beyond, from his residences in Austria, England, France, Germany, and Switzerland and from his trip around the world. A good deal of this knowledge is reflected in his books, so that reading them serves as an introduction to Clemens's three-quarters of a century. At its best this reflection was far from mere reportage, for the author mixed in his awareness of injustice and suffering as well as his nostalgic memories and often an appealing sense of the author's distinct personality. Wisely or otherwise, he journeyed beyond what he knew to the imagined world of King Arthur's Court or a drop of water or the life of a microbe; to the investigation of a new religion, Christian Science, and regrettably to the question of the authorship of Shakespeare's plays.

Mark Twain has been called America's best writer and its worst. What is his best? One group of choices would be "Jim Smiley and His Jumping Frog," "The Facts Concerning the Recent Carnival of Crime in Connecticut," *Tom Sawyer*, "Old Times on the Mississippi," "Captain Stormfield's Visit to Heaven," "Jim Baker's Blue Jay Yarn," *Huckleberry Finn*, "Early Days," "The Chronicle of Young Satan" (fragment though it is), and "Letters from the Earth." Among at least somewhat neglected works that deserve a reading are "Ye Sentimental Law Student" and "The Evidence in the Case of Smith vs. Jones," "Private Habits of Horace Greeley," "A True Story," the several McWilliams stories, "In Defense of Harriet Shelley," *Tom Sawyer Abroad* (but only in a good text), and "Eve's Autobiography" (soon to be published, complete).

But the Mark Twain devotee, even an unfanatical one, finds that in nearly everything that *his* author wrote, something attractive is to be found. Even in the midst of the most ordinary and undistinguished passages there are gems waiting to be discovered. Great pleasures await in such passages as these: the description of stewed oysters in *Which Was It?*, the characterization of Mary Baker Eddy's prose in *Christian Science*, and—buried very deep—the character vignettes in the unpublished "A Family Sketch" and the hilarious account, recorded in a recently published notebook, of Mark Twain's receiving as tribute to his wit the false teeth of a theater manager. One doesn't have to be an English professor to develop a taste for Mark Twain's writing. On the contrary, it is easy to become an admirer. Mark Twain's worldwide popularity is no mystery—even if one does not always encounter *The Authentic Mark Twain*.

Abbreviations

AD   Autobiographical dictation, Mark Twain Papers.

AL   *American Literature* (quarterly journal).

AQ   *American Quarterly.*

Berg   Henry W. and Albert A. Berg Collection, New York
            Public Library, Astor, Lenox, and Tilden Foundations.

BNYPL   *Bulletin of the New York Public Library.*

CG   *Contributions to "The Galaxy" 1868–1871 by Mark Twain.*
            Edited by Bruce R. McElderry Jr., Gainesville, Florida:
            Scholars' Facsimiles & Reprints, 1961.

CL1   *Mark Twain's Collected Letters*, Volume I. Edited by Lin
            Salamo et al. Berkeley, Los Angeles, London: University
            of California Press, forthcoming.

CL2   *Mark Twain's Collected Letters*, Volume 2. Edited by Dahlia
            Armon et al. Berkeley, Los Angeles, London: University
            of California Press, forthcoming.

CL3   *Mark Twain's Collected Letters*, Volume 3. Edited by
            Michael B. Frank. Berkeley, Los Angeles, London:
            University of California Press, forthcoming.

CofC   *Clemens of the "Call": Mark Twain in San Francisco.* Edited
            by Edgar M. Branch. Berkeley and Los Angeles:
            University of California Press, 1969.

CY   Twain, Mark. *A Connecticut Yankee in King Arthur's Court.*
            Edited by Bernard L. Stein, with an Introduction by
            Henry Nash Smith. Berkeley, Los Angeles, London:
            University of California Press, 1979.

ET&S1	Twain, Mark. *Early Tales & Sketches*. Volume 1, 1851–1864. Edited by Edgar M. Branch and Robert H. Hirst. Berkeley, Los Angeles, London: University of California Press, 1979.
ET&S2	Twain, Mark. *Early Tales & Sketches*. Volume 2, 1864–1865. Edited by Edgar M. Branch and Robert H. Hirst. Berkeley, Los Angeles, London: University of California Press, 1981.
FM	*Mark Twain's Fables of Man*. Edited by John S. Tuckey. Berkeley, Los Angeles, London: University of California Press, 1972.
HHR	Henry H. Rogers.
HH&T	*Mark Twain's Hannibal, Huck & Tom*. Edited by Walter Blair. Berkeley and Los Angeles: University of California Press, 1969.
ISLC	*Interviews with Samuel L. Clemens 1874–1910*. Edited by Louis J. Budd. Arlington, Tex.: American Literary Realism, 1977.
JHT	Joseph H. Twichell.
LAIFI	Twain, Mark. *Life as I Find It: Essays, Sketches, Tales, and Other Material, the Majority of Which Is Now Published in Book Form for the First Time*. Edited by Charles Neider. Garden City, N.Y.: Hanover House, 1961.
LAMT	Branch, Edgar M. *The Literary Apprenticeship of Mark Twain*. Urbana: University of Illinois Press, 1950.
LE	Twain, Mark. *Letters from the Earth*. Edited by Bernard DeVoto, with a preface by Henry Nash Smith. New York: Harper and Row, 1962.
LLMT	*The Love Letters of Mark Twain*. Edited by Dixon Wecter. New York: Harper and Brothers, 1949.
LOM(1944)	Twain, Mark. *Life on the Mississippi*. With an introduction by Edward Wagenknecht and a number of previously suppressed passages [from the Pierpont Morgan Library holograph manuscript], now printed for the first time, and edited with a note by Willis Wager. New York: Limited Editions Club, 1944.
MMT	Howells, William Dean. *My Mark Twain: Reminiscences and Criticisms*. Edited by Marilyn Austin Baldwin. Baton Rouge: Louisiana State University Press, 1967.
MS(S)	Manuscript(s).
MSM	Twain, Mark. *The Mysterious Stranger Manuscripts*. Edited by William M. Gibson. Berkeley and Los Angeles: University of California Press, 1969.

MTA	*Mark Twain's Autobiography.* 2 vols. Edited by Albert Bigelow Paine. New York: Harper and Brothers, 1924.
MTB	Paine, Albert Bigelow. *Mark Twain: A Biography.* 3 vols. New York: Harper and Brothers, 1912.
MTBus	*Mark Twain, Business Man.* Edited by Samuel C. Webster. Boston: Little, Brown and Co., 1946.
MTCH	*Mark Twain: The Critical Heritage.* Edited by Frederick Anderson. New York: Barnes and Noble, 1971.
MTCor	*Mark Twain: San Francisco Correspondent.* Edited by Henry Nash Smith and Frederick Anderson. San Francisco: Book Club of California, 1957.
MTE	*Mark Twain in Eruption: Hitherto Unpublished Pages About Men and Events.* Edited by Bernard DeVoto. New York: Harper and Brothers, 1940.
MT&EB	Hill, Hamlin. *Mark Twain and Elisha Bliss.* Columbia: University of Missouri Press, 1964.
MTEng	Welland, Dennis. *Mark Twain in England.* London: Chatto and Windus, 1978.
MTGF	Hill, Hamlin. *Mark Twain: God's Fool.* New York: Harper and Row, 1973.
MTHHR	*Mark Twain's Correspondence with Henry Huddleston Rogers.* Edited by Lewis Leary. Berkeley and Los Angeles: University of California Press, 1969.
MTHL	*Mark Twain–Howells Letters.* 2 vols. Edited by Henry Nash Smith and William M. Gibson. Cambridge: Harvard University Press, 1960.
MTJ	*Mark Twain Journal.*
MTL	*Mark Twain's Letters.* 2 vols. Edited by Albert Bigelow Paine. New York: Harper and Brothers, 1917.
MTLP	*Mark Twain's Letters to His Publishers.* Edited by Hamlin Hill. Berkeley and Los Angeles: University of California Press, 1967.
MTM	Mark Twain Memorial (Stowe-Day Library), Hartford, Connecticut.
MTMF	*Mark Twain to Mrs. Fairbanks.* Edited by Dixon Wecter. San Marino, Calif.: Huntington Library, 1949.
MTN	*Mark Twain's Notebook.* Edited by Albert Bigelow Paine. New York: Harper and Brothers, 1935.
MTP	Mark Twain Papers, Bancroft Library, University of California, Berkeley.
MTQH	*Mark Twain's Quarrel with Heaven: "Captain Stormfield's Visit to Heaven" and Other Sketches.* Edited by Ray B. Browne. New Haven: College & University Press, 1970.

MTS   *Mark Twain Speaking.* Edited by Paul Fatout. Iowa City: University of Iowa Press, 1976.

MTSH   *Mark Twain Speaks for Himself.* Edited by Paul Fatout. West Lafayette, Ind.: Purdue University Press, 1979.

MTSM   Brashear, Minnie M. *Mark Twain: Son of Missouri.* Chapel Hill: University of North Carolina Press, 1934.

MTTB   *Mark Twain's Travels with Mr. Brown.* Edited by Franklin Walker and Ezra C. Dane. New York: Alfred Knopf, 1940.

MTW   DeVoto, Bernard. *Mark Twain at Work.* Cambridge: Harvard University Press, 1942.

NEQ   *New England Quarterly.*

N&J1   *Mark Twain's Notebooks & Journals,* Volume 1 (1855–1873). Edited by Frederick Anderson, Michael B. Frank, and Kenneth M. Sanderson. Berkeley, Los Angeles, London: University of California Press, 1975.

N&J2   *Mark Twain's Notebooks & Journals,* Volume 2 (1877–1883). Edited by Frederick Anderson, Lin Salamo, and Bernard L. Stein. Berkeley, Los Angeles, London: University of California Press, 1975.

N&J3   *Mark Twain's Notebooks & Journals,* Volume 3 (1883–1891). Edited by Robert Pack Browning, Michael B. Frank, and Lin Salamo. Berkeley, Los Angeles, London: University of California Press, 1979.

OLC   Olivia L. Clemens.

PH   Photocopy.

PMLA   *Publications of the Modern Language Association of America*

P&P   Twain, Mark. *The Prince and the Pauper.* Edited by Victor Fischer and Lin Salamo. Berkeley, Los Angeles, London: University of California Press, 1979.

S&B   *Mark Twain's Satires and Burlesques.* Edited by Franklin R. Rogers. Berkeley and Los Angeles: University of California Press, 1967.

SLC   Samuel L. Clemens

Tenney   Tenney, Thomas A. *Mark Twain: A Reference Guide.* Boston: G. K. Hall and Co., 1977.

TG   Cardwell, Guy A. *Twins of Genius.* East Lansing: Michigan State College Press, 1953.

TJS   Clemens, Samuel L. *The Adventures of Thomas Jefferson Snodgrass.* Edited by Charles Honce. Chicago: Pascal Covici, 1928.

TS	Twain, Mark. *The Adventures of Tom Sawyer, Tom Sawyer Abroad, Tom Sawyer, Detective.* Edited by John C. Gerber, Paul Baender, and Terry Firkins. Berkeley, Los Angeles, London: University of California Press, 1980.
WDH	William Dean Howells.
WIM	Twain, Mark. *What Is Man? and Other Philosophical Writings.* Edited by Paul Baender. Berkeley, Los Angeles, London: University of California Press, 1973.
WWD	*Mark Twain's Which Was the Dream? and Other Symbolic Writings of the Later Years.* Edited by John S. Tuckey. Berkeley and Los Angeles: University of California Press, 1968.

Notes

PREFACE

1. "The Turning Point of My Life."
2. *Overland Monthly*, January 1870, pp. 100–110; reprinted in *MTCH*, p. 34. (For list of abbreviations, see pp. 279–83.)
3. *MTSH*, p. 156.
4. *WWD*, pp. 166–76.

CHAPTER ONE: THE CREATION OF MARK TWAIN

1. "Hannibal, Missouri," published March 25, 1852; *ET&S1*, pp. 67–68. (The population was closer to 1,000.) All the writings cited in this chapter appear in *ET&S1* unless otherwise identified.
2. *HH&T*, pp. 36, 33.
3. Ibid., pp. 39–40. This collection also includes the author's sketch of his mother, pp. 43–53.
4. *MTB*, I, 90.
5. *LAMT*, pp. 218–19.
6. Quoted in Dixon Wecter, *Sam Clemens of Hannibal* (Boston: Houghton Mifflin Co., 1952), p. 258.
7. *MTB*, III, 1445.
8. *TJS*, p. 32.
9. Ibid., pp. 38, 44.
10. AD, March 29, 1906; *MTA*, II, 289.
11. AD, September 10, 1906; *MTE*, p. 228.
12. Letter dated June 29, 1874, published in facsimile in *The Eighteenth Year Book 1919* (Boston: Bibliophile Society, 1919), following p. 123.
13. *Autobiographical Sketch* (written for Samuel Moffett, Clemens's nephew, privately printed, Worcester, 1918), p. 6.
14. See Edgar M. Branch, "Samuel Clemens, Steersman of the *John H.*

Dickey," *American Literary Realism* 15 (1982): 195–208, and Branch, "A New Clemens Footprint: Soleleather Steps Forward," *AL* 54 (1982): 497–510.

15. William C. Miller, "Samuel L. Clemens and Orion Clemens vs. Mark Twain and His Biographers," *MTJ* 16 (Summer 1973): 1–9.

16. *HH&T*, p. 34.

17. AD, October 2, 1906; *MTE*, pp. 390–91.

18. William C. Miller, "The Editor's Page," *Nevada Historical Society Quarterly* 5 (January–March 1962), inside back cover.

19. See William C. Miller et al., eds., *Reports of the 1863 Constitutional Convention of the Territory of Nevada* (Carson City: State of Nevada, 1972).

20. "A Couple of Sad Experiences," *The Galaxy*, June 1970, reprinted in *CG*, pp. 47–50. In a letter to Orion dated October 21, 1862, Clemens tells how he sent Sewell a copy of the California reprints each day to annoy him.

21. *Enterprise*, January 4, 1864; *Mark Twain of the "Enterprise": Newspaper Articles & Other Documents 1862–1864*, ed. Henry Nash Smith and Frederick Anderson (Berkeley and Los Angeles: University of California Press, 1957), p. 139.

22. Robert Regan, *Unpromising Heroes: Mark Twain and His Characters* (Berkeley and Los Angeles: University of California Press, 1966), pp. 32–33.

23. Copy in Scrapbook 2, p. 43, MTP.

24. July 9, 1863, *Call*, quoted in *CofC*, p. 8.

25. Reprinted in *The Twainian* 9 (March–April 1950), and *ET&S1*, p. 260.

26. Quoted in *MTL*, I, 89.

27. *CG*, pp. 47, 49–50.

28. Quoted in letter of protest by ladies of Carson City in Virginia City *Union*, May 26/27, 1864; reprinted in *Mark Twain of the "Enterprise,"* p. 200.

29. Both are quoted in Paul Fatout, *Mark Twain in Virginia City* (Bloomington: Indiana University Press, 1964), pp. 211, 242.

30. Useful criticism and scholarship dealing with the materials of this chapter include: Edgar M. Branch, *The Literary Apprenticeship of Mark Twain* (Urbana: University of Illinois Press, 1950); David E. E. Sloane, *Mark Twain as a Literary Comedian* (Baton Rouge: Louisiana State University Press, 1979); Paul Fatout, *Mark Twain in Virginia City* (Bloomington: Indiana University Press, 1964); Pascal Covici, Jr., *Mark Twain's Humor: the Image of a World* (Dallas: Southern Methodist University Press, 1962); Kenneth Lynn, *Mark Twain and Southwestern Humor* (Boston: Little, Brown, 1959); Paul Schmidt, "Mark Twain's Techniques as a Humorist, 1857–1872" (Ph.D. diss., University of Minnesota, 1951); Franklin R. Rogers, ed., *The Pattern for Mark Twain's "Roughing It"* (Berkeley and Los Angeles: University of California Press, 1961).

CHAPTER TWO: CALIFORNIA, HAWAII, AND THE EAST

1. June 26, 1864; quoted in *ET&S2*; this edition is quoted hereafter in this chapter unless otherwise noted.

2. Edgar M. Branch in *CofC*, p. 5.

3. Ibid., p. 40.

4. *ET&S2*, pp. 435–36.

5. AD, June 13, 1906; *MTE*, p. 256.

6. AD, July 7, 1908; *MTE*, p. 304.

7. See AD, June 13, 1906; *MTE*, pp. 254–92.

8. AD, May 26, 1907; *MTE*, pp. 360–61.

9. See *ET&S2*, p. 145.

10. Cyril Clemens, *Young Sam Clemens* (Portland, Me.: Leon Tebbets Editions, 1942), pp. 209–17. Cyril Clemens reports that his account is derived from his father, James Ross Clemens, who had talked with Samuel Clemens in 1897. See also Mark Twain's own "Private History of the Jumping Frog Story."

11. AD, February 20, 1906; *MTA*, I, 125.

12. *Mark Twain in Hawaii*, ed. Walter Francis Frear (Chicago: Lakeside Press, 1947), pp. 367, 412, 277.

13. Ibid., p. 288.

14. *Sketches of the Sixties, by Bret Harte and Mark Twain*, ed. John Howell, rev. ed. (San Francisco: John Howell, 1927), pp. 210–11. The sobriquet "moral phenomenon" appears as early as January 1864. See David Basso, ed., *Mark Twain in the "Virginia Evening Bulletin" and "Gold Hill Daily News"* (Sparks, Nev.: Falcon Hill Press, 1981), p. 49.

15. Quoted in Ivan Benson, *Mark Twain's Western Years* (Stanford: Stanford University Press, 1938), pp. 212–13.

16. *Alta California* of unknown date; reprinted in Yreka City (California) Yreka *Weekly Union*, March 23, 1867; *MTSH*, pp. 39–40.

17. *MTTB*, pp. 111–21.

18. Published in the Missouri *Democrat*, March 12, 13, 14; reprinted in *LAIFI*, pp. 10–21.

19. *MTTB*, p. 144.

20. Reprinted in *LAMT*, pp. 268–70.

21. *MTTB*, pp. 157–58. Hereafter page citations of this edition appear in the text.

22. Useful criticism and scholarship dealing with the materials of this chapter include: Edgar M. Branch, "'My Voice Is Still for Setchell': A Background Study of 'Jim Smiley and His Jumping Frog,'" *PMLA* 82 (1967): 591–601; Paul Baender, "The 'Jumping Frog' as a Comedian's First Virtue," *Philological Quarterly* 60 (1963): 192–200; S. J. Krause, "The Art and Satire of Twain's 'Jumping Frog' Story," *AQ* 16 (1964): 363–76; Walter Francis Frear, *Mark Twain and Hawaii* (Chicago: Lakeside Press, 1947); Robert Hirst, "The Making of *The Innocents Abroad*, 1867–1872" (Ph.D. diss., University of California, Berkeley, 1975).

CHAPTER THREE: THE TURNING POINT

1. *MTB*, I, 310.

2. AD, April 1904; *MTA*, I, 243.

3. *Traveling with the Innocents Abroad: Mark Twain's Original Reports from Europe and the Holy Land*, ed. Daniel Morley McKeithan (Norman: University of Oklahoma Press, 1958), p. 84. Hereafter page citations of this edition appear in the text.

4. Published in *The Galaxy*, May 1868, and reprinted in *Sketches New and Old*.

5. SLC to Mrs. Fairbanks, December 2, 1876; *CL*1.

6. Letter of December 4, published December 22, 1867; PH, MTP.

7. Letter of January 20, published February 19, 1868; PH, MTP.

8. Letter dated February, published March 7, 1868; PH, MTP.

9. Letter dated February 14 and published February 19, 1868; PH, MTP; reprinted in *Washington in 1868*, ed. Cyril Clemens (Webster Groves, Mo.: International Mark Twain Society, 1943), pp. 29–32.

10. Reprinted in *LAIFI*, pp. 5–9.

11. Reprinted in *The Twainian* 5 (May–June 1946):1, and, revised, in *Sketches New and Old*.

12. November 21, 1867; *MTL*, I, 140.

13. Chicago *Republican*, August 23, 1868; PH, MTP.

14. McKinney Papers, Vassar College, item A-22.

15. *MTS*, p. 26.

16. Quoted in Paul Fatout, *Mark Twain on the Lecture Circuit* (Bloomington: Indiana University Press), p. 90.

17. Published in the *Alta*, September 6, 1868; reprinted in *The Twainian* 7 (November–December 1948): 5–7.

18. Reprinted in *LAIFI*, p. 23.

19. December 1, 1868; quoted in *MTMF*, p. 53.

20. Buffalo *Express*, September 25, 1869; PH, MTP.

21. *CG*, p. 37.

22. Ibid., pp. 79–81; *A Pen Warmed Up in Hell: Mark Twain in Protest*, ed. Frederick Anderson (New York: Harper and Row, 1972), pp. 131–52; *LAIFI*, pp. 75–89. Eleven *Galaxy* pieces were collected in *The Curious Republic of Gondour and Other Whimsical Sketches* (New York: Boni and Liveright, 1919).

23. *CG*, p. 101.

24. SLC to Orion Clemens, March 11 and 13, 1871; *CL*3.

25. Auburn (California) *Stars and Stripes*, June 23, 1870; reprinted in *MTSH*, pp. 62–64.

26. Reprinted in *LAIFI*, pp. 38–42.

27. SLC to Samuel Moffett, April 25, 1899; MTP (†).

28. Howells, "The Man of Letters as a Man of Business," *Scribner's Magazine*, October 1893; collected in *Literature and Life* (New York: Harper, 1902), p. 15.

29. Howells, "Editor's Study," *Harper's Magazine*, December 1886, p. 162.

30. August 20, 1881; *MTL*, I, 402.

31. *Overland Monthly*, June 1872; reprinted in *MTCH*, p. 51.

32. Useful criticism and scholarship dealing with the materials of this chapter include: Leon T. Dickinson, "Mark Twain's Revisions in Writing *The Innocents Abroad*," *AL* 19 (1947–48); Robert Hirst, "The Making of The Innocents Abroad, 1867–1872" (Ph.D. diss., University of California, Berkeley, 1975); Philip D. Beidler, "Realistic Style and the Problem of Context in *The Innocents Abroad* and *Roughing It*," *AL* 52 (1980–81): 33–49; John Gerber, "The Relationship Between Point of View and Style in the Works of Mark Twain," in *Style in Prose Fiction*, English Institute Essays, 1958 (New York: Columbia

University Press, 1959); Hamlin Hill, *Mark Twain and Elisha Bliss* (Columbia: University of Missouri Press, 1964); Van Wyck Brooks, *The Ordeal of Mark Twain* (New York: Dutton, 1920); Henry Nash Smith, "Mark Twain as Interpreter of the Far West: The Structure of *Roughing It*," in *The Frontier in Perspective*, ed. W. D. Wyman and C. B. Kroeber (Madison: University of Wisconsin Press, 1957).

CHAPTER FOUR: SOMETHING OLD AND SOMETHING NEW

1. These documents are all in MTP.
2. *MTB*, I, 476–77.
3. C. D. Warner to Whitelaw Reid, April 7, 1873; in Royal Cortissoz, *Life of Whitelaw Reid* (New York: Scribner's, 1921), p. 273.
4. SLC to George McDonald, March 9, 1883; MTP (†).
5. December 2, 1870; *CL2*.
6. SLC to Robert S. MacKenzie, September 23, 1874; Hist. Soc. Pa. (†).
7. *Tribune*, February 1, 1874; quoted in *MT&EB*, p. 81.
8. Stoddard's reminiscences and an 1874 letter, quoted in George Wharton James, "How Mark Twain Was Made," *National Review*, February 1911, p. 12; and James, "Charles Warren Stoddard," *National Review*, August 1911, pp. 659–72.
9. Interview by Richard Whiteing, originally published in New York *World*, May 11, 1879; republished in *ISLC*, pp. 33–34.
10. Thus he charged on August 2, 1873, SLC to Elisha Bliss, *CL3*, and in DV268, notes to Samuel C. Thompson's 1909 letter, p. 12, MTP.
11. SLC to Elisha Bliss, July 7, 1873, *CL3*; *ET&S1*, p. 434.
12. See also SLC to Hartford *Post*, November 3, 1874, as published in that newspaper.
13. DV226; PH, MTP.
14. *TS*, p. 443.
15. SLC to Dr. John Brown, September 4, 1874; *MTL*, I, 224.
16. AD, August 30, 1906; *MTE*, p. 197.
17. Ibid.
18. *TS*, pp. 8–9.
19. See Brander Matthews's report on what Mark Twain told him in 1890 about the composition of *Tom Sawyer* in *The Tocsin of Revolt and Other Essays* (New York; Scribner's, 1922), pp. 265–66.
20. See *MTA*, I, 102, 105 (written 1897–98); II, 179 (AD, March 8, 1906).
21. Portland *Oregonian*, August 11, 1893; reprinted in *ISLC*, p. 52.
22. Thomas Sergeant Perry, in *Century Magazine*, May 1885, pp. 171–72; reprinted in *MTCH*, pp. 128–30.
23. Fatout, *Mark Twain on the Lecture Circuit*, p. 151.
24. SLC to Dr. John Brown, February 28, 1874; *MTL*, I, 215.
25. *MMT*, pp. 18, 41.
26. SLC to Moncure Daniel Conway, April 16, 1876, *MTLP*, p. 98.
27. *TS*, pp. 26–28; New York *Times*, January 13, 1877, p. 3; reprinted in *MTCH*, pp. 70–71.
28. SLC to WDH, December 8, 1874; *MTHL*, I, 50.

29. SLC to David Watt Bowser, March 20, 1880; "'Dear Master Wattie': The Mark Twain–David Watt Bowser Letters," ed. Pascal Covici, Jr., *Southwest Review* 45 (1960): 107.

30. *MTB*, III, 1368. Paine is reporting what Clemens told him late in life.

31. *N&J2*, pp. 449–50.

32. SLC to WDH, May 22 and June 7, 1875; *MTHL*, I, 85, 86.

33. SLC to Robert Watt, January 26, 1875; Berg (†).

34. *Atlantic Monthly*, December 1875; reprinted in *MMT*, p. 103.

35. March 23, 1878; *MTL*, I, 322.

36. *Atlantic Monthly*, December 1875; reprinted in *MMT*, p. 103.

37. Reprinted in *LAIFI*, p. 169.

38. Twichell journal, January 24, 1876; quoted in *MTHL*, I, 120.

39. SLC to J. Y. W. MacAllister, April 7, 1903; Univ. Va. Lib. (†).

40. SLC to Mary Benjamin Rogers, November 7, 1906; *Letters to Mary*, ed. Lewis Leary (New York: Columbia University Press, 1961), p. 86.

41. AD, July 31, 1906; *MTE*, p. 207. I quote from the Mark Twain Society edition of *1601* (Chicago, 1939).

42. *N&J2*, p. 303; AD, July 31, 1906; *MTE*, p. 204.

43. SLC to Pamela Moffett, undated, 1879; *MTBus*, p. 137.

44. SLC to Mollie Fairbanks, August 6, 1877; Huntington Lib. (†).

45. DV56, Paine 197; MTP.

46. A privately printed copy is in MTP. The story is similar to that of a sketch in *N&J1*, pp. 511–17 (1868).

47. SLC to WDH, June 21, 1877; SLC to JHT, June 27, 1877.

48. SLC to Mrs. Theodore Crane, undated; quoted in *N&J2*, p. 9.

49. Fulton to SLC, March 12, 1877; MTP.

50. *MTS*, p. 114.

51. *MMT*, pp. 50–51.

52. AD January 11, 1906; *Mark Twain's Speeches*, ed. Albert Bigelow Paine (New York: Harper, 1923), p. 68; AD, January 23, 1906; *MTA*, II, 5; AD, May 25, 1906; quoted in Henry Nash Smith, "'That Hideous Mistake of Poor Clemens's'" *Harvard Library Bulletin* 9 (1955): 175.

53. September 3, 1877; *MTMF*, p. 210.

54. February 17, 1878; *MTL*, I, 319–20.

55. *MTS*, p. 118.

56. Useful criticism and scholarship dealing with the materials of this chapter include: Robert Regan, "'English Notes': A Book Mark Twain Abandoned," *Studies in American Humor* 2 (1976): 157–70; Hamlin Hill, "The Composition and Structure of *Tom Sawyer*," *AL* 32 (1960–61): 379–92; Cynthia Griffin Wolff, "*The Adventures of Tom Sawyer*: Nightmare Vision of American Boyhood," *Massachusetts Review* 21 (1980): 637–52; Judith Fetterley, "The Sanctioned Rebel," *Studies in the Novel* 3 (1971): 292–304; Walter Blair, "On the Structure of *Tom Sawyer*," *Modern Philology* 37 (1939): 75–88; Tom T. Towers, "'I Never Thought We Might Want To Come Back': Strategies of Transcendence in *Tom Sawyer*," *Modern Fiction Studies* 21 (1975–76): 509–20; Edgar Burde, "Mark Twain: The Writer as Pilot," *PMLA* 93 (1978): 878–92; "'That Hideous Mistake of Poor Clemens's'," *Harvard Library Bulletin* 9 (1955): 148–80.

CHAPTER FIVE: THE DISAPPEARANCE OF MARK TWAIN

1. OLC to Mrs. Langdon, May 26, 1878; MTM.

2. Box 6, nos. 52, 46, 47; MTP (†).

3. SLC to Frank Bliss, July 13, 1878; *MTLP*, p. 108.

4. SLC to JHT, January 26, 1879; *MTL*, I, 349. SLC had paid his friend's expenses. SLC to JHT and Bissell and Co., May 23, 1878; MTP.

5. SLC to Frank Bliss, August 20, 1878; *MTLP*, p. 109.

6. SLC to JHT, November 3, 1878; *MTL*, I, 399.

7. Hartford *Courant*, September 4, 1879.

8. SLC to JHT, January 26, 1879; *MTL*, I, 350.

9. SLC to JHT, October 2, 1879; Beinecke Lib. (†).

10. SLC to Thomas Bailey Aldrich, November 7, 1879; Houghton Lib. (†).

11. SLC to JHT, June 2, 1879; Beinecke Lib. (†).

12. *MTB*, II, 668.

13. *Athenaeum*, April 24, 1880, pp. 529–30; reprinted in *MTCH*, pp. 73–76.

14. Quoted by Chester L. Davis in "Mark Twain's Religious Beliefs as Indicated by Notations in His Books," *The Twainian* 14 (September–October 1955): 5.

15. SLC to Mrs. Fairbanks, February 5, 1878; *MTMF*, p. 218.

16. February 26, 1880; Vassar Coll. Lib. (†).

17. SLC to Osgood, January 21, 1881; typescript, MTP (†).

18. SLC to Annie Lucas, January 31, 1881; *Mark Twain the Letter Writer*, ed. Cyril Clemens (Boston: Meador, 1932), p. 37.

19. *MTB*, II, 696; Paine quotes a letter from SLC to his mother.

20. Goodman to SLC, October 24, 1881; MTP. The letter was written before Goodman had seen the book.

21. July 26, 1880; MTP.

22. December 22, 1880; MTP.

23. AD, February 9, 1906; *MTA*, II, 88.

24. December 22, 1880; MTP.

25. *N&J3*, p. 287.

26. Goodman to SLC, October 24, 1881; MTP.

27. B. E. Purcell in *Academy*, December 20, 1881, p. 469; reprinted in *MTCH*, pp. 90–91.

28. Atlanta *Constitution*, December 25, 1881.

29. New York *Tribune*, October 25, 1881, p. 6.

30. SLC to Charles W. Stoddard, October 26, 1881; *MTL*, I, 404–5.

31. AD, August 30, 1906; quoted in *MTQH*, p. 19.

32. AD, August 29, 1906; *MTE*, p. 246. See also SLC to WDH, June 27, 1878; *MTHL*, 1, 236.

33. Published in *MTQH*, p. 33.

34. AD, August 29, 1906; *MTE*, p. 248.

35. *MTQH*, p. 50.

36. Ibid., p. 71.

37. SLC to Frederick Duneka, September 15, 1902; quoted in James M. Cox, "The Muse of Mark Twain," *Massachusettes Review* 5 (1963): 140.

38. SLC to Mrs. Jordan, March 10, 1905; N.Y. Pub. Lib. (†).
39. Quoted by Henderson, *Mark Twain* (New York: Stokes, 1912), p. 183.
40. *The Ordeal of Mark Twain* (New York: Dutton, 1920), p. 116.
41. SLC to Thomas Lounsbury, July 2, 1904; Beinecke Lib. (†).
42. *MTB*, II, 774.
43. Quoted in Walter Blair, *Mark Twain & Huck Finn* (Berkeley and Los Angeles: University of California Press, 1960), p. 325.
44. *LLMT*, p. 333.
45. September 15, 1899; MTP (†).
46. *MTB*, I, 524.
47. M. A. DeWolfe Howe, *Memoirs of a Hostess: A Chronicle of Eminent Friendships Drawn Chiefly from the Diaries of Mrs. James T. Fields* (Boston: Atlantic Monthly Press, 1922), p. 256.
48. *S&B*, p. 67; *MTHL*, I, 369.
49. Joseph H. Twichell's journal, Beinecke Rare Book and Manuscript Library, Yale University, includes the reunion program, pasted in at page 83 of volume 4. Twichell wrote in, below "RATIONS," "By Mark Twain." I cite the journal with the kind permission of the Beinecke Library. The menu is discussed more fully in my essay "Mark Twain: The Writer as Reader," *Thoughts* [Chulalongkorn University, Thailand] 3 (1983): 1–7.
50. SLC to Karl and Hattie Gerhardt, June 26, 1881; typescript, MTP (†).
51. SLC to Franklin G. Whitmore, August 8, 1881; MTM (†).
52. SLC to unidentified St. Louis newspaper, October 24, 1881; PH, MTP.
53. Quoted in *MTB*, II, 730.
54. July 17, 1881; *TG*, p. 81.
55. *LLMT*, p. 208.
56. Quoted as part of Item 123, AAA-Anderson Galleries, Sale No. 4228, January 29–30, 1936, catalog, p. 45; PH, MTP. All of the passage quoted in the catalog appears here; published in Horst H. Kruse, *Mark Twain and "Life on the Mississippi"* (Amherst: University of Massachusetts Press, 1981), p. 48.
57. *LOM*(1944), p. 411. Hereafter page citations of this edition appear in the text.
58. MTP.
59. SLC to Charles L. Webster; *MTBus*, p. 199.
60. Memo dated October 29, 1882; PH, MTP.
61. May 17, 1882; *MTL*, I, 419.
62. January 15, 1883; *MTLP*, p. 162.
63. November 27, 1871; *LLMT*, p. 166.
64. *Harper's Magazine*, October 1883, p. 799.
65. New Orleans *Times-Democrat*, May 30, 1883; reprinted in *MTCH*, pp. 109–10.
66. *Athenaeum*, June 2, 1883; reprinted in *MTCH*, p. 116.
67. Useful criticism and scholarship dealing with the materials of this chapter include: Walter Blair, "Mark Twain's Other Masterpiece: 'Jim Baker's Blue Jay Yarn,'" *Studies in American Humor* 1 (1975): 132–47; Leon T. Dickinson, "The Sources of *The Prince and the Pauper*," *Modern Language Notes* 64 (1949): 103–6; Howard G. Baetzhold, "Mark Twain's *The Prince and the Pau-*

per," *Notes and Queries* 199 (1954): 401–3; Tom T. Towers, "*The Prince and the Pauper*: Mark Twain's Once and Future King," *Studies in American Fiction* 6 (1978): 194–202; Hamlin Hill, "Mark Twain's Book Sales, 1869–1879," *BNYPL* 65 (1961): 371–89; Frederick Anderson and Hamlin Hill, "How Samuel Clemens Became Mark Twain's Publisher: A Study of the James R. Osgood Contracts," *Proof* 2 (1972): 117–43; Robert A. Rees, "*Captain Stormfield's Visit to Heaven* and *The Gates Ajar*," *English Language Notes* 7 (1970): 197–202; Van Wyck Brooks, *The Ordeal of Mark Twain* (New York: Dutton, 1920); Walter Blair, "When Was *Huckleberry Finn* Written?" *AL* 30 (1958–59): 1–24; Coleman O. Parsons, "Down the Mighty River with Mark Twain," *Mississippi Quarterly* 22 (1968–69): 1–18; Horst H. Kruse, *Mark Twain and "Life on the Mississippi"* (Amherst: University of Massachusetts Press, 1981); Arthur L. Scott, "Mark Twain Revises *Old Times on the Mississippi*," *Journal of English and Germanic Philology* 54 (1955): 634–38.

CHAPTER SIX: A NEW VOICE FOR SAMUEL CLEMENS

1. Vassar Coll. Lib. I quote with the permission of the University of California Press; the letter is copyrighted by the press (†).
2. From Boston *Transcript*, March 17, 1885.
3. Webster to SLC, April 21, 1884, quoted in Henry Nash Smith, ed., *Adventures of Huckleberry Finn* (Boston: Houghton Mifflin Co., 1958), p. 247; SLC to Webster, April 22, 1884; *MTBus*, pp. 249–50.
4. Quoted in *MTW*, p. 67.
5. Quoted in ibid., pp. 64–65.
6. *MTB*, II, 683.
7. *LOM*(1944), p. 392.
8. *Saturday Review*, January 31, 1885, pp. 153–54; reprinted in *MTCH*, pp. 122–23.
9. Notebook 35, typescript p. 35, MTP; quoted in part in Smith, ed., *Huckleberry Finn*, p. xvi (note) (†).
10. *MTA*, I, 131 (written around 1898).
11. Quoted in *MTW*, p. 75.
12. Reproduced from the manuscript in Smith, ed., *Huckleberry Finn*, pp. 265–66.
13. Tenney, p. 15; *MTCH*, pp. 126–30.
14. Tenney, pp. 14–15; *MTCH*, pp. 121–25.
15. Arthur L. Vogelback, "The Publication and Reception of *Huckleberry Finn* in America," *AL* 11 (1939–40): 269–72.
16. SLC to Webster, March 18, 1885; *MTL*, II, 452–53.
17. April 15, 1885; *MTBus*, p. 317.
18. AD, February 9, 1906; *MTA*, II, 88.
19. SLC to WDH, July 20, 1883; *MTHL*, I, 435–36.
20. SLC to J. R. Osgood, September 1, 1883; Phillips Mem. Lib. (†).
21. *MMT*, p. 221.
22. *MTMF*, p. 255.
23. February 8, 1885; *MTBus*, pp. 232–35.
24. SLC to Eustace Conway, August 14, 1876; quoted in *HH&T*, p. 245.

25. See Everett Emerson, "A Send-Off for Joe Goodman: The Carson Fossil-Footprints," *Resources for American Literary Study* 10 (1980): 71–78.

26. SLC to OLC, January 10, 1885; *LLMT*, p. 288.

27. June 6, 1884; *MTBus*, p. 258.

28. SLC to Webster, July 6, 1884; *MTBus*, pp. 264–65.

29. *MTBus*, p. 274.

30. *WIM*, pp. 26–59; see also p. 585.

31. Quoted in *MTB*, I, 412.

32. *MTA*, II, 13. See also *WIM*, pp. 585–86.

33. Useful criticism and scholarship dealing with the materials of this chapter include: Walter Blair, "When Was *Huckleberry Finn* Written?" *AL* 30 (1958–59): 1–24; Judith Fetterley, "Disenchantment: Tom Sawyer in *Huckleberry Finn*," *PMLA* 87 (1972): 69–74; Henry Nash Smith, "Introduction" to *Adventures of Huckleberry Finn* (Boston: Houghton Mifflin Co., 1958); Louis J. Budd, "The Southern Currents Under Huck Finn's Raft," *Mississippi Valley Historical Review* 46 (1959): 222–37; Walter Blair, "The French Revolution and *Huckleberry Finn*," *Modern Philology* 55 (1957): 21–35; Blair, *Mark Twain & Huck Finn* (Berkeley and Los Angeles: University of California Press, 1960); Arthur L. Scott, "The Century Magazine Edits *Huckleberry Finn*, 1884–1885," *AL* 27 (1955–56): 356–62; Arthur L. Vogelback, "The Publication and Reception of *Huckleberry Finn* in America," *AL* 11 (1939–40): 260–72; Jeanne M. Wagner, "*Huckleberry Finn* and the History Game," *MTJ* 20 (Winter 1979/80): 5–10; Paul J. Delaney, "You Can't Go Back to the Raft Huck Honey: Mark Twain's Western Sequel to *Huckleberry Finn*," *Western American Literature* 11 (1976): 215–29; Eugene McNamara, "Huck Lights Out for the Territory: Mark Twain's Unpublished Sequel," *University of Windsor Review* 2 (1966): 68–74.

CHAPTER SEVEN: A SWAN SONG—AND A RESUMPTION

1. AD, November 8, 1906; *North American Review*, August 2, 1907, p. 691.

2. *MTB*, II, 381.

3. *MTB*, II, 840; Paine quotes Susy's biography of her father.

4. SLC to Mrs. Fairbanks, November 16, 1886; *MTMF*, p. 258.

5. Johnson to SLC, March 16 and 18, May 11, July 16, August 15 and 22, November 13, 1885; MTP; SLC to Johnson, March 18, July 28, September 8, typescript, MTP.

6. December 16, 1885; *MTBus*, p. 343.

7. February 8, 1885; (†); the original does not survive; the text cited here is based on Susy's copy, Univ. Va. Lib.

8. February 13, 1886; *MTBus*, p. 355.

9. Susy's biography of her father, in *Susy and Mark Twain: Family Dialogues*, ed. Edith Colgate Salsbury (New York: Harper and Row, 1965), p. 219.

10. Edwin J. Park, "A Day with Mark Twain," *Chicago Tribune*, September 19, 1886, p. 12; reprinted in *ISLC*, p. 40.

11. *N&J3*, p. 456.

12. SLC to Clara Clemens, July 20, 1890, *LLMT*, p. 257.

13. SLC to Webster, August 3, 1887; *MTLP*, p. 222.

14. SLC to Fred J. Hall and Webster, August 15, 1887; *MTLP*, p. 244.

15. SLC to Chatto and Windus, January 16, 1889; *MTL*, II, 524.

16. *Century Magazine*, November 1889, p. 77.

17. Rejected preface, *CY*, p. 517.

18. July 7, 1889; quoted complete in ibid., pp. 519–22.

19. *CY*, p. 667. Hereafter page citations of this edition appear in the text.

20. Ibid., pp. 517. 518.

21. SLC to Chatto and Windus, July 16, 1889; *MTL*, II, 524.

22. Advertising prospectus of Charles L. Webster and Company quoted in *CY*, p. 18.

23. Tenney, pp. 17–19; *CY*, pp. 18–27.

24. New York *Standard*, January 1, 1890, pp. 8, 10.

25. *Scots Observer*, January 18, 1890; reprinted in *MTCH*, p. 165.

26. *MTL*, II, 525–28; *CY*, pp. 27–28.

27. *MTB*, II, 849 (note); Paine quotes from SLC's manuscript.

28. DV344, MTP; quoted in Howard G. Baetzhold, *Mark Twain and John Bull: The British Connection* (Bloomington: Indiana University Press, 1970), p. 165.

29. DV313A, MTP (†).

30. *MTB*, II, 917.

31. *MTL*, II, 541.

32. February 25, 1891; MTP (†).

33. February 27, 1891; *MTLP*, p. 269.

34. Box 32, MTP (†).

35. April [?] 1891; *MTL*, II, 546.

36. Box 32, MTP (†).

37. Paine no. 102A, MTP.

38. Useful criticism and scholarship dealing with the materials of this chapter include: Fred W. Lorch, "Mark Twain and the 'Campaign That Failed,'" *AL* 12 (1940–41): 454–70; John Gerber, "Mark Twain's 'Private Campaign,'" *Civil War History* 1 (1955): 37–60; C. J. Armstrong, "John L. RoBards—A Boyhood Friend of Mark Twain," *Missouri Valley Historical Review* 25 (1931): 293–98; J. Stanley Mattson, "Mark Twain on War and Peace: The Missouri Rebel and 'The Campaign that Failed,'" *AQ* 20 (1968): 783–94; Alan Gribben, "'The Master Hand of Old Malory': Mark Twain's Acquaintance with *Le Morte d'Arthur*," *English Language Notes* 16 (1978): 32–40; Hamlin Hill, "Barnum, Bridgeport, and the *Connecticut Yankee*," *AQ* 16 (1964): 615–16; Howard G. Baetzhold, "'The Autobiography of Sir Robert Smith of Camelot': Mark Twain's Original Plan for *A Connecticut Yankee*," *AL* 32 (1960–61): 456–61; James Russell, "The Genesis, Sources, and Reputation of Mark Twain's *A Connecticut Yankee in King Arthur's Court*" (Ph.D. diss., University of Chicago, 1966); Robert H. Wilson, "Malory in the *Connecticut Yankee*," *Texas Studies in English* 27 (1948): 185–206; James D. Wilson, "The Use of History in Mark Twain's *A Connecticut Yankee*," *PMLA* 80 (1965): 102–10; Louis D. Rubin, "Mark Twain and the Post-War Scene" in his *The Writer in the South* (Athens: University of Georgia Press, 1972); Henry Nash Smith, *Mark Twain's Fable of Progress: A Connecticut Yankee in King Arthur's Court* (New Brunswick, N.J.: Rutgers University Press, 1964); Everett Carter, "The Meaning of *A Connecticut Yankee*, "*AL* 50 (1978–79): 418–40; Jeffrey L. Dun-

can, "The Empirical and Ideal in Mark Twain," *PMLA* 95 (1980): 201–12; James D. Williams, "Revision and Intention in Mark Twain's *A Connecticut Yankee*," *AL* 36 (1964–65): 288–97; Paul J. Carter, "Mark Twain and the American Labor Movement," *NEQ* 30 (1957): 382–88; Harold Aspiz, "Lecky's Influence on Mark Twain," *Science and Society* 26 (1962): 15–25; Beverly R. David, "The Unexpurgated *A Connecticut Yankee*: Mark Twain and His Illustrator, Daniel Carter Beard," *Prospects* 1 (1975): 98–117; Ada M. Klett, "*Meisterschaft*, or The True State of Mark Twain's German," *German-American Review* 7 (December 1940): 10–11; Clyde L. Grimm, "*The American Claimant*: Reclamation of a Farce," *AQ* 19 (1967): 86–103.

CHAPTER EIGHT: EUROPEAN WANDERINGS

1. SLC to Hall, October 27, 1891; *MTLP*, pp. 287–89.
2. July 22, 1894; *LLMT*, p. 305.
3. "Mental Telepathy?" DV254, published in *MTQH*, p. 119. This collection includes "A Singular Episode."
4. April 25, 1892; *MTLP*, p. 310.
5. *MTLP*, pp. 313–15.
6. October 31, 1892; *MTLP*, p. 324.
7. *TS*, p. 302.
8. SLC to Hall, October 31, 1892; *MTLP*, p. 324.
9. SLC to Hall, August 10, 1892; *MTLP*, p. 314.
10. SLC to Hall, September 2, 1892; *MTLP*, p. 319.
11. Unpublished portion of "My Platonic Sweetheart," p. 36a recto, Box 15, no. 3A, MTP (†).
12. Box 8, no. 9, MTP (†), published in part in Arlin Turner, "Mark Twain and the South: An Affair of Love and Anger," *Southern Review* 4 (1968): 511.
13. SLC to Hall, December 12, 1892; *MTLP*, p. 328.
14. SLC to unidentified correspondent, June 23, 1895; quoted in Alan Gribben, *Mark Twain's Library: A Reconstruction* (Boston: G. K. Hall, 1980), I, 251.
15. SLC to Hall, December 12, 1892; *MTLP*, p. 328.
16. SLC to Laurence Hutton, January 2, 1893; Princeton Univ. Lib. (†).
17. SLC to Hall, February 3, 1893; *MTLP*, pp. 337, 340.
18. SLC to Hall, July 30, 1893; *MTLP*, p. 355.
19. Quoted in D. M. McKeithan, *The Morgan Manuscript of Mark Twain's "Pudd'nhead Wilson"* (Uppsala: American Institute, Uppsala University, 1961), p. 36.
20. SLC to Hall, July 30, 1893; *MTLP*, p. 354.
21. Quoted in McKeithan, *Morgan Manuscript*, p. 38.
22. SLC to OLC, January 12, 1884; *LLMT*, p. 291.
23. *Saturday Review*, December 29, 1894, p. 277; *Athenaeum*, January 19, 1895, pp. 83–84; reprinted in *MTCH*, p. 183; Tenney, pp. 22, 24.
24. SLC to Hall, November 24, 1892; *MTLP*, p. 326; see also p. 322.
25. Hall to SLC, August 7, 1893; *MTLP*, p. 352.
26. Charles S. Underhill, Jr., "Is the Garden of Eden at Niagara Falls?

Mark Twain Says 'Yes'," *The Gleaner* [published by the students of Nichols School, Buffalo, New York], (March 1928): 15 (copy at MTP).

27. SLC to S. M. Underhill, April 14, 1893, typescript, MTP (†).

28. Box 15, no. 4, PH, MTP.

29. SLC to Duneka; *MTL*, II, 775.

30. Box 15, no. 4 and no. 13, MTP.

31. SLC to Arthur S. Hardy, February 3, 1894; quoted in *MTHHR*, p. 10.

32. *LE*, p. 122.

33. *MTB*, I, 81–83; III, 1262.

34. Notebook 31, typescript pp. 6, 13, MTP [†]; cf. SLC to Chatto and Windus, October 13, 1892; PH, MTP.

35. *MTB*, II, 953–57; *MTL*, II, 580.

36. SLC to Mrs. Fairbanks, January 18, 1893; *MTMF*, p. 269.

37. SLC to Hall, January 28, 1893, [misdated 1892]; *MTL*, II, 579.

38. *MTL*, II, 615.

39. SLC to OLC, March 1, 1894; typescript, MTP (†).

40. SLC to OLC, July 13, 1894; *LLMT*, p. 302.

41. Alden to SLC, quoted in *Joan of Arc*, in *Mark Twain's Works*, Stormfield Edition (New York: Harper, 1929), p. viii.

42. SLC to OLC, July 31, 1894, and August 5, 1895; typescript, MTP; SLC to Henry Mills Alden, April 15, 1895; typescript, MTP.

43. *MTB*, II, 959.

44. SLC to Henry Harper, August 17 and August 21, 1895; in J. Henry Harper, *The House of Harper* (New York: Harper, 1912), pp. 575–76.

45. SLC to [Frank?] Harper, August 5, 1896; PH, MTP.

46. Michelet, *Jeanne D'Arc*, p. 10; Mark Twain's copy, MTP, quoted in Albert E. Stone, "Mark Twain's *Joan of Arc*: The Child as Goddess," *AL* 31 (1959–60): 6

47. Mark Twain's copy, MTP; quoted in Roger B. Salomon, *Twain and the Image of History* (New Haven: Yale University Press, 1961), p. 175.

48. *Joan* ms., vol. 2, pp. 341–42, 344; PH, MTP; a version is quoted in Salomon, *Twain and History*, p. 182.

49. Draft of memorial to Olivia Susan Clemens, Box 31, no. 4, p. 46½; MTP (†).

50. Quoted in *MTEng*, p. 166.

51. July 1896, p. 124.

53. *Idler*, August 1896, pp. 112–14.

53. *Bookman* [New York], May 1896, pp. 207–10.

54. *The Dial*, June 16, 1896, pp. 351–57.

55. *Harper's Weekly*, May 30, 1896, pp. 535–36; reprinted in *MMT*, pp. 129–35.

56. SLC to OLC, November 10, 1893; *LLMT*, p. 277.

57. SLC to Baroness Alexandra Gripenberg, December 27, 1888; *AL* 45 (1973–74): 376.

58. Useful criticism and scholarship dealing with the materials of this chapter include: Arthur L. Scott, "*The Innocents Adrift*, edited by Mark Twain's Official Biographer," *PMLA* 78 (1963): 320–37; O. M. Brack, Jr., "Mark Twain in Knee Pants: The Expurgation of *Tom Sawyer Abroad*," *Proof* 2 (1972): 141–

51; Bernard DeVoto, ed., *The Portable Mark Twain* (New York: Viking Press, 1946), pp. 31–32; Leslie Fiedler, *Love and Death in the American Novel*, rev. ed. (New York: Dell, 1966), pp. 403–9; F. R. Leavis, "Mark Twain's Neglected Classic: The Moral Astringency of *Pudd'nhead Wilson*," *Commentary* 21 (1956): 128–36; Robert A. Wiggins, "The Original of Mark Twain's 'Those Extraordinary Twains,'" *AL* 23 (1951–52): 355–57; Anne P. Wigger, "The Source of the Fingerprint Material in Mark Twain's *Pudd'nhead Wilson*," *AL* 28 (1956–57): 517–20; Hershel Parker and Henry Binder, "Exigencies of Composition and Publication: *Billy Budd, Sailor*, and *Pudd'nhead Wilson*," *Nineteenth-Century Fiction* 33 (1978): 131–43; Anne P. Wigger, "The Composition of *Pudd'nhead Wilson* and *Those Extraordinary Twins*: Chronology and Development," *Modern Philology* 55 (1957): 93–102; G. W. Spangler, "*Pudd'nhead Wilson*: A Parable of Property," *AL* 42 (1970–71): 28–37; Stanley Brodwin, "Blackness and the Adamic Myth in Mark Twain's *Pudd'nhead Wilson*," *Texas Studies in Language and Literature* 15 (1973): 167–76; Michael L. Ross, "Mark Twain's *Pudd'nhead Wilson*: Dawson's Landing and the Ladder of Nobility," *Novel* 6 (1973): 244–56; Sydney J. Krause, "Cooper's Literary Offenses: Mark Twain in Wonderland," *NEQ* 38 (1965): 291–311; "Fred J. Hall Tells the Story of His Connection with Charles L. Webster and Co.," *Twainian* 6 (November–December 1947): 1–3; Helen H. Salls, "Joan of Arc in English and American Literature," *South Atlantic Quarterly* 35 (1936): 167–85; Albert E. Stone, "Mark Twain's *Joan of Arc*: The Child as Goddess," *AL* 31 (1959–60): 1–20; William Searle, *The Saint and the Skeptics: Joan of Arc in the Works of Mark Twain, Anatole France, and Bernard Shaw* (Detroit: Wayne State University Press, 1976); J. Christian Bay, "*Tom Sawyer, Detective*: The Origins of the Plot," in *Essays Offered to Herbert Putnam*, ed. William Bishop and Andrew Keough (New Haven: Yale University Press, 1929), pp. 80–88.

CHAPTER NINE: DESPAIR

1. SLC to JHT, January 19, 1897; *MTL*, II, 641.
2. SLC to Frank Bliss, March 26, 1897; Beinecke Lib. (†).
3. SLC to J. Y. W. MacAllister, May 8, 1897; Univ. Va. Lib. (†).
4. SLC to Wayne MacVeagh, August 22, 1897; MTP (†).
5. *MTHHR*, pp. 249–50.
6. MS, *More Tramps Abroad*, p. 953, Berg (†).
7. Tenney, pp. 25–29; Francis J. Madigan, "Mark Twain's Passage to India: A Genetic Study of *Following the Equator*" (Ph.D. diss., New York University, 1974), pp. 22–23; *MTCH*, pp. 210–15.
8. January 19, 1897; *MTL*, II, 640.
9. Both appear in *FM*.
10. SLC to Mrs. Theodore Crane, March 19, 1893, typescript, MTP; a version appears in *MTL*, II, 581.
11. March 20, 1895; *LLMT*, p. 312.
12. AD, February 2, 1906; *MTA*, II, 34.
13. Ibid., 40.
14. Notebook 42, typescript pp. 28–34, MTP.

15. *FM*, p. 131.

16. Notebook 39, typescript p. 22; Notebook 41, typescript pp. 57–58, MTP, quoted in *HH&T*, p. 153.

17. Notebook 45, typescript p. 20; MTP (†).

18. *HH&T*, p. 170.

19. *S&B*, pp. 199, 187.

20. August 22, 1899; *MTHHR*, p. 407.

21. Paine no. 212, MTP.

22. *MTA*, I, 111–12.

23. "My Platonic Sweetheart," pp. 36a verso, 37–38; Box 15, no. 3A, MTP (†).

24. Ibid., MS pp. 43–44 (†).

25. Notebook 40, typescript p. 29, MTP; quoted in *LE*, p. 296.

26. *WWD*, p. 124.

27. Ibid., note.

28. Ibid., p. 556.

29. Notebook 40, typescript pp. 43–46, MTP; quoted in *WWD*, p. 19.

30. February 7, 1896; *LLMT*, p. 316.

31. SLC to Edward Day, March 21, 1903; West Va. Univ. Lib. (†).

32. November 8, 1899; MTP.

33. Notebook 40, typescript p. 50; quoted in *MSM*, p. 428.

34. *MSM*, p. 216.

35. Ibid., pp. 438ff.

36. *MTA*, I, 117.

37. Notebook 40, typescript p. 37, MTP; quoted in *MSM*, p. 17.

38. *MTTB*, pp. 252–53.

39. The text used is the only reliable one, that of *MSM*, hereafter cited in the text by chapter numbers.

40. *WWD*, p. 168.

41. Compare ibid., pp. 171–74 and *MTA*, II, 84–87.

42. *WWD*, p. 169.

43. Ibid., p. 167.

44. Isabel V. Lyon's Daybook, February 2, 1906–7; MTP: quoted in *MTGF*, p. 89.

45. *WWD*, p. 168.

46. SLC to Laurence Hutton, January 1, 1900; Princeton Univ. Lib. (†).

47. *MTA*, I, 127.

48. Ibid., 132.

49. Useful criticism and scholarship dealing with the materials of this chapter include: Francis J. Madigan, "Mark Twain's Passage to India: A Genetic Study of *Following the Equator*" (Ph.D. diss., New York University, 1974); Paul J. Carter, "Olivia Clemens Edits *Following the Equator*," *AL* 39 (1967–68): 325–51; Sydney J. Krause, "Olivia Clemens's 'Editing' Reviewed," *AL* 39 (1967–68): 325–51; St. George Tucker Arnold, "Mark Twain's Critters and the Traditions of Animal Portraiture of the Old Southwest," *Southern Folklore Quarterly* 40 (1977): 195–211; Dennis Welland, "Mark Twain's Last Travel Book," *BNYPL* 69 (1965): 31–48; Friedrich Schöenmann, "Mark Twain and Adolph Wilbrandt," *Modern Language Notes* 34 (1919): 372–74; Alexander E. Jones, "Mark Twain and the Determinism of *What Is Man?*" *AL* 29 (1957–58):

1–17; Sherwood Cummings, "Mark Twain's Social Darwinism," *Huntington Library Quarterly* 20 (1957): 163–75; Cummings, *"What Is Man?"*: The Scientific Sources," in *Essays in Determinism in American Literature*, ed. Sydney J. Krause (Kent, Ohio: Kent State University Press, 1964), pp. 108–16; Howard G. Baetzhold, *Mark Twain and John Bull: The British Connection* (Bloomington: Indiana University Press, 1970), pp. 217–26, 362; John Tuckey, "Mark Twain's Later Dialogue: The 'Me' and the Machine," *AL* 41 (1969–70): 532–42; Daryl E. Jones, "The *Hornet* Disaster: Mark Twain's Adaptation in 'The Great Dark,'" *American Literary Realism* 9 (1976): 243–47; Mary E. Rucker, "Morality and Determinism in 'The Man That Corrupted Hadleyburg,'" *Studies in Short Fiction* 14 (1977): 49–54; John R. May, "The Gospel According to Philip Traum: Structural Unity in 'The Mysterious Stranger,'" *Studies in Short Fiction* 8 (1971): 411–22; Paul Delaney, "The Dissolving Self: The Narrator of Mark Twain's *Mysterious Stranger* Fragments," *Journal of Narrative Techniques* 6 (1976): 51–65.

CHAPTER TEN: CITIZEN OF THE WORLD

1. Introduction at a Lotus Club dinner, November 10, 1900; *MTB*, III, 1116.

2. *The Academy*, September 29, 1900, p. 258; R. E. Phillips, "Mark Twain More Than Humorist," *The Book Buyer*, April 1901, p. 201; reprinted in *MTCH*, p. 242.

3. SLC to JHT, August 12, 1900; *MTL*, II, 699.

4. *LAIFI*, pp. 333–39; *ISLC*, pp. 16–17.

5. New York *Herald*, December 30, 1900, sec. 1, p. 7; quoted in *MTHL*, II, 726.

6. SLC to JHT, January 29, 1901; *MTL*, II, 704–5.

7. *FM*, pp. 403–19.

8. SLC to Rudolf Lindau, April 14, 1901; quoted in *MTGF*, p. 29.

9. Notebook 44, typescript p. 5, MTP (†).

10. SLC to Frederick Duneka, February 16, 1902; amanuensis copy, MTP (†).

11. *FM*, p. 321. Hereafter page citations of this edition appear in the text.

12. August 26, 1901; Univ. Texas Lib. (†).

13. August 29, 1901; Univ. Texas Lib. (†).

14. September 8, 1901; Beinecke Lib. (†). See also SLC to HHR, September 6, 1901; *MTHHR*, p. 469.

15. Notebook 45, typescript p. 24; MTP; quoted in *WWD*, p. 22.

16. AD, August 30, 1906; *MTE*, p. 198.

17. *N&J3*, pp. 88, 358–59.

18. Quoted in *MTB*, III, 1147.

19. *MTGF*, p. 39.

20. December 30, 1901, Houghton Lib. (†).

21. *LAIFI*, p. 249.

22. *FM*, p. 138.

23. *HH&T*, p. 17.

24. Notebook 45, typescript p. 14, MTP; quoted in *HH&T*, p. 18.

25. AD, August 30, 1906; *MTE*, p. 199.
26. February 11, 1903, MTP.
27. January 4, 1904; *MTL*, II, 748–50.
28. *MTA*, I, xv.
29. Amanuensis copy, MTP (†).
30. SLC to Clara Clemens, June 29, 1905; typescript, MTP (†).
31. AD, August 30, 1906; *MTE*, pp. 198–99.
32. *MTW*, p. 127.
33. *MSM*, pp. 342–43. Hereafter page citations of this edition appear in the text.
34. SLC to JHT, July 28, 1904; quoted in *MSM*, p. 30.
35. Useful criticism and scholarship dealing with the materials of this chapter include: Philip S. Foner, *Mark Twain: Social Critic* (New York: International Publishers, 1958); Louis J. Budd, *Mark Twain: Social Philosopher* (Bloomington: Indiana University Press, 1962); Kenneth Requa, "Counterfeit Currency and Character in Mark Twain's 'Which Was It?'" *MTJ* 17 (Winter 1974–75): 1–6; John Tuckey, Paper delivered at the December 1979 Modern Language Association convention, San Francisco, California.

CHAPTER ELEVEN: FINAL SOLILOQUIES

1. November 4, 1904; *MTL*, II, 761, 764.
2. *LAIFI*, p. 27.
3. *FM*, p. 422.
4. Elizabeth Jordan to SLC, March 22, 1905; MTP.
5. Quoted in *FM*, p. 157.
6. *MTB*, III, 1500.
7. SLC to Clara Clemens, June 29, 1905; typescript, MTP.
8. July 16, 1905; *MTL*, II, 775.
9. SLC to Clara Clemens, July 16, 1905; typescript, MTP (†).
10. SLC to Duneka, July 16, 1905; *MTL*, II, 775.
11. July 27, 1905; MTP.
12. Box 15, no. 5.
13. *MTB*, III, 1226.
14. September 26, 1905; MTP.
15. Box 15, no. 6, MTP (†).
16. Box 15, no. 2, MS p. 72; MTP (†).
17. Minnie Madden Fiske to SLC, September 18, 1905; MTP; *MTB*, III, 1246.
18. AD, August 29, 1906, MTP (†).
19. *MTA*, I, 269.
20. Isabel Lyon's diary, January 14, 1906; quoted in *MTGF*, p. 136.
21. *MTB*, III, 1268.
22. SLC to J. W. Y. MacAllister, February 21, 1907; quoted in *MTEng*, p. 50.
23. AD, October 4, 1906; MTP (†).
24. AD, May 19, 1907; MTP (†).
25. "Reflections on Religion," *Hudson Review* 16 (1963): 348–49.

26. Quoted in *MTB*, III, 1268.
27. AD, June 2, 1906; *MTE*, p. 195.
28. DV226, Doheny Lib. (†). In preparing this work, SLC drew on another unpublished work, written about the Clemens children in the 1870s and 1880s, "A Record of Small Foolishnesses," DV401, PH, MTP.
29. Quoted in *MTHHR*, p. 664.
30. *WIM*, p. 400.
31. AD, January 13, 1908; *MTE*, p. 316.
32. *WIM*, p. 439.
33. *MTB*, III, 1548.
34. Paine no. 278, PH, MTP. The original manuscript is in the Rare Books and Special Collections Department, Washington University Libraries, St. Louis, Missouri, whose permission to quote I gratefully acknowledge (†).
35. Useful criticism and scholarship dealing with the materials of this chapter include: Hunt Hawkins, "Mark Twain's Involvement with the Congo Movement: 'A Fury of Generous Indignation,'" *NEQ* 51 (1978): 147–75; William L. Andrews, "The Sources of Mark Twain's 'The War Prayer,'" *MTJ* 17 (Summer 1975): 8–9; Henry J. Lindborg, "A Cosmic Tramp: Samuel Clemens's 'Three Thousand Years Among the Microbes,'" *AL* 44 (1972–73): 652–57; Robert A. Rees and Richard D. Rust, "Mark Twain's 'The Turning Point of My Life,'" *AL* 40 (1968–69): 524–35; Alexander E. Jones, "Mark Twain and Sexuality," *PMLA* 71 (1956): 595–616.

CHAPTER TWELVE: A BACKWARD GLANCE

1. AD, August 29, 1906; *MTE*, p. 243.
2. SLC to Judge Horace Russell, December 12, 1884; typescript, MTP.
3. *MTB*, II, 785–86.
4. February 11, 1894; typescript, MTP (†).
5. Letter to Yale University on being awarded an honorary master's degree, Hartford *Courant*, June 29, 1889.
6. SLC to Edward Bok, October 10, 1898; Univ. Va. Lib. (†).
7. Published in "My Methods of Writing" in *MTJ* 8 (Winter–Spring 1949): 1, and from George Bainton's 1890 publication reprinted in *LAIFI*, p. 227.
8. Bombay *Gazette*, January 23, 1896; *MTSH*, p. 155.
9. AD, February 15, 1906; *MTE*, p. 251.
10. E.g., Clemens to William Walter Phelps, January 2, 1893 (PH at MTP), in which Mark Twain amusingly reveals his majestic plans for revamping the physical geography of the earth.
11. Many not-so-revealing comments in letters are marked "*private.*" Presumably Clemens's eagerness to appear frank, open, and all-revealing was compensation for his overwhelming fear that his iconoclastic ideas would hurt his career, a belief that must have stemmed from his recognition of his Western past, when he had been a severe critic of the same social order that he later became part of.

Bibliography

This list supplements the works in the list of abbreviations, above. *Note*: individual personal letters, published and unpublished, and some brief reviews are excluded.

MANUSCRIPTS

Unless otherwise stated, manuscripts are in the Mark Twain Papers, Bancroft Library, University of California, Berkeley. Some items are scheduled for publication, notably in *Autobiography of Eve and Other Sketches and Fragments*, edited by John S. Tuckey.

Samuel L. Clemens (Mark Twain)

"Adam's Diary," additions to, Box 15, no. 5.
"Adam's Diary," unpublished fragment of, Box 15, no. 6.
"Advice to Paine," Paine no. 278, Washington Univ. Lib.
"Aguinaldo," Paine no. 89 and no. 89a.
The American Claimant, manuscript of novel and summary, Box 32.
"The American Press," Paine no. 102A.
"Ashcroft-Lyon Manuscript," Box 48.
Autobiographical dictations and other portions of autobiography.
Boardinghouse novel fragment, DV55.
"The Case of the Rev. Dr. Ament, Missionary." Paine no. 21.
"A Defense of Royalty and Nobility," DV313a.
"Extract from Adam's Diary," from *The Niagara Book*. Buffalo, N.Y.: Underhill and Nichols, 1893. With author's holograph corrections, PH.

Extracts from Adam's Diary. New York: Harper and Brothers, 1904. With au-
thor's holograph corrections, PH.
"A Family Sketch." DV226. Doheny Lib.
"Girl Who Was Ostensibly a Man," DV325.
"Happy Memories of the Dental Chair," DV51.
"In Memory of Olivia Susan Clemens," draft, Box 31, no. 4.
The Innocents Abroad, manuscript drafts, McKinney Papers, Vassar College.
"Is He Dead?" Paine no. 126.
Joan of Arc, holograph manuscript, PH.
"Letters from a Dog to Another Dog Explaining & Accounting for Man:
Translated from the Original Doggerel," DV344.
Life on the Mississippi, holograph manuscript, Pierpont Morgan Library.
"Mental Telegraphy?" DV254.
"Mr. Brown and the Sergeant-at-Arms," McKinney Papers, Vassar College.
More Tramps Abroad, holograph manuscript, Berg Collection, New York Public
Library.
"My Platonic Sweetheart," Box 15, no. 3a.
"The Mysterious Chamber," DV56.
Notebooks, typescript of unpublished, MTP.
Notes on Samuel C. Thompson's 1909 letter, DV268.
"On Progress, Civilization, Monarchy, etc.," Paine no. 102b.
"Postal Service," Paine no. 73.
Pudd'nhead Wilson, manuscript notes, Box 8, no. 9.
"A Record of the Small Foolishnesses of Susie & 'Bay' Clemens (Infants),"
DV401, PH.
Sandwich Islands novel fragment, DV111.
Scrapbook 2, MTP.
"A Singular Episode," DV329. [Also known as "The Late Reverend Sam
Jones's Reception into Heaven."]
"A Thanksgiving Sentiment," DV370.
A Tramp Abroad, early drafts, Box 6, nos. 46, 47, 52.

Frederick A. Duneka

Twain, Mark. *Extracts from Adam's Diary.* New York: Harper and Brothers,
1904. With Frederick Duneka's holograph corrections, PH.

Joseph H. Twichell

Journals. Beinecke Rare Book and Manuscript Library, Yale University.

PUBLISHED WORKS

Samuel L. Clemens (Mark Twain)

Note: Many of the shorter uncollected pieces will appear in volumes now being readied for publication in the edition of the works of Mark Twain being released by the University of California Press.

"American Travel Letters, in *Alta California* [1867–1869]," reprinted in *The Twainian* 6 (May–June 1947): 1–3; 6 (July–August 1947): 4–6; 6 (September–October 1947): 3–4; 6 (November–December 1947): 3–4; 7 (January–February 1948): 3–5; 7 (March–April 1948): 3–5; 7 (May–June 1948): 3–5; 7 (July–August 1948): 3–4; 7 (September–October 1948): 3–4; 7 (November–December 1948): 5–7; 8 (January–February 1949): 3–6; 8 (March–April 1949): 4–7; 8 (May–June 1949): 3–6; 8 (July–August 1949): 3–6.

"Around the World," Buffalo *Express*, October 17, 30; November 13; December 11, 18, 1869; January 8, 22, 29, 1870; PH, MTP.

Autobiographical Sketch written for Samuel Moffett. Worcester: Privately printed, 1918.

The Autobiography of Mark Twain. Edited by Charles Neider. New York: Harper and Brothers, 1959.

"The Carson Fossil-Footprints," *The San Franciscan*, February 16, 1884 (copy at Bancroft Library, University of California, Berkeley); reprinted in *Resources for American Literary Study* 10 (1980): 74–78.

The Celebrated Jumping Frog of Calaveras County, and Other Sketches. Edited by John Paul. New York: C. H. Webb, 1867.

The Choice Humorous Works of Mark Twain. London: John Camden Hotten [1873].

The Choice Humorous Works of Mark Twain. Revised and Corrected by the Author. London: Chatto and Windus, 1874.

The Complete Essays of Mark Twain. Edited by Charles Neider. Garden City, N.Y.: Doubleday and Co., 1963.

The Complete Works of Mark Twain. "American Artists Edition." New York: Harper and Brothers, n.d.

Conversation As It Was at the Fireside of the Tudors [*1601*]. Chicago: Mark Twain Society, 1939.

"Correspondence," Memphis *Daily Appeal*, October 24, 1858; reprinted in *American Literary Realism* 15 (1982); 201–03.

The Curious Republic of Gondour and Other Whimsical Sketches. New York: Boni and Liveright, 1919.

"'Dear Master Wattie': The Mark Twain–David Watson Bowser Letters." Edited by Pascal Covici, Jr., *Southwest Review* 45 (1960): 104–21.

"Eve's Diary." In *Their Husbands' Wives*, edited by William Dean Howells and Henry Mills Alden. New York: Harper and Brothers, 1906.

Eve's Diary. New York: Harper and Brothers, 1906.

Eye Openers: Good Things, Immensely Funny Sayings & Stories That Will Bring a Smile upon the Gruffest Countenance. London: John Camden Hotten, [1871].

"The Facts Concerning the Recent Important Resignation," New York *Tribune*, February 1868; reprinted in *The Twainian* 5 (May–June 1946): 1.

"Fenimore Cooper's Further Literary Offenses," edited by Bernard DeVoto. *NEQ* 19 (1946): 291–311.

Following the Equator. Hartford: American Publishing Co., 1897.

"Happy Memories of the Dental Chair." In Sheldon Baumrind, "Mark Twain Visits the Dentist," *Journal of the California Dental Association* 46 (1964): 493–96, 502.

How to Tell a Story and Other Essays. New York: Harper and Brothers, 1897.

Letter from Hartford dated July 1, 1869, and published in the San Francisco *Alta California*, August 1, 1869; PH, MTP.

Letter to *Alta California*, September 6, 1868; reprinted in *The Twainian* 7 (November–December 1948): 5–7.

Letters in the Chicago *Republican*, 1868, PH, MTP.

Letters in the Virginia City *Territorial Enterprise*, 1867–1868, PH, MTP.

Letters to Mary. Edited by Lewis Leary. New York: Columbia University Press, 1961.

Letters to San Francisco *Call* from Nevada, 1863; reprinted in *The Twainian* 8 (September–October 1949): 1–2; 9 (March–April 1950): 3–4; 11 (January–February 1952): 1–2; 11 (March–April 1952): 1–4; 11 (May–June 1952): 1–4.

"Magdalen Tower." In *The Shotover Papers; or, Echoes from Oxford*, October 17, 1874; reprinted in *The Twainian* 2 (January 1943): 4–5.

The Mammoth Cod and Address to the Stomach Club. Edited by G. Legman. Milwaukee: Maledicta, 1976.

The Man That Corrupted Hadleyburg and Other Stories and Essays. New York: Harper and Brothers, 1900.

The Man That Corrupted Hadleyburg and Other Stories and Sketches. London: Chatto and Windus; Leipzig: Bernard Tauchnitz, 1900.

Mark Twain and Hawaii. Edited by Walter Francis Frear. Chicago: Lakeside Press, 1947.

Mark Twain of the "Enterprise": Newspaper Articles and Other Documents, 1862–1864. Edited by Henry Nash Smith and Frederick Anderson. Berkeley and Los Angeles: University of California Press, 1957.

Mark Twain: San Francisco Correspondent. Edited by Henry Nash Smith and Frederick Anderson. San Francisco: Book Club of California, 1957.

Mark Twain's (Burlesque) Autobiography and First Romance. New York: Sheldon and Co., [1871].

Mark Twain's Letters from Hawaii. Edited by A. Grove Day. New York: Appleton-Century, 1966.

"Mark Twain's Religious Beliefs as Indicated by Notations in His Books."

Edited by Chester L. Davis, *The Twainian* 14 (September–October 1955): 4.

Mark Twain's Sketches. Selected and Revised by the Author. London: George Routledge and Sons, 1872.

Mark Twain's Sketches, New and Old. Now First Published in Complete Form. Hartford and Chicago: American Publishing Co., 1875.

Mark Twain's Sketches. *Number One*. New York: American News Co., [1874].

Mark Twain's Speeches. Edited by Albert Bigelow Paine. New York: Harper and Brothers, 1923.

"Memphis—The Cotton Trade—Illinois Politics—What Tennessee Thinks of Them," *Missouri Republican*, October 22, 1858; reprinted in *American Literary Realism* 15 (1982); 199–200.

More Tramps Abroad. London: Chatto and Windus, 1897.

The New Pilgrim's Progress. London: Routledge, 1872.

"Our Special River Correspondence," *Missouri Democrat*, September 1, 1858; Reprinted in *American Literary Realism* 15 (1982): 197–98.

On the Poetry of Mark Twain. With Selections from His Verse. Edited by Arthur L. Scott. Urbana and London: University of Illinois Press, 1966.

The Pattern for Mark Twain's "Roughing It." Edited by Franklin R. Rogers. Berkeley and Los Angeles: University of California Press, 1961.

A Pen Warmed Up in Hell: Mark Twain in Protest. Edited by Frederick Anderson. New York: Harper and Row, 1972.

The Portable Mark Twain. Edited by Bernard DeVoto. New York: Viking Press, 1946.

Punch, Brothers, Punch! and Other Sketches. New York: Slote, Woodman and Co., 1878.

"Reflections on Religion," edited by Charles Neider. *Hudson Review* 16 (1963): 329–52.

Report from Paradise. Edited by Dixon Wecter. New York: Harper and Brothers, 1952.

Representative Selections. Edited by Fred Lewis Pattee. New York: American Book Co., 1935.

"Rev. H. W. Beecher: His Private Habits," Buffalo *Express*, September 25, 1869, p. 1 (PH, MTP).

Roughing It. Edited by Franklin R. Rogers and Paul Baender. Berkeley, Los Angeles, and London: University of California Press, 1972.

Screamers: A Gathering of Scraps of Humor, Delicious Bits, & Short Stories. London: John Camden Hotten, [1871].

"The Secret of Dr. Livingston's Continued Voluntary Exile," Hartford *Courant*, July 20, 1872.

Simon Wheeler, Detective. Edited by Franklin R. Rogers. New York: New York Public Library, 1963.

"Soleleather Cultivates His Taste for Music," New Orleans *Crescent*, July 21, 1859, reprinted in *AL* 54 (1982): 498–502.

"Some Recollections of a Storm at Sea," *The Bazaar Record* (Cleveland), January 18, 1876; reprinted in *The Twainian* 8 (July–August 1949): 1–2.
The Stolen White Elephant, Etc. Boston: James R. Osgood, 1882.
Tom Sawyer Abroad. London: Chatto and Windus, 1894.
"To the Person Sitting in Darkness," *North American Review*, February, 1901, pp. 161–76.
Traveling with the Innocents Abroad: Mark Twain's Original Reports from Europe and the Holy Land. Edited by Daniel Morley McKeithan. Norman: University of Oklahoma Press, 1958.
A True Story and the Recent Carnival of Crime. Boston: James R. Osgood and Co., 1877.
Wapping Alice. Berkeley, Calif.: Friends of the Bancroft Library, 1981.
Washington in 1868. Edited by Cyril Clemens. Webster Groves, Mo.: International Mark Twain Society, 1943.
The Writings of Mark Twain. "Definitive Edition." 37 vol. New York: Gabriel Wells, 1923–35.

Samuel L. Clemens (Mark Twain) and Bret Harte

"Ah Sin," a Dramatic Work. Edited by Frederick Anderson. San Francisco: Book Club of California, 1961.
Sketches of the Sixties, by Bret Harte and Mark Twain. Revised edition. San Francisco: John Howell, 1927.

Samuel L. Clemens (Mark Twain) and William Dean Howells

Howells, William Dean. *The Complete Plays of William Dean Howells.* Edited by Walter J. Meserve. New York: New York University Press, 1970. [Includes *Colonel Sellers as a Scientist.*]

SECONDARY SOURCES

The indispensable sources of this study of Mark Twain's career as a writer were his writings, published and unpublished, his correspondence, and his notebooks. Many other writings, especially recent scholarship and criticism, also proved helpful, as I have indicated in my notes. The works that follow, together with those above and in the list of abbreviations, provide a full record of my indebtednesses. To five books I owe an especially large debt. They are: Albert Bigelow Paine's 1912 biography, a primary source that includes information and quotations available nowhere else, though it is a secondary source as well; the seminal critical studies of Henry Nash Smith and James M. Cox; Alan Gribben's learned volumes on Mark Twain's reading; and my candidate for the best book yet written on our author, Walter Blair's *Mark Twain & Huck Finn*. I could only wish that my work were up to the standards of the model that indirectly inspired my study, Henry Nash Smith's superb introduction to his 1958 edition of *Adventures of Huckleberry Finn*.

Albasio, Christine. "Mark Twain: The Final Phase." Ph.D. diss., University of California, Davis, 1976.

[Alden, Henry Mills]. "Editor's Literary Record" [review of *Life on the Mississippi*]. *Harper's Magazine* 67 (1883): 799.

Aldrich, Thomas Bailey. *The Story of a Bad Boy*. Boston: Fields and Osgood, 1869.

Andrews, Kenneth R. *Nook Farm: Mark Twain's Hartford Circle*. Cambridge: Harvard University Press, 1950.

Andrews, William L. "The Source of Mark Twain's 'The War Prayer'," *MTJ* 17 (Summer 1975): 8–9.

Anonymous. "Mark's New Way." *Academy* (London), September 29, 1900, pp. 258–59.

Anonymous. Paragraphs on Mark Twain. *The Book Buyer*, April 1900, September 1900.

Anonymous. Review of Mark Twain's *Joan of Arc*. *Bookman* (London) 10 (July 1896): 124.

Armstrong, C. J. "John J. Robards—A Boyhood Friend of Mark Twain." *Missouri Historical Review* 25 (1931): 293–98.

Arnold, St. George Tucker. "The Twain Bestiary: Mark Twain's Critters and the Traditions of Animal Portraiture of the Old Southwest." *Southern Folklore Quarterly* 40 (1977): 195–211.

Aspiz, Harold, "Lecky's Influence on Mark Twain." *Science and Society* 26 (1962): 15–25.

Baender, Paul. "Alias Macfarlane: A Revision of Mark Twain Biography." *AL* 38 (1966–67): 187–97.

———. "The Date of Mark Twain's 'The Lowest Animal.'" *AL* 36 (1964–65): 174–79.

———. "The Jumping Frog as a Comedian's First Virtue." *Philological Quarterly* 60 (1963): 192–200.

———. "Mark Twain's Transcendent Figures." Diss., University of California, Berkeley, 1956.

Baetzhold, Howard G. "The Autobiography of Sir Robert Smith of Camelot: Mark Twain's Original Plan for *A Connecticut Yankee*." *AL* 32 (1960–61): 456–61.

———. "Found: Mark Twain's 'Lost Sweetheart.'" *AL* 44 (1972–73): 414–29.

———. *Mark Twain and John Bull: The British Connection*. Bloomington: Indiana University Press, 1970.

———. "Mark Twain's 'The Prince and the Pauper.'" *Notes and Queries*, n.s. 1 (1954): 401–3.

Baker, William. "Mark Twain in Cincinnati: 'A Mystery Most Compelling.'"

American Literary Realism 12 (1979): 229–315.

Basso, David, ed. *Mark Twain in the "Virginia Evening Bulletin" and "Gold Hill Daily News."* Sparks, Nev.: Falcon Hill Press, 1981.

Bates, Allen. "Mark Twain and the Mississippi River." Ph.D. diss., University of Chicago, 1968.

Bay, J. Christian. "Tom Sawyer, Detective: The Origin of the Plot." In *Essays Offered to Herbert Putnam by His Colleagues and Friends*, edited by William W. Bishop and Andrew Keough, pp. 80–88. New Haven: Yale University Press, 1929.

Beidler, Philip D. "Realistic Style and the Problem of Context in *The Innocents Abroad* and *Roughing It.*" *AL* 52 (1980–81): 33–49.

Bellamy, Gladys C. *Mark Twain as a Literary Artist.* Norman: University of Oklahoma Press, 1950.

———. "Mark Twain's Indebtedness to John Phoenix." *AL* 13 (1941–42): 29–43.

Benson, Ivan. *Mark Twain's Western Years.* Stanford: Stanford University Press, 1938.

Blair, Walter, "The French Revolution and *Huckleberry Finn.*" *Modern Philology* 55 (1957): 21–35.

———. *Mark Twain & Huck Finn.* Berkeley and Los Angeles: University of California Press, 1960.

———. "Mark Twain's Other Masterpiece: 'Jim Baker's Blue Jay Yarn.'" *Studies in American Humor* 1 (1975): 132–47.

———. "On the Structure of *Tom Sawyer.*" *Modern Philology* 37 (1939): 75–88.

———. Review of DeLancey Ferguson, *Mark Twain: Man and Legend. AL* 16 (1944–45): 143–45.

———. "When Was *Huckleberry Finn* Written?" *AL* 30 (1958–59): 1–24.

Blair, Walter, and Hamlin Hill. *America's Humor: From Poor Richard to Doonesbury.* New York: Oxford University Press, 1978.

Blues, Thomas. *Mark Twain & the Community.* Lexington: University Press of Kentucky, 1970.

Brack, O. M., Jr. "Mark Twain in Knee Pants: The Expurgation of *Tom Sawyer Abroad.*" *Proof* 2 (1972): 141–51.

Bradley, Ruth M. "The Making of *Personal Recollections of Joan of Arc.*" Ph.D. diss., University of California, Los Angeles, 1971.

Branch, Edgar M. "'The Babes in the Woods': Artemus Ward's 'Double Health' to Mark Twain." *PMLA* 93 (1978): 955–72.

———. *The Literary Apprenticeship of Mark Twain.* Urbana: University of Illinois Press, 1950.

———. "'My Voice is Still for Setchell': A Background Study of 'Jim Smiley and His Jumping Frog.'" *PMLA* 82 (1967): 591–601.

———. "A New Clemens Footprint: Soleleather Steps Forward." *AL* 54 (1982): 497–510.

――――. "Sam Clemens, Steersman on the *John H. Dickey*," *American Literary Realism* 15 (1982): 195–208.

Brashear, Minnie M. *Mark Twain: Son of Missouri.* Chapel Hill: University of North Carolina Press, 1934.

Brodwin, Stanley. "Blackness and the Adamic Myth in Mark Twain's *Pudd'nhead Wilson.*" *Texas Studies in Language and Literature* 15 (1973): 167–76.

――――. "The Useful and Useless River: *Life on the Mississippi* Revisited." *Studies in American Humor* 2 (1976): 196–209.

Brooks, Van Wyck. *The Ordeal of Mark Twain.* New York: E. P. Dutton, 1920. Revised edition, 1933.

Browne, Ray B. "Mark Twain and Captain Wakeman." *AL* 33 (1961–62): 320–29.

Buckle, Thomas Henry. *History of Civilization in England.* 2 vols. New York: Appleton, 1866.

Budd, Louis J. *Mark Twain: Social Philosopher.* Bloomington: Indiana University Press, 1962.

――――. "The Southern Currents Under Huckleberry Finn's Raft." *Mississippi Valley Historical Review* 46 (1959): 222–37.

Burde, Edgar. "Mark Twain: The Writer as Pilot." *PMLA* 93 (1978): 878–92.

Burg, David F. "Another View of *Huckleberry Finn.*" *Nineteenth-Century Fiction* 29 (1974): 299–319.

Cardwell, Guy A. "Samuel Clemens's Magical Pseudonym," *NEQ* 48 (1975): 175–94.

Carlyle, Thomas. *The French Revolution: A History.* 2 vols. New York: Harper, 1856.

Carter, Everett. "The Meaning of *A Connecticut Yankee.*" *AL* 50 (1978–79): 418–40.

Carter, Paul J. "Mark Twain and the American Labor Movement." *NEQ* 30 (1957): 382–88.

――――. "Mark Twain Describes an Earthquake." *PMLA* 72 (1957): 999–1004.

――――. "Olivia Clemens Edits *Following the Equator.*" *AL* 30 (1958–59): 194–209.

Clemens, Clara. *My Father, Mark Twain.* New York: Harper and Brothers, 1931.

Clemens, Cyril. *Young Sam Clemens.* Portland, Me.: Leon Tebbets Editions, 1942.

Covici, Pascal, Jr. *Mark Twain's Humor: The Image of a World.* Dallas: Southern Methodist University Press, 1962.

Cox, James M. *Mark Twain: The Fate of Humor.* Princeton: Princeton University Press, 1966.

――――. "The Muse of Mark Twain." *Massachusetts Review* 5 (1963): 127–41.

Crossman, Lester G. "Samuel L. Clemens in Search of Mark Twain—A Study of Clemens's Changing Conception of Himself as a Writer." Ph.D. diss., University of Washington, 1957.

Crowley, John W. "A Note on *The Gilded Age*." *English Language Notes* 10 (1972): 116–18.

Cummings, Sherwood. "Mark Twain's Social Darwinism." *Huntington Library Quarterly* 20 (1957): 163–75.

———. "*What Is Man?*: The Scientific Sources." In *Essays in Determinism in American Literature*, edited by Sydney J. Krause. Kent, Ohio: Kent State University Press, 1964.

David, Beverly R. "The Unexpurgated *A Connecticut Yankee*: Mark Twain and His Illustrator, Daniel Carter Beard." *Prospects* 1 (1975): 98–117.

Davis, Chester L. "Mark Twain's Religious Beliefs as Indicated by Annotations in His Books." *The Twainian* 14 (September–October 1955): 1–4.

Delaney, Paul. "The Dissolving Self: The Narrators of Mark Twain's *Mysterious Stranger* Fragments." *Journal of Narrative Techniques* 7 (1976): 51–65.

———. "'You Can't Go Back to the Raft A'gin Huck Honey!': Mark Twain's Western Sequel to *Huckleberry Finn*." *Western American Literature* 11 (1976): 215–29.

DeVoto, Bernard. *Mark Twain's America*. Boston: Little, Brown, 1932.

Dickinson, Leon T. "Mark the Twain: The Double Vision of Samuel Clemens." *Revue des Langues Vivantes*, special U.S. Bicentennial Issue, 1976, pp. 81–91.

———. "Mark Twain's Revisions in Writing *The Innocents Abroad*." *AL* 19 (1947–48): 139–57.

———. Review of Dewey Ganzel, *Mark Twain Abroad*. *Modern Philology* 68 (1970): 117–19.

———. "The Sources of *The Prince and the Pauper*." *Modern Language Notes* 64 (1949): 103–6.

Duckett, Margaret. *Mark Twain and Bret Harte*. Norman: University of Oklahoma Press, 1964.

Duncan, Jeffrey L. "The Empirical and Ideal in Mark Twain." *PMLA* 95 (1980): 201–12.

Eaton, Vincent L. "Mark Twain, Washington Correspondent." *Manuscripts* 11 (1959): 16–26.

Eliot, T. S. Introduction to *The Adventures of Huckleberry Finn*. London: Cressett Press, 1950.

Emerson, Everett. "Mark Twain: The Writer as Reader." *Thoughts* [Chulalongkorn University, Thailand] 3 (1983): 1–7.

———. "A Send-Off for Joe Goodman: Mark Twain's 'The Carson Fossil-Footprints." *Resources for American Literary Study* 10 (1980): 71–78.

Ensor, Alison. "The 'Tennessee Land' of *The Gilded Age*: Fiction and Reality." *Tennessee Studies in English* 15 (1970): 15–23.

Fatout, Paul. *Mark Twain in Virginia City*. Bloomington: Indiana University Press, 1964.

———. "Mark Twain, Litigant." *AL* 31 (1959–60): 30–45.

———. *Mark Twain on the Lecture Circuit*. Bloomington: Indiana University Press, 1960.

———. "Mark Twain's *Nom de Plume*." *AL* 34 (1962–63): 1–7.

Fender, Stephen. "'The Prodigal in a Far Country Chawing of Husks': Mark Twain's Search for a Style in the West." *Modern Language Review* 71 (1976): 737–56.

Ferguson, DeLancey. "Huck Finn Aborning." *The Colophon* 3 (1938): 171–80.

———. "Mark Twain's Comstock Duel: The Birth of a Legend." *AL* 14 (1942–43): 66–70.

———. "The Uncollected Portions of Mark Twain's *Autobiography*." *AL* 8 (1936–37): 37–46.

Fetterley, Judith. "Disenchantment: Tom Sawyer in *Huckleberry Finn*." *PMLA* 87 (1972): 69–74.

———. "The Sanctioned Rebel." *Studies in the Novel* 3 (1971): 293–304.

Fiedler, Leslie. *Love and Death in the American Novel*. Revised edition. New York: Dell, 1966.

Foner, Philip S. *Mark Twain: Social Critic*. New York: International Publishers, 1958.

French, Bryant Morey. *Mark Twain and the Gilded Age*. Dallas: Southern Methodist University Press, 1965.

Gale, Robert L. *Plots and Characters in the Works of Mark Twain*. 2 vols. Hamden, Conn.: Archon Books, 1973.

Ganzel, Dewey. *Mark Twain Abroad: The Cruise of the "Quaker City."* Chicago and London: University of Chicago Press, 1968.

Gardner, Joseph H. "Mark Twain and Dickens." *PMLA* 84 (1969): 90–101.

Gauvreau, Emile. *My Last Million Readers*. New York: Dutton, 1941.

Gerber, John. "Mark Twain's 'Private Campaign.'" *Civil War History* 1 (1955): 37–60.

———. "The Relationship Between Point of View and Style in the Works of Mark Twain." In *Style in Prose Fiction*, English Institute Essays, 1958, pp. 142–171. New York: Columbia University Press, 1959.

Grant, Douglas. *Mark Twain*. New York: Grove Press, 1962.

Gribben, Alan. "'It Is Unsatisfactory to Read to One's Self': "Mark Twain's Informal Reading." *Quarterly Journal of Speech* 62 (1976): 49–56.

———. *Mark Twain's Library: A Reconstruction*. 2 vols. Boston: G. K. Hall and Co., 1980.

———. "'The Master Hand of Old Malory': Mark Twain's Acquaintance with *Le Morte d'Arthur*." *English Language Notes* 16 (1978): 32–40.

———. "'A Splendor of Stars & Suns': Mark Twain as a Reader of Browning's Poems." *Browning Institute Studies* 6 (1978): 87–103.

Grimm, Clyde L. "*The American Claimant*: Reclamation of a Farce." *AQ* 19 (1967): 86–103.

Hall, Fred J. "Fred J. Hall Tells the Story of His Connection with Charles L. Webster & Co." *The Twainian* 6 (November–December 1947): 1–3.

Hansen, Chadwick. "The Character of Jim and the Ending of *Huckleberry Finn*." *Massachusetts Review* 5 (1963): 45–66.

Harbage, Alfred. *Conceptions of Shakespeare*. Cambridge: Harvard University Press, 1966.

Harris, Helen L. "Mark Twain's Response to the Native American." *AL* 46 (1974–75): 495–505.

Harris, Joel Chandler. Review of *Huckleberry Finn*. Atlanta *Constitution*, May 26, 1885, p. 4.

————. Review of *The Prince and the Pauper*. Atlanta *Constitution*, December 25, 1881, p. 11.

Hawkins, Hunt. "Mark Twain's Involvement with the Congo Movement: 'A Fury of Generous Indignation.'" *NEQ* 51 (1978): 147–75.

Hemingway, Ernest. *The Green Hills of Africa*. New York: Scribner's, 1935.

Hill, Archibald. *Mark Twain*. New York: Stokes, 1912.

Hill, Hamlin. "Barnum, Bridgeport, and *The Connecticut Yankee*." *AQ* 16 (1964): 615–16.

————. "The Composition and Structure of *Tom Sawyer*." *AL* 32 (1961–62): 379–92.

————. *Mark Twain and Elisha Bliss*. Columbia: University of Missouri Press, 1964.

————. "Mark Twain: Audience and Artistry." *AQ* 15 (1963): 25–40.

————. "Mark Twain's Book Sales, 1869–1879." *BNYPL* 65 (1961): 371–89.

Hill, Hamlin, and Frederick Anderson. "How Samuel Clemens Became Mark Twain's Publisher: A Study of the James R. Osgood Contracts." *Proof* 2 (1972): 117–43.

Hirst, Robert. "The Making of *The Innocents Abroad*: 1867–1872." Ph.D. diss., University of California, Berkeley, 1975.

Howe, M. A. DeWolfe. *Memoirs of a Hostess: A Chronicle of Eminent Friendships Drawn Chiefly from the Diaries of Mrs. James T. Fields*. Boston: Atlantic Monthly Press, 1922.

Howells, William Dean. *Literature and Life*. New York: Harper and Brothers, 1902.

Hyman, Stanley Edgar. "Half Mark, Half Twain." In *The Critic's Credentials: Essays and Reviews*, edited by Phoebe Pettingell. New York: Athenaeum, 1978.

James, George Wharton. "Charles Warren Stoddard." *National Review*, August 1911, pp. 659–72.

————. "How Mark Twain Was Made." *National Review*, February 1911, pp. 1–13.

Johnson, Merle. *A Bibliography of the Works of Mark Twain*. New York: Harper and Brothers, 1935.

Jones, Alexander E. "Mark Twain and Sexuality." *PMLA* 71 (1956), 595–616.

————. "Mark Twain and the Determinism of *What Is Man?*" *AL* 29 (1957–58): 1–17.

Jones, Daryl E. "The Hornet Disaster: Mark Twain's Adaptation in 'The Great Dark.'" *American Literary Realism* 9 (1976): 243–47.

Kahn, Sholom. *Mark Twain's Mysterious Stranger.* Columbia: University of Missouri Press, 1979.

Kaplan, Justin. *Mr. Clemens and Mark Twain.* New York: Simon and Schuster, 1966.

Klett, Ada M. "Meisterschaft; or The True State of Mark Twain's German." *German-American Review* 7 (December 1940): 10–11.

Krause, S. J. "The Art and Satire of Twain's 'Jumping Frog' Story." *AQ* 16 (1964): 363–76.

———. "Cooper's Literary Offenses: Mark Twain in Wonderland." *NEQ* 38 (1965): 291–311.

———. *Mark Twain as Critic.* Baltimore: Johns Hopkins University Press, 1967.

———. "Olivia Clemens's 'Editing' Reviewed." *AL* 39 (1967–68): 325–35.

Kruse, Horst H. *Mark Twain and "Life on the Mississippi."* Amherst: University of Massachusetts Press, 1981.

La Cour, Tage. "The Scandinavian Crime-Detective Story." *American Book Collector* 9 (May 1959): 22–23.

Leavis, F. R. "Mark Twain's Neglected Classic: The Moral Astringency of *Pudd'nhead Wilson.*" *Commentary* 21 (1956): 128–36.

Leisy, Ernest. "Mark Twain's Part in *The Gilded Age.*" *AL* 8 (1936–37): 445–47.

Lillard, Richard G. "Contemporary Reaction to the 'Empire City Massacre.'" *AL* 16 (1944–45): 198–203.

Lindberg, Gary. *The Confidence Man in American Literature.* New York: Oxford University Press, 1982.

Lindborg, Henry J. "A Cosmic Tramp: Samuel Clemens's *Three Thousand Years Among the Microbes.*" *AL* 44 (1972–73): 652–57.

Lorch, Fred W. "Mark Twain and the 'Campaign that Failed.'" *AL* 12 (1940–41): 454–70.

———. "Mark Twain in Iowa." *Iowa Journal of History and Politics* 27 (1929): 408–58.

———. "Mark Twain's Philadelphia Letters in *The Muscatine Journal.*" *AL* 17 (1945–46): 348–52.

———. *The Trouble Begins at Eight: Mark Twain's Lecture Tours.* Ames: Iowa State University Press, 1968.

Lynn, Kenneth. *Mark Twain and Southwestern Humor.* Boston: Little, Brown, 1959.

———. *William Dean Howells: An American Life.* New York: Harcourt Brace Jovanovich, 1971.

McKeithan, Daniel. *Court Trials in Mark Twain and Other Essays.* The Hague: Matinus Nijhoff, 1958.

———. *The Morgan Manuscript of Mark Twain's "Pudd'nhead Wilson."* Uppsala: American Institute, Uppsala University, 1961.

McNamara, Eugene. "Huck Lights Out for the Territory: Mark Twain's Unpublished Sequel." *University of Windsor Review* 2 (1966): 68–74.

Macnaughton, William G. *Mark Twain's Last Years as a Writer.* Columbia: University of Missouri Press, 1979.

McNutt, James C. "Mark Twain and the American Indian: Earthly Realism and Heavenly Idealism." *American Indian Quarterly* 4 (1978): 223–42.

Madigan, Francis J. "Mark Twain's Passage to India: A Genetic Study of *Following the Equator.*" Ph.D. diss., New York University, 1964.

Manierre, William R. "On Keeping the Raftsman's Passage in *Huckleberry Finn.*" *English Language Notes* 6 (1968): 118–22.

Matthews, Brander. *The Tocsin of Revolt and Other Essays.* New York: Scribner, 1922.

Mattson, J. Stanley. "Mark Twain on War and Peace: The Missouri Rebel and 'The Campaign That Failed.'" *AQ* 20 (1968): 783–94.

May, John R. "The Gospel According to Philip Traum: Structural Unity in 'The Mysterious Stranger.'" *Studies in Short Fiction* 8 (1971): 411–22.

Miller, William C. "The Editor's Page." *Nevada Historical Society Quarterly* 5 (January–March 1962), inside back cover.

———. "Samuel L. Clemens and Orion Clemens vs. Mark Twain and His Biographers (1861–1862)." *MTJ* 16 (1973): 1–9.

Miller, William, et al., eds. *Reports of the 1863 Constitutional Convention of the Territory of Nevada.* Carson City: State of Nevada, 1972.

Mobley, Lawrence E. "Mark Twain and the *Golden Era.*" *Publication of the Bibliographical Society of America* 58 (1964): 8–23.

Paine, Albert Bigelow. *Mark Twain: A Biography,* 3 vols. New York: Harper and Brothers, 1912.

Parker, Hershel, and Henry Binder, "Exigencies of Composition and Publication: *Billy Budd, Sailor,* and *Pudd'nhead Wilson.*" *Nineteenth Century Fiction* 33 (1978): 131–43.

Parsons, Coleman O. "The Devil and Samuel Clemens." *Virginia Quarterly Review* 23 (1947): 582–606.

———. "Down the Mighty River with Mark Twain." *Mississippi Quarterly* 22 (168–69): 1–18.

Pettit, Arthur G. *Mark Twain & the South.* Lexington: University Press of Kentucky, 1974.

Phelps, Elizabeth Stuart. *The Gates Ajar.* Boston: Fields, Osgood and Co., 1869.

Poirier, Richard. *A World Elsewhere: The Place of Style in American Literature.* New York: Oxford University Press, 1966.

Rees, Robert A. "*Captain Stormfield's Visit to Heaven* and *The Gates Ajar.*" *English Language Notes* 7 (1970): 197–202.

Rees, Robert A., and Richard Dilworth Rust. "Mark Twain's 'The Turning Point of My Life.'" *AL* 40 (1968–69): 524–35.

Regan, Robert. "'English Notes': A Book Mark Twain Abandoned." *Studies in American Humor* 2 (1976): 157–70.

———. "The Reprobate Elect in *The Innocents Abroad.*" *AL* 54 (1982–83): 240–57.

————. *Unpromising Heroes: Mark Twain and His Characters.* Berkeley and Los Angeles: University of California Press, 1966.

Requa, Kenneth A. "Counterfeit Currency and Character in Mark Twain's 'Which Was It?'" *MTJ* 17 (Winter 1974–75): 1–6.

Rideing, William H. *Many Celebrities and a Few Others* (Garden City, N.Y.: Doubleday, Page, 1912.

Rodney, Robert M., ed. and comp. *Mark Twain International: A Bibliography and Interpretation of His Worldwide Popularity.* Westport, Conn.: Greenwood Press, 1982.

Rogers, Franklin R. *Mark Twain's Burlesque Patterns.* Dallas: Southern Methodist University Press, 1960.

————. "The Road to Reality: Burlesque Travel Literature and *Roughing It.*" *BNYPL* 67 (1963): 155–68.

Ross, Michael L. "Mark Twain's *Pudd'nhead Wilson*: Dawson's Landing and the Ladder of Nobility." *Novel* 6 (1973): 244–56.

Rowlette, Robert, "'Mark Ward on Artemus Twain': Twain's Literary Debt to Ward." *American Literary Realism* 6 (1973): 13–25.

Rubin, Louis D. *The Writer in the South: Studies in a Literary Community.* Athens: University of Georgia Press, 1972.

Rucker, Mary E. "Moralism and Determinism in 'The Man That Corrupted Hadleyburg.'" *Studies in Short Fiction* 14 (1977): 49–54.

Russell, James. "The Genesis, Sources, and Reputation of Mark Twain's *A Connecticut Yankee in King Arthur's Court.*" Ph.D. diss., University of Chicago, 1966.

Salls, Helen H. "Joan of Arc in English and American Literature." *South Atlantic Quarterly* 35 (1936): 167–84.

Salomon, Roger B. *Twain and the Image of History.* New Haven: Yale University Press, 1961.

Salsbury, Edith Colgate. *Susy and Mark Twain.* New York: Harper and Row, 1965.

San Juan, Pastora. "A Source for *Tom Sawyer.*" *AL* 38 (1966–67): 101–2.

Schmidt, Paul. "Mark Twain's Techniques as a Humorist, 1857–1872." Ph.D. diss., University of Minnesota, 1951.

Schönemann, Friedrich. "Mark Twain and Adolph Wilbrandt." *Modern Language Notes* 34 (1919): 372–75.

Scott, Arthur L. "The *Century Magazine* Edits *Huckleberry Finn*, 1884–1885." *AL* 27 (1955–56): 356–62.

————. "*The Innocents Adrift*, Edited by Mark Twain's Official Biographer." *PMLA* 78 (1963): 320–37.

————. "Mark Twain Revises *Old Times on the Mississippi.*" *Journal of English and German Philology* 54 (1955): 634–38.

Searle, William. *The Saint and the Skeptics: Joan of Arc in the Works of Mark Twain, Anatole France, and Bernard Shaw.* Detroit: Wayne State University Press, 1976.

Seelye, John. "Introduction," to Mark Twain, *Personal Recollections of Joan of Arc*. Hartford, Conn.: Stowe-Day Foundation, 1980.

———. *Mark Twain in the Movies: A Meditation with Pictures*. New York: Viking Press, 1977.

———. *The True Adventures of Huckleberry Finn*. Evanston, Ill.: Northwestern University Press, 1970.

Shaw, George Bernard. *Saint Joan*. In *Complete Plays with Prefaces*, Volume 2. New York: Dodd, Mead, 1962.

Sloane, David E. E. *Mark Twain as a Literary Comedian*. Baton Rouge: Louisiana State University Press, 1979.

Smith, Henry Nash, ed. *Adventures of Huckleberry Finn*. Boston: Houghton Mifflin Co., 1958.

———. "Mark Twain as Interpreter of the West: The Structure of *Roughing It*." In *The Frontier in Perspective*, edited by W. D. Wyman and C. B. Kroeber. Madison: University of Wisconsin Press, 1957.

———. *Mark Twain: The Development of a Writer*. Cambridge: Harvard University Press, 1962.

———. *Mark Twain's Fable of Progress: "A Connecticut Yankee in King Arthur's Court."* New Brunswick, N.J.: Rutgers University Press, 1964.

———. "Mark Twain's Images of Hannibal: From St. Petersburg to Eseldorf." *Texas Studies in English* 37 (1958): 3–23.

———. "'That Hideous Mistake of Poor Clemens's.'" *Harvard Library Bulletin* 9 (1955): 145–80.

Smythe, Carlyle. "The Real Mark Twain." *Pall Mall Magazine* 16 (September 1898): 29–36.

Spangler, G. W. "*Pudd'nhead Wilson*: A Parable of Property." *AL* 42 (1970–71): 28–37.

Spengemann, William C. *Mark Twain and the Backwoods Angel: The Matter of Innocence in the Works of Samuel L. Clemens*. Kent, Ohio: Kent State University Press, 1966.

Stoddard, Charles Warren. *Exits and Entrances*. Boston: Lothrop Publishing Co., 1903.

———. "Mark Twain." San Francisco *Chronicle*, July 28, 1878.

Stone, Albert E. *The Innocent Eye: Childhood in Mark Twain's Imagination*. New Haven: Yale University Press, 1961.

———. "Mark Twain's *Joan of Arc*: The Child as Goddess." *AL* 31 (1959–60): 1–20.

———. "The Twichell Papers and Mark Twain's *A Tramp Abroad*." *Yale University Library Gazette* 29 (1955): 151–64.

Thompson, James Westfall. "The Maid of Orleans." *Dial* 20 (1896): 351–57.

Towers, Tom T. "'Hateful Reality': The Failure of the Territory in *Roughing It*." *Western American Literature* 9 (1974): 3–15.

———. "'I Never Thought We Might Want to Come Back': Strategies of

Transcendence in *Tom Sawyer.*" *Modern Fiction Studies* 21 (1975–76): 509–20.

———. "*The Prince and the Pauper*: Mark Twain's Once and Future King." *Studies in American Fiction* 6 (1978): 194–202.

Trachtenberg, Alan. "The Form of Freedom in *Adventures of Huckleberry Finn.*" *Southern Review* 6 (1970): 954–71.

Trent, William Peterfield. "Mark Twain as an Historical Novelist." *Bookman* (New York) 3 (May 1896): 207–10.

Tuckey, John S. *Mark Twain and Little Satan: The Writing of "The Mysterious Stranger.*" West Lafayette, Ind.: Purdue University Studies, 1963.

———. "Mark Twain's Later Dialogue: The 'Me' and the Machine." *AL* 41 (1969–70): 532–42.

Turner, Arlin. *George W. Cable: A Biography.* Durham, N.C.: Duke University Press, 1956.

———. "Mark Twain and the South: An Affair of Love and Anger." *Southern Review* 4 (1968): 493–519.

Underhill, Charles S. "Is the Garden of Eden at Niagara Falls? Mark Twain Says 'Yes.' *The Gleaner* [Buffalo, N.Y.], 1 (March 1928): 14–19.

Vogelback, Arthur L. "*The Prince and the Pauper*: A Study in Critical Standards." *AL* 14 (1942–43): 48–54.

———. "The Publication and Reception of *Huckleberry Finn* in America." *AL* 11 (1939–40): 260–72.

Wagner, Jeanne M. "*Huckleberry Finn* and the History Game." *MTJ* 20 (Winter 1979–80): 5–10.

Weber, Carl J. *The Rise and Fall of James Ripley Osgood: A Biography.* Waterville, Me.: Colby College Press, 1959.

Wecter, Dixon. *Sam Clemens of Hannibal.* Boston: Houghton Mifflin Co., 1952.

Welland, Dennis. "Mark Twain's Last Travel Book." *BNYPL* 69 (1965): 31–48.

Wigger, Anne P. "The Composition of Mark Twain's *Pudd'nhead Wilson* and Those Extraordinary Twins: Chronology and Development." *Modern Philology* 55 (1957): 93–102.

———. "The Source of the Fingerprint Material in Mark Twain's *Pudd'nhead Wilson.*" *AL* 28 (1956–57): 517–20.

Wiggins, Robert A. *Mark Twain: Jackleg Novelist.* Seattle: University of Washington Press, 1964.

———. "The Original of Mark Twain's 'Those Extraordinary Twins.'" *AL* 23 (1951–52): 355–57.

Williams, James D. "Revision and Intention in Mark Twain's *A Connecticut Yankee.*" *AL* 36 (1964–65): 288–97.

Wilson, James D. "The Use of History in Mark Twain's *A Connecticut Yankee.*" *PMLA* 80 (1965): 102–10.

Wilson, Robert H. "Malory in *The Connecticut Yankee.*" *Texas Studies in English* 27 (1948): 185–206.

Wolff, Cynthia Griffin. "*The Adventures of Tom Sawyer*: The Nightmare Vision of American Boyhood." *Massachusetts Review* 21 (1980): 637–52.

Yates, Norris. *William T. Porter and the "Spirit of the Times": A Study of the Big Bear School of Humor.* Baton Rouge: Louisiana State University Press, 1957.

Yu, Beongcheon. "The Immortal Twins—An Aspect of Mark Twain." *The English Language and Literature* [Korea], 23 (Summer 1967).

Index to the Works of Mark Twain/Samuel L. Clemens

Major entries are in italics.

Index of Personal Names